Travel and Travail

Early Modern Cultural Studies

SERIES EDITORS
Carole Levin
Marguerite A. Tassi

TRAVEL *and* TRAVAIL

Early Modern Women,
English Drama,
and the Wider World

Edited and with an introduction by
Patricia Akhimie *and* Bernadette Andrea

UNIVERSITY OF NEBRASKA PRESS
Lincoln and London

© 2019 by the Board of Regents of the University of Nebraska. All rights reserved. Manufactured in the United States of America. ♾

Library of Congress Cataloging-in-Publication Data
Names: Akhimie, Patricia, editor, writer of introduction. | Andrea, Bernadette Diane, editor, writer of introduction.
Title: Travel and travail: Early Modern women, English drama, and the wider world / edited and with an introduction by Patricia Akhimie and Bernadette Andrea.
Description: Lincoln: University of Nebraska Press, [2018] | Series: Early modern cultural studies | Includes bibliographical references and index.
Identifiers: LCCN 2018027855
ISBN 9781496202260 (pbk.: alk. paper)
ISBN 9781496210296 (epub)
ISBN 9781496210302 (mobi)
ISBN 9781496210319 (pdf)
Subjects: LCSH: English drama—Early modern and Elizabethan, 1500–1600—History and criticism. | Women travelers in literature. | English prose literature—Women authors—History and criticism. | Women travelers. | Travelers' writings, English—History and criticism.
Classification: LCC PR678.W6 T73 2018 | DDC 820.9/32082–dc23
LC record available at
https://lccn.loc.gov/2018027855

Set in Merope Basic by Mikala R. Kolander.

CONTENTS

List of Illustrations · viii
Acknowledgments · ix
Introduction: Early Modern Women, English Drama, and the Wider World · 1
PATRICIA AKHIMIE AND BERNADETTE ANDREA

Part 1
Early Modern Women Travelers:
Global and Local Trajectories

1. Desdemona and Mrs. Keeling · 19
   RICHMOND BARBOUR

2. A Stranger Bride: Mariam Khan and the East India Company · 41
   KAREN ROBERTSON

3. Sailing to India: Women, Travel, and Crisis in the Seventeenth Century · 64
   AMRITA SEN

4. Teresa Sampsonia Sherley: Amazon, Traveler, and Consort · 81
   CARMEN NOCENTELLI

5. The Global Travels of Teresa Sampsonia Sherley's Carmelite Relic · 102
   BERNADETTE ANDREA

6. Gender and Travel Discourse: Richard Lassels's "The Voyage of the Lady Catherine Whetenall from Brussells into Italy" (1650)   121
PATRICIA AKHIMIE

7. Advance and Retreat: Reading English Colonial Choreographies of Pocahontas   139
ELISA OH

8. Lady Anne Clifford's Way and Aristocratic Women's Travel   158
LAURA WILLIAMSON AMBROSE

Part 2
Early Modern Women and the Globe:
Gendered Travel on the English Stage

9. Mapping Women: Place Names and a Woman's Place   181
LAURA AYDELOTTE

10. Eroticizing Women's Travel: Desdemona and the Desire for Adventure in *Othello*   199
STEPHANIE CHAMBERLAIN

11. Desdemona's Divided Duty: Gender and Courtesy in *Othello*   215
MICHAEL SLATER

12. From Adventure to Danger in the Travels of Desdemona and Miranda   236
EDER JARAMILLO

13. Marian Mobility, Black Madonnas, and the Cleopatra Complex   250
RUBEN ESPINOSA

14. Precarious Travail, Gender, and Narration
in Shakespeare's *Pericles, Prince of Tyre*
and Margaret Cavendish's *The Blazing World*   273
DYANI JOHNS TAFF

15. Traveling Companions: Shakespeare's
As You Like It and the Book of Ruth   292
SUZANNE TARTAMELLA

16. English Women, Romance, and Global
Travel in Thomas Heywood's *The Fair Maid
of the West, Part I*   313
GAYWYN MOORE

Afterword: Looking for the Women in
Early Modern Travel Writing   331
MARY C. FULLER

Contributors   353
Index   357

ILLUSTRATIONS

Following page 157

1. Sandro Botticelli, *Venus and Mars*, ca. 1485
2. The Santa Casa and Madonna di Loreto, *The history of our B. Lady of Loreto*, 1608
3. Map depicting properties of Lady Anne Clifford's inheritance in northern England
4. Map of England depicting Lady Anne Clifford's many residences and properties
5. Natural history cabinet, Ferrante Imperato, *Dell'historia naturale*, 1599

ACKNOWLEDGMENTS

First and foremost, we thank the participants in our seminar on "Early Modern Women and Travel: Local Histories and Global Designs" at the 2016 Shakespeare Association of America conference in New Orleans. This collection has grown far beyond that seminar, with new contributors and substantially expanded (sometimes radically different) chapters. The collaborative spirit of the seminar happily extended throughout the editing of this collection, which led to the historical, interpretive, and methodological questions we raise in our introduction. We look forward to seeing how this conversation continues, guided by these questions and beyond them to sources, histories, and locales we could not cover.

Patricia would like to thank the Shakespeare Association of America for the invitation to propose a seminar on the topic of early modern women's travel, and, of course, Bernadette, for her steadfast partnership. Thanks also to Manu and to PJ, who was born not long before this book began.

Bernadette, in addition to her expressing her gratitude to Patricia for our several collaborations on early modern women and travel, would like to thank Brianne Dayley, who is completing her doctoral degree at the University of Texas–San Antonio, for her assiduous bibliographical work. And, as always, thanks to Ben.

Introduction

Early Modern Women, English Drama, and the Wider World

PATRICIA AKHIMIE AND BERNADETTE ANDREA

Traditionally, early modern women's travel has been construed as an "absent presence" due to the general ban on women's movement outside the domestic sphere. An influential articulation of this ban was disseminated in *The Traveiler of Jerome Turler* (1575), which intones: "the wide wandring of Weemen cannot want suspition, & bringeth some toke[n] of dishonestie. Whereupon the Tragicall and Comicall Poets, when they bring in any far traueiling Woman, for the most parte they feine her to be incontinent," or unchaste.[1] Another popular travel guide, Thomas Palmer's *An Essay of the Meanes how to make our Travailes, into forraine Countries, the more profitable and honorable* (1606), lists women in general—along with "Infants," "Decrepite persons," "Fooles," "Madmen," and "Lunaticke[s]"—under the category *"What persons* are inhibited trauaile," or prohibited from traveling.[2] By adducing new sources and examining familiar sources in new ways, the essays collected here confirm that a wide range of girls and women engaged in extensive movement within and beyond the British Isles during the sixteenth and seventeenth centuries despite these proscriptions.[3] Complementing this expanded focus on historical women travelers, contributors also engage the representation of women's travel on the English public stage and in other manuscript and printed works.[4] Such representations arguably function as a reproach to the travel ban promulgated in admonitory tracts and as further evidence of women's movement within and outside England, whether voluntary (recreational, educational, or at least self-willed) or involuntary (occurring as a result of political exile, religious persecution, capture, enslavement, or coercion).[5]

In focusing on historical and literary sources, this collection accordingly highlights and rectifies gendered lacunae in foundational studies such as Jaś Elsner and Joan-Pau Rubiés's *Voyages and Visions: Towards a Cultural History of Travel* (1999), which defines "travel" as "a culturally significant event rather than as mere physical movement."[6] Yet, this definition effaces the wide range of forms women's travel took in the premodern era, as the lone reference to a medieval woman pilgrim demonstrates.[7] Ivo Kamps and Jyotsna Singh's *Travel Knowledge: European "Discoveries" in the Early Modern Period* (2001), which pairs critical essays with excerpts from travel narratives to the Levant, India, and Africa, includes a section on the Ottoman travels of Lady Mary Wortley Montagu (1716–18).[8] Yet, the inclusion of the canonical Montagu only reinforces the widely held belief that women's travel begins in earnest only in the eighteenth century.[9] In this vein, Kristi Siegel's edited volume, *Gender, Genre, and Identity in Women's Travel Writing* (2004), includes a chapter on Montagu but focuses on travel narratives from the Victorian period so that Montagu comes to seem like the *terminus a quo* of early modern women's travel.[10] Andrew McRae in his influential study *Literature and Domestic Travel in Early Modern England* (2009) offers astute readings of Queen Elizabeth I's progresses at the end of the sixteenth century and Celia Fiennes's travels within Britain at the end of the seventeenth century.[11] However, because he asserts that "in the early modern period to 'travel' typically meant to leave the nation's shores," he does not account for women's travel to and from Britain as dependent wives, servants, and chattel.[12] More recently, in *Mind-Travelling in Early Modern England* (2013), David McInnis adduces Aphra Behn's "New World" writings to conceptualize travel in the period. However, he does not address female travelers or travel prior to the late seventeenth century.[13]

In dialogue with related critical studies, *Travel and Travail* features new historical material and new readings of familiar texts to account for the journeys of these various girls and women.[14] It thereby expands our understanding of "travel" in the period, as well as the archive of "travel writing," to account for the journeys of a diverse group of girls and women. To this end, the essays address a series of pressing conceptual, historical, literary, and methodological questions. To start, what constitutes "travel" for early modern women locally and globally? How is women's mobility accomplished and to what ends? How do we assess women's agency as "voluntary" and "involuntary" travelers? Furthermore, how do we understand "travel writing" as a genre with respect to early modern women's contributions? What archival questions emerge from a discussion of early modern women's distinctive modes of travel and/or forms of writing? What documentary sources should we consider or reconsider? And how do we weigh writing about the "voluntary" travel of primarily elite women given the relative absence of writing or archival traces from the "involuntary" travels experienced by women of lower status? Finally, how do literary works across genres, including Shakespeare's plays, illuminate women's travel and travel writing in the period?[15] And what critical and theoretical approaches do we bring to a study of women's "domestic travel" within the British Isles? Across continental Europe? To and from the Americas? From and to the Islamic world? What are the connections between the local histories of women's travel and the global designs of early modern imperialism and colonialism? Responding to these questions, this collection reassesses the nature of travel in the period, the experiences of historical women travelers, and imaginative representations of women's travel, pressuring conventional definitions that categorically exclude girls and women.

Considering "travel" through the lens of gender, which intersects with race, religion, ethnicity, sexuality, and other social vectors, several contributors adduce native women who journeyed from North America and the Islamic world to England, as well as English women who traveled within and beyond the British Isles.[16] They recover and reread a wide range of documentary sources by and about women travelers, including colonial archives, biographical treatises, biblical commentary, conduct books, sacred sites, and maps. Other contributors examine the ways in which women's travel is defined within or against the fantasies of adventure, capture, itinerancy, or elopement on the stage, in drama, utopian discourse, and encomia.[17] They engage these sources from multiple methodological perspectives, often contrapuntally, including literary critical, historical, and visual, extending into the digital humanities and intertextual studies. Together, they seek to build a vocabulary, a canon, and a comparative apparatus for discussing writing by women and about travel within borders and overseas, in Europe and the wider world, in the traditional "Age of Discovery" of the sixteenth century and through the turn of the seventeenth century and later in the seventeenth century and into the eighteenth century, when travel took on new meanings associated with tourism, science, and exile.[18] The collection as a whole thus resituates "travel" as a key term for these fields by restoring women to visibility in the history and literature of Shakespeare's era and, more broadly, of the early modern–colonial period.[19]

Part one features eight essays that document the travel of historical women between Europe and the Islamic world, including the Mughal (Indian) and the Safavid (Persian) empires; across the Atlantic as the English are initiating their first permanent settlement at Jamestown; from England through Continental Europe, with destinations in Italy and Spain; and within the British Isles, particularly England. This cluster of historically oriented essays is followed by eight essays that engage the literature of the era more pointedly, from Shakespeare's plays to the manuscripts and published writings of early modern Englishwomen. These essays recover and reconceptualize women's "travel" via an archive of historical documents and literary works to establish that, despite the ban in prescriptive literature on their mobility, women did indeed participate in the era's expansionist projects, whether global trade, colonialism, religious conversion, international humanism, or transnational literary genres. Our title reflects the gendered challenges of travel with the early modern pun, "travail," meaning labor, especially in childbirth.[20] Yet women did travel, even while pregnant, and therefore our attention to their agency as documented in the archives and imagined in the literature of the era adds significantly to critical conversations in Renaissance and early modern studies about emergent globalization.

Travel and Travail begins with a section on "Early Modern Women Travelers: Global and Local Trajectories," which extends from the British

Isles to the Islamic empires of the Mughals and Safavids, through Continental Europe and North America, and back to England, tracing the travels of women across classes, religions, ethnicities, and races. Richmond Barbour, in "Desdemona and Mrs. Keeling," draws our attention to a key distinction between private interests and corporate interests where women are associated with the private. Placing a famous literary scenario and a neglected historical incident in dialogue, he prompts us to consider the role of women both in travel for the purposes of settlement and in travel for the purposes of trade. As Barbour notes, women were welcome aboard ships of the Virginia Company, whose membership and management overlapped with the East India Company's. Why then, he asks, was Ann Broomfield denied her husband's Eastern voyage? His essay productively engages this historical and critical crux to launch further discussions of women's agency as travelers, even when thwarted. Also focusing on the forgotten women of the early seventeenth-century English trading companies, Karen Robertson, in "A Stranger Bride: Mariam Khan and the East India Company," documents the Mughal Armenian Miriam Khan's travels by combing through the East India Company records, asking whether women, rarely recognized as independent subjects, more readily fit into generic stereotypes when written about by English captains. Engaging the documentary record through generic tropes, Robertson effectively bridges the gap between the "shadows" of women travelers in the archives and the cultural forms that determine their participation, or lack thereof, in these ventures. Amrita Sen, in "Sailing to India: Women, Travel, and Crisis in the Seventeenth Century," similarly brings these forgotten women, especially those of the serving classes, to the fore, dwelling on the women who were part of the Sherley entourage, led by the "famous English *Persian*" Robert Sherley (in Thomas Middleton's words), who traveled on East India Company ships to the Safavid empire. Sen focuses on the (possibly) Persian wife of Sir Thomas Powell, who gave birth to a child, the first born to an "English" couple in India. She queries, did these traveling women draw the same type of criticism that the wives of East India Company members did? And how did considerations of class, ethnicity, religion, and race complicate or facilitate these relatively lower-status women's travels, even as it rendered them all but invisible in the archives?

Resonating with Sen's essay on the Sherley entourage, in "Teresa Sampsonia Sherley: Amazon, Traveler, and Consort," Carmen Nocentelli plumbs Italian and Latin sources to map the contours of what seventeenth-century Europeans understood as respectable, and perhaps even exemplary, female travel. This essay posits that the construction of Lady Sherley as a "consort," a full-fledged partner in the life and fortunes of her husband, is crucial to her representation as a woman traveler who was neither gender deviant nor sexually suspect. Visual and literary depictions of this globe-trotting Circassian reveal both the limits of, and the conditions of possibility for, early modern constructions of respectable female travel, which Michael Slater later explores in his essay on Desdemona. Bernadette Andrea, in "The Global Travels of Teresa Sampsonia Sherley's Carmelite Relic," offers another perspective on this cross-cultural exchange by unpacking the significance of the relic Teresa Sampsonia wore as a locket to ward off the dangers she faced after her husband died on their second return trip to the Safavid empire: a particle of flesh ("la partícula de carne") from the corpse of St. Teresa of Ávila, which she received from the hand of the Carmelite Mother Beatrice (Beatriz de Jesús, 1560–1639), who was a niece of the saint and prioress of the Convent of Santa Ana in Madrid. Deploying the "cultural biography perspective," Andrea establishes the significance of this Carmelite relic in terms of the networks it established between cloistered and cosmopolitan women from "East" and "West" by foregrounding material culture as a crucial constituent of women's connections across a wide range of Muslim and Christian domains. Continuing this attention to continental Europe in a global frame, Patricia Akhimie, in "Gender and Travel Discourse: Richard Lassels's 'The Voyage of the Lady Catherine Whetenall from Brussels into Italy,'" explores the work of gender in the early modern English discourse of travel, examining legal restrictions on women's travel and advice on (or rather against) women traveling in *ars apodemica* (art of travel) treatises. Explicating the trope of domesticity in the unpublished 1650 manuscript "The Voyage of the Lady Catherine Whetenall," a rare and early account of a woman's grand tour, Akhimie draws connections between the portrayal of Lady Whetenall as traveler and saintly wife and the English fascination with the Santa Casa (Holy House) in Loreto, near the Adriatic coast in Italy, whose purportedly miraculous journey Ruben Espinosa further explores in his essay. As Akhimie establishes, while gentlemen travelers were imagined to be transformed by sightseeing—their exposure to a series of edifying objects—women were imagined to be transformed into objects themselves as static exempla.

Elisa Oh's essay, "Advance and Retreat: Reading English Colonial Choreographies of Pocahontas," excavates the agency of the Native American (Powhatan) traveler known as Pocahontas, who served as a tenuous political bridge between the English colonizers and her nation, especially through her marriage to John Rolfe and voyage with him to visit the Jacobean court in 1616–17. Oh reads Pocahontas's nonverbal movements through space and between groups of people as evidence of her multiple identities, including ambassador, agent of colonial propaganda, and independent agent. In London court spaces, Pocahontas embodied both masque and antimasque, discourses of order and disorder, Englishwoman and "other." Yet, her pained silence and withdrawal from Smith when they reencountered each other in London introduces the possibility of resistance, rejection, and hostility from her and the nation for which she stands. The final essay in this section, Laura Williamson Ambrose's "Lady Anne Clifford's Way and Aristocratic Women's Travel," examines representations of seventeenth-century female aristocratic travel through one of the era's most notable women, Lady Anne Clifford. Ambrose contends that Clifford's collective and prolific textual outpourings (ca. 1603–76) offer multiple insights into a range of understudied practices, habits, and patterns of movement undertaken and represented by English women of the upper class. Ambrose's goal in this essay is twofold: first, to read Clifford's records *as* travel writing and, second, to see what new picture of women's mobility might emerge in doing so. Broader questions include: In what ways are the everyday spatial practices of elite women like Clifford gendered? How might we compare her experiences to those of racially marked female travelers like Mrs. Rolfe (Pocahontas), Lady Sherley (Teresa Sampsonia), or

Mrs. Hawkins/Towerson (Mariam Khan)? And, finally, how do atypical forms of travel writing like Clifford's inform our understanding of both travel practices and ideas about mobility in the early modern period?

The second section, "Early Modern Women and the Globe: Gendered Travel on the English Stage," shifts to literary representations of women's travel in the period to access their responses—whether imaginary or refracted from historical incidents—to the restrictions and possibilities of travel, both local and global. This section opens with an essay, Laura Aydelotte's "Mapping Women: Place Names and a Woman's Place," which looks at the locations encoded in six plays covering three genres: the comedy *A Midsummer Night's Dream*; the tragedies *Othello* and *Antony and Cleopatra*; and the history plays of the Henriad. As she inquires, what can we learn about the geographic places between which they travel, the places to which they refer, and the places names they use to metaphorically describe themselves and others? Do the number or kind of places referred to by male and female characters differ? Aydelotte's essay deftly unpacks the ways women in the plays relate to place names and, at the same time, she explores the potentials and limits of a data driven methodological approach to such questions. Stephanie Chamberlain, in "Eroticizing Women's Travel: Desdemona and the Desire for Adventure in *Othello*," situates Desdemona's fascination with the exotic world in terms of early modern modes of travel with all their attendant perils: from the educational travel favored by humanists to global trade and expansionism, both of which marginalized women and "others." Desdemona's attraction to the exotic, instantiated in her dual longing to listen to Othello's travel tales and to travel herself, is reconfigured as desire for the erotic. In the patriarchal worlds that collide in her marriage, her desire to travel poses numerous gendered dangers, ultimately leading to her tragic end. Yet her own "traveller's tale," as Chamberlain shows, excavates the possibilities, imaginative and otherwise, that the expanded scope of travel in the early modern period promised women.

Indeed, Michael Slater, in "Desdemona's Divided Duty: Gender and Courtesy in *Othello*," argues that Desdemona's mode of travel, as an aristocratic woman from Renaissance Italy, was encouraged, not prohibited, as critical attention to conduct manuals oriented toward the domesticated English "bourgeois wife" have led us to believe. Slater seeks to reconcile critical perspectives on the two seemingly incompatible visions of Desdemona that the play provides: the one aggressively defiant, the other meekly acquiescent. By situating Desdemona's behavior—her speech, her education, and her travel—within a set of courtly conduct manuals or courtesy books from Baldesar Castiglione's *Il Cortegiano* (*The Courtier*, trans. 1561) to Stephano Guazzo's *La Civil conversazione* (*The Civil Conversation*, trans. 1581), Slater argues for a fundamental rethinking of the nature of Desdemona's tragedy. Further nuancing this crucial play for a consideration of early modern travel, especially as inflected by gender, race, religion, and sexuality, Eder Jaramillo, in "From Adventure to Danger in the Travels of Desdemona and Miranda," elaborates a layered reading of stage representations of early modern women's travel experiences. Engaging with intertextual and interimperial methodologies, Jaramillo investigates a series of parallels between Shakespeare's *The Tempest* and *Othello* to show how the common trope of land as a woman awaiting ravishment melds with patriarchal anxieties over women's desires to travel, manifested through their projected attraction and vulnerability to a ravishing "other": Caliban in the first instance, Othello in the second. Jaramillo illustrates the intertextual dynamic wherein women's attraction to travels and adventure are overwritten by the dangers that the sexual threats of non-European cultures are designed to represent.

Continuing an investigation of Shakespeare's engagement with the question of women's travel, but shifting to a less-discussed play, Ruben Espinosa, in "Marian Mobility, Black Madonnas, and the Cleopatra Complex," evokes early modern French essayist and traveler Michel de Montaigne's description of his visit to the Holy House of Loreto—believed to be the house where the Virgin Mary was born—and details the miraculous conveyance of the house from Galilee to Slavonia and ultimately to Loreto itself. The travels surrounding this house thus register the religious desire for a material Marian connection, but the mobility behind both the history of the house and the various visitors who journey to see this Marian site (including Lady Whetenall, on whom

Akhimie focuses) also registers its cross-cultural energies. Of rather significant weight, as Espinosa underscores, is the fact that Loreto houses a black image of the Virgin Mary. As he proposes, when considered alongside Shakespeare's *Antony and Cleopatra*, Black Madonna narratives in European and trans-Atlantic settings offer a neglected nexus through which to explore the influence of an original black, foreign femininity on perceptions of a Christian identity that was increasingly coded as white. Dyani Johns Taff, in "Precarious Travail, Gender, and Narration in Shakespeare's *Pericles, Prince of Tyre* and Margaret Cavendish's *The Blazing World*," the latter published in 1666, productively ventures even farther afield in Shakespeare's oeuvre and into a direct engagement with early modern women's utopian writing, adducing two works that represent the stage as a sea and the sea as a stage. Pressuring the difficulties and failings of this chiasmus, Taff argues that Shakespeare and Cavendish invite their audiences to dwell on the precariousness faced by travelers, by narrators and playwrights who represent sea travel, and by characters who traverse gender boundaries. Shakespeare's Thaisa and Cavendish's Empress, in particular, seem simultaneously to control and to be shaped by the maritime environments through which they travel, enmeshed in a fluctuating power relationship with their male counterparts and with the environment itself.

Suzanne Tartamella, in "Traveling Companions: Shakespeare's *As You Like It* and the Book of Ruth," examines underappreciated references to the Book of Ruth in Shakespeare's celebrated comedy, arguing that the biblical text not only serves as a source for the play, but also helps frame its exploration of female identity, alienation, and adaptability. As Tartamella points out, although the Book of Ruth remains one of the most beloved stories of the Old Testament, it has made surprisingly few direct inroads in Western literature, especially prior to the eighteenth century. Drawing on an anonymous poetic retelling entitled *Ruth Revived* (1639), she explores why the Book of Ruth constitutes an important backdrop for the play, how Shakespeare (and consequently his contemporaries) would have interpreted that text, and what allusions to Ruth's story reveal about the role of female travelers in effecting cultural change. Moving even farther beyond Shakespeare, the final essay in this section, Gaywyn Moore's "English Women, Romance, and Global Travel in Thomas Heywood's *The Fair Maid of the West, Part One*," offers a situated reading of Bess, the tavern wench turned tavern owner turned cross-dressing pirate in Heywood's play, written circa 1600 and published 1631, arguing that her travels present a narrative of transformation from domestic laborer to upwardly mobile woman. "Mobile" in this case signifies both an improvement in class status and movement into a foreign space. As Moore concludes, the play's historical backdrop, the Islands Voyage (the 1597 Essex-Raleigh expedition), completes the transformation of Bess into a world-traveling pirate by erasing her dead (or so she believes) fiancé's body. Phrased otherwise, Bess's encounter with the Azores, a port of call that functions as the crossroads to world commerce within the play, erases her future domestic plans in England and allows her to commit fully to her high-seas adventures. Bess thereby presents early modern audiences with both an extension of Queen Elizabeth as a world traveler through her state-sanctioned pirates, and a commoner who substantially alters her identity through increasing geographic distance from England.

Moore's essay returns us to the question of historical women's agency as travelers in the early modern period, with the fantasy projection of Bess and her global travels set alongside the historical movements of Queen Elizabeth within her realm, which she never left. One of our framing questions was about the way women's travel is represented on stage and about whether women's travel is necessary or desirable. Clearly women's travel is marked as transgressive, but does it also serve a purpose? Why do women keep traveling on stage if they are "not supposed to"? The essays in this collection, whether focusing on historical women travelers or representations of women's travel in literary and cultural productions, advance a historically grounded, theoretically informed, and critically incisive array of responses to this crucial question, ones that are meant to launch further investigations into this neglected topic. Together, they affirm that women's travel *was* culturally significant and copious, even if proscribed.

Notes

1. Turler, *Traveiler*, 9. For more on the *ars apodemica* or guidebooks on the "art of travel," of which Turler's tract is exemplary, see Stagl, *History*, 47–94.
2. Palmer, *Essay*, 16. For more on travel advice books, including Palmer's, see Games, *Web*, 18–46. For a discussion of Palmer in terms of travel and ethnographic literature, see Suranyi, *Genius*, 15–17.
3. For an important group of Englishwomen travelers from the mid-seventeenth century, see Wiseman, "Read Within." For more on early Quaker women's Mediterranean travels, see Andrea, *Women and Islam*, 53–77.
4. For a brilliant analysis of "traveling boys," both historical travelers (usually involuntary) and literary representations in English and Ottoman texts, see Arvas, "Travelling Sexualities."
5. On the vexed issue as to whether "coerced journeys" (of exiles, refugees, transported slaves, vagrants, etc.) should count as travel, see Buzard, "What Isn't Travel?," 55. For more, see Borm, "Defining Travel."
6. Elsner and Rubiés, *Voyages and Visions*, 7. Other foundational studies, such as Hadfield, *Literature, Travel, and Colonial Writing*, and Maquerlot and Willems, *Travel and Drama*, similarly efface women as historical travelers and traveling characters.
7. Elsner and Rubiés mention Egeria or Etheria, whose narrative of her pilgrimage to Jerusalem in the 380s was widely read (*Voyages and Visions*, 17–20). Campbell, *Witness*, discusses Egeria's pilgrimage in a study that otherwise focuses on male travelers' journeys into Asia, the Middle East, and the Americas (20–33). Margery Kempe (ca. 1373–1438), whose dictated narrative has been labelled the first autobiography in English, is an English female traveler who predates the period we cover. Her travel narrative was framed in terms of the medieval pilgrimage tradition.
8. Montagu, *Turkish Embassy Letters*, was published posthumously in 1763 as *Letters of the Right Honourable Lady M—y W—y M—e: Written, during her Travels in Europe, Asia and Africa*. For conflicting approaches to Montagu as traveler, see Andrea, *Women and Islam*, 118–12. For a more recent treatment, see Dadabhoy, "'Going Native.'"
9. Recent anthologies of early modern travel writing regularly cite Montagu as one of the earliest example of travel writing by a woman (Foster and Mills, *Anthology of Women's Travel Writing*; Bohls and Duncan, *Travel Writing*). Several recent anthologies of women's travel writing aimed at a broader readership also offer Montagu as the earliest example (Morris and O'Connor, *Maiden Voyages*; Robinson, *Unsuitable for Ladies*). Other anthologies, such as Hadfield's *Amazons, Savages and Machiavels*, do not include any discussion of women's travel or travel writing.

10. For details, see Bannerjee, "Lady Montagu."
11. In some anthologies, Fiennes's diary appears as an example of early women's travel writing (Foster and Mills, Bohls and Duncan). For more on the travels of Queen Elizabeth I see Archer, Goldring, and Knight, *Progresses*; Cole, *Portable Queen*; and Goldring et al.'s new edition. For the mobile poor during the same period, with consistent attention to women's travel, see Fumerton, *Unsettled*.
12. McRae, *Literature and Domestic Travel*, 14. For an investigation of "the often elided role of huswifery [women's domestic labour] in early modern English colonial discourses," see Akhimie, "Travel, Drama, and Domesticity."
13. Cf. Paravisini-Gebert and Romero-Cesareo's *Women at Sea*, which likewise begins an examination of women's travel writing in the Caribbean with essays on early travel writing by men and on Aphra Behn.
14. Our collection reflects the trend in studies of women's writing and lived experience in the early modern period that has given rise to treatments of understudied texts including new scholarly editions such as Hind's edition of Anna Trapnel and Owens's edition and translation of Madre María Rosa, along with new studies such as Dursteler's *Renegade Women*, Andrea's "'Travelling Bodyes,'" Christensen's "Guides to Marriage," and Singh's "Boundary Crossings." See also Cary, "New Directions."
15. See also Degenhardt, "Foreign Worlds," especially her sections on "Travel Writing and the English Traveller" (441–43) and "Theatrical Contrivances of Travel" (453–57).
16. For an important recent study with consistent attention to indigenous women travelers, see Thrush, *Indigenous London*.
17. Even though they focus primarily on later periods, Lawrence's *Penelope Voyages* and Frederick and McLeod's *Women and the Journey* similarly bring together studies of literary and historical women's travel. For a more recent study, see O'Loughlin, *Women, Writing, and Travel in the Eighteenth Century*.
18. A significant intervention is Kinsley, *Women Writing the Home Tour*.
19. For recent work on early modern Dutch and Spanish women's transatlantic travels respectively, see Romney, *New Netherland Connections*, and Poska, *Gendered Crossings*.
20. Yates, in *Error, Misuse, Failure*, offers an incisive reading of Thomas Nashe's *The Unfortunate Traveller* through "the various senses of the word 'travel' permitted in early modern English" (104). For more, see Andrea, *Women and Islam*, 65–66; Snader, *Caught Between Worlds*, 13–61; and Vitkus, "Labor and Travel," 229–30.

Bibliography

Akhimie, Patricia. "Travel, Drama, and Domesticity: Colonial Huswifery in John Fletcher and Philip Massinger's *The Sea Voyage*." *Studies in Travel Writing* 13, no. 2 (2009): 153–66.

Andrea, Bernadette. "'Travelling Bodyes': Native Women of the Northeast and Northwest Passage Ventures and English Discourses of Empire." In *Rethinking Feminism in Early Modern Studies*, edited by Ania Loomba and Melissa Sanchez, 135–48. London: Routledge, 2016.

———. *Women and Islam in Early Modern English Literature*. Cambridge: Cambridge University Press, 2007.

Archer, Jayne Elisabeth, Elizabeth Goldring, and Sarah Knight, eds. *The Progresses, Pageants, and Entertainments of Queen Elizabeth I*. Oxford: Oxford University Press, 2007.

Arvas, Abdulhamit. "Travelling Sexualities, Circulating Bodies, and Early Modern Anglo-Ottoman Encounters." PhD diss., Michigan State University, 2016.

Bannerjee, Sukanya. "Lady Montagu and the 'Boundaries' of Europe." In Siegel, *Gender*, 31–54.

Bohls, Elizabeth, and Ian Duncan, eds. *Travel Writing 1700–1830: An Anthology*. Oxford: Oxford University Press, 2005.

Borm, Jan. "Defining Travel: On the Travel Book, Travel Writing and Terminology." In *Perspectives on Travel Writing*, edited by Glenn Hooper and Tim Youngs, 13–26. New York: Routledge, 2004.

Buzard, James M. "What Isn't Travel?" In *Unravelling Civilisation: European Travel and Travel Writing*, edited by Hagen Schulz-Forberg, 43–61. Brussels: P.I.E.-Peter Lang, 2005.

Campbell, Mary. *The Witness and the Other World: Exotic European Travel Writing, 400–1600*. Ithaca NY: Cornell University Press, 1988.

Cary, Daniel. "New Directions in the Study of Travel Writing." *Études anglaises* 70, no. 2 (2017): 131–37.

Christensen, Ann. "Guides to Marriage and 'Needful Travel' in Early Modern England." In *Mapping Gendered Routes and Spaces in the Early Modern World*, edited by Merry Weisner-Hanks, 271–89. Farnham UK: Ashgate, 2015.

Cole, Mary Hill. *The Portable Queen: Elizabeth I and the Politics of Ceremony*. Amherst: University of Massachusetts Press, 1999.

Dadabhoy, Ambereen. "'Going Native': Geography, Gender, and Identity in Lady Mary Wortley Montagu's *Turkish Embassy Letters*." In *Gender and Space in British Literature, 1660–1820*, edited by Mona Narain and Karen Gevirtz, 49–66. Farnham UK: Ashgate, 2004.

Degenhardt, Jane Hwang. "Foreign Worlds." *The Oxford Handbook of Shakespeare*, edited by Arthur F. Kinney, 433–57. Oxford: Oxford University Press, 2011.

Dursteler, Eric. *Renegade Women: Gender, Identity, and Boundaries in the Early Modern Mediterranean*. Baltimore: Johns Hopkins University Press, 2011.

Elsner, Jaś, and Joan-Pau Rubiés, eds. *Voyages and Visions: Towards a Cultural History of Travel*. London: Reaktion Books, 1999.

Foster, Shirley, and Sara Mills, eds. *An Anthology of Women's Travel Writing*. Manchester: Manchester University Press, 2002.

Frederick, Bonnie, and Susan H. McLeod, eds. *Women and the Journey: The Female Travel Experience*. Pullman: Washington State University Press, 1993.

Fumerton, Patricia. *Unsettled: The Culture of Mobility and the Working Poor in Early Modern England*. Chicago: University of Chicago Press, 2006.

Games, Alison. *The Web of Empire: English Cosmopolitans in an Age of Expansion, 1560–1660*. Oxford: Oxford University Press, 2008.

Goldring, Elizabeth, Faith Eales, Elizabeth Clarke, and Jayne Elisabeth Archer, eds. *John Nichols's "The Progresses and Public Processions of Queen Elizabeth I."* Oxford: Oxford University Press, 2014.

Hadfield, Andrew, ed. *Amazons, Savages and Machiavels: An Anthology of Travel and Colonial Writing, 1550–1650*. Oxford: Oxford University Press, 2001.

———. *Literature, Travel, and Colonial Writing in the English Renaissance*. Oxford: Oxford University Press, 1998.

Hinds, Hilary, ed. *Anna Trapnel's Report and Plea: Or, a Narrative of Her Journey from London into Cornwall*. Toronto: Iter, 2016.

Kinsley, Zoë. *Women Writing the Home Tour, 1682–1812*. Aldershot UK: Ashgate, 2008.

Lawrence, Karen. *Penelope Voyages: Women and Travel in the British Literary Tradition*. Ithaca NY: Cornell University Press, 1994.

Macquerlot, Jean-Pierre, and Michèle Willems. *Travel and Drama in Shakespeare's Time*. Cambridge: Cambridge University Press, 1996.

McRae, Andrew. *Literature and Domestic Travel in Early Modern England*. Cambridge: Cambridge University Press, 2009.

Montagu, Mary Wortley. *The Turkish Embassy Letters*. Edited by Teresa Heffernan and Daniel O'Quinn. Peterborough ON: Broadview, 2013.

Morris, Mary, and Larry O'Connor, eds. *Maiden Voyages: Writings of Women Travelers*. New York: Vintage, 1993.

O'Loughlin, Katrina. *Women, Writing, and Travel in the Eighteenth Century*. Cambridge: Cambridge University Press, 2018.

Owens, Sarah, ed. and trans. *Madre María Rosa: Journey of Five Capuchin Nuns*. Toronto: Iter, 2009.

Palmer, Thomas. *An Essay of the Meanes how to make our Trauailes*. London, 1606.
Paravisini-Gebert, Lizabeth, and Ivette Romero-Cesareo, eds. *Women at Sea: Travel Writing and the Margins of Caribbean Discourse*. New York: Palgrave, 2001.
Poska, Allyson. *Gendered Crossings: Women and Migration in the Spanish Empire*. Albuquerque: University of New Mexico Press, 2016.
Robinson, Jane. *Unsuitable for Ladies: An Anthology of Women Travellers*. Oxford: Oxford University Press, 1994.
Romney, Susanah. *New Netherland Connections: Intimate Networks and Atlantic Ties in Seventeenth-Century America*. Chapel Hill: University of North Carolina Press, 2014.
Sherman, William H. "Stirrings and Searchings (1500–1720)." In *The Cambridge Companion to Travel Writing*, edited by Peter Hulme and Tim Youngs, 7–36. Cambridge: Cambridge University Press, 2002.
Siegel, Kristi, ed. *Gender, Genre, and Identity in Women's Travel Writing*. New York: Peter Lang, 2004.
Singh, Jyotsna G. "Boundary Crossings in the Islamic World: Princess Gulbadan as Traveler, Biographer, and Witness to History, 1523–1603." *Early Modern Women: An Interdisciplinary Journal* 7 (2012): 231–40.
Snader, Joe. *Caught Between Worlds: British Captivity Narratives in Fact and Fiction*. Lexington: University Press of Kentucky, 2000.
Stagl, Justin. *A History of Curiosity: The Theory of Travel, 1550–1800*. Amsterdam: Harwood, 1995.
Suranyi, Anna. *The Genius of the English Nation: Travel Writing and National Identity in Early Modern England*. Newark: University of Delaware Press, 2008.
Thrush, Coll. *Indigenous London: Native Travelers at the Heart of Empire*. New Haven: Yale University Press, 2016.
Turler, Jerome. *The Traveiler of Jerome Turler*. London, 1575.
Vitkus, Daniel. "Labor and Travel on the Early Modern Stage: Representing the Travail of Travel in Dekker's *Old Fortunatus* and Shakespeare's *Pericles*." In *Working Subjects in Early Modern English Drama*, edited by Michelle Dowd, Natasha Korda, and Jean Howard, 225–42. Burlington VT: Ashgate, 2011.
Wiseman, Susan. "Read Within: Gender, Cultural Difference and Quaker Women's Travel Narratives." In *Voicing Women: Gender and Sexuality in Early Modern Writing*, edited by Kate Chedgzoy, Melanie Hansen, and Suzanne Trill, 153–71. Pittsburgh PA: Duquesne University Press, 1997.
Yates, Julian. *Error, Misuse, Failure: Object Lessons from the English Renaissance*. Minneapolis: University of Minnesota Press, 2003.

PART 1

Early Modern Women Travelers

Global and Local Trajectories

1

Desdemona and Mrs. Keeling

RICHMOND BARBOUR

The tragic outcome of *Othello* requires Desdemona's journey to Cyprus, a dangerous liminal zone at the peripheries of Venetian and Ottoman power. Her voyage is the product of her own initiative. Anticipating a Turkish invasion, when the duke and senate commission Othello to take charge of the island's defenses, everyone but for her expects his bride to remain in Venice. "I crave fit disposition for my wife," Othello requests,

> Due reference of place, and exhibition,
> With such accommodation and besort
> As levels with her breeding. (1.3.236–39)[1]

It is Desdemona who first proposes that she accompany Othello. Beginning with her willful act of voyaging, and then investigating at greater length the like efforts of an East India Company (EIC) general's wife to join her husband on an expedition, this essay of cultural criticism juxtaposes the stage and the boardroom to historicize constructions of women and travel in both discursive fields. My aim is to delineate occasions of women's sexual and geographic agency, as represented in Shakespeare and contemporaneously debated in EIC councils, during a pivotal and disruptive interval: the founding generation of the London-based corporation that globalized the work of imperial capitalism.

With a siege of Cyprus imminent, Desdemona's petition is unusual: shall she be exposed to the hazards of war and possible capture by the Turks, even enslavement in a seraglio? The request's irregularity remains implicit in the rhetoric mobilized in its advocacy, not in any voiced objections. Claiming boldly "That I did love the Moor to live with him," declaring her "soul and fortunes consecrate[d]" to "his honors and his valiant parts," she insists upon her right to join him in the field, where he has earned these honors: "Let me go with him" (1.3.248, 253–54, 259). Her independent resolve recalls that of Emilia in *The Comedy of Errors*, who, left behind in Syracuse by her merchant husband Egeon, surprises him by voyaging, pregnant, to join him in Epidamnus.

    Shakespeare's primary source for *Othello*, Giovanni Battista Giraldi Cinthio's *Gli Hecatommithi* (1565), frames the question of Desdemona's travel rather differently: here, the couple alone, not the Venetian senate, ponder her options. The Signoria does not concern itself with their domestic arrangements. No siege or naval skirmishes loom. The precipitating occasion is not a Turkish threat but "a change in the forces" occupying the island, with the Moor, "a gallant man," to take command. The default assumption is that she will go. Yet as he foresees that "the length and dangers of the voyage" will greatly trouble her, the prospect of his wife's company saddens the Moor. Grieved by her husband's distress, she asks him what provokes his melancholy. He explains,

> The love I bear you spoils my pleasure at the honour I have received, because I see that one of two things must happen: either I must take you with me in peril by sea, or, so as not to cause you hardship, I must leave you in Venice. The first alternative must inevitably weigh heavily on me, since every fatigue you endured and every danger we met would give me extreme anxiety. The second . . . would be hateful to me, since, parting from you I should be leaving my very life behind.[2]

As the thought of her company provokes anxiety over her welfare, so that of her absence depresses him. Cinthio's Disdemona arrests this neurotic spiral. Spurning ambivalence, she professes the courage to take whatever comes and insists that their love requires her participation:

> Why do you let such ideas perturb you? I want to come with you wherever you go, even if it meant walking through fire in my shift

instead of, as it will be, crossing the water with you in a safe, well-furnished galley. If there really are to be dangers and fatigues, I wish to share them with you; and I should consider myself very little beloved if, rather than have my company on the sea, you were to leave me in Venice, or persuaded yourself that I would rather stay here in safety than be in the same danger as yourself.[3]

Her forceful clarity decides the matter.

Strikingly, Shakespeare frames Desdemona's travel as a question of public concern. She shares her precursor's resolve to undertake the journey. Moreover, as she speaks before the full senate, she addresses social anxieties and cultural fears deeper than a husband's confused despondency. By adding the geo-strategic vicissitudes of Christian-Ottoman conflict to the environmental hazards of her passage (we might note that, while a storm scatters the Turkish fleet in the play, Cyprus fell to the Ottomans in 1571, as London's theatergoers would have known), Shakespeare raises the stakes of the debate over her travel. Given the military urgency of Othello's commission, the default assumption is that she will stay in Venice—protecting her from danger and saving him, a wartime general, from the presumable distractions of her company. Thus, while Othello's account of wooing Desdemona without witchcraft is altogether self-assured, some edginess marks his support of her proposal, for he fends off the tacit suspicion that their lust will impede the discharge of his duties. Unlike Cinthio's Moor, who worries over his wife's comfort and safety, Othello dwells on his motives and reputation:

> Let her have your voice.
> Vouch with me, heaven, I therefore beg it not
> To please the palate of my appetite,
> Nor to comply with heat—the young effects
> In me defunct—and proper satisfaction;
> But to be free and bounteous to her mind. (1.3.260–65)

As she "saw Othello's visage in his mind" (1.3.252), so he elevates attention from her body to her mind. Yet some anxiousness underlies the sublimation. Sweepingly, Othello rejects the racist supposition that Moors are prone to lust and the misogynistic premise that sexual indulgence with a woman may undo a man, empowering her and making him womanly. He is too old for that, he claims. He will not be unmanned as Hercules was by Omphale, who took up his club and lion skin while he spun her distaff, or Antony was by Cleopatra, who boasts, "I drunk him to his bed; / Then put my tires and mantles on him, whilst / I wore his sword Phillippan" (*Ant.* 2.5.21-23). Enobarbus predicts that Cleopatra's "presence needs must puzzle Antony" (*Ant.* 3.7.10) at Actium, and it does. Shakespeare voices a classic instance of such dominion in Venus's boast to Adonis of her conquest of Mars:

> I have been wooed, as I entreat thee now,
> Even by the stern and direful god of war,
> Whose sinewy neck in battle ne'er did bow,
> Who conquers where he comes in every jar;
> Yet hath he been my captive and my slave,
> And begged for that which thou unasked shalt have.
> (*Ven.* 97–102)

Botticelli's rendering of the pair shows a naked, postcoital, utterly enervated Mars asleep opposite an alert, reattired Venus, eyeing him as if impatient for more action. His phallic lance, now aimed at his head, and his helmet are the toys of infantile satyrs (fig. 1).

Ironically, Othello's assertion that his "heat" is now "defunct" envenoms a suspicion with which Iago later infects him: that he is incapable of satisfying his lustful wife, whose choice of him in the first place proves her desires to be unnatural, ungoverned. Othello continues:

> And heaven defend your good souls that you think
> I will your serious and great business scant
> When she is with me. No, when light-winged toys
> Of feathered Cupid seel with wanton dullness
> My speculative and officed instruments,
> That my disports corrupt and taint my business,

> Let housewives make a skillet of my helm,
> And all indign and base adversities
> Make head against my estimation! (1.3.266–74)

Speaking in public as a general, Othello fixates on his forthcoming performance in Cyprus—on Desdemona's likely effects upon him—not on her likely troubles there. Rejecting the premise that something like Mars's fate awaits him in her embrace, his hyperbolic rhetoric ("Let housewives make a skillet of my helm") betrays the strain of the argument. The state's "serious and great business," whose prosecution requires keen "speculative and officed instruments," opposes the "wanton dullness" induced by "light-winged toys / Of feathered Cupid." Sexual "disports" necessarily contradict "business." Will the general keep each activity in its place, or will they commingle? The terms and force of the denial insinuate the suspicion that Desdemona might, indeed, distract him—as, given Iago's toxic intimacies on Cyprus, she assuredly does. Shakespeare's plot requires her to join Othello at that outpost—there would be no play else. Her loving, meddlesome presence there makes for tragedy. Depressingly, the play cannot refute the misogynistic premise that its leading couple would deny: that a wife should not accompany the general her husband on a critical mission eastward. Desdemona is attractively bold in her declaration of love for Othello. Her insistence that she enjoy the right to live with him is stirring. It excites his love and admiration. Their happiest moment is their reunion on Cyprus: "O my fair warrior!" he declares, admiring her potent, transgressive allure—his first words there (2.1.181). Yet her presence opens both of them to Iago's plotting and their undoing.

Desdemona's insistence that she accompany her husband to Cyprus should have resonated powerfully for the women in the play's original audiences. The question of "fit disposition" for wives, and the risks of including them on voyages east, was a matter of recurrent concern in Shakespeare's England, whose London-based trading companies proliferated during his lifetime. Making regular circuits around the Cape of Good Hope to the Indian Ocean, the London East India Company, chartered in 1600, complemented the Mediterranean pursuit of Asian exotica that the Levant Company initiated in the 1580s. Perhaps a decade after the play was first staged, EIC authorities heard an appeal like Desdemona's for a general's wife to embark on an important mission, and their response held something like *Othello*'s pessimism on the matter.

East-Indian voyages removed mariners from their families for up to three years and often left dependents in hard circumstances. Needful wives petitioning for assistance crowded the halls of EIC governor Sir Thomas Smythe's house on Philipot Lane, the company's initial home.[4] Salaries earned at sea were paid in London, and the directors made it their practice, at the close of a voyage, to give widows the wages due their late husbands.[5] They also eventually systematized benefits for wives of active sailors. By 1632 when Walter Mountfort, homeward bound from Persia, penned *The Launching of the Mary*, or *The Seaman's Honest Wife*, the EIC annually distributed to spouses one-sixth of a husband's pay: "And two monthes pay theyr wives are yearly payd / the better to mayntayne theyr poore estate / during the discontinuance of theyr husbands."[6]

Another possible solution to the problem—to let sailors' wives travel with their husbands—was, for the EIC's London magnates, out of the question. On February 1, 1614, for instance, three Indian mariners who reached London in the summer or fall of 1613 on the *Hector* in the company's Eighth Voyage (1611–14), "Salvador, Samuell Mounson and Anth. Delebber, together with their wives," requested that they "bee permitted to goe all into the East Indies" on the forthcoming voyage. The directors recoiled: "the Company knowinge howe inconvenient and unfitting it is for such woemen to goe among soe many unrulie sailors in a ship, by noe meanes would give way thereto." Class-based—and perhaps racialized—mistrust of "such women" and the potential swarms of "unrulie sailors" contending for their favors ignited managerial fears of promiscuous disorder at sea.

The directors counterbalanced their denial of this petition with solicitude for the couples' welfare in London. Recognizing that "they are not able to mayntaine their wives and themselves here" on their "small" wages, in evident desire to foster London's nascent Indian community and international good will, "for the better encouradgment of strangers," the directors offered the Indian sailors a respectable twenty shillings a month on the next voyage. Moreover, considering "their former paines taken in the *Hector*," the committees—a "committee" was an elected shareholder-director—also gave them a collective bonus of six pounds and individual gratuities of twenty shillings. They distributed the same sums to the wives, "for their household provisions." In a generous vein, they further offered each wife an annual stipend of five pounds "for soe longe tyme as they [their husbands] shall continue in the Companies service."[7]

The wealth, social status, and personal connections of the petitioner were critical to the EIC's comportment towards her. In rare instances, a woman of distinction might earn the committees' blessing to embark with her husband. In this volume, Amrita Sen and Karen Robertson recount the story of one such woman, Mariam Khan, an Armenian Christian who Emperor Jahangir arranged to marry England's ersatz ambassador to India, William Hawkins. Her companionship had steadied Hawkins there: "I lived content and without fear," he wrote, "she being willing to goe where I went, and live as I lived."[8] He died on the pestilential *Thomas* on the voyage home, and the richly left Mariam was wooed by Captain Gabriel Towerson of the *Hector*, another ship in the fleet. When she first arrived in London, the directors declared themselves "charitablie affected towards the widdowe, that is a straunger and to be married very shortlie" to Towerson.[9] They forgave her the sums they found due from her late husband. Thinking fit "to give her some token of there [sic] love (which happilie she will signifie unto her freindes in Cambaia)," Governor Smythe presented her with a wedding gift of "200 Jacobus in a purse" (about £240) in the company's name, a substantial sum.[10] Three years later, she and Towerson successfully petitioned the company to travel together as private passengers on a 1617 voyage to India. There they hoped, William Foster explains, "to improve their fortunes by the aid of her relatives."[11] EIC magnates endorsed her return in hopes that her connections would likewise enhance the company's fortunes in India. Though amiable and internationalist in spirit, their motives were business based.

As the denial of the Indian mariners' February 1614 request indicates, however, Mrs. Towerson's case was extraordinary. As a rule, the London

Company was somewhat queasy about passengers on its vessels. To permit the embarkation of an Englishwoman of upper-middling station with no overseas connections, the wife of a prosperous and respected merchant captain, was a vexing question. Late in 1614, as the fleet designated to carry Ambassador Sir Thomas Roe to India prepared to sail under the command of General William Keeling (1577/8–1620), the Court of Committees heard a petition from the general and his pregnant wife, Ann Broomfield Keeling, that she join the expedition. They had married in 1610, the year he returned as the general of the EIC's Third Voyage, and he had not shipped out since.[12] Keeling now held a critical assignment projected to occupy five years: to re-organize and oversee the EIC's several factories in the Indian Ocean.

The prospect of his wife's suasive presence in these distant markets raised swarms of patriarchal anxieties in London. After protracted debate, the directors effectively denied the couple's request by referring it to a vote of the general assembly of shareholders, where it was likely to lose. At this point, Keeling withdrew the petition. Yet as the fleet prepared to leave English waters, Ann boarded the flagship off Sandwich. Advised of this, the alarmed committees ordered Keeling to put her ashore or resign his commission. Otherwise, they were prepared to invest Sir Thomas Roe with "full power (in place of Captaine Keelinge) to undertake his charge with the government and power over the whole fleete." On the question of migratory wives, Roe, though just married, was a safer bet.[13] As Sen has shown, the ambassador vigorously opposed the company of wives in India and depicted female appetites as an engine of extravagance that unhinged the masculine frugality of the corporate body.[14] The balance of this essay will interrogate the rhetoric ignited by the Keelings' petition, discern its misogynistic premises and documentation of undaunted female resolve, and observe that the dominant faction's patronizing constructions of women and travel destabilized the corporate loyalties they sought to enforce.

Women, Travel, and the East India Company

Important marriages are a tool of state in Shakespeare and Tudor-Stuart England, yet in *Othello*, the state of Venice leaves it to the couple to choose Desdemona's arrangements: "Be it as you shall *privately* determine," the duke concludes (1.3.275, emphasis added). The EIC itself functioned as a kind of state: "thus we keepe / a little, but well governed Common weale / (by the permission of our soveraigne liege) / within our selves," declares the EIC's deputy governor in Mountfort's play.[15] This ministate, however, consecrated itself to commercial aims: it was above all a profit-seeking entity that harnessed individual interests and investments to the aims of the (male-gendered) corporate body. Unlike the duke, therefore, Governor Smythe refused to countenance the marital privacy of personnel: the maximization of profit made middle- and even lower-class marriages communal concerns. "Private trade" among mariners and factors was a perpetual bane to shareholders, and as they strived to contain it, the specter of invigorated private motives—which wives might fuel—haunted them. The joint-stock system was premised upon the identification of personal and collective investments: money and individual initiative earned legitimacy in the service of joint stock, not outside it. Capital strength derived from that merger. The prospect that Ann Broomfield's presence on the voyage might tilt the precarious balance of Keeling's fealties troubled company magnates in London.

Their disapproval struck some shareholders as outrageous. Indeed, many leading EIC investors held shares in the Virginia Company, which routinely included women on its voyages. But because a commander's wife—unlike a female passenger to America, single or married—enjoyed unique proximity to the mission-critical man, the prospect of her presence at his ear and in his bed concerned leading shareholders, who desired, and were perpetually frustrated of, their agents' absolute fidelity to corporate purposes abroad. Sailing east was profoundly different from sailing west in 1615. The Virginia Company was in the business of (hopefully profitable) colonization, the EIC the business of trade. Wives, strengthening domestic solidarities, bearing children, are clear assets in the process of "plantation." But many in the EIC saw Mrs. Keeling as a threat to their commerce.

The initial entry on Mrs. Keeling in the *Court Book of the EIC* indicates that the couple—like Shakespeare's and like the Indian mariners and their wives that year—made a joint appeal: "Mr. Governor acquainted this Courte wth a suite wch Captain Keelinge and his wife doe both make unto the Company, for leave for her to goe with him, to remayne in the Indies soe longe time as he shall staie there."[16] When first proposed, "Some approved of the motion, supposing yt to be very fitting in reguard of the quiet of his mynde, and good of his soule, which otherwise could hardlie be setled to live soe longe from his wife and as *a curse befalleth those that keepe man and wife asunder*, soe this Company cannot butt expect a blessing in giveinge way for them to contynue together."[17] In this view, his wife's steadying influence would invigorate Keeling's clearheaded pursuit of company purposes. Otherwise, restless longing for her would distract and demoralize him, perhaps drive him "to retourne sooner then the Company woulde be willing wthall." Echoing language from the marriage service of *The booke of common praier of 1559*, "Those whome God hath joyned together, let no man putte a sunder," these shareholders believed it a Christian imperative to grant the couple's request.[18]

That conviction, however, was firmly contradicted by others on the court. Some found it, "very inconvenient in reguard of the danger may befall him thereby, by the people of the Countrye whoe will attempt to abuse her, and shee *being a weake woman, and unfitt for travaile, wilbe a means to keepe him by her* and soe hinder the maine buysiness that hee is employed for, of passing from Porte to Porte."[19] By this proto-orientalist construct, Keeling would be burdened by the defense of white womanhood against dark desires. Moreover, unlike a colonist or a resident factor, he was commissioned to knit together trading depots throughout the Indian Ocean. He would stay on the move, a voyager par excellence. And women, in this view, being weak, are "unfitt for travaile."

The implicit pun is germane: a woman's "travail" is obstetric, not maritime. Mrs. Keeling's proposal to commix these labors is received with skepticism: she will probably desire to nest somewhere, thus retarding her husband's movements: "shee goinge soe longe a voyage to dwell upon the sea, will ... be a meanes to disswade him from passing from place to place of danger and *detaine him in some place where a good aire shalbee*."[20] This patriarchal speculation frames travel as a masculine performance, home-keeping a feminine one: thus Odysseus traverses the seas while Penelope works her loom in Ithaka. Eric J. Leed awkwardly valorizes such gendered travel as "the *spermatic* journey [which] has its classical form in the myths of the traveling gods, heroes, and patriarchs."[21] Moreover, even if Mrs. Keeling contented herself to "dwell upon the sea," some saw trouble there as well: she "shalbe exposed to many and sundrye dangers that may followe, and be an occasion of discord betwixt his people and him, if ought should be attempted against her honor."[22] We are suddenly very near *Othello* here: might the flagship harbor an attractive lieutenant and an Iago?

The Keelings rejected these concerns. William insisted, "that his wife and hee have dulie weighed together all objections and inconvenyences, wch wilbe rather to themselves then [to] the Company." Ann might well be "inconvenienced" by bearing and raising a child within the unsteady, testosterone-thick environment of a ship at sea, but the couple were willing to face that challenge to stay together. Dismissing the directors' fears, Keeling desired the committees "not to stand upon shadowes wth him." He assured them "that his care of the publique good shall oversways any private respect whatsoever."[23] Four days later, he renewed the petition: "The motion was againe approved by some, and distasted by others, supposinge thatt where shee shall conceyve any daunger may bee towards her husband, either in fight (yf any should happen) or in passing from porte to porte in the Companyes service, *shee will bee a meanes to daunte him by her feares, or detaine him* and make him neglect those Actions hee is espetiallye employed for."[24] Opponents of the plan hit upon a range of misogynistic tropes to justify their opposition. Now the assumption that women are innately timorous—prone to seek protection from men and thus to keep them nearby, shunning risks—drove the inference that Mrs. Keeling would "detain" him from performing his duty.

Keeling answered that he had already raised these objections with his wife. "Yet shee contynueinge her earnest and ymportunate suite, hee craveth their consentes."[25] This explanation offered small reassurance to the skeptics, for it showed Keeling unable to dissuade his wife. *Her* "earnest and ymportunate suite" has renewed *his*. If he defers to her here, what will he do abroad? In any case, he assured them again, "uppon the faith and protestations of an honest man, that noe private respectes whatsoever shall bee any occasion to him to hinder their publique service."[26] He declared himself confident that her companionship "should enable him to perform the better service for them." The directors "rested upon indifferent tearmes for the present, rather enclyneinge [inclining] to graunte her leave to goe, then to keepe them asunder."[27]

Discerning progress, Keeling pressed the case again three days later by elaborating the argument that her presence would foster "the quiet of his mynde": he hoped that, through his wife, "God will give him the better blessinge in his labors, havinge this meanes to free his mynde from *sundrye corrupt thoughts.*"[28] Here, the general outflanks the misogynist premise that women instigate bad male behavior. To the contrary: like a good angel, Ann will allay his demons. Fidelity to his wife, Keeling suggests, shall strengthen his performance of the company's pious purposes. Unable to claim "young effects / In me defunct," he offers a variant of Othello's argument: a man in his late thirties will crave sexual release one way or another. Lust is less corrosive of self-discipline within the holy bonds of marriage than in onanism, sodomy with shipmates, or random and unsanctified liaisons abroad. In the memorable words of Saint Paul, "But if they cannot contain themselves, let them marry: for it is better to marry than to burn. . . . Let not the wife depart from her husband."[29]

Not warming to this argument, Governor Smythe and his faction, concerned that acquiescence would reflect badly upon their judgment, continued to find it "very inconvenyent" for Mrs. Keeling to go. Others insisted to the contrary "that the greatest Inconvenyence [of her staying] will bee to [the couple] themselves, and therefore [they] beinge both younge and not fit to bee parted for soe longe time, wisht that they might be gyven thereunto and their requests graunted."[30] Largely sympathetic yet divided, anxious to project piety in their affairs, the November 15 court referred the matter of Mrs. Keeling to a plenary shareholder meeting, a political move that covered, and advantaged, Smythe's faction: "This Court could be contented to give waye to their suite. Yet findinge that the matter is like to prove doubtfull hereafter, and *distastfull unto the generalitie*, therefore they would willinglie have the consent of the generalitie to joyne with them."³¹ Keeling saw which way the winds were blowing. At the general court on December 6, he withdrew his request. Greatly relieved, the committees granted him one hundred pounds to compensate his lengthy stay abroad without his wife.³²

Three days later in Deptford, however, Smythe heard from Keeling's rival for the 1615 appointment, Thomas Best, the general of the recently returned Tenth Voyage, "some doubtfull speeches . . . concerning Mrs. Keelinge goinge wth her husband" after all. At Smythe's response "that the Company would not give waye thereunto, hee [Best] objected, what if shee will goe, whether the Company will or noe?" Best hinted at a plot to exploit Ann's pregnancy: "to gett her aboard by some meanes from whence she would nott willinglie retourne. That then it might bee supposed she should not bee violentlie forced, being in the case shee is in, and soe must necessarilie bee permitted to accompany him." To induce miscarriage by muscling her off the ship could ignite terrible publicity for an oft-maligned corporation that preferred to think itself charitable to mariners' wives and families.

Upset by the report, anxious to prevent its dissemination, the court requested "Mr Governor to deale privatelie wth him [Keeling], to consider of a direct answere against the next Courte, and not to goe aboute to hoodwinke the Companie."³³ At the following court, Keeling—in a strikingly awkward position now, having requested and accepted a hundred-pound bonus in confirmation of his good faith—turned defensive and apologetic. He insisted that he would never have requested his wife's company had not reputable shareholders first urged the idea upon him, "as a thinge fitting, laudable, honest and convenyent." With apologies, he also confessed to personal queasiness about the proposal: "hee conceyved it from the beginning very prejudiciall unto the Companie and himselfe. And beinge nowe . . . that he finds it distastfull unto them in such high measure, he professed, protested, and affirmed upon his credit that he will nott presse it any further."³⁴

To take Keeling at his word is to infer that Ann, as he indicated on November 12, was the plan's prime mover. Following the crisis in December, Keeling conducted himself as if the couple had accepted that she must stay in England. In light of this concession, he negotiated a raise of one hundred pounds a year and secured the company's pledge to pay her from his salary fifty pounds annually for her housekeeping.[35] Yet, whatever her husband's inward thoughts, Ann had not relinquished hope of sailing to India. In February, word reached London from the Downs that Keeling "hath his wife aboard, wth an Intent to carry her wth him."[36] For reasons noted above, the court hesitated to remove her by force: "yf she should miscarrye . . . yt would nott onelie bee a greate greyfe unto the Company, but some ymputacion [imputation] would fall upon them for there severitie." Some now argued that they should simply let the Keelings go. But the dominant group, angered at the couple's subterfuge, "held yt a great indignitie to bee circumvented in this manner, taxing her of great immodestie, and him of indiscretion to be soe carryed away, wch must hange as a Continuall disgrace upon him, And call his reputation in question more then any thinge that ever hee did."[37] Their indignation recalls the opening complaint of Shakespeare's *Antony and Cleopatra*: "Nay, but this dotage of our general's / O'erflows the measure" (1.1.1–2) — a rebuke provoked by an extravagant liaison, not an insistent marriage.

A few days later, the cashier Richard Atkinson, dispatched to the coast to manage her, reported Mrs. Keeling to be "on shore, wth an intent to make for London."[38] Atkinson remained suspicious, however, his mistrust confirmed in a February 19 letter describing, "the pretended shewe made by Mrs Keelinge of retourning for London; and yet that she dealt underhand wth a midwife at Deale to have gone wth her into the Indyes."[39] At this report, the committees directed Atkinson to deliver to Keeling the governor's "sharpe" letter commanding him to send her ashore or resign his commission. Writing in response, Keeling "taxt [taxed] the Companie of great unkindness towards him."[40] The Court then entreated Smythe to write him another letter, "wherein they wisht to have some lines of comfort to be remembred. Being all of one minde, That yf he retourne his wife to London, and procede wthout her, that then they hould there former opinions firme: That none can be employed fitter then himselfe. But yf she accompanie him, they hould him unworthie their service or place of charge wherein hee is."⁴¹ Their supposedly comforting words confirmed a stunning intrusion of corporate imperatives into the domestic sphere. Keeling's entire office and authority hinged upon a single issue: his submission to the court's patriarchal will that he govern his wife and put her ashore.

The committees prevailed. Yet the resilience of this married woman's determination, recalling that of several Shakespearean wives, warrants our attention. Like the heavily pregnant Emilia of *Errors*, who sails to Epidamnus in the attempt to raise her offspring with her husband (1.1.43–48), or Pericles's bride Thaisa, who, "with child, makes her desire— / Which who shall cross?—along to go," together with her nurse, Lychorida (*Per* 3. Cho. 40–41)—Ann Keeling evidently plotted her own bold course. Her gendered desire to travel expressed more than a will to experience the great world. Like Desdemona, Emilia, and Thaisa, she took independent action to enjoy her husband and preserve her nascent family. By securing a midwife in the coastal town of Deale—a serving woman who would have been to her something as *Othello's* Emilia, another traveling wife, was to Desdemona—she made provision for her long and perilous journey. Childbirth at sea, as *Pericles* dramatized that event, would be unusually risky.⁴² Ann would need a midwife and a companion to help her care for the child. The surviving evidence in the EIC papers indicates that she took the initiative to exercise her own sexuality and reproductive agency: to bear children while she could and to determine who would father them. If she wanted more offspring by William, then it made far better sense to join him than to wait several years for a return that might fail. Thus, while her husband vacillated and apologized, and either colluded with her to mislead the company or found himself unable to dissuade her or both, the pregnant and "immodest" Ann Broomfield Keeling held firm in the conviction that she must go with him to India.

With the voyage in progress, the couple persisted in their appeals. In letters of February 28 and March 3 drafted in Portland, Dorset, just before the fleet left England, Keeling widened the rationale for her inclusion. He and his merchants had discussed wives on voyages. They concurred that the presence of their spouses would make married men of "special place" more effective company agents than single men. Wives would consolidate corporate loyalties and healthier lifestyles abroad: for "indeed there are very few [men] ... whoe are able (notwithstanding there best endevors) to live wthout the Companie of woemen." Wives might curb "the great disorder of the factors nowe living at Bantam," for instance, a disease-wracked port city on Java whose English factory, the EIC's first, was notorious for the devastating mortality, sexual license, and private trading of personnel—outcomes London understood as intervolved.[43] Factors' wives, Keeling reasoned, would mitigate these problems. He duly requested that, "after she shalbe delivered" of their child, Ann be sent on the next available ship to join him in Bantam. His following letter "earnestlie desir[ed]" the same.[44]

Unmoved, the company found "noe possibilitie att present to give any satisfaction." Keeling's fleet was already at sea, and the next, not scheduled to depart until Christmas, would take a roundabout course to Java. Speculating that "it will bee too tedyous for her to fetch so greate a compasse"—that she lacked the stamina to endure a circuitous voyage—the court referred the proposal to future consideration.[45] At the next meeting, Smythe reported that he and an associate had called on Mrs. Keeling to discuss her husband's letters. Undaunted by the prospect of the unusually "longe and wearisome" voyage they described, she forcefully renewed her request: "shee tooke her opportunity to second her husbands last mocion [motion] ... and prest [pressed] her said suite very earnestlie, notwithstanding the many discouradgments and almost impossiblities alledgd, ... all those objections nothinge prevailinge to make her desiste."[46] She was as ardent as Cinthio's Disdemona to bear the full burdens of travel in order to join her husband. While impressed that both Keelings argued "earnestlie," the committees again referred the appeal to future consideration.

Keeling's next missive of June 19, 1615, from South Africa, does not survive. But its digest includes, amongst a litany of complaints about the company's hiring and provision for the voyage ("Batten, a master's mate, wholly unfit for the voyage and place; your stewards more fit to be under tutors and a rod than in charge"), one item whose phrasing indexes his vehemence on the theme of reunion with Ann: "Wonderful many arguments and requests to have his wife sent unto him or to permit him to come home (in what fashion soever) in your next ship from Bantam." He had begun to consider resignation if denied the appeal. In implicit caustic critique of the court's misogyny, the summary continues: "Wishing you not to suffer any gentleman passenger to go along in any of your ships. Merland, whom some of the Lords commended, is the veriest villain in the world."[47] The injustice of the court's decisions vexed Keeling deeply: the company invited an ill-disposed, volatile gentleman aboard while denying Ann access to her husband's person for five years.

But their separation did not last that long. The minority on the court, who suggested that the general's longing for his spouse would damage him and drive him to return prematurely, were intuitive. In their patronizing appraisals of the distractive potential of a traveling wife, Smythe's faction had miscalculated. Their aim—that the talented Keeling should advance their interests in the East for five years—would likelier have been fulfilled if they had honored the couple's will to cohabitate. Their unease over the intrusion of women and domestic fealties into the corporate sphere curtailed the general's performance in the latter. Having requested the directors' blessing to return, Keeling was thrilled in September 1616 to receive in Bantam their letter accepting his resignation. At the end of May 1617 the *Dragon* reached the Downs, where Ann had stolen aboard two years before. Attended by two dignitaries of the court, she was among the first to board the ship and embrace her husband.[48]

Keeling prospered during his years of EIC service, yet his health had suffered. Having come to the attention of the Isle of Wight's governor, the Earl of Southampton, Shakespeare's patron, Keeling was installed there as the captain of Cowes Castle and made a Groom of the Bedchamber to James I.[49] The couple entertained generously, adapting global skills of shipboard hospitality to their new circumstances. Sir John Oglander (1585–1655), the island's resident gossip, reports that Keeling, "was a brave and noble fellow and one that gave the royalest entertainment, when he did invite, that ever I saw, with all sorts of wine, perfumed ginger and all other dainties that London could yield."[50] The family enjoyed just three years together there. Late in

1620, the year originally set for his return, Keeling, aged forty-two or forty-three, died, leaving four children. He was buried in Carisbrooke church, where a monument commissioned by his "loveing & sorrowful wife" is puzzlingly antedated to September 1619.[51] Ann's April 1621 marriage to another islander, John Hobson, restored the fortunes of the Hobson family. Oglander reports an intriguing anecdote of the initial visit of Lord Edward Conway, appointed secretary of state in 1623 and governor of the Isle of Wight in 1625, to the island on September 14, 1627: "When he came to Newport I caused Elgor, the schoolmaster, to provide an oration, which was made unto him by Keeling, one of the scholars."[52] The well-spoken lad, evidently Elgor's star pupil, was perhaps the unborn child Ann carried when she climbed aboard the *Dragon* in hopes of sailing to India. In 1627 he would have been twelve years old.

The Keelings' story offers one measure of the human costs of the anxious masculinity of nascent imperial capitalism — a transnationally fraught elaboration of the patriarchic vexations that Shakespeare tested variously on the London stage. General Keeling finally found those costs too high. As if anticipating his mortality, he resigned from corporate service to share the remainder of his life with his wife. Their story, I submit, contests *Othello*'s tragic pessimism on the consequences of women's travel: Ann's company might have invigorated the general's aborted command. Misogynistic speculation on the tactical and commercial risks supposedly embodied in wandering women, and corporate dominion over personal and family relations, added avoidable damage and dysfunction to the EIC's inherent exploitation of its servants in the East, who risked their lives for London's gain. By its refusal to accommodate Ann's desire to share her husband's journey, a controlling masculinist mentality over-taxed the corporate fealties it thereby sought to fortify.

Notes

I thank Nancy Staton Barbour for her suggestions throughout this essay's composition, including the inference that Ann Keeling's resolve to travel with her husband expressed the will to exercise her own sexual and reproductive agency.

1. All quotations of Shakespeare are from Orgel and Braunmuller, *The Complete Pelican Shakespeare*.

2. Bullough, *Narrative*, 7: 242–43.
3. Bullough, *Narrative*, 7: 243.
4. Foster, *John Company*, 1–31.
5. On December 19, 1609, for instance, the Court of Committees ordered the cashier Richard Atkinson to "pay the deceased mariners' wages to their wives, so far as the same shall appear due unto them" (India Office Records [hereafter IOR] B/3, 161, December 31, 1606– January 26, 1610). My transcripts of *Court Book* entries exchange "i" for "j" and "u" for "v" where appropriate, but otherwise preserve original spelling and many contractions. Thus "wth" reads "with," "wch" reads "which," throughout; italics mark an expanded contraction. Some punctuation has been adjusted.
6. Mountfort, *The Launching*, p. 74, ll. 1718–20. On the play, see Christensen, "'Absent, Weak, or Unserviceable,'" as well as Christensen, *Separation Scenes*. On the familial consequences of long-range trade, see Fury, *Tides*, and Fumerton, *Unsettled*.
7. IOR B/5, 25, February 1, 1613/14. I thank Amrita Sen for drawing my attention to this entry. Fisher, *Counterflows*, 41–42 also treats these mariners.
8. Foster, *Early Travels*, 85.
9. IOR B/5, 33, February 11, 1613/14. I thank Karen Robertson for drawing my attention to this entry.
10. IOR B/5, 38, February 21, 1613/14.
11. Foster, *Early Travels*, 69.
12. Laughton, "Keeling." On his prior command, see Barbour, *Third Voyage Journals*.
13. IOR B/5, 365, February 11, 1614/15. Roe married a young widow, Lady Eleanor Beeston, on December 15, 1614; see Strachan, "Roe."
14. See Sen, "Traveling Companions." Some of Roe's hostility to Mrs. Steele and Mariam Khan may have derived from his sense of virtuous self-sacrifice in leaving his own bride in England. She joined him on the subsequent embassy to Constantinople, 1621–29. On the Keeling's petition, see also Schleck, "The Marital Problems of the East India Company," an essay that came to my attention too late to engage here. Schleck frames the relation between EIC agents and their employers as a virtual marriage bond; I see it rather as a corporate variant of the master-servant bond, a highly charged relation that often foreclosed marriage for the servant in the early modern period.
15. Mountfort, *The Launching*, p. 14, ll. 189–92. On this theme, see Stern, *The Company-State*.
16. IOR B/5, 263, November 8, 1614.
17. IOR B/5, 263; emphasis added.

18. *The booke of common praier*, n. p.
19. IOR B/5, 263; emphasis added.
20. IOR B/5, 263; emphasis added.
21. Leeds, *The Mind*, 114; emphasis added.
22. IOR B/5, 263.
23. IOR B/5, 263.
24. IOR B/5, 272, November 12, 1614; emphasis added.
25. IOR B/5, 272.
26. IOR B/5, 272.
27. IOR B/5, 263.
28. IOR B/5, 263; 277, November 15, 1614; emphasis added.
29. 1 Cor. 7:9–10, King James Version.
30. IOR B/5, 276, November 15, 1614.
31. IOR B/5, 277; emphasis added.
32. IOR B/5, 305, December 10, 1614.
33. IOR B/5, 310, December 13, 1614.
34. IOR B/5, 314, December 16, 1614.
35. IOR B/5, 339, January 14, 1614/15.
36. IOR B/5, 364, February 11, 1614/15.
37. IOR B/5, 365, February 11, 1614/15.
38. IOR B/5, 369, February 16, 1614/15.
39. IOR B/5, 372, February 22, 1614/15.
40. IOR B/5, 373, February 22, 1614/15.
41. IOR B/5, 373.
42. For a detailed assessment of these risks, see Taff's essay on *Pericles* in this volume.
43. IOR B/5, 385, March 10, 1614/15.
44. IOR B/5, 385; IOR B/5, 417, April 28, 1615.
45. IOR B/5, 417.
46. IOR B/5, 419–20, May 5, 1615.
47. Danvers, *Letters*, 2:190.
48. Strachan and Penrose, *East India Company Journals*, 6, 42, 44, 168. On September 21, 1616, Keeling wrote in his journal, "The *Swann's* skiffe came to Bantam bringing me l[etter]s from England, and in them to my most content licence for my retourne for Engl[an]d: Thy m[e]rcye therin O lord, let me never forgett" (150).
49. Laughton, "Keeling"; Strachan and Penrose, *East India Company Journals*, 6–7.
50. Bamford, *A Royalist's Notebook*, 154.
51. Laughton, "Keeling"; Jewitt, *Reliquary*, 89–90.
52. Bamford, *A Royalist's Notebook*, 24.

Bibliography

Bamford, Francis, ed. *A Royalist's Notebook: The Commonplace Book of Sir John Oglander Kt. of Nunwell*. London: Constable, 1936.

Barbour, Richmond. *The Third Voyage Journals: Writing and Performance in the London East India Company, 1607-10*. New York: Palgrave Macmillan, 2009.

The booke of common praier, and administration of the Sacramentes, and other rites and ceremonies in the Churche of Englande. London, 1559.

Bullough, Geoffrey, ed. *Narrative and Dramatic Sources of Shakespeare*. 7 vols. London: Routledge, 1973.

Christensen, Ann C. "'Absent, Weak, or Unserviceable': The East India Company and the Domestic Economy in *The Launching of the Mary, or The Seaman's Honest Wife*." In *Global Traffic: Discourses and Practices of Trade in English Literature and Culture from 1550 to 1700*, edited by Barbara Sebek and Stephen Deng, 117-36. New York: Palgrave Macmillan, 2008.

———. *Separation Scenes: Domestic Drama in Early Modern England*. Lincoln: University of Nebraska Press, 2017.

Danvers, Frederick Charles, ed., *Letters Received by the East India Company from its Servants in the East, 1613-16*. 6 vols. 1897. Reprint, Amsterdam: N. Israel, 1968.

Fisher, Michael H. *Counterflows to Colonialism: Indian Travellers and Settlers in Britain 1600-1857*. Delhi: Permanent Black, 2004.

Foster, William, ed. *Early Travels in India, 1583-1619*. London: Oxford University Press, 1921.

———. *John Company*. London: John Lane, 1926.

Fumerton, Patricia. *Unsettled: The Culture of Mobility and the Working Poor in Early Modern England*. Chicago: University of Chicago Press, 2006.

Fury, Cheryl. *Tides in the Affairs of Men: The Social History of Elizabethan Seamen, 1580-1603*. Westport: Greenwood, 2002.

Jewitt, Llewellynn, ed. *The Reliquary, Quarterly Archaeological Journal and Review*, 14 (1873-74).

India Office Records. East India Company Minutes of the Court of Directors and Court of Proprietors 1599-1858. British Library, London.

Laughton, J. K. "Keeling, William (1577/8-1620)," *Oxford Dictionary of National Biography*. Oxford University Press, 2004; online edition, January 2008.

Leeds, Eric J. *The Mind of the Traveler: From Gilgamesh to Global Tourism*. New York: Basic, 1992.

Malieckal, Bindu. "Mariam Khan and the Legacy of Mughal Women in Early Modern Literature of India." In *Early Modern England and Islamic Worlds*, edited by Bernadette Andrea and Linda McJannet, 97–122. New York: Palgrave Macmillan, 2011.

Mountfort, Walter. *The Launching of the Mary*. Edited by J. H. Walter. London: Malone Society Reprints, 1933.

Schleck, Julia. "The Marital Problems of the East India Company." *Journal for Early Modern Cultural Studies* 17, no. 3 (2017): 84-105.

Sen, Amrita. "Traveling Companions: Women, Trade, and the Early East India Company." *Genre* 48, no. 2 (2015): 193–214.

Shakespeare, William. *The Complete Pelican Shakespeare*. Edited by Stephen Orgel and A. R. Braunmuller. New York: Penguin, 2002.

Strachan, Michael. "Roe, Sir Thomas (1581–1644)," *Oxford Dictionary of National Biography*. Oxford University Press, 2004; online edition, May 2011.

Strachan, Michael, and Boies Penrose, eds. *The East India Company Journals of Captain William Keeling and Master Thomas Bonner, 1615–1617*. Minneapolis: University of Minnesota Press, 1971.

Stern, Philip J. *The Company-State: Corporate Sovereignty and the Early Modern Foundations of the British Empire in India*. Oxford: Oxford University Press, 2011.

2

A Stranger Bride

Mariam Khan and the East India Company

KAREN ROBERTSON

Mariam Khan, during the second decade of the East India Company's long-distance trade, married two EIC captains: William Hawkins in 1610 and then, after Hawkins's death, Gabriel Towerson in February 1613/14. Between 1611 and 1616 this *stranger* (foreign) bride, a woman raised in the palace of the Mughal emperor Jahangir, made a round-trip voyage from the court at Agra to London and back again.[1] Though travel by wives on company ships was unusual, her passage was subsidized. Her voyage from Agra to the Red Sea, to Saldania (currently South Africa), Ireland, and London tested her tenacity and fortitude when disease swept the ship and many including her husband died. Unusually, on her trip back to India she was accompanied by two other women, a trio that caused a great deal of trouble.[2] Her marriages brought her two English husbands into intimate contact with a wife raised in the women's quarters of the Mughal court. The mystery of her connections to that feminine space from which most men were excluded and, even more importantly, her links to the highest noblewomen of the palace of Jahangir provoked hope and caution on the part of the directors of the company. My recent transcription amplifies the printed East India Company Minutes of the directors to follow their debates in London as they assessed Mariam Khan's economic, social, and even spiritual capital over nearly a decade.[3] This story coincided with the prohibition on the attempts of Ann Broomfield to join her EIC husband on his ship discussed by Richmond Barbour in his essay in this volume. The trio of wives caused so much trouble in Surat that Sir Thomas Roe, ambassador to the Mughal court, fulminated against such "encumbrances," a story Amrita Sen details in her essay in this volume.[4]

Though ultimately enormously successful, in its earliest years the company, as K. N. Chaudhuri explains in his economic history of the East India Company, was undercapitalized and weakly organized; its first decades to 1640 "relatively weak," and the death rate of employees abroad shocking.[5] Its central goal was to maximize profit by establishing trading posts called factories in locations in the East. Corporate responsibility for employees and their families was under strain as the movement of large numbers of English men abroad for years complicated notions of patriarchal domesticity and disturbed the English by the notion of English profit earned from the blood of so many employees abroad.[6] Guilds had always had some responsibilities for the families of freemen, and joint-stock companies had experience in handling the inheritance of stock by widows, but this developing overseas mercantile corporation urgently needed to develop policy about the dependents of its employees. The company's responsibility to "stranger wives" as well as widows was brought to the fore by the petitions of Mariam Khan as they debated her marriages.

This story forms a prelude to the company's continuing struggles to formulate policy about wives. Sir Thomas Roe, the first official English ambassador to India, was so frustrated by his dealings with Mariam Khan and her companions that he called wives "encumbrances" and demanded they be prohibited.[7] The troubles provoked by Mariam Khan may have influenced the refusal of permission for Ann Broomfield to join her husband, Captain Keeling. Company interactions with these wives preceded the organizational ideals of the midcentury that linked good bookkeeping with social order and banned wives from the factories.

The court minutes of the Committee of Committees, recording the weekly meeting of the directors of the company, reveal their cautious treatment of Mariam Khan. Wary about setting precedents about wives, they repeatedly assessed her economic and social capital, particularly her potential influence at the court of Jahangir, through both her relatives and the women of the court. Fantasies of the *haram* as an exotic location of highly sexualized female bodies had not yet fully developed, but Mariam Khan's connections to the fabulous riches and the wealthy women of the Indian court were her greatest asset and caused the company to treat her cautiously. Ruby Lal rightly contests the orientalist fantasy of the *haram* as a static location of sexual pleasure; nonetheless, the restriction of English men from such spaces did mystify the nature of women's power.[8] Both Bindu Malieckal and Amrita Sen deepen our understandings of the power and independence of Mughal noblewomen, an independence that might have baffled the English merchants. Moreover, as a Christian Armenian in a Mughal court, from a community that survived through its deep knowledge of Eastern trading routes, Mariam Khan was both insider and outsider. By reading against the grain of the company records, the story of her friendship with other wives detailed by Amrita Sen in this volume shows that she crossed religious and national boundaries to form informal networks of Christian and Mughal women, actions that may reflect her experience in the *haram*. A family practice of transnational connection is further suggested by the marriages of her mother and aunt to Dutch and Portuguese traders.

Chaudhuri's phrase "decision-making under uncertainty" barely conveys the uncertainties that long-distance trade posed to the directors of the company in its earliest decades.[9] The directors, who met regularly in Sir Thomas Smythe's house in Philpot Lane, were required to make market decisions over thousands of miles, across years of time, and about cultures they barely knew. The directors had to assess the exchange value of commodities and predict the English market primarily for textiles and spices, over distance and time, as their captains and factors plunged into a world of extraordinary diversity unfamiliar to Londoners. In the early days the directors were forced to make judgments in a mist. They relied on "intelligence" through the medium of journals and letters sent from multiple sources.[10] Daniel Vitkus, in his challenge to the binaries of postcolonial theory in *Turning Turk*, quotes William Lithgow, a Scottish traveler, who lists fourteen different varieties of Christians he encounters in Cairo in 1612 and an "infinite number of Infidels, whose sorts are these, Turkes, tawny Moores, white Moores, black Moores, Nigroes, Musilmans, Tartars, Persians, Indians, Sabunks, Berdoanes, Jewes, Arabians, Barbares, and Tingitanian Sarazens."[11] For the directors exchange rates and prices were perhaps easier to quantify than assessment of their employees' interactions with such diversity. Yet to survive the company needed to ally with strangers. Barbour observes that "without the widespread collusion of indigenous groups, Britain lacked the demographic strength to impose their will on Asian populations."[12] The company was also struggling with the extraordinary death rate of its employees abroad. Its directors expected their captains to establish trading networks and outposts on land, leaving men, called factors, who often settled for years. In the first years, factors went out as single men, and though young they died at a great rate. The death rate at Bantam from 1603 to 1605, where six of eight men died, was so great that Gabriel Towerson's survival invites comment by John Keay in *The Honourable Company*: "Gabriel Towerson must have been blessed with a constitution of concrete for he would outlast all of his contemporaries, only to succumb twenty years later to the cruelest cut of all" (as we shall see).[13]

During the "messy and contingent" institutional development during the earliest decades of the company, the reality of their captains' marriages challenged the simple naval rule that excluded wives from ships.[14] English wives were expected to stay at home, even though the long absence of husbands could leave families destitute.[15] This early story of the stranger bride reveals the directors struggling with the challenges of translation of terms of religious and racial diversity across oceans and also disturbances to the English ideology of domestic patriarchalism that wives were under the control and rule of their husbands. The court minutes provide varied scrutiny of Mariam Khan's spiritual, cultural, economic, and social capital, the last a mystery that guaranteed their continuing caution.

The company learned of this stranger widow when she arrived in London and demanded compensation for her dead husband's expenses. On the two-year journey back to England, Hawkins had recorded the story of his marriage in the Mughal court in a "journal of intelligence," presumably the one produced by Nicholas Ufflet during the earliest exchanges between the court and the widow in February 1613/14 and subsequently printed by Samuel Purchas.[16]

Captain Hawkins had left his ship and traveled eight hundred miles to the court at Agra seeking a *firman* (imperial edict) for trade and found a new emperor, Jahangir, who four years earlier had inherited the throne from his father, Akbar. Jahangir developed a fondness for the eccentric Englishman who arrived in April 1609, possibly because Hawkins could speak Turkish, or because he was a satisfactory drinking companion. However, Hawkins's rise as favorite provoked such hostility at the court that an attempt was made on his life. He remonstrated with the emperor, who after blaming the Jesuits made the Englishman an unexpected offer: "This past, the King was very earnest with me to take a white Mayden out of his Palace, who would give her all things necessary with slaves, and he would promise me she should turn Christian: and by this means my meats and drinks should be looked unto by them, and I should live without fear."[17] Taken aback by this shift from murder to marriage, Hawkins tries to refuse. He objects he will not take a "Moor" and insists he must have a Christian born, "little thinking" a Christian daughter could be found. Jahangir foils the Englishman by producing a Christian born. When Jahangir withdraws the first bride, we never learn what "white mayden" he had in mind. He may simply have been using "white" as a signifier of beauty, as was common both East and West. Or he may have been using "white" in the Portuguese fashion to describe "Arabs and light-skinned Asians." The unnamed "mayden" and convert-to-be disappears from the story as Jahangir surveys his court and selects a woman with an impeccable Christian lineage, the daughter of an Armenian. Her lineage is in fact superior to that of the Englishman, since Armenians established one of the earliest Christian communities, antedating Anglo-Saxon conversion by centuries.[18]

To Jahangir, the gift of an Armenian bride to a Christian trader may have seemed perfectly logical. The Armenians had been invited by Akbar to settle in Mughal lands and had established an Armenian church in Agra in 1562.[19] Chaudhuri explains that "the Armenian traders were a group of highly skilled arbitrage dealers who were forced through historical circumstances to develop very flexible and geographically mobile forms of commerce." Expert in the "multiplicity of money and weights, and even government fiscal regulations," Armenians linked with the Portuguese trading networks as intermediaries.[20]

While the participants in the discussion seem to understand the substitution of *Moor* for a white convert, the word injects into the exchange the somatic associations around *Moor* developing in English and raises questions about color consciousness in the Mughul court. To dissolve the black/white binary subsequently established so firmly, I recall Vitkus's argument about the "gallimaufry" of differences that English merchants encountered in Jahangir's empire.

"Colorism," Alice Walker's useful term, did exist at the Mughal court. Perhaps by offering a white convert, Jahangir was simply attempting to suit the complexions of the couple. A contemporary allegorical painting by the court artist Bichitr, *Jahangir preferring a Sufi mystic to three kings* (ca. 1615–18), differentiates five different skin colors, from the pasty English king to the dark complexioned Hindu Bichitr, the "king of painting."[21]

By rejecting a *Moor*, Hawkins raises the associations of phenotype that were accumulating around *Moor* in England, a question investigated in the extensive scholarship on the "race" of Othello.[22] Jean Feerick's recent argument in *Strangers in Blood: Relocating Race in the Renaissance* shows the older discourse of race as lineage colliding with an emergent discourse of race as phenotype.[23] By shifting to the word *Moor*, Hawkins entangles the two discourses. Dennis Britton's recent study of the "converted infidel trope" adds considerable assistance to the interpretation of what Hawkins was saying to his employers. Britton argues that the theological and political debate over infant baptism in the Reformed Anglican Church, with its focus on infants born of Christian parents, had the secondary ramification of racializing Christian communities, though the process was slow in India.[24] (Carl Nightingale, in *Segregation*, observes that two areas of Madras previously called Hindu and Christian were not renamed Black Town and White Town on a map until 1711.[25]) By naming and rejecting a potential Muslim convert as a *Moor* and accepting a Christian born, Hawkins was affirming the whiteness of his Armenian Christian bride.

Hawkins further emphasizes the legitimacy of his marriage by detailing his two wedding ceremonies. The first ceremony merged the traditional practice of spousals, the announcement *per verba de presenti* in which a couple simply pledge to one another, with the simulacrum of a wedding service, presided over by his servant, Nicholas Ufflet, about whom we will hear more soon. When, some months later, Hawkins joined Sir Henry Middleton's fleet, he learned that the Anglican church now rejected such private rituals. Although the recent parliamentary statute (3 Jac. 1606) insisting on church weddings was primarily aimed at preventing recusant and Puritan weddings from evading Anglican services, Hawkins hastily organized a second wedding, this time presided over by the Anglican chaplain of the fleet.[26]

The story of his two weddings to a white Christian carefully distinguishes his lawful union from an interracial liaison or, even more troubling, intermarriage with a Catholic. For English merchants in India in 1615, differentiation by race may have been emerging, but the dominant rival and demonized "other" remained Catholic: the Spanish, enemies during the long war of the 1580s and 1590s, and the Portuguese, whose trade they were challenging in the Indian Ocean. Portuguese Jesuits, his Catholic antagonists, had been accused of his attempted murder. For English sailors *Christian* referred to fellow Protestants, which in the East primarily meant the Dutch. Even as they were trying to distinguish themselves from the Dutch by parading in red costumes, the English sailors welcomed Dutch ships, traded for necessary supplies and specie, and expected charity and Protestant solidarity. Capt. Nicholas Downton, in need of sturdy rope, hoped "at Bantam to meet with some Hollanders, from whom he might find some Christian feeling to relieve our need."[27] George Ball referred to the "bands of amity" between the English and the Dutch.[28] Such naiveté about the bonds formed during English support against Spain in the Low Countries forty years earlier was shattered in 1623 when rough commercial conflict gave way to torture and executions by the Dutch at Amboyna.

Hawkins ends the story of his marriage with a phrase echoing the biblical Book of Ruth, saying his wife was content "to go where I went and live as I lived."[29] When he left Agra, he shook off his mother-in-law and his wife's brother, who were demanding that he leave her in Goa and provide her with a dowry.[30] The double ceremonies legalizing the marriage and the effort to evade her relatives suggest that Hawkins felt some satisfaction with his bride. Her collusion in the evasion of her relatives suggests her acquiescence, and possible content. Malieckal assures us that women at the Mughal court did have the right to refuse marriage, so she may have found the marriage acceptable.[31] For Hawkins, too, was a Christian, even if a Protestant.

For their part, the company never questioned Mariam's status as a wife nor her spiritual capital. The "stranger wife" who had grown up in a Mughal court was unquestionably a suitable Christian. Six years later, the company directors compared her to the wife of Captain Giles, who had made an error in judgment by marrying a Spaniard. Giles, whose Catholic bride made him "suspected for his religion," promised to hurry his unfortunate wife down to live in Wales in order to appease the directors.[32]

Mariam (now Mrs. Hawkins) participated in her husband's scrambling escape from her relatives in Agra and followed her husband on an uncertain route. To trick her relatives, Hawkins obtained two licenses from the Portuguese, one for Goa and one for travel on Portuguese ships, then changed his plan and joined the EIC fleet of Sir Henry Middleton's Sixth Voyage, traveling to the Red Sea and Bantam.

On arrival in the Red Sea, Middleton's fleet met the Eighth Voyage under the command of Capt. John Saris, a meeting that produced a great deal of conflict and a great deal of paper. The "wrangling"—Captain Downton's word—between Sir Henry and Saris was extensive, with arguments over precedence, authority, purposes and profits, and particularly shares.[33] Multiple reports reveal that both Hawkins and Towerson successfully intervened with Middleton. Hawkins intervened in a parley between Sir Henry and Captain Saris.[34] When Towerson, an amiable man,[35] assisted in calming Middleton's fury, he was invited to join Sir Henry for dinner on his ship, perhaps an event where he met Mrs. Hawkins.[36] Middleton sent Towerson back to England as captain of the *Hector*, and Hawkins and his wife sailed on the *Thomas*.[37]

We hear nothing directly of the voyage of the *Thomas* after the ships left Saldania Bay, May 21, 1613, though Downton, who was following on the *Peppercorn*, wrote of his difficult voyage back after the ships were separated. Downton's account of his voyage, including the decimation of his crew, his expectation of death, and their final inability to reach Plymouth against contrary winds conveys a misery similar to that which swept the *Thomas* when many died, including Hawkins, who was buried in Ireland.

Downton probably learned about the deaths on the *Thomas* when he, too, was forced to land in Ireland. Later he reported to Sir Robert Sherley that Hawkins had died, as did "most on the ship."[38] Mariam, now Hawkins's widow, survived that epidemic, and she was sufficiently lively or sympathetic that she acquired a new fiancé between the burial of her husband in Waterford and the February meeting of the directors. By the time of their first discussion of the widow, Mariam was engaged to none other than Captain Towerson. Robert Markley suggests it was a marriage of convenience for an isolated woman.[39] Towerson's hope that he had snapped up a rich widow is suggested by the rumors of wealth that surrounded his fiancée and by his subsequent disappointments.

Some of the fantasies of the wealth of Jahangir's court seem to accumulate around her.[40] As they read the journal, the directors learned that his bride was white, a Christian, and also possibly rich. Threaded throughout Hawkins's history of Jahangir's court is the story of a ballas ruby, a rare, delicate rose-pink stone found near Samarkand, one Jahangir is seeking from a dealer in Gujarat. Hawkins exclaims in the text that he, too, has a ruby, and ends with an extensive catalogue of the riches of Jahangir.[41] Though Hawkins's journal was written solely for the directors, the catalogue of Mughal wealth may have leaked, for sailors talk as well as write. On the long voyage, surely he spoke of the hunt for the ruby or described Jahangir's wealth. Such descriptions may have suggested to his companions that his wife, produced from the palace, was not only a treasure, but possessed treasure. Certainly, other Englishmen saw his bride as wealthy, or in the words of Proverbs, a wife "more precious than rubies," as the new King James translation put it.[42]

From "Stranger Wife" to Widow

Her emotions of either grief or joy remain unmentioned when Mariam, as Hawkins's widow and administrix, enters the court minutes. Nor do her reasons for remarriage. In London in February 1613/14, the widow came under scrutiny by the Committee on Committees. The company was accustomed to dealing with widows as executors, though this widow made an extraordinary claim of £2000 for her deceased husband's expenses in India.[43] She had obtained the support of his brother, Charles Hawkins, who himself made a £300 pound claim, as well as the support of her new fiancé, Gabriel Towerson. No one described how the couple met, but by the time the widow was seeking repayment for her first husband's expenses in India, her potential wealth had riveted many eyes, including Towerson's, and certainly the jealous servant, Nicholas Ufflet.

Ufflet, who had followed and shared his master's adventures at Agra, officiated at the first wedding, and attended his master's burial in Ireland, may have resented the change in the household order. Urvashi Chakravarty, in her compelling reading of Hamlet's "More than Kin, less than Kind," reminds us of the shifting definitions of the word *family* and changing understandings of affiliation in the period. "Family" could mean the servants and master who make up the household. Like Feerick, Chakravarty sees that definition giving way to a blood-based definition of kinship, perhaps stimulated by the admission of strangers into households.[44] Ufflet's intervention was hostile to his mistress, although the company initially was welcoming.

The support of her brother-in-law as well as her captain fiancé, assisted her welcome. Hawkins had created an illusion of wealth by claiming an annual payment of £3,200 from Jahangir on his appointment as a khan, extensive expenses owed to him by the company, and profit from his private trade. It took Sir Thomas Roe, as the official ambassador, years to dispel these illusions, which were, no doubt, supported by seamen's awed description of the wealth of Jahangir and by the mysteries surrounding the *haram*. Mrs. Hawkins seemed a rich widow as well as one protected by the Mughal emperor.

The power and wealth of the leading noblewomen of Jahangir's family had become known to European traders, particularly after a Portuguese captain seized the *Rahimi*, the ship belonging to Jahangir's mother, in 1613, an incident of piracy that caused a severe reaction from Agra. Among other acts, Jahangir cancelled all trade through Surat.[45] Just where Mariam Khan fit in that hierarchy of women was difficult to assess, particularly from Philpot Street, though the dangers of court women remained in another captain's mind four years later as he warned the company: "[I]f they had taken the [queen mother's] junk [ship] and known to be English ... all your goods in this could not have made satisfaction."[46]

The second decade of the company's existence also brought challenges about its responsibility for the widows of employees, particularly given irregular bookkeeping around wills and estates, problems intensified by the unprecedented death rate. Mariam, as a stranger bride, was handled cautiously. Keeping a tight control over the budget, the directors rejected her claim for Hawkins's expenses. Yet, after their ruthless accounting and reminder that she owed £300 for the removal of goods from Agra, their language shifts to charity and love: "The company be charitably affected towards the widow that is a stranger and to be married very shortly they thought it fit to give her some token of their love," and they decide to give her a purse of two hundred gold sovereigns.[47] Simultaneously, lest charity be carried too far, they demanded that she, her brother-in-law, and her fiancé sign a release for all claims for Hawkins's expenses.

In an unusual intrusion by a lower-level employee, Nicholas Ufflet interrupted these deliberations over her economic capital.[48] The servant, trying to ingratiate himself with the directors and to persuade them to give him a raise and promotion, provided the secret information that the widow was wealthy, rather than pitiful. He reported that he had spied on her and had seen a bag of gems, containing a huge diamond worth £2,000, and some lesser stones worth £4,000 pounds. At first the directors accepted his claims of superior loyalty to the company.[49]

When the group parted on that cold February day, they congratulated Ufflet for "his honest and civil carriage" and members were adjured to keep the information secret.[50] Yet Ufflet's self-exposure as a spying servant troubled them. Within a week, perhaps after considering their lives conducted under the eyes of their own servants, the directors turned against him. The servant who had justified his exposure of his mistress with an emergent discourse of corporate loyalty had violated too deeply the dominant discourse of service. Caught in the collision of these discourses, Ufflet's betrayal of his mistress ultimately did him no good. The committee's previous decision about their gift of two hundred sovereigns was upheld; Ufflet, "suspected both for his honesty and sufficiency . . . of whom much ill was spoken and little good," was not promoted. Yet, acutely aware of the danger of London gossip, the directors recognized they could not leave him in England to discourage others. They sent him abroad to Jakarta to serve as a scribe. And they warned him "that if he carried not himself honestly and well then to ship him home as an ordinary man" (reduced to the lowest seaman).[51] The directors' wariness about Ufflet's character was proven astute; when he arrived at his new post, he boasted about his superiority to the irritation of his companions. Like so many, he died young on the ship home.

In the February debates, the spiritual and social standing of Mariam Khan as Christian was unquestioned. Transformed by marriage, she was recognized both as Hawkins's widow and his legal administrix. They also noted her position as the fiancée of another captain, Towerson. Her status as a stranger invites charity. No discussion is raised about color. Once brought into the Hawkins household, she has become kin. Chosen by two Englishmen, she is a suitable wife. Her Christian faith is impeccable, unlike that of Mrs. Giles, the Spanish Catholic.

The news of Mariam Khan's bag of gems seemed only to increase her attractions. Lubricated by that morning's gift of two hundred crowns, she and Captain Towerson wed at St. Nicholas Acons parish church on February 21, 1614.[52] The company's reason for their generous wedding present explicitly concerns her social capital. They explained, "it may be for the honor of the company if she shall signify their bounty and kind resort towards her, unto her friends in those parts."[53] Her friends at court, veiled in mystery, were her greatest asset. Her social connections with the court, particularly with the women's quarters inaccessible to men, and her possible influence with Nur Mahal, Jahangir's powerful favorite wife, led the company to pay for her passage back to India.

The second marriage began well. Ufflet's information, instead of exposing his mistress as a fraud, may have served to elevate her status and increase her husband's hopes. Nicholas Downton's letter to Sir Robert Sherley telling about the progress of the widow from one husband to the next includes the information that Captain Towerson visited the

Sherley family at Wiston and had seen Sherley's son, Henry, who had been left behind to be raised by his English grandmother. Mariam (now Mrs. Towerson) is not named, but presumably the newlyweds traveled together and set eyes on the healthy boy.[54]

The couple married on the day that the widow with her bag of jewels received her purse of gold sovereigns. As mentioned above, she and her husband returned to India at company expense, with the explicit expectation that her court connections would assist their trade negotiations, in particular her connections with Nur Mahal. As they said, "to signify their bounty ... unto her friends."[55]

Roe's Prohibition of "Encumbrances"

When Mariam Khan Towerson boarded the *Anne* for the voyage back to India, she was accompanied by two other women, her maid Frances Webbe and a Mrs. Hudson. The return voyage involved a scandal worthy of a Jacobean city comedy, one that caused a great deal of merriment for a number of EIC captains. The plot includes young lovers, disguise exposed by pregnancy, marriage, and a birth. The incidents that caused such a stir among the company suggest that Mariam Khan organized her life on principles different from the status hierarchies of English ladies, as she encouraged independence on the part of the two other women, a widow and a servant.[56]

In his edition of Roe's embassy, William Foster suggests that Mrs. Hudson was the Indian widow of a lesser factor, William Hudson.[57] Sen sees her as an Englishwoman, perhaps because of her bold claims of permission from Sir Thomas Smythe.[58] She engaged in private trade, though lacking documentary permission, and did finally return to England with a cargo of indigo.[59] She, like Mrs. Towerson, had managed to return to India on company charge, though she subsequently had to pay for her cargo. If Foster is correct, then Mrs. Towerson had made friends with another "stranger bride." Mrs. Towerson's husband's status as captain was higher than that of William Hudson and also that of Richard Steele, one of the central parties in the ensuing scandal; yet Mrs. Towerson in her support of the two women did not seem to discriminate on the basis of rank.[60]

Though Mrs. Hudson irritated Sir Thomas Roe, she was by no means the center of the scandal, which blew up around Mrs. Towerson's maid, Frances. Before the ship had reached the Cape of Good Hope, it became obvious the maid was pregnant. In a theatrical *anagnorisis*, she cast off her disguise and announced herself as the fiancée of Richard Steele, a young man full of projects that failed. Letters from captains flew about as they reported the discovery of her pregnancy. Captain Salmon reports, "her belly told the tale," and claims that the Towersons had been tricked: "Captain Towerson and his wife were ignorant . . . but her [Frances's] belly . . . could no longer be hid under a timpany (swelling)."[61] Richard Steele honorably stepped forward to claim his pregnant bride, and Captain Towerson supervised the couple's wedding, one Roe later described as "at the Cape under a bush."[62]

Mrs. Towerson's involvement in Frances Webbe's masquerade as a servant is difficult to assess. Perhaps she was tricked, as Salmon claimed, and Webbe had disguised the early stages of pregnancy as seasickness, but collusion is suggested by Towerson's supervision of the Webbe-Steele wedding and Mrs. Towerson's continuing support of Mrs. Steele. The bride gave birth at Surat just after the ship docked in 1616. Edward Monox, a junior factor, puns, "Mrs Steele shortly after her sea travel travailed on shore, and brought forth to the no small joy of her husband a goodly young son."[63] Ambassador Roe notes Mrs. Towerson's support of the young couple: "His wife I have bound to Mrs. Towerson at her suit."[64] Steele quickly broke his promise to Roe that his wife would remain as a servant with Mrs. Towerson and speedily set up his own household, excusing his behavior as "affection."[65]

The friendship of the women continued, and in December to save money, they with their husbands and servants moved into the factory at Surat. The disruption to company affairs is made explicit when Monox, lower in the hierarchy, complains he had "no chamber to lie in and no place to write in."[66] This incident provoked Roe to exclaim against "these encumbrances."[67]

This threat to the steady production of scribal reports may have pushed the company to issue an edict forbidding wives. One captain wryly observes, Richard Steele had done "what Captain Keeling durst not presume to do."⁶⁸ At first, Roe welcomed the Towersons, hoping that Mariam Khan would assist in his approaches to Nur Mahal: "his [Towerson's] haste to court will be convenient, for his wife may assist me to Normahal [sic] better than all this court."⁶⁹ Yet such hopes for assistance were undermined by the extraordinary effect the women had on Golding, a ship's chaplain. His behavior epitomizes the disturbances provoked by the women: he abandoned his ship, disguised himself as a Moor, and followed the women to the court at Ahmadabad. (Despite his flagrant disobedience, he was taken back into service.⁷⁰) Roe exclaimed, "You know not the danger, the inconvenience of granting these liberties."⁷¹ Roe's desire to be rid of the women was frustrated by the fertility of Mrs. Steele: "she hath one child sucking (as they say) forward of another; it were unfit to send her home alone among men."⁷²

The ostensible purpose of Mrs. Towerson's support by the company was also in shreds. Within months, Roe had penetrated the various social and economic fantasies about Mrs. Towerson. He vanquished the illusions of enormous loans that were to be repaid to Hawkins—"the money had fallen from 2000 rupees to 200."⁷³ He described her familial connections as naught: "His father[-in-law] will do little, nor is able; his mother-in-law poor at Agra and he will be consumed if he fall to travel on his own purse . . . his wife's aunt promised in marriage to Frans Swares, the prodigal Portugal and finally nothing before him but consumption."⁷⁴ Accurately intuiting the company's reasons for their support, he wrote, "perhaps they thought her greatness could do them some pleasure."⁷⁵ Having himself successfully won the patronage of Nur Mahal, he dismissed any need for Mariam Khan's assistance.⁷⁶

As the Towerson marriage frayed, Roe assessed the economic and social standing of Mrs. Towerson: "Captain Towerson and his wife find cold reception here. Her friends are poor and mean and weary of them. He came with hopes of great diamonds and they look for gifts of him. I am sorry for him and his little vanity. I have used my best advice to persuade his return. . . . He thought to be esteemed here a great man."⁷⁷ His description of the failing marriage is bleak: "They fence one upon another and are both weary."⁷⁸ Yet, however disappointed Captain Towerson was in his fantasies of wealth and status, his wife still had friends at court. Though Roe had found his own way to ingratiate himself with Nur Mahal, Sen observes in her essay in this volume that Mrs. Towerson may have fostered a friendship between Mrs. Steele and the daughter of Jahangir's commander in chief.[79]

Finally, Roe persuaded Mrs. Hudson, Mrs. Steele, and Captain Towerson to return to England with him on the *Anne*, but Mrs. Towerson refused to accompany her husband. As the directors feared, the needs of the wife who lived apart became an economic charge. In 1619 she sought a loan from the factors at Surat and was allowed two hundred rupees "for this year to supply her necessities . . . but seeing she stayeth behind her husband, not much to his liking [and] that he hath not given warrant to relieve her, it is in his choice whether he will repay it or no, notwithstanding her bill."[80] She continued to be both an economic and social threat. Her vocal complaints elicited money from the factors who warned that she and her mother "railed upon her husband and nation, but principally her mother which is no small discredit to our nation. So if the next year her husband come not nor send her means she will breed much trouble to your factors in Agra and the court with their exclamations; therefore [it] is needful you take some course with her husband for her maintenance, or send for her to him to avoid expense, trouble and scandal; which if [she] remain here and want means will follow in the end."[81] In the same month as that warning, Towerson in London applied to the company for another contract. His experience and honesty were warmly commended but were weighed against the expense of his wife. "It was objected that his wife taking knowledge of his being at Banta will go to him in some Indian ship" and the company would be charged.[82]

Despite their separation, Mrs. Towerson's social capital continued to worry employees in India. In 1621 she approached the factors for money again, while still refusing to join her husband in England: "Mr. Towerson's wife hath no mind for England. We deny her maintenance. She complaineth of her husband."[83] The company had not, however, identified the real threat.

Towerson probably repaid her debts, though the couple did not reconcile. In 1623 dispatched to Amboyna, he moved toward his confrontation with the Dutch who were more ruthless than the English in defense of trade. Accused of attempting to capture the Dutch fort at Amboyna, Towerson was waterboarded, then executed, along with others. His stoic courage earned his apotheosis as an English hero and the company withdrew from the spice trade in the Moluccas. The Privy Council wept when the report of his death was read to them. His Armenian wife, her mother, and her aunt disappear from the court minutes, only to be transmuted into Quisara in Fletcher's play *The Island Princess* in 1619 and into Yasbinda in Dryden's *Amboyna, or the Cruelties of the Dutch to the English Merchants during the third Anglo-Dutch war* (1673).[84]

These stories from the chaotic and deadly early decades of EIC trade are far from the supposed stability and clear purposes of the British Raj. By the 1640s the overseas trade was so unprofitable that the company was forced to sell its London properties in Deptford and Blackwall and to cease building ships. The need for reorganization was recognized. When the company charter was renewed in 1657 and territorial acquisition granted subsequently by Charles II, inspectors were sent out to the East. Miles Ogborn in *Indian Ink* shows how the necessity to regularize bookkeeping was intimately linked to the social order of the factories. Ogborn details the ideals of William Puckle, who envisioned transferring the masculine hierarchy of a grammar school or university to India, with all members dining together, seated at table by rank, no wives allowed. Streynsham Master, who did succeed in improving bookkeeping, toured the factories and attempted to enforce an "idealized Christian moral order."[85] Yet these efforts could not regulate the behavior of young men so far from the tight surveillance of England. Finally, Josiah Child, major shareholder from 1679 and governor of the company in the 1680s, encouraged junior employees to marry Indian women, a policy subsequently reversed, but which contributed to the growth of the large Anglo-Indian population.[86]

Notes

1. Maleickal, "Miriam Khan," places her within the context of Mughal noblewomen. Fisher, *Counterflows*, provides a chronology of her life (22–29) and unearths the parish record of her second marriage. I am grateful

to Richmond Barbour, who first told me about this stranger bride, and to Bindu Maleikal who told me her name.
2. Sen, "Traveling Companions," details the actions of the trio in India and amplifies Malieckal's argument about the significance of the trading models provided by Mughal noblewomen.
3. I have silently modernized the spelling in my transcriptions of the India Office Records, East India Company Court Minutes, hereafter IOR (primarily IOR B/5, February 11–February 21, 1614) and in most printed sources.
4. Roe, *Embassy*, 455.
5. Chaudhuri, *Trading World*, 20, and Barbour "'English Nation,'" 174–76.
6. Barbour, "'English Nation,'" 176–77.
7. Roe, *Embassy*, 455.
8. Lal, *Domesticity*, 6–14. Peirce criticizes the inadequacy of the Western dichotomy of public and private for understanding the interactions between Ottoman spatial boundaries and the inner sphere (*Imperial Harem*, 6–12).
9. Chaudhuri, *Trading World*, 20–21.
10. Ogborn studies the history of the multiple kinds of writing that make up the East India Company archives (*Indian Ink*, 6). Barbour, in "'English Nation,'" epitomizes that history (165–68). William Hawkins's journal is called his "book of intelligence." See IOR B/5, February 17, 1614.
11. William Lithgow, *The Total Discourse of the Rare Adventures* (1632), cited by Vitkus, *Turning Turk*, 15.
12. Barbour, "'English Nation,'" 175.
13. Keay, *Honourable Company*, 30.
14. Ogborn, *Indian Ink*, 70.
15. Christensen, "'Absent,'" examines a 1632 play that addresses the pauperization of families by long distance trade, *The Launching of the Mary, or The Seaman's Honest Wife*.
16. Hawkins, "Captain," 15–16. Hawkins recounts the story in his "journal of intelligence" which his servant Nicholas Ufflet passed on to the directors who passed it on to Samuel Purchas (IOR B/5 34–35, February 17, 1613/14). See Malieckal, "Miriam Khan," for extensive analysis of the terms (102–5), and Habib, *Black Lives*, for further examples of Indians in the archive.
17. Hawkins, "Captain," 16.
18. The Armenians were the first nation to make Christianity the official religion in 301 CE, on which see Ayvazyan, "Armenia's Conversion." The pagan Anglo-Saxons who conquered England were slowly converted by the mission led by Augustine in 597, a conversion completed over the next century, on which see Higham, "Tribal Chieftains."

19. Panossian, *Armenians*, records the settlement of Armenians in Agra and their establishment of the Armenian Church in 1562 (80–81).
20. Chaudhuri, *Trading World*, 137. I am grateful to Ainslie Embree for guiding me toward the place of the Armenians in India.
21. Das discusses the portrait in "Apes of Imitation." Kapadia analyzes the details in "Bichitr." For the pasty complexion of King James I, Bichitr copied a portrait presented by Ambassador Roe.
22. For instance, Hall, *Things of Darkness*; Bartels, *Speaking of the Moor*; MacDonald, "Black Ram."
23. Feerick, *Strangers*, 5.
24. Britton, *Becoming Christian*, 8–9.
25. Nightingale, *Segregation*, 68; Giddings, *When and Where*, 33–39.
26. Sokol and Sokol, *Shakespeare* 13–14.
27. Danvers and Foster, *Letters*, 6:191.
28. Danvers and Foster, *Letters*, 6:308.
29. "Whither thou goest I will go, and where thou lodgest I will lodge" (Ruth 1:16, King James Version [KJV]). For more, see Suzanne Tartamella's essay in this volume.
30. In a personal conversation, Bernadette Andrea noted that this dowry demand is the Muslim form of the *mahr*, given directly by the husband to the bride.
31. Malieckal, "Miriam Khan," 105.
32. IOR E/4, December 1–3, 1619.
33. Barbour tells the story in "'English Nation,'" 171–73, For a less sympathetic view of Saris, see Nicholas Downton in Danvers and Foster, *Letters*, 1:183.
34. Danvers and Foster, *Letters*, 1:220.
35. Downton reports that Captain Saris, Towerson's master, said he loved the man, Danvers and Foster, *Letters* 1:182.
36. Downton in Danvers and Foster, *Letters*, 1:189.
37. Danvers and Foster, *Letters*, 1:230.
38. Danvers and Foster, *Letters*, 1:259–68.
39. Markley, *Far East*, 162.
40. Malieckal, "Miriam Khan," 113.
41. Hawkins, "Captain," 25.
42. Proverbs 3:15, KJV. The comparison made between the wife and rubies could startle those familiar with the Geneva Bible version: "Wisdom is more precious than rubies."
43. For example, Sir Henry Middleton's sister-in-law Alice handled his estate when he died in 1619.
44. Chakravarty, "More than Kin," 24.

45. Findly, "Capture," 228–29.
46. Danvers and Foster, *Letters*, 6:174.
47. IOR B/5, 32–33, February 11, 1613/14.
48. The company maintained a system of hierarchical and vertical communication, on which see Chaudhuri, *Trading World*, 30. Only the Court of Committees had full knowledge.
49. IOR B/5, 34–35, February 17, 1613/14.
50. IOR B/5, 34–35, February 17, 1613/14.
51. IOR B/5, 34–35, February 17, 1613/14.
52. Fisher, *Counterflows*, was misled by the "1613" in the parish records, forgetting that the English still dated the beginning of the year at the end of March, 25.
53. IOR B/5, 38–39, February 21, 1613/14.
54. For a discussion of this meeting, see Andrea, *Lives*.
55. IOR B/5, 38–39, February 21, 1613/14.
56. Both Sen in "Traveling Companions," 196–200, and Malieckal, "Miriam Khan," agree on the differences and independence of women's actions modeled by Mariam Khan.
57. Roe, *Embassy*, 391.
58. Sen, "Traveling Companions," 194.
59. Roe, *Embassy*, 486n.
60. Roe, *Embassy*, 391n.
61. Danvers and Foster, *Letters*, 6:291.
62. Roe, *Embassy*, 468.
63. Danvers and Foster, *Letters*, 6:277.
64. Roe, *Embassy*, 447.
65. Roe, *Embassy*, 455.
66. Danvers and Foster, *Letters*, 6:277.
67. Roe, *Embassy*, 455.
68. *Calendar* 139 (no. 320).
69. Roe, *Embassy*, 393.
70. Roe, *Embassy*, 462n.
71. Roe, *Embassy*, 407.
72. Roe, *Embassy*, 447.
73. Roe, *Embassy*, 448.
74. Danvers and Foster, *Letters*, 6:141.
75. Danvers and Foster, *Letters*, 6:228.
76. Roe, *Embassy*, 412.
77. Roe, *Embassy*, 459.
78. Roe, *Embassy*, 448.
79. Roe, *Embassy*, 469.

80. Foster, *English Factories*, 1:155.
81. Foster, *English Factories*, 1:169.
82. IOR B/6, 463, February 21, 1619.
83. Foster, *English Factories*, 1:327.
84. Malieckal in "Mariam Khan" discusses the connections to Quisara and Ysabinda (114–17). For more on Fletcher's *Island Princess*, see Loomba, "'Break her will'" Discussing the same play, Markley considers the translation of the Pocahontas myth to the Spice Islands and the recasting of what may have been a marriage of convenience to a "Manichean theatrics of heroic sacrifice" (*Far East*, 162).
85. Ogborn, *Indian Ink*, 83–89, esp. 87.
86. Nightingale, *Segregation*, 73. For the changing history of interracial concubinage and marriage in India, see Ghosh, *Sex and the Family*, and Dalrymple, *White Mughals*. Cohen, *Family Secrets*, traces the early history of intermarriage in India and follows the transformation of eighteenth-century English acceptance of mixed-race children to the shame of the nineteenth century. Stoler's key work, *Carnal Knowledge*, examines the social sanctions against such relationships in the nineteenth-century Raj.

Bibliography

Andrea, Bernadette. *The Lives of Girls and Women from the Islamic World in Early Modern British Literature and Culture*. Toronto: University of Toronto Press, 2017.

Ayvazyan, Arman. "Armenia's Conversion to Christianity." In *Ancient History Encyclopedia*, April 15, 2015, http://www.ancient.eu/article/801/. Accessed December 17, 2016

Ayyar, Varsha, and Lalit Khandare. "Mapping Color and Caste Discrimination in India Society." In *The Melanin Millennium: Skin Color as 21st Century International Discourse*, edited by Ronald Hall, 71–96. Dordrecht NL: Springer, 2012.

Barbour, Richmond. "'The English Nation at Bantam': Corporate Process in the East India Company's First Factory." *Genre* 48, no. 2 (2015): 159–92.

Bartels, Emily. *Speaking of the Moor: From Alcazar to Othello*. Philadelphia: University of Pennsylvania Press, 2008.

Britton, Dennis. *Becoming Christian: Race, Reformation, and Early Modern English Romance*. New York: Fordham University Press, 2014.

Calendar of State Papers, Colonial Series East Indies, China and Japan, 1617–1622, edited by W. Noel Sainsbury. 3 vols. London, 1860.

Chakravarty, Urvashi. "More than Kin, Less than Kind: Similitude, Strangeness, and Early Modern Homonationalisms." *Shakespeare Quarterly* 67, no. 1 (2016): 14–29.

Chaudhuri, K. N. *The Trading World of Asia and the East India Company, 1660-1760*. Cambridge: Cambridge University Press, 1978.

Christensen, Ann. "'Absent, Weak, or Unserviceable': The East India Company and the Domestic Economy in *The Launching of the Mary, or The Seaman's Honest Wife*." In *Global Traffic: Discourses and Practices of Trade in English Literature and Culture from 1550 to 1700*, edited by Barbara Sebek and Stephen Deng, 117–36. New York: Palgrave Macmillan, 2008.

Cohen, Deborah. *Family Secrets: Shame and Privacy in Modern Britain*. New York: Oxford University Press, 2013.

Dalrymple, William. *White Mughals: Love and Betrayal in Eighteenth-Century India*. London: Penguin, 2004.

Danvers, F. C., and W. Foster, eds. *Letters Received by the East India Company from Its Servants in the East*. 6 vols. London: Sampson Low, Marston and Company, 1896–1902.

Das, Nandini. "'Apes of Imitation': Imitation and Identity in Sir Thomas Roe's Embassy to India." In *A Companion to the Global Renaissance*, edited by Jyotsna Singh, 114–28. Malden MA: Wiley-Blackwell, 2009.

Feerick, Jean E. *Strangers in Blood: Relocating Race in the Renaissance*. Toronto: University of Toronto Press, 2010.

Findly, Ellison. "The Capture of Maryam-Uz Zamani's Ship: Mughal Women and European Traders." *Journal of the American Oriental Society* 108, no. 2 (1988): 227–38.

Fisher, Michael. *Counterflows to Colonialism: Indian Travellers and Settlers in Britain, 1600-1857*. New Delhi: Permanent Black, 2004.

Foster, William, ed. *The English Factories in India, 1618-1669*. 13 vols. Oxford: Clarendon, 1906–27.

Ghosh, Durba. *Sex and the Family in Colonial India*. New York: Cambridge University Press, 2006.

Giddings, Paula. *When and Where I Enter: The Impact of Black Women on Race and Sex in America*. New York: Morrow, 1984.

Habib, Imtiaz. *Black Lives in the English Archives, 1500-1677*. Aldershot, UK: Ashgate, 2008.

Hall, Kim F. *Things of Darkness: Economies of Race and Gender in Early Modern England*. Ithaca NY: Cornell University Press, 1995.

Hawkins, William. "Captain William Hawkins, His Relations." In *Hakluytus Posthumus or Purchas His Pilgrimes*, edited by Samuel Purchas, 3:1–51. Glasgow: James MacLehose and Sons, 1905.

Higham, Nicholas. "From Tribal Chieftains to Christian Kings." In *The Anglo-Saxon World*, edited by Nicholas Higham and Martin Ryan, 126–78. New Haven: Yale University Press, 2013.

Holland, Sharon. *The Erotic Life of Racism*. Durham NC: Duke University Press, 2012.

India Office Records. East India Company Minutes of the Court of Directors and Court of Proprietors 1599–1858. British Library, London.

Kapadia, Roshna. "Bichitr, Jahangir Preferring a Sufi Shaikh to Kings." www.khanacademy.org/humanities/art-islam/islamic-art-late-period/a/bichtir-jahangir-preferring-a-sufi-shaikh-to-kings. Accessed December 31, 2016.

Keay, John. *The Honourable Company*. New York: Harper Collins, 1993.

Lal, Ruby. *Domesticity and Power in the Early Mughal World*. Cambridge: Cambridge University Press, 2005.

Loomba, Ania. "'Break her will, and bruise no bone sir': Colonial and Sexual Mastery in Fletcher's *The Island Princess*." *Journal for Early Modern Cultural Studies* 2, no. 1 (2002): 68–108.

MacDonald, Joyce Green. "Black Ram, White Ewe: Shakespeare Race and Women." In *A Feminist Companion to Shakespeare*, edited by Dympna Callaghan, 188–207. Oxford: Blackwell, 2001.

Malieckal, Bindu. "Mariam Khan and the Legacy of Mughal Women in Early Modern Literature of India." In *Early Modern England and Islamic Worlds*, edited by Bernadette Andrea and Linda McJannet, 97–122. New York: Palgrave Macmillan, 2011.

Markley, Robert. *The Far East and the English Imagination, 1600–1730*. Cambridge: Cambridge University Press, 2006.

Nightingale, Carl. *Segregation: A Global History of Divided Cities*. Chicago: University of Chicago Press, 2012.

Ogborn, Miles. *Indian Ink*. Chicago: University of Chicago Press, 2007.

Panossian, Razmik. *The Armenians*. New York: Columbia University Press, 2006.

Peirce, Leslie. *The Imperial Harem*. New York: Oxford University Press, 1993.

Roe, Thomas. *The Embassy of Sir Thomas Roe to India, 1615–1619*, edited by William Foster. London: Oxford University Press, 1926.

Sen, Amrita. "Traveling Companions: Women, Trade, and the Early East India Company." *Genre* 48, no. 2 (2015): 193–214.

Sokol, B. J., and Mary Sokol. *Shakespeare, Law and Marriage*. New York: Cambridge University Press, 2008.

Stoler, Ann. *Carnal Knowledge and Imperial Power*. Berkeley: University of California Press, 2002.

Subrahmanyam, Sanjay. "Frank Submission: The Company and the Mughals." In *The Worlds of the East India Company*, edited by H. V. Bowen, Margarette Lincoln, and Nigel Rigby, 69–96. Rochester NY: Boydell, 2003.

Vitkus, Daniel. *Turning Turk: English Theater and the Multicultural Mediterranean, 1570–1630*. New York: Palgrave Macmillan, 2003.

3

Sailing to India

Women, Travel, and Crisis in the Seventeenth Century

AMRITA SEN

In what has become a truism, the East India Company during the early years of its operation did not encourage women to travel onboard its ships. As Richmond Barbour and Karen Robertson demonstrate in the preceding essays, this active discouragement often led to conflicts between the company and its male employees who sought to make the journey to the East Indies with their wives. Women, both English and Asian, did, however, travel back and forth between Europe and the East, either directly under the aegis of the company or independently with their spouses or friends. Nonetheless, the number of women who succeeded in securing a passage to the East Indies was significantly lower than the number of men, a difference that has resulted in an interesting linguistic discrepancy. Whereas the term "sahib," commonly used to denote an Englishman or other Europeans in the Indian subcontinent, entered the English lexicon in the late-seventeenth century, its gendered counterpart "memsahib" would be first recorded almost two centuries later.[1] What further decenters women from traditional historiography is the absence of any documents written by them during these early years. Instead, the women surface only when they are spoken about by English factors or diplomats associated with the company. But why did the women at all break into correspondences and reports dominated by concerns of trade and the company's uncertain footing in India? This question is especially pertinent when we consider women who were not actually involved in commercial exchange.[2] In this essay, I am interested in tracing what might best be described as "moments of crisis" that force women, but particularly traveling women, to become visible in the archive.

Specifically, this essay defines these moments of gendered crisis as the sexual anxieties and threats of transculturation that the traveling women seemed to embody for the company. While the presence of women onboard company ships would have immediately registered as anomalies, in the two different case studies that follow, they were alternately seen as either triggers or victims of real and imagined sexual advances from both Englishmen and foreigners that ultimately threatened to disrupt the company's routine operations. At the same time the traveling women themselves appeared to expose the company to dangerous foreign influences. The complex narratives surrounding these women, however, expose the inherently heterogeneous nature of the company, revealing the richly diverse cultural exchanges that geographically mobile Europeans embarked upon during the early seventeenth century and that ran counter to the deliberately monolithic descriptions forwarded by people like Sir Thomas Roe, King James I's ambassador to the Mughal emperor Jahangir, and his chaplain Edward Terry.

The two groups of women that I will examine here were among the earliest to travel between Europe and Asia. The first includes Lady Teresa Sampsonia Sherley and Lady Tomasin Powell, who arrived in the Indian subcontinent around 1613. While Carmen Nocentelli will discuss Lady Teresa Sherley in the following essay, I will here focus on Lady Tomasin Powell, whose son was later identified by William Foster as the first English child to be born in India.[3] The second group comprised Mariam Khan, the wife of Cap. Gabriel Towerson and widow of Cap. William Hawkins, as well as her friends Frances (Webbe) Steele and Mrs. Hudson, who together journeyed to Mughal India in 1617. The journeys of these women often intersected, and it is highly probable that Mariam Khan had met Lady Powell and Lady Sherley.[4] The women, in fact, belonged to a cosmopolitan circle, mostly connected by their husbands who had traveled to and lived in common geographical regions. Sir Robert Sherley, William Hawkins, Gabriel Towerson, as well as Richard Steele knew (or at least knew of) each other from their days in the greater Middle East. For instance, Cap. Nicholas Downton in a 1614 letter to Sir Robert Sherley, before introducing Steele as the new company agent in Persia, goes on to break the news of Hawkins's death off the coast of Ireland. He also informs him of Mariam Khan's remarriage in London before disclosing that her new husband, Towerson, had recently visited Henry, the only son of Sir Robert and Lady Sherley, during the absence of his parents.[5] Despite its friendly tone however, Downton's letter situates itself against the physical and material dangers or crises that usually accompanied such long voyages: he notes, for instance, the deadly outbreak of disease on Hawkins's ship before going on to express his knowledge of Sherley's own misadventures in India and the loss of his companions.

Downton effortlessly combines crucial personal anecdotes with details of company affairs, suggesting how the survival of the English joint-stock venture depended on negotiating these two aspects of its factors' lives. It also reveals the tightly organized transcontinental networks of trade and personal friendship within which the women traveling to the East operated. The crises which prompted these women to become legible thus were similarly inflected with the dual concerns of the personal and the fiscal, marking the female bodies as sites where questions regarding familial, national, as well as corporate well-being could be staged.

In recent years, the turn towards unraveling the connected histories of European and Asian polities has also allowed us to recognize how, in fact, a much wider demographic participated in the new opportunities of trade and discovery that marked the "global renaissance."[6] As Bernadette Andrea has demonstrated, women formed a crucial component in these transnational exchanges. The women that we will consider here, moreover, *themselves* constituted a cosmopolitan group, offering us an important glimpse into the heterogeneity of early modern women travelers and the relationships they forged. Lady Sherley was, of course, a Circassian; with her traveled Lady Powell, generally believed to be a Persian, as well as various other Persian and English companions. Mariam Khan, an Armenian, similarly did not travel alone but was accompanied by Frances Steele and Mrs. Hudson. As Andrea importantly argues, most of these women were "dependent wives" and as such "cannot be considered completely 'voluntary' travellers ... however, neither can they be considered 'involuntary' travelers."[7] For the company these uncertainties regarding the women extended not only to their relationship with their husbands but also to the other men traveling with them. The anxieties regarding the company's own status as a new player in the Indian Ocean region thus often got deflected onto the bodies of these traveling women, ironically allowing them to become visible at these moments. As we shall see below, in its early years the company wrestled with a broad set of issues ranging from interference from King James I to concerns over the conduct of its employees. Although women were not employed by the company, it was within this tightly bound economic context and its perceived disruption that they surfaced, allowing them to become legible in the archive.

Lady Tomasin Powell and the Construction of the East India Company Archive

While the phrase "absent presence" has frequently been used to denote the status of women within the early colonial archive, perhaps no one fits the role better than Lady Tomasin Powell. Compared to Lady Sherley or Mariam Khan, very few traces of her remain. Unlike Mariam, we do not know the exact circumstances under which Tomasin met Thomas Powell, but it was likely during his stay in Persia. We do know that, like the other women, she traveled back and forth across continents in the company of her husband. Some of the first definitive records of her historical presence are from her voyage to the East Indies onboard the company ship the *Expedition*. The circumstance of this journey was unusual since the company was "ordered to transport to the kingdom of Persia, at [its own] cost" Sir Robert Sherley and his entourage. It is likely that this burden of expense had been placed on it by King James himself, and the company's relationship with Sherley and his group was to remain that of a wary mediator. Sherley, after a notable stay in the Safavid empire, had returned to England in 1611 as the ambassador of Shah Abbas I.[8] Now, in 1613, he was on his way back to Persia in the same capacity. Accompanying him was his friend Capt. Thomas Powell, who had also been in the employment of the Persian shah, and like him had fought against the Turks.[9] King James knighted both Sherley and Powell before appointing the latter as his own ambassador to Persia.[10]

What to begin with might have seemed a highly unusual though important group of passengers was thus made even more remarkable by the inclusion of women. It is through Walter Payton's description of these unexpected passengers onboard a company ship that we learn of Lady Powell: "The names of the Ambassadour, and his people, are these. Sir Robert Sherley, the Ambassadour. Teresha, his ladie, a Circasian. Sir Thomas Powell. Tomasin his Ladie. Leylye, a Persian Woman. Morgan Powell, Gentleman."[11] Payton refrains from providing any further information about the women. He does, though, go on to list the other men who formed part of Robert Sherley's entourage and were drawn from various professions (musicians and apothecaries) and ethnicities (Englishmen, Armenians, and Persians). That this group of travelers was remarkable—not only because of the different sexes and demographics of the people involved, but also because of their uneasy relationship with the company—is evident from Payton's subsequent comments on the embassy of Sir Thomas Roe. Only a few years later he found himself part of the fleet responsible for transporting King James's official ambassador to the Mughal court. In stark contrast, Payton is far more reserved, only mentioning that Roe had arrived onboard the *Lion* with "fifteene followers."[12] Presumably, Roe's companions did not arouse Payton's curiosity.

While the company did not support (and at times openly opposed) Sherley's plans for Persian trade, its relation with Roe was entirely different.[13] After much deliberation it had chosen Roe as a man of "suffitient [sufficient]" standing to take on the role of the official English ambassador at the Mughal court.[14] Unlike Sherley's entourage, Roe's passage onboard a company ship would have been more easily anticipated. Moreover, although Roe had secretly married Lady Eleanor Cave Beeston shortly prior to heading off for the East Indies, she did not accompany him.[15] Roe's wife, therefore, never became a problem for the company in the way that the other women did. Furthermore, it is likely that the reason the company allowed the women in Sherley's entourage passage on its ship was because their travel had, in part at least, been brokered by King James. This, of course, did not change the company's attitude towards them. One of the chief reasons that the company repeatedly cited in supporting its prohibition on women traveling on its ships was the perceived sexual danger—whether from their own crews or from outsiders. This sexual crisis transcended class: if the English wives of ordinary Indian sailors could not be allowed to travel because it was dangerous "for such women to go among so many unruly sailors in a ship,"[16] then neither could Ann Keeling in case "people of the Countrye . . . attempt to abuse her."[17]

Not surprisingly, the next time that Payton mentions the women onboard the *Expedition* it is precisely within this context of sexual anxiety. What occasioned this crisis was the difficulty in finding a safe landing place for the passengers headed for Shah Abbas's court. The dangers arose both from the Portuguese who controlled the Indian Ocean as well as from the scant knowledge of the English regarding the regional political configurations in Asia. When in September 1613, the *Expedition* anchored off the coast of Baluchistan, the crew as well as a small exploratory party led by Powell mistakenly believed that they were in friendly territory. The ruler of Makran, Malik Mirza, despite professing loyalty to Shah Abbas, had in fact rebelled against him. The arrival of a Persian ambassador thus must have offered a rare opportunity for political retaliation, with the added lure of seizing the considerable amounts of money that Sherley was carrying. In his account Payton reveals their timely discovery of Malik Mirza's heinous plot involving "the Massacre of us all (except the Chirurgions [surgeons], Musitians [musicians], Women and Boyes)."[18] While death awaited most of the men, the women and the boys faced sexual violence. This, of course, was precisely the scenario that the company feared most. As Julia Schleck argues, the company's concerns regarding the welfare of traveling women was ultimately deeply connected with its own concerns for profit.[19] For the company, the sexual vulnerability of women tainted or affected the men accompanying them, making the husbands and mariners more concerned with protecting the women than carrying out their financial duties. The very presence of women thus made the men ineffective. However, Payton's account shows that when faced with the threat of death and sexual violation, the Sherley entourage showed no signs of weakness or hesitation. Following Sherley's orders, the crew retrieved both his wife's trunk and his bags of money before the ship quietly raised anchor and sailed away, foiling Malik Mirza's plot.[20]

Nonetheless, Payton's journal reinforces the company's concerns regarding the sexual dangers of transporting women. While in Malik Mirza's conspiracy the surgeon and musicians also become prized commodities, it is the young boys and the women who provoke stereotypical fears regarding profligate eastern appetites. For our current purposes, these moments of crisis prove illustrative of a larger "logic of recall" that informs the colonial archive.[21] If these crises—whether it be the English crown forcing the company to transport passengers or the threats of murder and rape—allow the women to become briefly legible, what we are left with are incomplete narratives of their journeys. We never learn, for instance, how the women might have spent their time onboard the ship or if they got to interact with anyone outside of their immediate circle of friends. This fragmentary nature becomes especially apparent when Payton informs us of Lady Powell's childbirth and death: "The Ladie Powell in this space was delivered of a Sonne, but Shee and it together with Master Michael Powell, Brother to Sir Thomas, lost their lives in this tedious expectation, in Boats, for that great man aforesaid."[22] Payton's revelation of Lady Powell's pregnancy comes as an afterthought, as part of a later voyage that he undertook with Roe. Ironically, Tomasin Powell during her time onboard the *Expedition*, and subsequently in Baluchistan and in Diul-Sind where the Persia-bound party finally disembarked, would have embodied the multiple meanings of travel as movement and (womanly) labor. As scholars such as Daniel Vitkus and Bernadette Andrea remind us, during the early modern period the words "travel" and "travail" were still intimately linked "in spelling, pronunciation, [and] meaning."[23] To travel then, was to labor, and to suffer: the consequence of the postlapsarian condition that saw man's exile from Eden.[24] But travail also implied the "labor of child-birth." Thus, in William Shakespeare's *Pericles*, which Dyani Johns Taff discusses in her essay later in this volume, the eponymous hero, worried about his pregnant wife, cries out to Lucina, the Roman goddess of childbirth to "convey thy deity / Aboard our dancing boat; make swift the pangs / Of my queen's travails" (3.1.12–14)! What makes Thaisa's labor even more arduous is that it takes place on a ship, thus literally doubling her travails. She, of course, is famously presumed dead and set adrift in a caulked chest with jewels and spices. Pericles, quick to gauge the low life expectancy of a newborn in the open seas, changes course to Tarsus to give his daughter Marina a chance at life. While this early seventeenth-century dramatic representation of pregnancy and childbirth at sea has a happy ending, in reality such conclusions were far from certain. What both Shakespeare's play and Payton's journal attest to, however, are the additional dangers that pregnant women had to endure while traveling. Lady Powell's travails had resulted in a successful childbirth—the first English infant to be born in the Indian subcontinent. The circumstances of her labor must indeed have been harrowing, for Thomas Powell died in Diul-Sind. The exact circumstances of his death remain unclear since Sherley and his entourage had to overcome Portuguese machinations as well as the hostility of local Mughal officials before they could finally get to the capital city of Agra. It was in Tutta, "in tedious expectation in Boats," waiting for a safe convoy to Jahangir's court that both Lady Powell and her son seem to have succumbed.[25]

Lady Powell's fragmented appearance is illustrative of the way that the company archive understood and represented its traveling women. While Payton does not comment on Lady Powell's pregnancy in the preliminary part of his account, this contrasts sharply with the treatment of Frances Steele. Her pregnancy, because it was the subject of controversy, was made visible repeatedly in the company reports. For instance, in a letter to Sir Thomas Smith, governor of the East India Company, Roe complained about "Master Steele, who brought to sea a mayd, Captain Towersons seruant, but great with Child and married her at the Cape vnder a bush."[26] At around the same time he wrote to the company that Frances Steele had "one Child sucking and (as they say) forward of a Nother."[27] Thus, in contrast to Lady Powell whose pregnant body was rendered invisible until its tragic end, Frances became an open spectacle, her pregnancies the visible markers of the company's failure at regulating its employees' sexuality. Furthermore, although we know Lady Powell was not traveling alone, Payton's later account does not allow us any glimpse into her friendships with the other women of her group, especially Lady Sherley. These friendships, as I have noted elsewhere, were essential in helping women negotiate the new geographical and cultural contexts they encountered during their travels.[28] We can only speculate on the nature of Lady Powell's relation with her companions. All that we learn from Payton is of the small group of survivors who finally made it to Persia with Sherley: "There remayned with him of his old Followers only his Ladie, and her Woman, two Persians, the old Armenian and the Chircassian."[29] Here too, we get tantalizing clues regarding female companionships. Lady Sherley's "Woman," presumably Leylye, had shared her "travails" across Asia and Europe—yet, again our understanding of this relationship remains incomplete. In the next section, I focus on the more fully developed case studies of Mariam Khan and France Steele to argue that the gendered crisis that traveling women triggered in the company archives arose not only from their perceived physical vulnerabilities (either from sexual assault or childbirth), but also from the company's estimation of their roles as unregulated sexual agents who might corrupt otherwise obedient and god-fearing chaplains and factors.

Mariam Khan, Frances Steele and Scandal in the Archive

The crises which prompted traveling women to become legible in the archive were not solely restricted to political intrigues threatening the loss of men and ships. They could also take the form of a breach in decorum which threatened the outward appearance of the company and its operations. In 1617, almost three years after Lady Powell's death, Mariam Khan returned to India accompanied by two other women, Mrs. Hudson and Frances (Webbe) Steele. Frances had nominally, at least, been Mariam's maid, and the discovery of her relationship with Richard Steele caused a scandal that continued to haunt them for the duration of their stay. It was this scandal that caused the crisis in the archive: a series of sexual and other indiscretions that as the story unfolded did not remain confined to the unfortunate husband in question. For Roe, who was left to resolve the situation, the women were seen as a dangerous influence and an impediment to the smooth functioning of the company. Their presence itself constituted a crisis; not surprisingly, the women surfaced again and again in Roe's frantic letters as he was confronted by their unorthodox movements.

Most likely Steele already knew Frances and had arranged for her transportation to India by attaching her to Mariam Khan, a ploy which effectively subverted the company's prohibition on allowing its employees' wives to travel with them. Mariam's journey back was itself an exception, and possibly permitted by the company because she was a Mughal subject.[30] Whatever the status of their prior relationship, Richard Steele and Frances were publicly married at the Cape. Officiating the ceremony was Reverend Mr. Golding, the chaplain of the *Anne*. Roe would subsequently try his best to keep Frances away from her husband and even to send her back home to England, all to no avail. I suggest that the ambassador's hostility toward the three women should be read within the larger context of his own uncertain position within the Mughal court. Prior to Roe, there had been other unofficial ambassadors, one of the first and most famous being Hawkins, Mariam's first husband. Roe thus had to struggle to establish his own legitimacy while at the same time trying to reconcile "his royal functions" with "his commercial ones."[31] Unlike other Englishmen who had claimed the position of ambassador—Roe did not know any Asian languages—his experience in overseas expeditions had been restricted to the New World.[32] Similarly, while the cosmopolitan circle within which Mariam Khan and Frances Steele operated could more easily access the Mughal codes of behavior, Roe found himself struggling at Jahangir's court.[33] At the same time Roe felt himself to be, in some degree at least, responsible for the conduct of the other Englishmen around him.

Unfortunately, for Roe, the problems that the women caused did not remain confined to their spouses. Mr. Golding who had officiated the wedding at the Cape of Good Hope, now attached himself to the women, causing quite a scandal amongst the factors in Surat. To make matters worse, when Golding was asked to return to his ship he refused and "slipped out of the city disguised as a native, and went 'after the women' to Ahmadabad."[34] A distraught Roe wrote to Capt. Martin Pring: "In assurance of right I rest quiett, as farr as Master Steele, the woemen and the indiscretion of Master Goulding will suffer mee. I woonder to see him here and shall soon resend him. I must labor to mend all. I gaue consent for the best to Mistress Steele, but neuer for the minister. Now her husband discouers himself; but one of vs must breake in this business."[35] The significance of this "indiscretion" cannot be underestimated. While religious conversion was not high on the agenda of the East India Company, the chaplains still fulfilled an important function, "administering to English souls."[36] Such care would have seemed especially important given that the English merchants, especially at the Mughal court and in the port cities, lived among not only Hindus and Muslims with whom they had to trade on a daily basis, but also the Portuguese and their Jesuit priests who would have been seen as no less of a corruptive influence. Ironically, Roe had initially greeted the news of the arrival to Surat of two chaplains—Reverend Patrick Copland and Mr. Golding—quite enthusiastically, hoping that at least one would stay back and tend to the English factors: "You have come two ministers. My desire is that one of them that shall be willing may live with you ashore at Suratt, that you may have the Word and Sacraments, and that in outward show we may live to profess the service of our gracious God, who keepeth us among His and our enemies."[37] The purpose of the chaplain for Roe was thus not merely a matter of inner spiritual upliftment through religious instruction, but also that of "outward show." Given the ambassador's own efforts at putting forward a performance of Englishness at the Mughal court, it is hardly surprising that he would want the company factors to publicly present themselves as pious practitioners of their Protestant faith.[38] What was therefore particularly distressing about the Golding episode was its public nature: specifically, the spectacle of an English clergyman "going native" in pursuit of three women. Golding, of course, was not alone in picking up eastern attire; Thomas Coryate had previously done the same, and on a more permanent basis.[39] Unlike Coryate, however, who had built his reputation as a jester in Prince Henry's court and had walked overland to India independent of the company, the chaplain was another matter.[40] The company and Roe, even while providing Coryate shelter and support, could and did distance themselves from his antics.[41] Golding, on the other hand, was a company chaplain, and his unexpected behavior spoke directly to the company's fears regarding the dangerous influence of traveling women.

That Golding managed to pass himself off as a native on his journey from Surat to Ahmedabad, where Jahangir's peripatetic court was stationed, reveals the liminal nature of English identity in the Indian subcontinent. Frances Steele herself once at court would set up a household complete with eastern accessories such as the *Palinke* or palanquin.[42] Her friend and erstwhile mistress, Mariam Khan, was, of course, a member of the larger Mughal community. The anxiety that Roe expresses is thus layered with fears of not only sexual transgression, but also transculturation. As scholars have frequently pointed out, Roe assiduously resisted the Mughal cultural influence, dismissing its court etiquettes as inconsequential theatricality.[43] Even his personal chaplain, Terry, while describing Mughal India and its charms, repeatedly undercut his praise by describing the land as postlapsarian and its customs as degenerate.[44] Golding, apparently influenced by the women, presented a counter model of engaging with the East. An English chaplain arriving at the city where Jahangir was holding court, dressed in native clothes, naturally would have registered as a crisis that Roe had to "labor to mend." Contrary to Roe's assertions, however, it was not easy to be rid of Golding, for he proved singularly stubborn in his desire to remain in the company of the women. Even after being sent back from Ahmedabad with English factors the chaplain escaped. He would eventually seek pardon for his "loose carriage" and express "penitence for the past, and promise of amendment for the future."[45] The company Court Book reveals that the matter reached London, where the indiscretions of Mariam Khan, Frances Steele, and Mr. Golding were duly noted. As Roe described it, the women had caused a "scandal already... not easely wiped off."[46]

To conclude, the danger that Mariam Khan and her fellow women travelers presented to the company combined the lure of sexual license and transculturation. Although it remains unclear whether Golding formed any specific relationship with any of the women, his general attachment to the group was well known and commented upon. This sexual anxiety is also evident in the company's dealings with the Sherley entourage. However, the women, as we have seen, were part of a cosmopolitan circle that drove early English trading and diplomatic alliances with Asian empires. The women, in other words, were as much part of the "global renaissance" as their male counterparts. Nonetheless, the gendered corporate logic of the East India Company retained an uneasy relation with them throughout the seventeenth century. As Nocentelli demonstrates in *Empires of Love*, the company's hostility extended to women who were not seeking to travel. In 1625 when the company discovered John Leachland's relationship with an Indian woman named Manya, it immediately attempted to separate them, hoping that he would eventually become "sensible of his own Errors."[47] The company's prohibition on allowing women to travel during these initial years was thus part of a larger discourse that sought to exclude women from directly participating in its overseas operations. It is this exclusion that manifests itself in other ways in the archive, allowing us to access only the fragmentary traces of the company women. One of the ways that the women surfaced at all was when they were seen to interrupt or threaten the routine functions of the company and its factors. It is these moments of crisis that allow us to better understand company attitudes towards its traveling women.

Notes

1. "Sahib" was only one of the terms used for Europeans, drawn from the Urdu-Arabic "çāḥib." The other word used almost exclusively for Europeans was "Feringhee" derived from the Persian-Arabic term for Franks. Both "Feringhee" and "sahib" entered the English language during the seventeenth century, the former a few years prior. Unlike "Feringhee," however, the word "sahib" eventually prompted a specifically gendered counterpart, the prefix "mem" coming from "ma'am." During the colonial period "memsahib" was used exclusively to denote English women. For more see "sahib, *n*.," "memsahib, *n*.," and "Feringhee, *n*.," OED Online. See also Harris, *First Firangis*, 18.
2. Although the East India Company did not employ women as factors, it did enter into various trading arrangements with them, renting warehouses for instance or paying out the wages for their husbands. See Sharpe, "Gender at Sea," 58–62, and Sen, "Traveling Companions," 201.
3. Roe, *Embassy*, 439n.

4. Andrea, "'Presences of Women,'" 302.
5. Downton, "Captain Downton to Sir Robert Sherley," 209–10.
6. Singh, "Introduction," 2–4. For more, see Subrahmanyam, "Connected Histories."
7. Andrea, *Lives*, 37, 124–30.
8. For more on Sherley's life in Persia and his embassy in Europe, as well the arrival of the rival ambassador Naqd Ali Beg, see Andrea, *Women and Islam*, 43–44.
9. Briggs, "Sherley Family," 77–104; Sainsbury, *Calendar*, 164.
10. Briggs, "Sherley Family," 99; Anderson, *English in Western India*, 9.
11. Payton, "Journall," 180.
12. Payton, "Journall," 289.
13. Penrose, *Sherleian Odyssey*, 185.
14. Roe, *Embassy*, iii.
15. She would, however, later accompany Roe on his subsequent diplomatic mission to Constantinople. See Roe, *Embassy*, lv, 255n.
16. Sainsbury, *Calendar*, 275.
17. Schleck, "Marital Problems," 89
18. Payton, "Journall," 195.
19. Schleck, "Marital Problems," 87–90
20. Payton, "Journall," 196.
21. Stoler, "Colonial Archives," 100.
22. Payton, "Journall," 297.
23. Vitkus, "Labor and Travel," 229; Andrea, *Women and Islam*, 65–67.
24. Vitkus, "Labor and Travel," 229–30.
25. Payton, "Journall," 297.
26. Roe, *Embassy*, 500.
27. Roe, *Embassy*, 477.
28. Sen, "Traveling Companions," 205–7.
29. Payton, "Journall," 297.
30. Hawkins in his own report to the East India Company reveals that Jahangir, worried about his safety, had given him in marriage "a white mayden" out of his haram ("William Hawkins 1608-13," 84). In keeping with Hawkins's request the woman in question, Mariam Khan, was a Christian.
31. Barbour, *Before Orientalism*, 146.
32. Singh, *Colonial Narratives*, 29; Barbour, *Before Orientalism*, 152.
33. For more on Roe's difficulties at the Mughal court, including his difficulty finding interpreters, see Barbour, *Before Orientalism*, 151–87, and Teltscher, *India Inscribed*, 17–21.

34. Roe, *Embassy*, 490n.
35. Roe, *Embassy*, 491.
36. Singh, *Colonial Narratives*, 28.
37. Roe, "Sir Thomas Roe to Thomas Kerridge," 122.
38. Barbour, *Before Orientalism*, 176
39. Barbour, *Before Orientalism*, 136.
40. Barbour, *Before Orientalism*, 115–16; Singh, *Colonial Narratives*, 40.
41. Coryate, who found himself chronically short of money while in Mughal India, relied on the hospitality of the company factors. Incidentally, he knew Robert and Teresa Sherley, as well as Richard Steele, and had encountered them during his journey to India (Roe, *Embassy*, 103–4n). For more, see Singh, *Colonial Narratives*, 40–41; Barbour, *Before Orientalism*, 141; Andrea, *Women and Islam*, 47.
42. Roe, *Embassy*, 483; Sen, "Traveling Companions," 206.
43. Teltscher, *India Inscribed*, 21; Barbour, *Before Orientalism*, 178.
44. Teltscher, *India Inscribed*, 24–26.
45. Sainsbury, *Calendar*, 232.
46. Roe, *Embassy*, 484.
47. Nocentelli, *Empires of Love*, 1.

Bibliography

Anderson, Philip. *The English in Western India: Being the Early History of the Factory at Surat, of Bombay, and the Subordinate Factories on the Western Coast*. Bombay: Smith, Taylor, 1854.

Andrea, Bernadette. *The Lives of Girls and Women from the Islamic World in Early Modern British Literature and Culture*. Toronto: University of Toronto Press, 2017.

———. "The 'Presences of Women' from the Islamic World." In *Mapping Gendered Routes and Spaces in the Early Modern World*, edited by Merry Wiesner-Hanks, 291–306. Burlington VT: Ashgate, 2015.

———. *Women and Islam in Early Modern English Literature*. Cambridge: Cambridge University Press, 2007.

Barbour, Richmond. *Before Orientalism: London's Theatre of the East, 1576–1626*. Cambridge: Cambridge University Press, 2003.

Briggs, [John], Major-General. "A Short Account of the Sherley Family." *Journal of the Royal Asiatic Society of Great Britain and Ireland* 6, no. 1 (1841): 77–104.

Downton, Nicholas. "Captain Nicholas Downton to Sir Robert Sherley." In *Letters Received by the East India Company from Its Servants in the East,*

1613–1615, vol. 2, edited by William Foster, 209–11. London: Sampson Low, Marston, 1897.

"Feringhee, n." *The Oxford English Dictionary Online*. Oxford: Oxford University Press. www.oed./view/Entry/69344?redirectedFrom=firingi#eid. Accessed December 22, 2016.

Harris, Jonathan Gil. *The First Firangis: Remarkable Stories of Heroes, Healers, Charlatans, Courtesans & Other Foreigners Who Became India*. New Delhi: Aleph, 2015.

Hawkins, William. "William Hawkins 1608–13." In *Early Travels in India 1583–1619*, edited by William Foster, 60–121. Delhi: Low Price, 1999.

"memsahib, n." *The Oxford English Dictionary Online*. Oxford: Oxford University Press. www.oed./view/Entry/116367#eid37235945. Accessed December 22, 2016.

Nocentelli, Carmen. *Empires of Love: Europe, Asia, and the Making of Early Modern Identity*. Philadelphia: University of Pennsylvania Press, 2013.

Payton, Walter. "A Journall of all principall matters passed in the twelfth Voyage to the East Indies . . . Anno 1612." In *Hakluytus Posthumus or Purchas His Pilgrimes*, vol. 6, edited by Samuel Purchas, 488–500. Glasgow: James MacLehose and Sons, 1905.

Penrose, Boies. *The Sherleian Odyssey*. Taunton, UK: Wessex, 1938.

Roe, Sir Thomas. *The Embassy of Sir Thomas Roe to the Court of the Great Mogul 1615–1619*, vol. 2, edited by William Foster. London: Hakluyt Society, 1899.

———. "Sir Thomas Roe to Thomas Kerridge and other Factors at Surat. Mandoa, October 11, 1617." In *Letters Received by the East India Company from its Servants in the East*, vol. 6, edited by William Foster. London: Sampson Low, Marston, 1902.

"sahib, n." *The Oxford English Dictionary Online*. Oxford: Oxford University Press. www.oed.com/view/Entry/169785#eid24660606. Accessed December 22, 2016.

Sainsbury, W. Noel, ed. *Calendar of State Papers, Colonial Series: East Indies, China, and Japan, 1617–1621*. 1870. Reprint, Vaduz, Liechtenstein: Kraus, 1964.

Schleck, Julia. "The Marital Problems of the East India Company." In "The Alternative Histories of the East India Company," edited by Julia Schleck and Amrita Sen. Special issue, *Journal of Early Modern Cultural Studies* 17, no. 3 (Summer 2017): 83–104.

Sen, Amrita. "Traveling Companions: Women, Trade, and the early East India Company." In "Transcultural Networks in the Indian Ocean, Sixteenth–Eighteenth Centuries: Europeans and Indian Ocean Societies in Interaction," edited by Su Fang Ng. Special issue, *Genre: Forms of Discourse and Culture* 48, no. 2 (July 2015): 193–214.

Shakespeare, William. *The Riverside Shakespeare*, edited by G. Blakemore Evans. Boston: Houghton Mifflin, 1997.

Sharpe, Pamela. "Gender at Sea: Women and the East India Company in Seventeenth Century London." In *Women, Work and Wages in England, 1600–1850*, edited by Penelope Lane, Neil Raven, and K. D. M. Snell, 47–67. Woodbridge, UK: Boydell, 2004.

Singh, Jyotsna G. *Colonial Narratives/Cultural Dialogues: "Discoveries" of India in the Language of Colonialism*. London: Routledge, 1996.

———. "Introduction: A Global Renaissance." In *A Companion to the Global Renaissance: English Literature and Culture in the Era of Expansion*, edited by Jyotsna Singh, 1–27. Malden MA: Wiley-Blackwell, 2009.

Stoler, Ann Laura. "Colonial Archives and the Arts of Governance." *Archival Science* 2 (2002): 87–109.

Subrahmanyam, Sanjay. "Connected Histories: Notes Towards a Reconfiguration of Early Modern Eurasia." *Modern Asian Studies* 31, no. 3 (1997): 735–62.

Teltscher, Kate. *India Inscribed: European and British Writing on India 1600–1800*. Delhi: Oxford University Press, 1995.

Vitkus, Daniel. "Labor and Travel on the Early Modern Stage: Representing the Travail of Travel in Dekker's *Old Fortunatus* and Shakespeare's *Pericles*." In *Working Subjects in Early Modern English Drama*, edited by Michelle Dowd and Natasha Korda, 225–42. Burlington VT: Ashgate, 2011.

4

Teresa Sampsonia Sherley

Amazon, Traveler, and Consort

CARMEN NOCENTELLI

The European colonization of America, the expansion of long-distance trade, and the emergence of the Grand Tour significantly increased the rate and scale of geographical mobility during the early modern period. Men and women alike voyaged in unprecedented numbers, going farther and staying away longer than ever before. Yet while the travels of men were generally appreciated, the travels of women met with prejudice and suspicion. Across linguistic and national boundaries, women were told to stay home, lest their voyages compromise their gender or jeopardize their chastity. "[M]en have the freedom to travel with honor in foreign lands. . . . Women, on the other hand, are . . . more useful when they sit still," wrote Leon Battista Alberti in the mid-fifteenth century, voicing a sentiment that would resonate, over a century later, in works as diverse as Jean de Sainte-Fère's *La Republique Chrestienne* (The Christian republic), Georg Loys's *Pervigilium Mercurii* (Mercury's vigil), and Fynes Moryson's *Itinerary*.[1] "Women for suspition of chastity are most unfit for [travel]," ruled Moryson, even as he admitted that some "masculine women" traveled both far and often.[2]

Representations of the woman traveler were thus subject to a double bind. On the one hand, conventional markers of femininity—emotionality, weakness, passivity, and submissiveness—emphasized her vulnerability and sexual availability, inviting skepticism on her claims to propriety. On the other hand, the very traits that should have deemphasized vulnerability and sexual availability—rationality, strength, activity, and dominance—cast her in the mold of the masculine woman, thereby exposing her as a gender transgressor. Whether she adopted a male disguise or retained female dress, journeyed under male protection or ventured forth solo, the female traveler was a woman at risk, unceasingly liable of breaching decorum if not also natural and divine law.

Not all representations of the woman traveler fell prey to this impasse, however. Focusing on the figure of Teresa Sampsonia Sherley (ca. 1589–1668), a polyglot Circassian who traveled extensively through Europe and Asia, this chapter maps the contours of what seventeenth-century writers construed as respectable, and even exemplary, female mobility. Such a construal required something of a paradox: an on-the-move subject who epitomized proper femininity while also embodying the (hyper)masculinity so often associated with traveling.

Teresa's early biographers tackled this paradox by tapping into discursive repertoires as diverse as Greco-Roman mythology, chivalric romance, and conduct literature. From classical mythology, they drew the figure of the Amazon as a synecdoche for female strength and power; from chivalric romance, they borrowed the ethical convention of travel as service; from conduct literature, and more generally from certain strains of early modern culture, they derived an understanding of marriage as a partnership founded on mutual affection and commitment. By melding these disparate elements together, Teresa's biographers sought to imagine the respectable woman traveler as straddling the gap between the Amazon and the wife—as a subject strong enough to overcome travel's toils and perils, yet feminine enough to use that strength in the service of patriarchy.

In what follows, I propose that Teresa's representation as a traveling *consort*, a partner in her husband's life and fortunes, was crucial to her construction as an on-the-move female subject who was neither gender deviant nor sexually suspect. Like the gender-specific "wife," the gender-neutral "consort" could imply marital relations predicated on female subservience; unlike "wife," it unlocked a range of positionalities that could be subject to change and negotiation. From this perspective, being a consort emancipated the woman traveler from too strict an adherence to conventional feminine scripts. At the same time, being a consort translated the away from home into private and domestic terms, thus harnessing female mobility to conventional gender roles.

From this perspective, the traveling consort theorized women's geographical mobility as an extension of domesticity. In so doing, the traveling consort also revealed some of the forms, limits, and conditions of respectable female travel during the seventeenth century.

A Different Sherley Myth

Like Teresa de Ávila, the sixteenth-century Spanish mystic whose name she came to bear and to whom she seems to have been especially devoted, Teresa Sampsonia Sherley traveled for much of her life, both literally and figuratively.[3] In the version of events favored by her Continental biographers, she was barely four years old when she left her native Circassia for the Persian capital, following an aunt into Shah 'Abbas I's royal harem.[4] Ten years later, having emerged from the seraglio "well instructed in all qualities pertaining to her greatness and a woman of the noblest condition," she met the English adventurer Robert Sherley, who was immediately charmed by her virtues and good looks.[5]

Robert had arrived in Persia in 1598 in the company of his brother Anthony, who had then convinced 'Abbas to send him back to Europe as his ambassador. Left behind "as a pledge" for Anthony's return, Robert seems to have been "kindly intreated" for a few years.[6] But when it became evident that his brother had no plan to return, Robert's position in Persia deteriorated. By report, he was maintained begrudgingly, often mistreated, and repeatedly pressured to convert to Islam.[7] Still, he must have had freedom enough *not* to convert to Islam, since he officially became a Catholic at some point during his stay in Persia. And while his standing at 'Abbas's court had perhaps grown less secure, he evidently enjoyed favor enough to marry Teresa, who was reputedly a princess as well as a niece to Shah 'Abbas's favorite wife.[8]

On February 2, 1608, Teresa was baptized and joined in marriage to Robert "in the form prescribed by the Council of Trent."[9] Ten days later, the newlyweds set out for Europe "with Camels and Horses ... and many attendants both men and women."[10] Robert's mission, like his brother's before him, was to establish diplomatic and commercial ties between Persia and the powers of Europe, with an eye to forming an alliance against the Ottoman Empire. Teresa went along, allegedly to keep him company but in all likelihood also as a deterrent should he think of defecting.[11] It was the beginning of an itinerant life that the couple would share until Robert's sudden death in 1628.

Between 1608 and 1635, the year in which she settled near the Carmelite Church of Santa Maria della Scala in Rome's Trastevere district (where she would eventually be buried), Teresa made the trip between Persia and Europe no less than five times, visiting Poland, Spain, Italy, England, India, and many other places besides.[12] "Countess Sherley, a Circassian lady of high quality and great spirit, is currently in Europe as Ambassadress of the King of Persia," wrote the Roman Pietro della Valle in a letter dated April 22, 1619. And if one tallied up all the trips she had taken to date, della Valle added with admiration, she could easily be said to have already "rounded little less than the whole world several times over."[13]

Between journeys, Teresa seems to have been quite active in both official and unofficial networks of diplomacy. She paid and received visits, proffered and accepted gifts, attended official audiences, and engaged in formal correspondence. While in Spain, she became intimate with Beatriz de Jesús, niece of Teresa de Ávila and prioress of the Carmelite convent in Madrid, and received from her a relic of Saint Teresa's flesh.[14] Between 1613 and 1615, she traveled in the Mughal Empire, visiting Jahangir's court and bestowing "forty shillings . . . in Persian money" on the indefatigable Thomas Coryate.[15] In 1622 she was a guest of the Archduchess Maria Maddalena of Austria in Florence, where she presented her hostess with a gift of her own embroideries and was in turn presented with a laudatory sonnet. From Florence, she traveled to Rome, where she met privately with the Pope and had her portrait painted by Anthony van Dyck, then in the patronage of the powerful Cardinal Guido Bentivoglio. Early in 1624, she was at her sister-in-law's in Suffolk, where she likely came into close contact with King James I. In 1627, after Robert was accused of imposture, she wrote in his defense, petitioning the Privy Council for safeguards to his dignity and well-being.[16]

Within the English archive, the figure of Teresa has been generally obscured by those of her male relatives.[17] Whether she is identified as

"Sir Robert Sherley... his Persian Lady," "the Sophies Neece," or "the King of Persia his cousin Germaine," she is little more than a prop in the so-called Sherley myth, a tale of masculine globe-trotting featuring Robert and his two older brothers, Anthony and Thomas, as exemplars of English prowess and entrepreneurism.[18]

In Anthony Nixon's *The Three English Brothers*, for instance, Teresa stands metonymically for the "honour and estimation" enjoyed by the Sherleys on the global stage.[19] Similarly, in John Day, William Rowley, and George Wilkins's *The Travailes of the Three English Brothers*, she helps encode the brothers' voyages as an export of English virility.

Even in Thomas Herbert's account of Dodmore Cotton's embassy to Persia—a text far less invested in the Sherley myth than either Nixon's pamphlet or Day, Rowley, and Wilkins's adventure drama—the role Teresa plays is effectively instrumental. Ill, brokenhearted, and defenseless in the wake of Robert's sudden death, she is at once an object of pity and an opportunity for rescue. In short, she is the foil against which the ethics of the men around her can be assessed and evaluated. Pitting "a faithfull honest" Englishman against a greedy Dutchman and a malicious Persian bent on plundering the Sherleys' possessions, Herbert's account of Teresa's early widowhood is less about honoring her "deserving Memorie," as the author claims to be doing, than about praising the members of England's first accredited embassy to Persia, of whom Herbert himself was one.[20] As it happens, it is not Teresa but one of Herbert's colleagues, the "worthy Gentleman" Robert Hedges, who stands at the center of the episode. It is Hedges who uncovers the plot to dispossess Teresa, absconds with her valuables, and returns them to her in the end along with "words of comfort."[21] What begins as a celebration of the "thrice worthy and undaunted Lady [Sherley]" ends as a self-congratulatory account of English masculinity.[22] If Teresa appears at all, it is because her weakness and vulnerability—her "feeble hands" and "pathetique virtue"—give shape and substance to the account.[23]

Outside of England, however, Teresa Sampsonia Sherley was a figure of note in and of her own right. Pietro della Valle, for one, described her as an "Ambassadress of the King of Persia," thereby placing her on equal footing with her husband.[24] The Medici courtier Cristoforo

Bronzini extolled her as "the ornament, glory, and honor of this century," while the poet and historian Gian Vittorio Rossi (also known as Ianus Nicius Erythraeus) featured her along with such celebrities as the Neapolitan polymath Margherita Sarrocchi, the Flemish intellectual Justus Lipsius, the Scottish satirist John Barclay, and the Tuscan astronomer Galileo Galilei.[25] For his part, the Carmelite chronicler Pierre de Saint-André devoted a lengthy chapter of his *Historia generalis fratrum discalceatorum* (General history of the Discalced Brothers) to Teresa's exploits. Decades later, another Carmelite, Martial de Saint Jean-Baptiste, praised her effusively for her "extraordinary devotion" as well as "heroic perseverance, indomitable courage, [and] well-known language skills."[26]

Placing Teresa Sampsonia Sherley within this larger archive means uncovering the contours of a very different Sherley myth. In this myth, globe-trotting is still central, but it is Teresa—not her acquired English family or the members of Cotton's embassy—who stands front and center. Here England is hardly mentioned, Anthony and Thomas Sherley are nowhere in sight, and Robert is conspicuous only for his helplessness. Teresa, by contrast, looms larger than life, at once a fierce Amazon, a stout she-Samson, a loving wife, and a Christian champion fighting in the defense of the weak and the oppressed.

The Roman Catholic Church undoubtedly had a hand in the construction of this myth: as a prized early fruit of the Carmelite mission in Persia, Teresa had an important role to play in Counter-Reformation historiography, especially after the anti-Christian persecutions of the 1620s.[27] And yet, even at their most obviously hagiographic, seventeenth-century accounts of Teresa's life and travels exceed the confines of ecclesiastical propaganda. In fact, what seems most at stake in these accounts is the elaboration of an agential femininity borne of the melding of conventional female traits such as grace, chastity, and devotion with male attributes such as courage, assertiveness, and physical strength.

Nowhere is this melding more evident than in a biographical sketch written as part of Bronzini's *Della dignità e nobiltà delle donne* (Of the dignity and nobility of women), a multivolume *querelle des femmes* partially published between 1624 and 1632.[28] On the one hand, Bronzini presents

Teresa as a paragon of conventional femininity. Not only is she "modest, chaste, and honest," she is also as beautiful as Venus, as devoted to her husband as Hypsicratea was to Mithridates, and more skilled at needlework than the mythical Arachne.[29] On the other hand, both Bronzini and the anonymous sonneteer he quotes construe Teresa as an exemplar of masculine virtue rivaling Cicero in eloquence, Mars in swordsmanship, Atlas in strength, and that byword of chivalric excellence, the knight Orlando, in spear throwing.

Bronzini and his unidentified poet were by no means the only seventeenth-century writers to portray Teresa as an androgyne. The English clergyman Thomas Fuller—whose *Worthies of England* is usually cited for noting that Teresa "had more of Ebony, then Ivory, in her Complexion"—pointedly referred to her as combining feminine amiableness with masculine valor, "a quality considerable in that Sex, in those Countries."[30] For their part, the Roman writer Gian Vittorio Rossi and the anonymous author of the "Breve relatione" (A short relation) described her as a woman "of manly spirit."[31] Excelling in the "arts and labors appropriate to her sex," was never enough for Teresa, noted the French ecclesiastic Pierre de Saint-André; instead, she constantly "strove to surpass, or at least to equal, the strongest of men and the most valiant of warriors."[32]

In this regard, it is significant that Teresa's Circassian name, Sanphluf, should be routinely rendered as Sampsonia.[33] On the surface, Sampsonia was merely a translation for Sanphluf—which, as an Italian relation recites—"is the same as Sampson in our language."[34] Yet in replacing one name with the other, seventeenth-century writers also associated Teresa with the biblical Sampson, thus endowing the former with the latter's exceptional brawn. Bronzini was simply making this inference explicit when he noted that the woman once known as Sanphluf was "a veritable she-Sampson, and very strong in both spirit and body."[35]

Equally significant is the repeated claim that Teresa's native Circassia was the land of the ancient Amazons, which made Teresa an Amazon by extension. Bronzini's manuscript describes her as a "compatriot" of the Amazons, while the tombstone in Santa Maria della Scala (which Teresa herself might have had a hand in composing) refers to her as a "native of the land of the Amazons."³⁶ Carrying these geographical premises to their logical conclusion, Saint-André's *Historia generalis* explicitly identifies Teresa as an Amazon, dubbing her variously as an "Amazon worthy of eternal praise," an "illustrious Amazon," a "Circassian Amazon," or a "Christian Amazon."³⁷

As these associations with both the biblical Sampson and the classical Amazons may have already suggested, seventeenth-century writers construed Teresa as a manlike or heroic woman—a type known as *mujer varonil* in Spain, *femme forte* in France, and *donna forte* in Italy. Aided by the increased visibility of women as political, spiritual, and military leaders—Queen Isabella and Saint Teresa de Ávila in Spain, Archduchess Maria Maddalena in Tuscany, Queens Elizabeth and Henrietta Maria in England, Queen Christina in Sweden, Queens Catherine de' Medici, Marie de' Medici, and Anne of Austria in France—by the mid-seventeenth century the heroic woman had become a figure of both unease and fascination through much of Europe. Rossi and Saint-André were undoubtedly nodding in this figure's direction when they wrote that Teresa was known in Persia as a "Tattzin," "which is to say, strong woman."³⁸

Service and the Ethics of Women's Travel

The traits attributed to Teresa made her especially well suited to the challenges of early modern travel. By all reports, she spoke between seven and nine languages, without counting her native Circassian.³⁹ She "neither fretted nor frighted" the way most women did and thought nothing of pain and discomfort.⁴⁰ True to her Amazonian heritage, she was also an indomitable warrior, an accomplished equestrian, and a formidable archer. "She shoots the bow so masterfully that from the back of a running horse she can hit an animal in the fields or a fruit on a tree . . . with the same accuracy others would have if they stood near the target," wrote Bronzini in this regard, noting that Teresa's abilities in hunt and combat were by no means inferior to those of knights-errant.⁴¹ She could break wild horses, draw heavy bows, throw the spear, and shoot arrows in volleys, echoed Saint-André, who ranked Teresa among the finest of hunters and warriors.⁴²

These abilities found concrete exemplification in two travel episodes that were often rehearsed by Teresa's biographers. In one episode, the Sherley party is on the road when Robert is suddenly surrounded by unidentified enemies, who overcome his servants and take him captive. But just as he is being forced to drink poison—or, in Rossi's variant, just as he is being carried away—Teresa throws herself into the fray. And although she is alone against many, she wreaks such a slaughter that she soon forces Robert's captors to relinquish him. Having thus pried her semiconscious husband from the hands of his enemies, she carries him to a safe place, and tends his wounds with such care and affection that in a short time she restores him to health.[43]

In another travel episode, Robert and Teresa's lodging at Lahri Bandar (a now-vanished port about twenty-eight miles south of modern Karachi) is set on fire by an armed throng.[44] As it happens, most of the Sherley entourage is in bad shape. Robert himself lies ill, too weak to defend himself or even run away. Taking charge of the situation, Teresa grabs an "Amazonian battle-ax," rounds up six servants, and rushes to the defense.[45] With seventy-odd ruffians seeking to do harm, the odds are ten to one against her party. But such are "the strength and ardor" with which Teresa fights that in the space of two hours she kills fourteen attackers, wounds "an incredible number" of them, and puts the remainder in flight. As for the Sherley party, it remains virtually unscathed: no one is killed, and Teresa herself comes out of the mêlée "with three wounds only."[46] Even the lodging suffers but minor damages: three crossbeams burn and collapse, yet "without causing any hurt to either [Teresa's] husband or the servants who were inside."[47]

With their overtly melodramatic language, exaggerated odds, and improbable casualty numbers, these episodes may well strike modern readers as ironic if not outright parodic. Indeed, the very excessiveness of these textual moments could easily be read as a sign of their authors' unease. If Robert's conspicuous frailty disrupts the binary of masculine potency and feminine vulnerability, Teresa's spectacular victimization of her (male) opponents challenges the equation between maleness and power, showing how women could intervene in the constitution and performance of patriarchal authority.

Nevertheless, there are indications that Teresa's Continental biographers took these episodes seriously. In Saint-André's *Historia generalis*, for instance, Teresa's violent acts are those of a "pious Maenad" possessed by God's spirit; in Bronzini's *querelle des femmes*, they stand for the "heroic and magnanimous acts of which strong and most loving consorts are capable."[48] Both secular and religious writers thus deployed these episodes in support of their larger claims. For Saint-André, they confirmed God's participation in the militancy of Counter-Reformation Catholicism. For Bronzini, they proved a thesis already advanced in the first volume of *Della dignità e nobiltà delle donne*: namely, that there was no obvious relationship between sexed bodies and gendered acts. Men and women might differ in the body parts "needed for procreation," but still enjoyed "the same vigor" and the exact same "faculty to pursue ... honorable endeavors."[49]

This is not to say that the excessiveness of these textual moments is accidental. Melodrama, exaggeration, and improbability in fact mark these episodes' indebtedness to chivalric romance, from which they borrow cherished conventions such as the travel through a foreign land, the combat of one against many, and the equation between invincibility and nobility. This formal aspect is important to note, and not only because chivalric romance was especially well suited to emplot the life of an Amazon who was at times explicitly compared to the eponymous knight-errant of *Orlando Furioso*. Since saints' lives and knightly tales had overlapping features, the conventions of chivalric romance nicely doubled as hagiographic devices, helping writers such as Saint-André enshrine Teresa within the heroic pantheon of Counter-Reformation Catholicism.[50] Above all, since chivalric romance thematized globe-trotting as honorable service, its conventions encoded female travel as an activity that need not be inherently suspect.

As any Latin dictionary will confirm, the primary meaning of the verb *errare*—from which the English adjective "errant" ultimately derives—is "to wander freely."[51] By definition, then, knights-errant were travelers; or to be more precise, travel was integral to the construction of knightly identity. Travel exposed knights to solitude, difficulty, and danger, testing their spiritual and physical mettle. It mapped their potentialities across space and time, piecing scattered experiences into coherent selfhoods. More important, travel inscribed knights within an ethos of service, manifesting thereby their nobility of purpose. Whether they roamed the land to defend the church, uphold the faith, obey their kings' commands, or prove their love to their beloveds, honorable knights traveled in the service of others. It was precisely this service ethos that made them honorable.

By the seventeenth century, knights-errant lived only in the pages of chivalric romances, and even those had gone out of fashion in many quarters. Yet the service ethos of chivalry was still central to the ways that travel was imagined, experienced, and represented.[52] Merchants may travel for profit and profligates for pleasure, but gentlemen traveled for honor, which was best acquired by placing others first.[53] Honorable travel thus privileged the good of the community, the *utilitas publica*, over what was good for the individual, the *utilitas singulorum*. This communal payoff may be immediate, as in the case of travel one embarked upon to broker peace or other political agreements; or it may be deferred, as in the case of educational travel one embarked upon in order to better serve in the future. Either way, honorable travel was predicated on a service ethos that subordinated the traveler's interest to the interests of those for whom he traveled, if not in practice then at least in appearance.

It is this service ethos that Samuel Purchas had in mind when he praised Robert Sherley for "directing [his] . . . private Genius for publike benefit"—which is to say, for traveling in pursuit of the common good.[54] "Let mee admire such a Traveller," Purchas expounded, "which travells not of and for some vaine discourse, or private gaine or skill, but still travelleth and is delivered of the publike good, accounting his Countrey his Garden, Christendome his Orchard, the Universe his Field, for this happy seed of publike beneficence."[55]

In celebrating Teresa's travels, seventeenth-century biographers adopted a similar strategy, going to great lengths to underscore the altruism that subtended them. Not only did Teresa accompany her husband wherever he went, she also served him with devotion and dedication. Her main concern throughout was his preservation, which she "always attended to far more carefully than her own life."⁵⁶ When he was ill or wounded, she nursed him back to health. And when he was in danger, she defended him with the fury of a "tiger deprived of her cubs."⁵⁷ For this reason, Robert "derived no small profit" from having Teresa by his side: his very success as a traveler depended largely on Teresa's presence.⁵⁸ As some Continental writers pointedly noted, he would have neither traveled so far nor lived so long if he had been without her. Thanks to her polyglossia, he escaped fraud and deceit despite his "ignorance of languages."⁵⁹ Thanks to her care and attention, he survived injury and disease. Thanks to her courage and strength, he dodged more than one assassination attempt.

Both Robert's and Teresa's travels were thus presented as service missions. There was, however, a crucial difference. As Purchas had it, Robert traveled to serve England, Christendom, and the world at large. As her biographers had it, Teresa traveled to serve Robert. Their journeys might have been identical in scope, similar in the demands they made of them, and even parallel in their ethical dimensions. Yet they ultimately diverged in purpose and inspiration. Robert's travels sprung from "desire of glorie"; Teresa's travels sprung from the "honorable and devoted love" she bore her husband.⁶⁰

Teresa's seventeenth-century biographers are unanimous in associating her travels with love—or, to be more precise, with the kind of love that tied consorts to one another.⁶¹ Love prompted her to follow Robert rather than stay safely behind. Love made her serve him with "affection, magnanimity . . . diligence, and care."⁶² Love prompted her to think of him first, and of herself last. Finally, love inspired her every deed of valor. Saint-André, for one, goes so far as to describe Teresa's massacre at Lahri Bandar as a sacrifice performed at the altar of marital love.⁶³ Bronzini closes the same episode by noting that Teresa's exploits were but the acts of a "consort"—or better yet, the "acts of which strong and most loving consorts" were capable.⁶⁴

Bronzini's pointed deployment of the term "consort" deserves underscoring, if for no other reason than that it helps tease out what is only implicit in other seventeenth-century biographies of Teresa. Derived from the Latin *consors, consortis*—literally, "one who shares the lot of another"— "consort" once had a general meaning that applied equally well to mates, colleagues, and relatives. With the early modern period, however, its usage became increasingly limited to the marital domain, where it came to denote both the husband and the wife.[65] Far more explicitly than any of its available synonyms, "consort" invoked the idea of marriage as *consortium omnis vitae*, a "partnership of all life." From a juridical point of view, the phrase concerned the rights and duties to which spouses were contractually bound, including cohabitation, marital fidelity, and reciprocal support. From an ideological point of view, though, marital consortium was more than a bundle of rights and duties. It postulated a relationship borne of equal commitment, shared responsibilities, and a pursuit of common goals. It envisioned the marital couple as a dyadic unit operating symbiotically in thought, feeling, and behavior. In short, it imagined matrimony as a joint enterprise where "a husband ought to suffer along with his wife's sufferings, and the wife with those of her husband, and in the same way they ought to share all their duties and activities."[66]

The insertion of marital consortium within the framework provided by knight-errantry allowed for a specifically feminine version of travel as service. As I have already mentioned, travel gave knights not just an opportunity to test their mettle but also a means of proving their identity. When it came to women, however, the conventions of chivalric romance could only go so far. In the case of Teresa, they were sufficient to test her altruism, Samson-like strength, and "brave Amazonian blood."[67] But they were insufficient to prove Teresa's identity as an honorable woman traveler. "Consort" came to the rescue by providing a subject position that was both agential and gender appropriate. Simply put, everything Teresa did was imagined by her biographers as something done out of consortship. In Bronzini's words, "in her every action she always sought to demonstrate how heartily she loved . . . her truest lord and beloved consort."[68]

Ultimately, it was Teresa's performance as a consort that seventeenth-century Continental writers found especially praiseworthy. While they certainly appreciated the distances she traveled, the sheer audacity of her actions, and the worthiness of her qualities and abilities, what they seem to have been most impressed with was Teresa's devotion to Robert. Celebratory accounts of Teresa's life can thus be read as part of a larger attempt to promote European understandings of family life—with their attendant emphasis on marital consortium—as natural and universal. By showcasing a non-European woman who embraced the affective values of seventeenth-century Europe, Teresa's biographers effectively proposed those values as globally valid norms. "And for the true love that she bore her husband, and for being her dear and faithful companion in every situation," concluded Bronzini in his encomium of Teresa, "[she] deserves . . . perpetual splendor and immortal glory."[69]

That a globe-trotter such as Teresa Sampsonia Sherley should earn praise more as a wife than as a traveler goes a long way toward highlighting the limits of her biographies as theorizations of women's mobility. Yet it would be a mistake to dismiss these theorizations as inherently oppressive. In extending the reach of the domestic well beyond the narrow confines of a woman's home, Teresa's biographers went against the grain of popular opinion to envision a typology of female mobility that was respectable and even exemplary. In linking this mobility to matrimony as *consortium omnis vitae*, moreover, they made it implicitly available to every woman who could lay claim to being a consort. This is what Bronzini seems to have had in mind when he referred to Teresa's on-the-road derring-dos as being but the "acts of which strong and most loving consorts are capable."[70] Far from being an exception to the rule of female frailty and passivity, they were a confirmation of female strength and agency. Far from being the exclusive preserve of a few Amazons, they represented the honorable travel experiences of which all women consorts could partake.

Notes

1. Alberti, *Family*, 3:77. See also Sainte-Fère, *La Republique*, 2:104–10; Loys, *Pervigilium Mercurii*, E4r; and Moryson, *Itinerary*, 3:1.
2. Moryson, *Itinerary*, 3:1.
3. As recorded in her autobiography, Teresa de Ávila traveled extensively to implement her religious reforms. The parallels between the Spanish saint and Teresa Sampsonia Sherley were not lost on Carmelite chroniclers: Berthold-Ignace de Sainte-Anne, for one, characterized the life of the lat-

ter as being marked by the same "toils, trials, bravery, and virtues" as the life of the former (*Historie,* 258).

4. By "Continental biographers," I mean seventeenth-century writers such as Cristoforo Bronzini, Gian Vittorio Rossi, and Pierre de Saint-André (also known as Jean-Antoine Rampalle), whose accounts of Teresa Sampsonia's character and accomplishments are far more detailed and generally more substantial than English ones. While these biographers were all Catholic, they were not all men of the cloth. They also wrote in different languages and in different literary genres.

5. [Bronzini], "Della contessa." Unless otherwise noted, all translations from non-English sources are my own.

6. Cartwright, *Preachers Travels,* 70.

7. Chick, *Chronicle,* 1:119–20.

8. Saint-André, *Historia,* 375. Bronzini identifies Teresa's father as "Ismicaón" [i.e., Isma'il Khan], "prince of the great province of Upper Circassia," and Teresa's aunt as a woman so beloved of the shah that she was "granted the title of first Queen and Wife" ("Della contessa," 1–2). Other seventeenth-century sources suggest a different story, however. A 1608 letter refers to Teresa as "an ill woman" with whom Robert Sherley lived *more uxorio* (quoted in Alonso and López, "Due lettere," 199); along similar lines, a report attributed to the Jesuit Francisco da Costa identifies Teresa as a "slave . . . of the Mohammedan faith," whom Robert had bought and kept as a concubine until pressured into marrying her (quoted in Piemontese, "I due ambasciatori," 387; see also Chick, *Chronicle,* 1:143). For English reports to the same effect, see Sainsbury, *Calendar,* 225.

9. Saint-André, *Historia,* 377.

10. Coverte, *True Report,* 54.

11. "Breve relatione," 2; see also Saint-André, *Historia,* 376.

12. Scattered references to European and Persian women in the Sherley entourage suggest that Teresa's travel experiences were not altogether exceptional, as Amrita Sen's essay in this collection makes clear. What seems exceptional, or at least uncommon, is the relative abundance of traces that these experiences left behind.

13. Della Valle, *Viaggi,* 1:463.

14. On the global career of this relic and its significance as an object of exchange between women, see Bernadette Andrea's essay in this collection.

15. Coryate, *Thomas Coriate,* 14. Coryate recorded meeting the Sherleys "betwixt Spahan and Lahore, just about the Frontiers of Persia & India." In this meeting, Robert promised to show Coryate's books to the Shah, so

that he might have "more gracious accesse unto him" in the future; being more practical, Teresa chose to give him money (14–15).

16. A transcription of this letter can be found in Shirley, *Sherley Brothers*, 95.
17. Andrea, *Lives*, 62–3. See also Andrea, "Lady Sherley," 283–87, and Tuson, "Scholars and Amazons," 18–20.
18. Purchas, *Pilgrimes*, 1:312; Day, Rowley, and Wilkins, *Travailes*, C2r; Nixon, *Three English Brothers*, H2v. Most English sources erroneously identify Teresa as a direct relative of Shah 'Abbas. Exceptions are Herbert, *Some Yeares*, 203, and Finet, *Finetti Philoxenis*, 175, according to which Teresa was "no kin of the King," "but the Queens kinswoman." For recent studies on the Sherley myth as a set of tales that served the self-aggrandizing purposes of the Sherley family just as much as the propaganda needs of England's expansionism, see Andrea, "Lady Sherley," 281–83; Schleck, *Telling True Tales*, 61–92; and Schwartz, "Sherleys and the Shah."
19. Day, Rowley, and Wilkins, *Travailes*, L4r.
20. Herbert, *Some Yeares*, 203.
21. Herbert, *Some Yeares*, 204.
22. Herbert, *Some Yeares*, 203.
23. Herbert, *Some Yeares*, 204.
24. Della Valle, *Viaggi*, 1:463. As scholars have observed, by the seventeenth century the title of "ambassadress" identified the accompanying spouse of an ambassador, thereby acknowledging the role that women could play in early modern diplomacy. See Santaliestra, "Lady Anne Fanshawe," 68.
25. [Bronzini], "Della contessa," 3.
26. Saint Jean-Baptiste, *Bibliotheca scriptorum*, 262.
27. The climax of these persecutions was the 1622 execution of five Persian converts, as detailed in the *Breve relatione del martirio di cinque Persiani*.
28. Conceived at the Medici court during the regency of Grand Duchess Christine of Lorraine and the Archduchess Maria Maddalena of Austria (to the latter of whom the first two volumes are dedicated), Bronzini's *Della dignità e nobiltà delle donne* should have related a series of conversations stretching over the course of twenty-four days. Teresa Sampsonia should have featured in the eleventh day, but the published work never got beyond the eighth.
29. [Bronzini], "Della contessa," 4. Hypsicratea, wife of King Mithridates VII of Pontus (died 63 BC), fought by her husband's side in battle and followed him into exile after he was defeated.
30. Fuller, *History*, 107.
31. Rossi, *Pinacotheca*, 3:254; "Breve relatione," 5.

32. Saint-André, *Historia*, 375.
33. Chick, *Chronicle*, 1:144 has "Sampsuff," but this may be a backformation. Early modern sources spell Teresa's name as "Samphuff" (tombstone in S. Maria della Scala), "Samflut" ("Breve relatione," 2), "Samphut" (Rossi, *Pinacotheca*, 3:253), "Sampluf" ([Bronzini], "Della contessa," 3), or "Sanphluf" (Saint-André, *Historia*, 370; Saint Jean-Baptiste, *Bibliotheca scriptorum*, 261). For consistency, I have adopted Sanphluf throughout. There is also some confusion in the sources as to whether Sanphluf was Teresa's name ("Breve relatione," 2; [Bronzini], "Della contessa," 3–4; Saint-André, *Historia*, 370, 375) or her father's (Rossi, *Pinacotheca*, 3:253; tombstone in S. Maria della Scala). I take this to suggest that Sanphluf was a patronymic or clan name.
34. "Breve relatione," 2.
35. [Bronzini], "Della contessa," 4.
36. [Bronzini], "Della contessa," 8.
37. Saint-André, *Historia*, 374, 376, 377.
38. Rossi, *Pinacotheca* 3: 259; Saint-André, *Historia*, 380.
39. "Breve relatione," lists "Turkish, Persian, Armenian, Indian, Russian, English, and Spanish" as the languages in which Teresa was conversant (3). Other accounts also include French, Italian, and Polish; see [Bronzini], "Della contessa," 8; Rossi, *Pinacotheca*, 3:254; Saint-André, *Historia*, 377.
40. "Breve relatione," 4.
41. [Bronzini], "Della contessa," 8.
42. Saint-André, *Historia*, 375.
43. [Bronzini], "Della contessa," 4–5; Rossi, *Pinacotheca*, 3:254; Saint-André, *Historia*, 377.
44. Variants of this episode are detailed or hinted at in a number of sources, including [Bronzini], "Della contessa," 5; Purchas, *Pilgrimes*, 1:484, Rossi, *Pinacotheca*, 3:254; Saint-André, *Historia*, 377–78. I follow Purchas in identifying Lahri Bandar, an entrepôt in the Kingdom of Sind, as the site of the attack; Bronzini, Rossi, and Saint-André refer more generally to either Sind or the Mughal empire, of which Sind was then part. Continental sources are consistently silent as to the reasons for the attack; English sources routinely blame it on Portuguese malice. See Purchas, *Pilgrimes*, 1:484, and Sainsbury, *Calendar*, 317.
45. Rossi, *Pinacotheca*, 3:255.
46. [Bronzini], "Della contessa," 6. Teresa's three wounds curiously parallel the three wounds allegedly received by Robert while fighting against the Turks, "a triple testimony of his love and service to Christendom" (Purchas, *Pilgrimes*, 2:1805). In both cases, these triple injuries appear to invoke the threefold wounds suffered by Christ on the cross.

47. [Bronzini], "Della contessa," 6.
48. Saint-André, *Historia*, 378; [Bronzini], "Della contessa," 4.
49. Bronzini, *Della dignità*, 1: 124. On Bronzini's contribution to the *querelle des femmes* tradition, see Giochi, "Un femminista"; Jordan, *Renaissance Feminism*, 266–69; Ross, *Birth of Feminism*, 107–9.
50. On the connections between hagiography and chivalric romance, see Cazelles, *Lady as Saint*, 30–38.
51. The secondary meaning of *errare*—"to miss the right way," "to err"—is now the dominant one; during the early modern period, however, the two meanings coexisted.
52. Goodman, *Chivalry and Exploration*, provides a helpful introduction to some of the ways that chivalric romance inflected early modern understandings of travel.
53. For an explicit application of these traditional ethical categories (profit or *bonum utile*, pleasure or *bonum jucundum*, honor or *bonum honestum*) to travel, see Leigh, *Gentlemans Guide*, 4.
54. Purchas, *Pilgrimes*, 2:1805.
55. Purchas, *Pilgrimes*, 2:1805. While Purchas does not explicitly compare Robert to a knight-errant, he reproduces verbatim the imperial grant that named Robert "a true and a lawfull Knight" by virtue of the "commendable Services" performed during the course of his travels (2:1807).
56. [Bronzini], "Della contessa," 5.
57. Saint-André, *Historia*, 378.
58. Rossi, *Pinacotheca*, 3: 254.
59. Rossi, *Pinacotheca*, 3: 354. Rossi's claim is belied by a number of sources vouching for Robert's linguistic abilities, including Herbert, *Relation*, 125; Middleton, *Sir Robert*, 1; and Francesco Simonetta's 1609 letter to Scipione Borghese (quoted in Piemontese, "I due ambasciatori," 367).
60. Middleton, *Sir Robert*, 2; Saint-André, *Historia*, 377.
61. Saint-André, *Historia*, 377.
62. [Bronzini], "Della contessa," 7.
63. Saint-André, *Historia*, 378.
64. [Bronzini], "Della contessa," 4.
65. Nowadays "consort" usually identifies the spouse of a ruling monarch (*consors regni*, literally "a sharer of the kingdom"), but in the early modern period the term could be just a synonym for "spouse" (*consors thalami* or bedfellow). The sixteenth-century dramatist George Chapman, for one, described marriage as a union of consorts (*Sir Gyles Goosecappe Knight*, K1r), while the Puritan divine Thomas Gataker referred to his wife as his "deer consort" (*Vindications*, 92).

66. Tasso, *Il padre*, 31.
67. Saint-André, *Historia*, 375.
68. [Bronzini], "Della contessa," 7.
69. [Bronzini], "Della contessa," 7.
70. [Bronzini], "Della contessa," 5.

Bibliography

Alberti, Leon Battista. *The Family in Renaissance Florence*. Translated by Renée Neu Watkins. 4 vols. Long Grove IL: Waveland Press, 2004.

Alonso, Carlos, and Saturnino López. "Due lettere riguardanti i primi tempi delle missioni agostiniane in Persia." *Analecta Agustiniana* 24 (1961): 152–201.

Andrea, Bernadette. "Lady Sherley: The 'First' Persian in England?" *The Muslim World* 95, no. 2 (2005): 279–95.

———. *The Lives of Girls and Women from the Islamic World in Early Modern British Literature and Culture*. Toronto: University of Toronto Press, 2017.

"Breve relatione delle conditioni della S.ra Contessa Teresa circassa . . . et de travagli da lei patiti per la fede di Christo nel regno di Persia nella città d'Aspahan." 263/e, no. 3, General Archive of the Carmelite Order, Rome.

Breve relatione del martirio di cinque persiani, nuovamemente battezzati dalli PP. *Carmelitani Scalzi*. Rome, 1622.

[Bronzini, Cristoforo]. "Della contessa Tiresia circassa, moglie del Conte Roberto Scherley, Ambasciadore." 263/e, no. 5, General Archive of the Carmelite Order, Rome.

———. *Della dignità e nobiltà delle donne*. 4 vols. Florence, 1622–32.

Cartwright, John. *The Preachers Travels*. London, 1611.

Cazelles, Brigitte. *The Lady as Saint: A Collection of French Hagiographic Romances of the Thirteenth Century*. Philadelphia: University of Pennsylvania Press, 1991.

Chapman, George. *Sir Gyles Goosecappe Knight: A Comedie Presented by the Children of the Chappell*. London, 1606.

Chick, Herbert, ed. *A Chronicle of the Carmelites in Persia: The Safavids and the Papal Mission of the 17th and 18th Centuries*. 2 vols. London: Eyre and Spottiswoode, 1939.

Coryate, Thomas. *Thomas Coriate Traveller for the English Wits*. London, 1616.

Coverte, Robert. *A True and Almost Incredible Report of an Englishman*. London, 1612.

Day, John, William Rowley, and George Wilkins. *The Travailes of the Three English Brothers*. London, 1607.

Della Valle, Pietro. *Viaggi di Pietro della Valle il Pellegrino . . . La Persia*. 2 vols. Rome, 1658.

Finet, John. *Finetti Philoxenis, Som[e] Choice Observations . . . Touching . . . Forren Ambassadors in England*. London, 1656.

Fuller, Thomas. *The History of the Worthies of England*. London, 1662.
Gataker, Thomas. *Vindications of the Annotations*. London, 1653.
Giochi, Filippo M. "Un femminista ante litteram del XVII secolo: Cristoforo Bronzini anconitano." *Atti e Memorie della Deputazione di Storia Patria delle Marche* 98 (1993): 175–97.
Goodman, Jennifer R. *Chivalry and Exploration, 1298–1630*. Rochester NY: Boydell and Brewer, 1998.
Herbert, Thomas. *A Relation of Some Yeares Travaill*. London, 1634.
———. *Some Yeares Travels into Divers Parts of Asia and Afrique*. London, 1638.
Jordan, Constance. *Renaissance Feminism: Literary Texts and Political Models*. Ithaca NY: Cornell University Press, 1990.
Leigh, Edward. *The Gentlemans Guide, in Three Discourses*. London, 1680.
Loys, Georg. *Pervigilium Mercurii: In quo agitur de praestantissimis peregrinantis virtutibus*. Hof, 1598.
Middleton, Thomas. *Sir Robert Sherley . . . His Royall Entertainment into Cracovia*. London, 1609.
Moryson, Fynes. *An Itinerary Written by Fynes Moryson, Gent.* 3 vols. London, 1617.
Nixon, Anthony. *The Three English Brothers*. London, 1607.
Piemontese, Angelo M. "I due ambasciatori di Persia ricevuti da Papa Paolo V al Quirinale." *Miscellanea Bibliothecae Apostolicae Vaticanae* 12 (2005): 357–425.
Purchas, Samuel. *Purchas His Pilgrimes*. London, 1625.
Ross, Sarah G. *The Birth of Feminism: Woman as Intellect in Renaissance Italy and England*. Cambridge MA: Harvard University Press, 2009.
Rossi, Gian Vittorio. *Pinacotheca imaginum illustrium doctrinae vel ingenii laude virorum*. 3 vols. Cologne, 1643–48.
Sainsbury, Noel. *Calendar of State Papers, Colonial Series, East Indies, China and Japan, 1513–1616*. London, 1862.
Saint-André, Pierre de. *Historia generalis fratrum discalceatorum, ordinis B. Virginis Mariae de Monte Carmelo Congregationis S. Eliae. Tomus Secundus*. Rome, 1671.
Sainte-Anne, Berthold-Ignace de. *Historie de l'établissement de la mission de Perse par les Pères Carmes-Déchaussés*. Brussels, 1885.
Saint Jean-Baptiste, Martial de. *Bibliotheca scriptorum utriusque congregationis et sexus Carmelitarum Excalceatorum*. Bordeaux, 1730.
Sainte-Fère, Jean de. *La Republique Chrestienne*. Paris, 1578.
Santaliestra, Laura Oliván. "Lady Anne Fanshawe, Ambassadress of England at the Court of Madrid (1664–1666)." In *Women, Diplomacy and International Politics Since 1500: Women and Diplomacy in Renaissance Italy*, edited by Glenda Sluga and Carolyn James, 68–85. New York: Routledge, 2016.

Schleck, Julia. *Telling True Tales of Islamic Lands: Forms of Mediation in English Travel Writing, 1575-1630*. Selinsgrove PA: Susquehanna University Press, 2011.

Schwartz, Gary. "The Sherleys and the Shah: Persia as the Stakes in a Rogue's Gambit." In *The Fascination of Persia: The Persian-European Dialogue in Seventeenth-Century Art and Contemporary Art of Teheran*, edited by Axel Langer, 78–99. Zürich: Scheidegger and Spiess, 2013.

Shirley, Evelyn Philip. *The Sherley Brothers*. Chiswick, 1848.

Tasso, Torquato. *Il padre di famiglia*. Venice, 1583.

Tuson, Penelope. "Scholars and Amazons: Researching Women Travellers in the Arabian Gulf." *Liwa: Journal of the National Center for Documentation and Research* 5, no. 9 (2013): 18–20.

5

The Global Travels of Teresa Sampsonia Sherley's Carmelite Relic

BERNADETTE ANDREA

In this contribution to rethinking the category of "women and travel" in the early modern period, I focus on the overdetermined thing ("cosa") that Lady Teresa Sampsonia Sherley (1589–1668) "wore on her breast" to ward off the dangers she faced after the death of her husband, the "English Persian" Robert Sherley (1581–1621), while they were en route to the Safavid court following their second European embassy: namely, "a small relic of the flesh of S[t]. Teresa [of Ávila, 1515–82], given her in Madrid by the Carmelite Mother Beatrice, niece of the saint" and prioress of the Convent of Santa Ana.[1] Teresa Sampsonia, a Circassian subject of the Safavid Shah 'Abbas, traveled with her husband to Russia, Poland, Germany, Italy, Spain, Portugal, France, and England.[2] Their travels were well documented in contemporaneous English, Italian, Latin, and Spanish sources, as well as in a series of portraits painted of them while in Italy and England.[3] However, the circulation of this significant item and its significance for Teresa Sampsonia's position as what Roxanne L. Euben, in *Journeys to the Other Shore: Muslim and Western Travelers in Search of Knowledge*, calls a "'translated person' negotiating multiple worlds, languages, and practices," has not been addressed in the burgeoning scholarship on the Sherleys.[4] While Teresa Sampsonia's residence in England on two occasions has begun to receive more attention, I seek to situate her Carmelite relic in terms of the networks it mediated between cloistered and cosmopolitan women from "East" and "West" across Muslim and Christian domains. In so doing, I deploy a material culture approach to women's increasingly global connections during the early modern period.

In particular, I engage the meaning (or, rather, the meanings) of this relic as a "thing-in-motion" by drawing on theories articulated by anthropologist Arjun Appadurai in relation to early modern material culture. As Appadurai asserts in his groundbreaking study, *The Social Life of Things*, these meanings "are inscribed in their forms, their uses, [and] their trajectories" and "[i]t is only through the analysis of these trajectories that we can interpret the human transactions and calculations that enliven things."[5] My investigation further participates in "the global turn" that historians Anne Gerritsen and Giorgio Riello, extending Appadurai's methodology, have advanced in *The Global Lives of Things: The Material Culture of Connections in the Early Modern World*. I concur with their general analysis in arguing that this relic and other items from the renewed contact between Safavid Persia and Western Europe, which made Teresa Sampsonia's journeys possible, "are not just things with social lives, but with global trajectories."[6] Prior to assessing this relic and its importance for comprehending its bearer's cross-cultural and cross-confessional travels, I survey its "human and social context," as Appadurai advises, through a condensed history of the diplomatic exchanges between the Safavid dynasty and the sovereigns of Western Christendom during the sixteenth century and into the first decades of the seventeenth century.[7] These exchanges, meant to forge an alliance against the expansionist Ottoman empire, culminated in a series of diplomatic missions from the Safavid court led by Robert Sherley, whose Persianate wife accompanied him on two extended sojourns.[8] I subsequently foreground salient details from Teresa Sampsonia's life before considering the Carmelite relic she received in Madrid and carried back to Isfahan, where it served to protect her against charges from high-ranking members of the court who accused her of the capital crime of apostasy and confiscated her property after Robert's death. My conclusion returns to the methodological questions that this "thing-in-motion" raises for a broader study of Teresa Sampsonia's life before, during, and after her European "embassies" with Robert.[9]

The Travels of the Sherley Brothers and the Travails of Teresa Sampsonia Sherley

If the task of a material culture approach that attends to "cross-border connections and interactions" is, as Gerritsen and Giorgio assert, "to identify the 'things' [under analysis] as global things and trace their trajectories, so that we see the accumulation of meanings that objects acquire as they travel," then the attempted rapprochement between the Safavid shahs and Western European rulers from the beginning of the sixteenth century and into the seventeenth century maps a crucial site of circulation and transformation.[10] Initiating this series of diplomatic exchanges, the progenitor of the Safavid dynasty, Shah Ismail I, sent a letter to the Venetian Doge in 1506, followed by an envoy three years later, to broach an alliance against the Ottomans. While "friendship and an intention for an alliance was repeatedly reaffirmed, . . . nothing actually happened, neither with Esmāʿīl [Ismail] (r. 1501–24), nor with his successor Shah Ṭahmāsb (r. 1524–76)," despite the 1539 embassy led by the Venetian-Cypriot Michele Membré.[11] Portuguese and Spanish envoys traveled to Shah Ismail's, and later Shah Tahmasp's, court, with uneven results. During their reigns, bilateral diplomatic missions also were attempted with the kingdom of Hungary and the Holy Roman Empire, with many assurances of friendship and little success in forming an effective alliance.

Emerging from the decade of political instability resulting from the succession struggles after Shah Tahmasp's death, Shah ʿAbbas (r. 1588–1629) continued to foster strategic alliances with Christian communities inside and outside his realm. Internally, he cultivated the Armenian community at New Julfa in Isfahan for their mercantile relations with Western Europe. He allowed Augustinian and Carmelite friars to engage in limited activities in his domains, with the former mission established at Isfahan in 1602 and the latter established in 1608. Having received overtures from the Holy Roman Emperor Rudolf II and Pope Clement VII regarding the combination of the Safavids "and the Christian princes . . . in a league against the Turk," Shah ʿAbbas initiated a series of diplomatic missions to Europe, three of which involved the expatriate English brothers Anthony and Robert Sherley.[12]

In the first of these missions (1599–1602), the older brother, Anthony Sherley (1565–ca.1633/36), was enlisted as the shah's "ambassador" or, more accurately, his emissary.[13] A suite of Safavid retainers—Husain ʿAli Beg and his four secretaries (Uruch Beg, his chief secretary; ʿAli Quli Beg, his nephew; and two others)—accompanied Anthony as far as Rome, after which the mission disintegrated.[14] Anthony's disputes with Husain ʿAli Beg, which began almost as soon as their journey commenced, came to a head over who would have the first audience with the pope (in this case, Clement VIII). Anthony prevailed in this matter of diplomatic precedence, with Husain ʿAli Beg departing separately for an audience with King Philip III of Spain. Ostensibly intending to return to Safavid domains, Anthony instead lingered in Venice for over three years. There he faced accusations that (to quote the English Jesuit Robert Parsons) "while he was in Persia he was of the Persian Religion [Shiʿa Islam], which Sir Anthony utterly denyeth to be true, though he confesseth he went in Persian apparel the better by that conforming himself to be amongst Turks [the Western European term for Muslims in general] and Christians."[15] Anthony eventually did convert, but to Roman Catholicism. Afterwards, he made his way to Spain, where he served the Spanish crown on several expeditions to Morocco and Sicily; he died in Madrid, impoverished and estranged from his family, sometime in the mid-1630s.[16]

The youngest Sherley, Robert, resided in Iran from 1599 to 1608 after his elder brother Anthony abandoned him. During this decade, he gained mastery of the Persian language and advised the shah on military matters. In recompense for his service, he was matched with the "daughter [Teresa Sampsonia] of a Circassian chieftain named Sampsuff Iscaon," with questions raised about whether she was Robert's slave.[17] It is certain, however, that the two were married at the Carmelite house in Isfahan on February 2, 1608, with both having converted to Roman Catholicism.[18] On his first embassy across Europe (1608 to 1615), Robert insisted on wearing his "Persian habit" (or apparel) topped with a large turban. In his audience with Pope Paul V, he accommodated Catholic sensibilities by affixing a crucifix to his headwear.[19] He was sent on his second embassy (1615 to 1628) almost immediately upon his return to Iran. Robert, with Teresa Sampsonia, spent substantial time in Spain on both journeys, passing through Barcelona and living in Madrid. He died on July 13, 1628 in Qazvin—probably of dysentery, but perhaps of poisoning—on his second return trip to report to the shah, leaving Teresa to fend for herself against their enemies at court. She later arranged for his body to be transported to Rome, where it was interred at the Church of Santa Maria della Scala in 1658. She was buried alongside him ten years later.

While both Sherley brothers epitomize to varying degrees the "chameleon," "cosmopolitan," and "renegade" that Sanjay Subrahmanyam theorizes in *Three Ways to Be Alien: Travails and Encounters in the Early Modern World*, the "Persians" of various ethnicities who accompanied them also fashioned hybrid and shifting identities out of the opportunities and constraints they encountered.[20] On the first diplomatic mission led by Anthony Sherley and Husain 'Ali Beg, several of the Safavid subjects (including Husain 'Ali Beg's cook) embraced Catholicism while in Rome and refused to return to Iran. Two others, including Husain 'Ali Beg's nephew, 'Ali Quli Beg, and his chief secretary, Uruch Beg, converted as the embassy continued in Spain: "the king of Spain [Philip III] and his wife, Queen Margarita," acted "as their godparents."[21] Uruch Beg, afterwards known as "Don Juan of Persia," recorded his extraordinary physical and spiritual journey in the Spanish-language narrative *Relaciones de Don Juan de Persia*, which was published in 1604. In this account he also details how 'Ali Quli Beg, afterwards known as Don Philip of Persia, "resolved to become a Christian and be baptized."[22]

Teresa Sampsonia's travels and travails overlap with those of the Persian men who converted in Rome with a pension from the pope and those who converted in Spain with a pension from the king.[23] These men assimilated into Western European culture to varying degrees by marrying or entering religious orders. All of them—many of whom were Turkoman retainers of the shah—were indisputably Muslim. However, pursuant to her Circassian background, Teresa's natal religion is not entirely clear. Circassians began to convert to Islam on a significant scale in the sixteenth century, but given the Russian influence at the same time, she may have been from an Orthodox Christian background.[24]

Sources such as Sir Thomas Herbert, who accompanied the Sherleys on their second return journey from England to Iran, asserted that "her Faith was euer [ever] Christian, her parents so."[25] Yet, the records of the Carmelites suggest she may have been born a Muslim, which is plausible as rebaptism is generally not permitted under canon law.[26] A Latin account of her first trip to Rome also claims she was a Muslim prior to embracing Christianity.[27]

Whatever her natal religion may have been, these sources concur that she was baptized as a Roman Catholic by the Carmelites of Isfahan, after which she married Robert and departed on their first European embassy. Her "Christian" name, Teresa (sometimes rendered Teresia), derives from the founder of the Discalced Carmelites, Teresa of Ávila. As "translator-editor" Herbert Chick conveys, she "wore on her breast a small relic of the flesh of S[t]. Teresa, given her in Madrid by the Carmelite Mother Beatrice, niece of the saint."[28] In Father Florencio del Niño Jesús's rendition, the relic is described as "la joya más preciosa" (the most precious jewel) and its gifting to Teresa Sampsonia is authorized by the voice of the saint herself to her niece—"Dale la condesa la partícula de carne mía que tienes" (Give the countess the particle of my flesh that you have)—thus adding another layer to this connected history between women across the Islamic East and the Christian West as mediated by this significant thing.[29]

As suggested above, after her husband's death Teresa Sampsonia suffered intense persecution, including the threat of the capital charge of apostasy from Islam.[30] In recounting "her impassioned defence and constancy" during her interrogations, Carmelite witnesses observed the relic exuding blood, a key moment to which we will return.[31] Subsequently, she hid in an Augustinian church in Isfahan and then at an Armenian convent in New Julfa, just outside the city. After receiving a special permit to travel, which was otherwise forbidden for a woman without a male guardian, she went to Istanbul, where she remained for three years. There, she received "a certificate from the Commissary General of the Dominicans in the East as to her pious and good conduct during her residence," which enabled her move to Rome.[32] She finally settled near the Carmelite church of Santa Maria della Scala, where she remained until her death over three decades later.³³ Having established Teresa Sampsonia's life history and its cross-cultural contexts, I now turn to the relic she carried on her travels with an emphasis on the methodological tools derived from "the so-called 'return to things', 'back to things' and 'turn to the non-human' which has become visible in the humanities since the late 1990s."³⁴ We are turning, that is, to the biography of the thing itself.

The "Career" of Teresa Sampsonia's Relic

In unpacking the significance of the Carmelite relic gifted to Teresa Sampsonia in Madrid by Beatriz de Jesús, niece of the saint, which she wore during her travails in the Safavid empire after her husband's death and which traveled with her across Eurasia, I have found the "cultural biography perspective," innovated by Igor Kopytoff, to be especially productive for shifting, in Ewa Domańska's formulation, "attention *from subjects* who create relations *to the relations* created by subjects."³⁵ As Appadurai develops, unlike a broad "*social history* of things," this perspective focuses on "*specific* things, as they move through different hands, contexts, and uses, thus accumulating a specific biography, or a set of biographies." As he underscores, this approach does not grant things "meanings apart from those that human transactions, attributions, and motivations endow them with." As such, it is only though the analysis of "their forms, their uses, [and] their trajectories . . . that we can interpret the human transactions and calculations that enliven things."³⁶ For my mapping of this relic's travels across cultural and religious registers, Patrick Geary's use of the term, "career," from "Sacred Commodities: The Circulation of Medieval Relics," is even more apposite.³⁷ This term, which derives from the Latin for "carriage-road," avoids the potential anthropocentrism of "biography" and the attendant debates in material cultural studies over the "agency" of things.³⁸ Rather, "career," particularly in the early modern period, signified "[t]he course over which any person or thing passes," as well as "a person's course or progress through life (or a distinct portion of life)."³⁹ I apply both meanings to this relic and the ways it illuminates Teresa Sampsonia's multilayered negotiation of her journey from the Mediterranean kingdoms of Spain and Italy across Eurasia to the Safavid empire and back again.

To recall, the form of the thing under consideration is described in the Carmelite records as a small piece of flesh from the deceased body of Teresa of Ávila, founder of the Discalced Carmelite order that established a mission in Isfahan during the reign of Shah 'Abbas I.[40] Although the decision was controversial and would result in a break between the Spanish and Italian branches of the order, the missionary impulse was one that Teresa of Ávila herself felt from the time she was a young girl who dreamt of traveling to North Africa to convert the Moors. As a nun post-Trent, her mobility was theoretically restricted by the requirement for strict claustration.[41] Practically, she traveled extensively throughout the Iberian peninsula founding and maintaining monasteries for women and men—so much so that she was accused by the papal nuncio (Filippo Sega) of being a "restless, disobedient, and contumacious gadabout."[42]

Indeed, Teresa of Ávila's travels were decisive for the form of the relic Teresa Sampsonia received, as the future saint was in transit to her foundation at Alba de Tormes, near Salamanca, when she died on October 4, 1582. Immediately, her sanctity was confirmed as her face and body shed its wrinkles (she was sixty-seven years old), exuded a sweet fragrance, and cured the ailments of the nuns who kissed it. Nevertheless, as Charles Freeman details in *Holy Bones, Holy Dust: How Relics Shaped the History of Medieval Europe*, "The problem facing the nuns of Alba was that Teresa had died far from home and they knew they would [be] challenged for possession of her remains by the nuns of Ávila [sic]." Due to a hasty burial deemed unseemly for a saint, with the "heavy mix of stones, bricks and lime" intended to secure the grave actually shattering the coffin, Father Jerónimo Gracián, the first provincial of the Discalced Carmelites (1581–85), arranged to exhume the body nine months after Teresa's death.[43]

At this time, Father Gracián "cut off Teresa's left hand [which he presented to the Discalced Carmelite house in Ávila] and took a finger from this for himself"; he then had the rest of the body reburied.[44] Three years later, Gracián again ordered the body exhumed, this time for its "translation," or ceremonial transfer, to Ávila. The nuns at Alba de Tormes were compensated with the left arm. However, they took their case to the Dukes of Alba, who in turn petitioned Pope Sixtus V, who ordered the body back to Alba, where it now rests. As Freeman concludes, "Once the body was back there, the nuns of Àvila [sic] grumbled that the body was continually raided for more parts and that flesh was handed out by their sisters in Alba to those who asked for them." This dismembered and dispersed body continued to inspire "healing miracles" for decades afterwards, which supported the canonization of Teresa in 1622.[45] As macabre as this phase of the relic's career appears to a post-Enlightenment reader, its protocols followed the practices of legitimating, distributing, and even stealing relics sanctioned by law and practice throughout the medieval and into the early modern era.[46]

The form of the thing, as the career of this relic thus far suggests, is inextricably tied to its uses. In the case of Teresa Sampsonia, she "wore [the relic] on her breast" (small relics were often set in lockets) and, in one recounting, it was "to fortify her at a critical juncture in her life": namely, the persecution she experienced in Qazvin, when she was accused of apostasy from Islam and threatened with death if she did not recant or a forced marriage if she did.[47] Her property, in any case, was confiscated, and she became a fugitive, hiding in an Augustinian church in Isfahan and an Armenian convent just outside the Safavid capital, as noted above. As documented in the 1631 "Brief narrative of a noteworthy event, which occurred at the Persian Court to Donna Teresa Sherley, together with the Discalced Carmelite Fathers," the Carmelite friars sought a permit for her to leave the shah's realms for Christendom, as women on their own were not allowed to travel.[48] She nevertheless was prevented from leaving pending her trial.

Summoned to appear before the shah and interrogated "as to the reasons why they [her persecutors] were so incensed at her," she remained silent as her best line of defense. As the Carmelite friars convey, "In order not to harm by her replies those men who were persecuting her, she gave him no answer at all: on which account her fortitude was much commended by the Shah: and he told her not to be afraid, for it would be harder for him to put a woman to death than 100 men."[49] In a subsequent examination by "a chief Mulla," or religious judge, who was adjudicating the charge of apostasy from Islam and the request that Teresa Sampsonia be permitted to travel, she similarly "persevered, steadily confessing the Faith of Christ, and confounded the hopes of the Mulla."[50] After this incident, the persecution intensified and necessitated her going into hiding. At a subsequent interview by "Rustam Khan, governor of Qazwin," a judge "told her that she lied [about her Christian faith] and he would have her burnt alive, if she did not make profession of the Muhammadan religion," or else he would "have her thrown down from a tower." In this instance, she "upbraided him severely and seriously, saying that this ill-treatment was not the reward deserved by her husband for his service to the Shah."[51] The persecution ceased thenceforth and she was allowed to leave.

During Teresa Sampsonia's interrogation by Safavid religious and political leaders, the relic of Teresa of Ávila's flesh that she wore as a locket "was observed by several persons to be wet with tiny spots of blood" or, in another account, "sangre fresca [fresh blood]."[52] Such exudations were not only commonly reported, but requisite, for the efficacy of a relic. As "an actual physical embodiment" of divine blessings or, to draw on Islamic terminology, *baraka*, relics operated across religious registers "as a locus and conduit of power," which Alexandra Walsham, in her introduction to the collection *Relics and Remains*, identifies as "supernatural, salvific, apotropaic, and magical."[53] As a source of inspiration and protection, then, Teresa Sampsonia's relic facilitated her deft and dangerous negotiations across religious and cultural divides as mediated by gender and geography.[54] Yet, its efficacy also points to a "shared affinity," as Rudi Matthee puts it, between Catholic Europe and the Shi'a empire of the Persian shahs, where the use of religious talismans was widespread.[55] As Josef Meri emphasizes in his study of "devotional objects or relics (Arab. *āthār*) (literally, traces or remnants)," "The experience of medieval Muslims, Christians, and Jews is largely one of cross-fertilization of similar yet unique devotional practices enriched by a shared belief in the efficacy of holy places and persons." As he concludes, "In Islam as in Christianity, relics conferred divine blessings on their possessors and those who came into contact with them seeking relief from adversity, cures, and the fulfilment of supplications."[56] Teresa Sampsonia was therefore able to operate in a familiar cultural register when relying on her Carmelite relic as a sacred item with the power to heal and protect.[57]

Embedded in the form and the uses of this relic, as suggested above, is its trajectory. The first part of its "career"—in the sense of the path it takes—commenced with the death of Teresa of Ávila in 1582 through the progressive dismemberment and distribution of her body. This drama took place primarily at Alba de Tormes, where Beatriz, niece of the saint, was born and bred. Beatriz "entered the Discalced Reform, at Alba, on October 28, 1584, and was professed on November 10, 1585."[58] She was thus at exactly the right place at the right time, with the right connections, to receive pieces of her aunt's flesh, which were preserved as relics. Beatriz eventually became prioress at Ocaña in 1600, at Toledo in 1607, and at the Discalced Carmelite convent of Santa Ana in Madrid from 1615 to 1619, 1626 to 1630, and 1633 to 1636. Teresa Sampsonia first traveled to Madrid in 1611, from March to June, with her husband Robert. At this time, she often visited the nuns at Santa Ana, with whom she established a close friendship ("amistad, y muy estrecha por cierto").[59] Teresa Sampsonia later lived in Madrid from 1617 to 1622, where she continued to cultivate these bonds with the nuns—especially their prioress. During one of these encounters, Beatriz gifted the relic to Teresa, who had a burning desire ("un deseo ardiente") to possess something from her namesake. As we have seen, the deceased saint herself intervenes after the nuns initially demurred.[60]

Returning to questions of methodology, this dramatic scenario ultimately enables us to comprehend this relic as a "thing-in-motion" through a range of theorists from Marcel Mauss to Claude Lévi-Strauss, with the former foregrounding the potential competition inherent in gift giving and the latter extending Mauss's model into the controversial exchange of women between men which rendered women "objects that speak."[61] Maurice Godelier establishes the limits of both models in favor of Anne Weiner's intervention in *Inalienable Possessions: The Paradox of Keeping-while-Giving*, which remains a key text for feminist studies. This category applies specifically to "sacred objects" and it foregrounds the "role of women and/or the feminine in the production and exercise of the political power from which they seem to be excluded or in which they seem to occupy an altogether minor place."[62] Following the career of Teresa Sampsonia's relic likewise highlights an exchange *amongst* women that connects the early modern Mediterranean and Safavid empires beyond the patriarchal discourses of militarism, trade, and diplomacy that have hitherto defined the story of the Sherleys' travels. Facilitating these feminocentric bonds between East and West, this "thing-in-motion" also speaks.

Notes

1. For a discussion of the "many ways the terms 'thing' and 'object' overlap," see Hodder, *Entangled*, 7–8, and on "the objectness of things," 13–14. On "this famous English Persian," see Thomas Middleton, "Sir Robert," 677. For this description of the relic, see Chick, *Chronicle*, 1:293. For a more detailed account, see Florencio, *Biblioteca*, 29, 39–40. Both draw on a lost primary source, as I indicate below. For more on Beatriz [Beatrice] de Jesús (1560–1639), see Peers, *Handbook*, 129. I thank Professor Alison Weber for her generosity in sharing this reference with me and others from her wealth of knowledge about Teresa of Ávila.
2. As Herbert, who traveled with Robert and Teresa Sherley [Shirley] on their second return trip to the Safavid empire, specifies: "her Countrey *Circashia* [Circassia], which joynes to *Georgia*, and to *Zuiria*, neere the *Euxine* [Black] and *Caspian* Seas" (*Relation* 125). A later seventeenth-century source situates these places as follows: "Between the *Black Sea* and the *Caspian*, lies *Georgia*. . . . Under the general Name whereof, we comprehend *Mingrelia, Gurgistan, Zuiria*, and *Comania*: Provinces which the ancient *Romans* could not subdue by reason of the ruggedness of the Mountains, which were known to the Ancients by the Name of *Caucasus*" (Morden, *Geography*, 365).
3. For an analysis of the primary sources in English, see Andrea, *Women and Islam*, 30–52; Schleck, *Telling True Tales*, 61–92; and López-Peláez, "The Travailes." For sources in other Western European languages, see Carmen Nocentelli's contribution to this collection. On the scarcity of source material in Persian, see Schwartz, "The Sherley Brothers," 83–84, and Sefatgol, "Farang," 359.
4. Euben, *Journeys*, 140.
5. Appadurai, "Introduction," 5.

6. Gerritsen and Riello, "The Global Lives," 2–3.
7. Appadurai, "Introduction," 5.
8. For the term "Persianate," see Hodgson, *Venture*, 3:46–52; for related terminology, see 1:57–60.
9. For more on Teresa Sampsonia's life and impact, see Andrea, *Lives*, 29–35.
10. Gerritsen and Riello, "The Global Lives," 3, 8.
11. Matthee, "Iran's Relations," describes Membré's travelogue as "the first to offer a credible, first-hand account of life at the Safavid court" (10). For an English translation, see Membré, *Mission*.
12. Schwartz, "The Sherley Brothers," 80. For a list of these rulers, see Penrose, *The Sherleian Odyssey*, 76–77. Matthee, "Iran's Relations," records that Shah 'Abbas sent "seven ambassadors to Europe in 1603/04 alone" (13). See also Quinn, *Shah 'Abbas*.
13. Robert is described as an *"ilchi"* (translated as "an envoy or ambassador") in "the 'fiat' or 'farman' bearing the seals of 'Abbas I," on which see Chick, *Chronicle*, 1:217.
14. Schwartz, "The Sherley Brothers," lists in this "fully credited embassy of Persia to eight European courts . . . [f]ifteen Englishmen (fifteen others and Robert [Sherley] were left behind as hostages), the Persian ambassador Husain [Hossein, Husayn] 'Ali Beg, four secretaries, fifteen servants, five interpreters, and a Franciscan and a Dominican monk" (80). Savory, *Iran*, describes Husain 'Ali Beg as "a *qizilbash* officer" (109). As Blow, *Shah Abbas*, explains, "[t]he Safavid Turkoman tribesmen were known as *Qizilbash*, a Turkish word meaning 'red-head', because they wore a red bonnet with twelve folds, symbolizing the Twelve Shi'i Imans" (3).
15. Ross, *Sir Anthony*, 53. Ross includes the complete letter from "the celebrated Jesuit, Father Parsons [Persons], and dated Rome, April 30th, 1601" (52).
16. López-Peláez, "*The Travailes*," 254n2. For studies that attend to Anthony Sherley's global connections, see Subrahmanyam, *Three Ways*, 72–132, and Şahin and Schleck, "Courtly Connections."
17. Chick, *Chronicle*, 1:144.
18. As Raiswell, "Shirley," explains, "Probably about 1603, while in the shah's service, he [Robert] was converted to Catholicism by the Augustinian friar Antonio de Gouveia" (399–400).
19. On Robert's turban, see Schwartz, "The Sherley Brothers," 91–93. On the couple's "hybrid" costumes, see Arthur, "'You will say they are Persian.'"
20. Subrahmanyam, *Three Ways*, 21–22.
21. Lockhart, "European Contacts," 387.
22. Uruch Bey, *Don Juan*, 292.

23. On the Spanish pensions, see Uruch Bey, *Don Juan*, 308, and on the papal pensions, see 337n12.
24. According to Jaimoukha, "During this period, it was common to find both Muslim, Christian and even pagan members in the same family" (*Circassians*, 149).
25. Herbert, *Relation*, 125.
26. After asserting "[t]hat she was baptized by the Carmelites on 2.2.1608 is a definite fact," Chick wonders, "had she not been baptized by Orthodox rite in Circassia, then?" (*Chronicle*, 1:291n2). To clarify, the *Code of Canon Law*, prohibits rebaptism as per Canon 84.1, which provokes questions about whether Teresa Sampsonia was a Muslim prior to her conversion to Roman Catholicism. Provisions are listed for conditional baptism if the validity of the first is in doubt as per Canon 869.1. Carmen Nocentelli, in a personal communication, shared that some Italian sources state Teresa was baptized "di cautela" (i.e., as a precaution).
27. Erythræi, "Teresa Comitissa ex Persia" ["Countess Teresa from Persia"], in *Pinacotheca*, 253–63.
28. Chick, *Chronicle*, 1:293; Matthee, Introduction, ix.
29. Florencio, *Biblioteca*, 29.
30. In documenting this persecution, Chick, *Chronicle*, transcribes "an enclosure to a letter addressed by the Visitor General of the Carmelites, Fr. Epiphanius of S. John Baptist, from Goa on 25.12.1631, to the Secretary of the Sacr. Congregation in Rome [S.R., vol. 104 (Lettere di Spangna, Armenia, etc.), p. 299 *et seq.*]" (1:290–91). S.R. stands for "the manuscript series *Scritture Riferite* in the archives of the Sacred Congregation of de Propaganda Fide" (1:xxiii). He explains that "[t]he account with full details—presumably forwarded to Rome by the Vicar Provincial of the Carmelites, then Fr. Dimas of the Cross—either is no longer available among the archives of the Order, or has escaped the notice of the present compiler of these annals" (1:290). He speculates that "perhaps the author of *En Perse* [Florencio, *Biblioteca*, 3:35–42] drew on it for the animated description of the scenes which he paints (not without discrepancies, however)" (1:290). While Florencio does not mention this lost source, he explicitly references the account in Sancto Andrea, *Historia*, 374–84.
31. Chick, *Chronicle*, 1:293.
32. Chick, *Chronicle*, 1:294. Florencio, *Biblioteca*, 41 ("un certificado de buena y santa conducta" [a certificate of good and saintly conduct]), which she received on June 21, 1634. For a detailed chronology of this period in Teresa Sampsonia's life, see Piemontese, *La Persia Istoriata*, 306–7.

33. Florencio, *Biblioteca*, records that she arrived in Rome ("la Ciudad Eternal" [the Eternal City]) on December 27, 1634; she died there in 1668, at the age of seventy-nine (42).
34. Domańska, "The Return," 171. Gosden and Marshall, "The Cultural Biography," offers a useful survey.
35. Appadurai," "Introduction," 34; Kopytoff, "Sacred Commodities," 66–68; Domańska, "The Return," 180 (emphasis in original).
36. Appadurai," "Introduction," 34, 5.
37. Geary concludes: "Thus one can well apply Kopytoff's suggestion that one examine the career or biography of objects as they pass from ordinary remains to treasured relics, and then perhaps back again" ("Sacred Commodities," 177).
38. On the debate over the "agency" of things, see Hodder, *Entangled*, 32, 215–16.
39. "career, n.," *OED*, 1b, 5a.
40. Chick, *Chronicle*, 1:293; Florencio, *Biblioteca*, 29.
41. Hsai, *The World*, 33.
42. Peers, *Handbook*, 54; Weber, *Teresa of Avila*, 3–4, 100, 126.
43. Freeman, *Holy Bones*, 263. On the relationship between Teresa of Ávila and Gracián, who was her spiritual director, see Luti, "'A Marriage Well Arranged.'" I thank Professor Claire Gilbert for this reference.
44. Freeman, *Holy Bones*, 263.
45. Freeman, *Holy Bones*, 264. Hsai, *The World*, has a similar assessment (135–36).
46. See Geary, *Furta Sacra*, on the theft of relics. For another approach to Teresian relics, see Sanjuán-Pastor, "When Flesh Becomes Word."
47. Chick, *Chronicle*, 1:293, 1:146. Florencio, *Biblioteca*, offers a more detailed description: "el relicario que siempre llevaba colgado al pecho, en donde había una reliquia de Santa Teresa, cubierta por una pequeña y devota imagen de la Santa" (the reliquary that always hung to the chest, where there was a relic of Santa Teresa, covered by a small and devout image of the saint) (39).
48. Chick, *Chronicle*, 1:291–92.
49. Chick, *Chronicle*, 1:291.
50. Chick, *Chronicle*, 1:292.
51. Chick, *Chronicle*, 1:293.
52. Chick, *Chronicle*, 1:293; Florencio, *Biblioteca*, 40. Del Niño Jesús offers a more detailed account of the bleeding relic, including Teresa Sampsonia's fear that the thing was demonic ("Por miedo a que no fuese cosa del demonio"), which she allayed by consulting a Carmelite friar stationed in Persia, Fray Dimas de la Cruz (de la Croix), who was reputed

to be a very saintly missionary ("muy santo Misionero") (40). For more on these fears, especially with respect to women's religiosity during the Counter-Reformation, see Hsia, *The World*, 151–54.
53. Walsham, "Introduction," 12–13.
54. Euben, *Journeys*, 140.
55. Matthee, "Iran's Relations," 18.
56. Meri, "Relics," 100, 101–2, 118. For "Connections with Christianity" in the Persianate context, see Hanaoka, *Authority and Identity*, 173, 180–81, 196–97, 201, 255–59. For similar connections on a broader scale, see Wheeler, *Mecca and Eden*. On Safavid relics, see Membré, *Mission*, xviii, 41–42.
57. For the influence Islamic mysticism, or Sufism, on Teresa of Ávila, see Netton, *Islam, Christianity and the Mystic Journey*, 124–31; Childers, "Spanish Mysticism and the Islamic Tradition"; and López-Baralt, *Islam in Spanish Literature*, 91–142.
58. Peers, *Handbook*, 129.
59. Florencio, *Biblioteca*, 28.
60. Florencio, *Biblioteca*, 29.
61. Irigaray, *Speculum*, 135.
62. On Mauss and Lévi-Strauss, see Godelier, *The Enigma*, 10–107; on Weiner, see 8, 32.

Bibliography

Andrea, Bernadette. *The Lives of Girls and Women from the Islamic World in Early Modern British Literature and Culture*. Toronto: University of Toronto Press, 2017.

———. *Women and Islam in Early Modern English Literature*. Cambridge: Cambridge University Press, 2007.

Appadurai, Arjun, ed. "Introduction: Commodities and the Politics of Value." In Appadurai, *Social Life*, 3–63.

———. *The Social Life of Things: Commodities in Cultural Perspective*. Cambridge: Cambridge University Press, 1998.

Arthur, Kate. "'You will say they are Persian but let them be changed': Robert and Teresa Sherley's Embassy to the Court of James." In *Britain and the Muslim World*, edited by Gerald MacLean, 37–51. Newcastle-upon-Tyne: Cambridge Scholars, 2011.

Blow, David. *Shah Abbas: The Ruthless King Who Became an Iranian Legend*. London: I. B. Tauris, 2009.

"career, n." *Oxford English Dictionary*, March 2018. Online edition, last accessed April 2, 2018.

Chick, Herbert, ed. *A Chronicle of the Carmelites in Persia and the Papal Mission of the XVIIth and XVIIIth Centuries*. 2 vols. London: Eyre and Spottiswoode, 1939. Reprinted with an Introduction by Rudi Matthee, New York: I. B. Tauris, 2012.

Childers, William. "Spanish Mysticism and the Islamic Tradition." In *Approaches to Teaching Teresa of Ávila and the Spanish Mystics*, edited by Alison Weber, 57–66. New York: Modern Language Association, 2009.

Code of Canon Law. Vatican: Libreria Editrice Vaticana, 1983. Online edition, last accessed April 2, 2018.

Domańska, Ewa. "The Return to Things." *Archaeologia Polona* 44 (2006): 171–85.

Erythræi, Iani Nicii [Gian Nicio Vittorio]. *Pinacotheca Tertia, Imaginum, Virorum, aliqua ingenii & eruditionis fama illustrium, qui, auctore superstite, è vita decesserunt*. Cologne, 1648.

Euben, Roxanne L. *Journeys to the Other Shore: Muslim and Western Travelers in Search of Knowledge*. Princeton: Princeton University Press, 2006.

Florencio, Del Niño Jesús. *Biblioteca Carmelitano-Teresiana de Misiones*. Vol. 3: *En Perse*. Pamplona: Ramon de Bengaray, 1930.

Freeman, Charles. *Holy Bones, Holy Dust: How Relics Shaped the History of Medieval Europe*. New Haven: Yale University Press, 2011.

Geary, Patrick J. *Furta Sacra: Thefts of Relics in the Central Middle Ages*. Princeton: Princeton University Press, 1990.

———. "Sacred Commodities: The Circulation of Medieval Relics." In Appadurai, *Social Life*, 169–91.

Gerritsen, Anne, and Giorgio Riello. "The Global Lives of Things: Material Culture in the First Global Age." In *The Global Lives of Things: The Material Culture of Connections in the Early Modern World*, edited by Anne Gerritsen and Giorgio Riello, 1–28. New York: Routledge, 2016.

Godelier, Maurice. *The Enigma of the Gift*. Translated by Nora Scott. Chicago: University of Chicago Press, 1999.

Gosden, Chris, and Yvonne Marshall. "The Cultural Biography of Objects." *World Archaeology* 31, no. 2 (1999): 169–78.

Hanaoka, Mimi. *Authority and Identity in Medieval Islamic Historiography: Persian Histories from the Peripheries*. Cambridge: Cambridge University Press, 2016.

Herbert, Thomas. *A Relation of Some Yeares Travaile, Begvnne Anno 1626. Into Afrique and the Greater Asia, especially the Territories of the Persian Monarchie*. London, 1634.

Hodder, Ian. *Entangled: An Archaeology of the Relationships between Humans and Things*. Malden MA: Wiley-Blackwell, 2012.

Hodgson, Marshall G. S. *The Venture of Islam*. 3 vols. Chicago: University of Chicago Press, 1974.

Hsai, R. Po-Chia. *The World of Catholic Renewal, 1540–1770*. Cambridge: Cambridge University Press, 2005.
Irigaray, Luce. *Speculum of the Other Woman*. Translated by Gillian C. Gill. Ithaca NY: Cornell University Press, 1985.
Jaimoukha, Amjad. *The Circassians*. New York: Palgrave, 2001.
Kopytoff, Igor. "The Cultural Biography of Things: Commoditization as Process." In Appadurai, *Social Life*, 64–91.
Langer, Alex, ed. *The Fascination of Persia: The Persian-European Dialogue in Seventeenth-Century Art and Contemporary Art of Teheran*. Zürich: Scheidegger and Spiess, 2013.
Lockhart, Laurence. "European Contacts with Persia, 1350–1736." In *The Cambridge History of Iran, Vol. 6: The Timurid and Safavid Periods*, edited by Peter Jackson and Laurence Lockhart, 6:373–410. Cambridge: Cambridge University Press, 1986.
López-Baralt, Luce. *Islam in Spanish Literature: From the Middle Ages to the Present*. Translated by Andrew Hurley. Leiden: Brill, 1992.
López-Peláez Casellas, Jesús. "*The Travailes of the Three English Brothers* and the Textual Construction of Early Modern Identities." *Interlitteraria* 21, no. 2 (2016): 253–74.
Luti, Mary. "'A Marriage Well Arranged': Teresa of Avila and Fray Jerónimo Gracián de la Madre de Dios." *Studia Mystica* 10 (1989): 32–46.
Matthee, Rudi. "Iran's Relations with Europe in the Safavid Period: Diplomats, Missionaries, Merchants, and Travel." In Langer, *Fascination*, 6–39.
Membré, Michele. *Mission to the Lord Sophy of Persia (1539–1542)*. Translated by A. H. Morton. Warminster, UK: Gibb Memorial Trust, 1999.
Meri, Josef W. "Relics of Piety and Power in Medieval Islam." *Past and Present* 206, no. s5 (2010): 97–120.
Middleton, Thomas. *Sir Robert Sherley, Sent Ambassadour in the Name of the King of Persia*. London, 1609.
Morden, Robert. *Geography Rectified: or, A Description of the World*. London, 1700.
Netton, Ian Richard. *Islam, Christianity and the Mystic Journey*. Edinburgh: Edinburgh University Press, 2011.
Peers, E. Allison. *Handbook to the Life and Times of St. Teresa and St. John of the Cross*. London: Burnes Oates, 1954.
Penrose, Boies. *The Sherleian Odyssey*. London: Simpkin Marshall, 1938.
Piemontese, Angelo Michele. *La Persia Istoriata in Roma*. Vatican: Biblioteca Apostolica Vaticana, 2014.
Raiswell, Richard. "Shirley, Sir Robert." In *Oxford Dictionary of National Biography [ODNB]*, edited by H. C. G. Matthew and Brian Harrison, 399–410. Oxford: Oxford University Press, 2004.

Quinn, Sholeh A. *Shah 'Abbas: The King Who Refashioned Iran*. London: Oneworld, 2015.

Ross, E. Denison. *Sir Anthony Sherley and His Persian Adventure*. London: Routledge, 1933.

Şahin, Kaya, and Julia Schleck. "Courtly Connections: Anthony Sherley's *Relation of his travels into Persia* (1613) in a Global Context." *Renaissance Quarterly* 69, no. 1 (2016): 80–115.

Savory, Roger. *Iran under the Safavids*. Cambridge: Cambridge University Press, 1980.

Sancto Andrea, Petro [Pierre de Saint-André]. *Historia Generalis Fratrum Discalceatorum . . . Tomas Secundus*. Rome, 1671.

Sanjuán-Pastor, Nuria. "When Flesh Becomes Word: Teresa of Avila's Handwritten Relics." In "Carta Blanca: Representations of Self in Sixteenth Century Epistolary Fictions," 97–144. PhD Diss., Princeton University, 2011.

Schleck, Julia. *Telling True Tales of Islamic Lands: Forms of Meditation in English Travel Writing, 1575-1630*. Selinsgrove PA: Susquehanna University Press, 2011.

Schwartz, Gary. "The Sherley Brothers: Persia as the Stakes in a Rouge's Gambit." In Langer, *Fascination*, 78–99.

Sefatgol, Mansur. "Farang, Farangi and Farangestan: Safavid Historiography and the West (907–1148/1501-1736). In *Iran and the World in the Safavid Age*, edited by Willem Floor, and Edmund Herzig, 357–63. London: I. B. Tauris, 2015.

Subrahmanyam, Sanjay. *Three Ways to Be Alien: Travails and Encounters in the Early Modern World*. Waltham MA: Brandeis University Press, 2011.

Uruch Bey. *Don Juan of Persia, A Shi'ah Catholic, 1560-1604*. Translated by Guy Le Strange. New York: Harper, 1926.

Walsham, Alexandra. "Introduction: Relics and Remains." *Past and Present* 206, no. S5 (2010): 9–36.

Weber, Alison. *Teresa of Avila and the Rhetoric of Femininity*. Princeton: Princeton University Press, 1990.

Weiner, Annette B. *Inalienable Possessions: The Paradox of Keeping-While-Giving*. Berkeley: University of California Press, 1992.

Wheeler, Brannon. *Mecca and Eden: Ritual, Relics, and Territory in Islam*. Chicago: University of Chicago Press, 2006.

6

Gender and Travel Discourse

Richard Lassels's "The Voyage of the Lady Catherine Whetenall from Brussells into Italy" (1650)

PATRICIA AKHIMIE

In the 1650 manuscript "The Voyage of the Lady Catherine Whetenall from Brussells into Italy," the familiar characterization of women's travel as a movement away from domesticity and thus from chastity is refigured. "The Voyage"—as I will call it—is most similar in its form and content to the Grand Tour travel diaries composed by young wealthy men, documenting the movements, encounters, and impressions of Lady Catherine Whetenhall during her tour of Italy. Lady Catherine, a member of the prominent English Catholic family the Talbots, traveled to the European continent to live and study but also to escape mounting anti-Catholic restrictions and sentiments in England.[1] After meeting and marrying her husband, Thomas Whetenhall, she devised a plan to travel to Rome for the final Jubilee Year of Pope Innocent X, accompanied by her newly wedded husband and their entourage, including Richard Lassels, a Catholic priest and tutor, as their guide.[2] Thomas Whetenhall was reluctant to agree to the trip, having only recently returned from his own tour of France and Italy in 1645–47. He was also concerned for the risk to his wife's health should she become pregnant while traveling, a fear that proved to be well-founded when Lady Catherine became ill and died after delivering a stillborn child in 1650 in Padua, a stop on the return leg of their tour.

The manuscript was written by Richard Lassels, and as Edward Chaney has demonstrated, "The Voyage" is likely the earliest draft of Lassels's well-known *Voyage of Italy* (1670).[3] This is most surprising because, while "The Voyage" describes the Grand Tour of a young lady, *Voyage of Italy*, which is often considered to be a founding text of the Grand Tour tradition, is written expressly "to young men and for them."[4] *Voyage of Italy*, like other early guidebooks and treatises on the art of travel—*ars apodemica*—builds on widely accepted ideas about the role of educational travel in the production of genteel masculinity. At a time when women were dissuaded or actively prohibited from educational travel, "The Voyage" is invested in a project of exoneration and adoration; it offers a model for a woman's travels as exceptional and therefore acceptable. Through Lassels's artistry, Lady Catherine manages both to travel and to remain saintly in her static domesticity. This model is made possible—or palatable—however, in part because the saintly female traveler is lost, returning to a heavenly rather than an earthly home. In this unique text, popular objections to women's travel are both acknowledged and contested.

In this chapter, I will explore the gendered discourse of travel including, on the one hand, legal restrictions and cultural limitations on women's movements and, on the other hand, the representational strategies employed to protect women's travel from disparagement. In the case of "The Voyage," Richard Lassels transports domesticity and chastity along with his lady traveler and transforms her, after her death, into a monument to those very virtues. This combination of travel and domesticity may seem paradoxical as a model of women's travel, but as I suggest by way of conclusion, early modern readers, and Grand Tour travelers in particular, would have been familiar with the figure of the traveling saintly mother, as embodied in the image the Madonna di Loreto and the story of the repeated transportation of the Virgin Mary's home, or Santa Casa, from the Holy Land to its final location in Loreto, an important stop on the Grand Tour.[5] The Santa Casa is usually shown in midflight and with the Virgin and Christ child mounted atop the house. In an image from an English translation of an earlier Italian history of Loreto and the Holy House (fig. 2), the Virgin Mary is hovering above Loreto, where ships can be seen in the harbor and pilgrims in the foreground. What is fascinating is that this quintessentially domestic object, Mary's one-room house complete with simple hearth and stone walls, is on the move in this striking manner. The image couples the stillness, the staying-put-ness that characterizes the domestic sphere, distinguishing it from the dangers and opportunities of the world at large, with the dynamism of travel beyond borders and overseas. In Lassels's account, Lady Catherine is akin to the Madonna di Loreto. She herself is a monument to domestic virtue.

Restrictions on Women's Travel

From the late sixteenth to early seventeenth century, for men of means, continental travel gained value both as an important form of vocational education or cultural refinement and as a luxury commodity, a pleasurable pastime. The period from the mid-sixteenth century on saw an outpouring of guidebooks and *ars apodemica* treatises—like Robert Dallington's *A Method for Trauell* (1605), Francis Bacon's "Of Travaile" (1625), and Fynes Moryson's "Of Travelling in Generall" (1617)— aimed at those genteel travelers whose continental wanderings were considered "educational."[6] In these prescriptive and didactic works, travel is figured as a masculine pursuit undertaken in anticipation of the social advancement travel might earn one at a later date through the acquisition of languages, polished manners, practical knowledge, and a network of powerful connections. It was said that one might travel for profit or for pleasure (a common refrain), but authors often conflated material and social gains. As the avid traveler Fynes Moryson points out in his *Itinerary* (1617), "We permit Merchants and Mariners... to take long voyages for gaine, neither can Gentlemen more inrich themselues, then by the knowledge of military and politicall affaires."[7] The families and households of genteel travelers were personally and financially invested in the success of the endeavor, believing that the potential gains outweighed the dangers associated with travel: loss of innocence, loss of fortune, and loss of faith.

At the same time, already heavy restrictions on travel increased, and it became more difficult to obtain written permission (travel licenses or passports) to leave England and travel overseas.[8] Statutes and proclamations enacted and issued in the period caution would-be travelers not to attempt to leave the country without a license and particularly to avoid those countries with which England was at odds. *A Procla-*

mation touching Passengers (1606) states that it has been enacted "That no woman nor any childe under the age of one and twenty yeeres ... should be permitted to passe over the Seas," and exempts just "Saylers or Shipboyes or Apprentice or Factor of some Merchant in trade of Merchandize."[9] The proclamation clarifies an earlier statute directing those few women and children who "have from time to time just and necessary causes and occasions to go and passe over the Seas" to seek a license from officers stationed in certain ports.[10]

The short list of exempted occupations—sailors and apprentices or factors of merchants—were those same offices and occupations that enabled young men to enter the world, even going into those cities, countries, and regions that presented the greatest imagined risk of danger or religious conversion (to Catholicism or Islam, for example). As a widely acknowledged addition to this list of accepted "passengers," young gentlemen had long been permitted to travel to the Continent with tutors or small entourages. Even such exalted travelers required licenses like the one signed by Charles I "giving license to Robert Lord Willoughby of Eresby, eldest son of Montagu earl of Lindsey, Lord Great Chamberlain," to "travel beyond the seas for his better improvement in foreign experience for 3 years" and to "let him pass to any part with four servants, apparel & necessaries not prohibited, and embark for overseas."[11]

The language of licenses permits travel by emphasizing its aims—"better improvement"—and limiting its duration in order to mitigate its potential negative effects. In the same vein, the authors of *ars apodemica* treatises attempt to advise readers on how to ensure that travel will be beneficial and edifying rather than corrupting. Generally these texts emphasize the importance of demonstrating all the outward signs that travel has successfully added something to a man's worth: he has kept a journal, he has kept up a correspondence with a network of contacts overseas, and he has learned foreign languages.

So great were the risks that many authors advocated travel only for certain individuals and under certain conditions. Many stated unequivocally that women should not travel under any circumstances. Moryson makes clear that "women for suspition of chastity are most unfit for this course," a claim that Thomas Palmer illustrates graphically in *An essay of the meanes how to make our travailes* (1606) with a table of the kinds and objectives of travel and travelers in which women appear on a list of those who are "inhibited" (prohibited) from travel along with "Infantes, Decrepite Persons, Fooles, Madmen, and Lunatickes."[12] As Palmer explains, "Nature" prohibits the very young and old from travel by "defect of understanding" in the young and physical "insufficencie" in the elderly, "Imperfection" prevents all those with "disabilities of minde," while it is their very "Sex" that "in most countries prohibiteth women, who are rather for the house then the fielde; and to remaine at home, then travaile into other Nations."[13] Travel could make or break a person depending upon the strength of their morals, faith, and good judgment. Women, as the discussion of statutes restricting their movements shows, were already assumed to be incapable of good judgment regarding travel and vulnerable to conversion and temptation. Thus, in works of travel advice women are excluded from travel both explicitly and implicitly.

The threat travel presents to women's chastity, and the link between women's chastity and domesticity (immobility), is clearly articulated in *ars apodemica* treatises. Authors frequently employ gendered metaphors in describing the dangers associated both with traveling abroad and with staying home for male travelers. Those writing in praise of travel imagine it as a journey toward male adulthood, a movement away from a domestic sphere associated with suffocating wives, mothers, and nurses. As Lassels explains, "Traueling preserues my yong nobleman from surfeiting of his parents, and weanes him from the dangerous fondness of his mother."[14] He exhorts readers to embody the wise Ulysses rather than his son Telemachus who "is held for a very shallow witted man . . . because his mother *Penelope*, instead of sending him abroad to see forrain countryes, had allwayes kept him at home."[15] Authors of travel advice often hold up the example of Ulysses as the quintessential traveler, quoting the favorite phrase, "Qui multos hominum mores cognovit et urbes" (For he knew many men's manners and saw many cities).[16] For women the commonplace was opposite, as Moryson illustrates with a different classical example: "Thou wilt say, he hath lived well who hath spent his time retyred from the world. . . . This may be true in women; and thus among many Roman Gentlemen, when one praised Fulvia, another Claudia, a third with good judgement preferred a Senators unknowne wife to both these, and many other severally commended, because she was no lesse good and faire, yet was knowne to few or none . . . but it is the part of an industrious man, to acct their affaires in the world, tho sluggards lie by the fire."[17] In defining travel as appropriate to men, Moryson also defines domesticity as appropriate to women. Travelers are improved the more they come to "know" the world. Women, though, are less estimable the more they themselves are "known," an adjective that implicitly links social acquaintance with sexual intimacy.

In *ars apodemica* treatises, travelers are imagined to be moving through a field of edifying exempla, gaining knowledge through exposure to the sights and sounds of an unfamiliar world. Women themselves are explicitly excluded from travel as an educational process. And women who do travel are seen as available to view and for review, as if travel itself were a sexually illicit act for women. Women's travel is transformative in that it converts them into edifying objects. To put it more succinctly: men sightsee, women become sights to be seen. The presumption underlying the gendered discourse of travel is that while women might travel, the act would be inadvisable and the negative result irremediable.

"The Voyage" offers an unusually positive representation of women's travel, but it is not a first-hand account, and scholars have sometimes defined only first-person narratives as belonging to the genre of travel writing.[18] Though "The Voyage" is not in her own hand or directly dictated, it is clearly identified as Lady Catherine Whetenhall's own tour and not her husband's. Specifically, the 1649–50 tour to Rome for the Jubilee celebrations was made at Lady Catherine's express request having been "infinitly & most zealously desired" (fol. 8r).[19] The written relation of the journey was also made "att *the* entreaty" of Lady Catherine (fol. 3r). Lassels's account features Lady Catherine as the central mover in a deeply personal and pious journey, self-willed though not self-recorded. With its authoritative woman traveler and once-removed authorial voice, "The Voyage" exemplifies the awkward and unfamiliar narrative modes required to recount early modern women's travel.

The male travelers of the "The Voyage" disappear into its background. Lady Catherine's husband, Thomas Whetenhall, appears seldom in the account, and Lassels is at some pains to explain this seeming oversight to him in the dedicatory epistle (Lassels gifted Thomas with the manuscript after Catherine's death). As he writes, "I call it therefore her voyage and abstract from you both in regard it was a voyage infinitly & most zealously desired by her contrary almost to your inclination, and the advise of those few friends she acquainted with it (who were as few as possible, lest she should not be able to stemme the streme of theire diswasions) as alsoo because you having formerly made itt more rather a compaynon & guide to her then the first mover in it" (fol. 8r). Lassels's apology by way of explanation lays bare the extent to which the journey was Lady Catherine's design.

Lassels's apology also reveals the extent to which the journey fell outside the bounds of accepted practice when it came to women's travel, even among the more cosmopolitan Catholic émigrés living in Ghent. In this passage Lassels describes Thomas Whetenhall in much the same terms as he would have described himself, as a "compaynon & guide." Indeed, in the text of "The Voyage" the whole cast of traveling companions, husband and venerable guide included, fade into the background as part of the faceless "trayne" mentioned in Lassels's lengthy title. Instead, Lassels's account is devoted to Lady Catherine's actions, impressions, and responses during the trip, as well as the most remarkable sites, holy and secular, in each town she visits.

The "Diary by John Pridgeon of Lord Willoughby's travels in France" provides a particularly useful comparison. Pridgeon, like Lassels, seems to have been charged with acting as guide and chaperone as well as tutor, and with recording the young man's daily experiences during his travels in France from 1647 to 1649.[20] At times, both "The Voyage" and Pridgeon's diary resemble guidebooks—didactic and detail oriented, even mundane. Other entries detail the sightseeing of their charges, and such passages can be sensational. At St. Denys, Lady Catherine grasps the sword of Jean d'Arc in her own hands; in Rome she touches her beads to St. Peter's Chair, ascends the steps of the Sancta Soala on her knees, kisses the Pope's foot, and hears the incomparable voice of a nun singing on St. Benedict's Day. Similar episodes appear in contemporaneous Grand Tour diaries written by young gentleman who visited the same towns and churches and viewed the same interactive sites.

Pridgeon dutifully records Lord Willoughby's visit to St. Denys, where he "had the same sword in his hand there with which the Pusilla d'Orleans drove all the English outt of France."[21] Written for a small audience of friends and family and as a memento for the traveler himself or herself, travel diaries like Pridgeon's for Lord Willoughby and Lassels's for Lady Whetenhall document the (manufactured) wonder of such encounters. Travel diaries also serve as proof that the risks associated with educational travel on the Continent (risks to fortune, health, and soul) have been worthwhile by providing a real-time narrative of the edification process the traveler has undergone. In this endeavor, Pridgeon's task is not difficult precisely because young gentlemen were permitted and expected to travel, to sightsee, and to interact with the world in this way. For Lassels, as I will discuss, producing a narrative justification of Lady Whetenhall's travels is more difficult, since educational travel for women was in no way accepted, but was instead dubiously exceptional.

Justifying Women's Travel

How did the authors of written accounts of women's travels combat the negative connotations associated with such travel? Women's travel is often subsumed by larger narratives of family, religion, and state—the needs and demands of parents, husbands, children, churches, masters, and monarchs necessitate women's movement from one place to another, across borders and even oceans. Accounts combat the stigma by first of all being subsumed by these other narratives, legitimating travel by linking it with domestic and with familial duties (wifely, motherly), and thus with the ideological imperatives (service to the state, religious devotion) that spurred male travelers to venture overseas with their families in tow.

Lassels's challenge is more complex: to commemorate but also excuse Lady Catherine Whetenhall's travels. This rhetorical dilemma gives rise to a central contradiction within the "The Voyage": the characterization of Lady Catherine's travel as both a movement abroad and staying still. In a dedicatory epistle addressed to Thomas Whetenhall, now a widower, Lassels remembers a scene of domestic bliss: "I could have witnessed with what haste you used to returne home when any business had detayned you longer than ordinary & run upp the stayres to prevent her, good Lady, from makeing as much haste downe to meet you, which she ever endeavoured to doe, as soone as ever she heard your voyce, or saw you out o[f] th[e] window, to which purpose she would frequently look out and sett her servants to watch" (fol. 6r). Catherine and Thomas were married just a month before leaving Ghent to go on tour, and Catherine never had the chance to return with her husband to his estate in Peckham during her life. Nevertheless, Lassels paints a picture of Lady Catherine as ensconced in the domestic space of the household, an image that belies the combination of piety and recklessness that Lassels attributes to her just a few lines earlier when describing her marital "proposal of travel" to Thomas. Lassels writes: "I would have even given colours to the conflict of your thoughts (when your Lady proposed her earnest desire of undertakeing the holy pilgrimage I here describe) betwixt your desire of condescending to all her requests; and a feare of what dangers might attend such great attempts" (fol. 5r). Here Lassels acknowledges that Lady Catherine's desire for travel was unconventional, even eccentric. Speaking directly to Thomas Whetenall, Lassels attests to the fact that Thomas was conflicted, that he did his husbandly duty by "fearing the danger" of travel for a woman in his charge.

Lassels wrestles with the gendered discourse of travel prevalent in the period and, through his evocative language, Lady Catherine maintains a saintly domesticity. At times the gestures are almost heavy-handed. Lassels refers to the tour as a "holy pilgrimage" in the dedicatory epistle. He finds an opportunity for biblical allusion when, on the road to Loreto, Lady Catherine begins riding horseback for greater safety, having now discovered that she is pregnant. On the road from Loreto to Venice the party stops at a small village to stay the night but finds no room at the inn, as it were. Lassels casts Lady Catherine and her husband (making one of his brief appearances) as Mary and Joseph in Bethlehem: "[They] tooke up there lodging in the hay loft and there upon a bed of hay, slept better then they had done in ma[n]y greate Innes" (fol. 40v). By patterning Lady Catherine's travels after the Virgin Mary's, Lassels is able to access a more palatable model for women's travel that allows a woman traveling to remain a wife and mother by remaining, in essence, at home: the Santa Casa.

This journey of the saintly mother or traveling *domus* is paradoxical but acceptable to the pious as a miraculous impossibility like the journey of the Santa Casa. It is important to note, however, that this miraculous journey is one for which there is no earthly "return." There is no socioeconomic reward for this kind of travel—as with young gentlemen's educational travel—and, in fact, no physical, geographic return home either. Instead the returns are imagined to be internal and eternal. The dynamic that Lassels is creating here, then, is one in which women's travel is permissible and even venerable only if the woman herself is lost.

The Santa Casa as a Model of Static Mobility

Reproduced in a broad range of representations across Europe and throughout the medieval and early modern periods, images of the Madonna di Loreto, or the Madonna of the Santa Casa (holy house) in Loreto, run the gamut from humble woodcuts to marble sculptures. The miracle of the holy house describes how angels transported the childhood home of the Virgin Mary—the home in which the Annunciation and Immaculate Conception takes place—from Nazareth to eastern Europe, and possibly a few other locations, before finally settling it on a lonely highway in Italy. As the story goes, the town of Loreto then grew up around the shrine, which drew pilgrims from all over Europe. For seventeenth-century English travelers, the shrine at Loreto was becoming a key attraction and a common stop on the developing Grand Tour. As royalist John Raymond puts it in *Il Mercurio Italico: A Voyage made through Italy* (1648): "Great is the Lady of Loreto. Loreto is of itselfe but a little Bourg or Village, yet by the noise it makes through Christendome, especially in the Catholike Regions, tis as much frequented as Saint Peters Chaire. Hee's no zealous Romanist hath not made one pilgramage thither, or sent some Offering to the Virgin here ador'd."[22]

The dynamic and mobile vision of the Virgin Mary in flight is most often to be found in descriptions written by faithful Catholics. Protestant travelers were far less commendatory, but they, too, were fascinated. William Lithgow, a Scottish Protestant and world traveler, repeats the words purportedly spoken by the Virgin Mary regarding the house and recorded in a book given him by Italian pilgrims, a passage Lithgow refers to as "A Papisticall dream'd-of Oration":

> It was in this Chamber my Mother Anna conceived me, nourished me and brought me up . . . and also I kept in this roome the blessed infant Iesus . . . brought him up with all diligent observation. . . . These cinders in the Chimney touch not, because they ar the fragments of the last fire I made on earth: And that Shelfe wheron my linen cloathes, and prayer Bookes lay, Let no person come neere it: for all these places are sanctified and holy.[23]

Lithgow's account of the Virgin Mary's pronouncement emphasizes the simplicity of the Santa Casa as a household—a chimney full of cinders, a shelf for linens and books—and as a shrine to the extended Holy Family, including Anna and John and the infant Christ.

The conflation of home and shrine is visible in the architecture of the larger structure that surrounds the Santa Casa, an elaborate marble casing built around the Santa Casa like a gigantic reliquary.[24] I see a potent contrast here between the dynamic image of the Santa Casa in flight, and the heavy and heavily ensconced Santa Casa as relic, buried in such a way as to suggest the impossibility of further or future flights. The Santa Casa memorializes a woman (wife and mother) once on the move at will and now essentially, eternally, and emphatically confined to a domestic sphere, a location that only others, devout pilgrims and curious adventurers, may travel toward and away from. This transformation occurs in "The Voyage" as well.

While in Loreto, Lady Catherine viewed the Santa Casa encased within what Lassels calls "an adoracon of white marble with exquisite statutes" (fol. 37v). He later describes Lady Catherine's own tomb—commissioned in Venice by a grief-stricken Thomas Whetenall—in very similar terms: "That hansom monument of White marble with a fair Bordue or Decoration of fine Marble . . . On which he caused to be engraven the ensuing Epitaph, as an eternall record of his love and grief" (Brussels, fol. 32v–33r). In the epitaph, given in both Latin and English, Lady Catherine is honored equally as dutiful wife and pious traveler:

> Disdaining to be confind & as it were separated
> From *the* rest of *the* world by Narrow British Seas.
> After hauing with great Courage, greater Piety
> But aboue all with a transcendant loue to her Husband
> Traueled thro *the* Low Countreys, France & Italy
> In *the* Jubily Year, arriued at Rome,
> Wher not content to haue only seen *the* Keys
> of Heauen
> She conceiued a Noble ambition of entring heauen
> it self, & passing thro a more Holy gate, euen to
> *the* Holy of Holies. (Brussels, fol. 33v)

The epitaph manages to convey some sense of the spontaneity and willfulness of Lady Catherine's decision to travel without offense by recasting what Lassels describes previously as an "almost contrary" and "zealous desire" as instead a "noble ambition" to move *with* her husband toward *heavenly* sites and ultimately, toward heaven. As if to underscore the incongruity of a memorial to a wife who is both an itinerant and domestic saint, a Santa Casa on the move, we later learn that, at Whetenall's request, "Her heart was embalmed and brought home to his domestic Chapel at Peckham," in Kent, returning Lady Catherine to the English estate of which she was mistress, but which she had never seen or visited in her lifetime.[25]

Lassels, too, waxes poetic in his last description of Lady Catherine in the final pages of "The Voyage": "As shee was comeing home, full fraught with the vertues of other Countreis like a full shipp loaden with forraign marchandize shee sunke in the haven, and defeated the expectacion of all her Trayne" (fol. 44v–45r). Here, Lassels employs a metaphor common in *ars apodemica* treatises, comparing travelers to ships that venture great risk in the hopes that their return will bring profit and drawing on a biblical allusion praising the virtuous wife or woman: "She is like the merchants' ships; she bringeth her food from afar."[26] Lassels's reiteration likens not only two journeys of proportionate length but also two vessels, with a subtle reference to Lady Catherine's pregnancy. Lady Catherine is both the virtuous wife of Proverbs (laden with goods and also with child) and the merchant ship. The vessel that is Lady Catherine is full-fraught with "the vertues of other Countreis," like Ulysses, so highly praised in the rhetoric of the *ars apodemica* treatises because he "knew many men's manners and saw many cities." Skirting the discursive taboo against women's travel, Lassels's final image of Lady Catherine disappearing from sight enables him to return her to the relative safety of anonymity. She becomes once again like the "Senators unknowne wife" cited by Fynes Moryson, "commended, because she was no lesse good and faire, yet was knowne to few or none."

Through Lassels's strategic revision of the taboos surrounding women's travel, Lady Catherine escapes the suggestion of a loss of chastity. Nevertheless, she does come to be "known" in a very different way. Lady Catherine herself is included as early as 1654 on the Grand Tour traveler's itinerary. Lassels's "Description of Italy," a manuscript prepared for David Murray, Lord Balvaird, is written just four years after the events of "The Voyage" and is closely based on that text.[27] In the 1654 manuscript, Lassels has added Lady Catherine's monument to the list of the "cheif things to be seen" in Padua for the edification of his genteel reader.[28] Number 14 on the list is the Oratorians Church: "In the midst of which lyeth buryed the noble and gallant Lady the Lady Catherin Whitenhall daughter of the Earle of Shrewsbury: who returning from Rome in the holy yeare with her husband, fell sick in Padua and there dyed to the shame of all Padua physitians, and the grief of all those that knew her."[29] Ultimately, Lady Catherine becomes a literal monument, a sight to be seen.[30]

The passage is expanded in the printed *Voyage of Italy* (1670), where Lassels exhorts travelers to see the vault and read the epitaph. He offers his own praise of Lady Catherine as a model woman and a model traveler, even as he acknowledges that such a combination is unusual:

> For my part, having had the honour to see her often in her Travels, I cannot but make honorable mention of her here in mine; She having so much honoured my profession of Traveling by her generous humour of Travelling. She was as nobly borne as the house of Shrewbury could make her & as comely, as if Poets had made her. Her behaviour was such, that if she had not bien noble by birth, she would have passed for such by her carriage. Her good qualityes were so many, that if they had been taken in pieces, they would have made several women Noble, and Noble women happy. She was wise beyond her yeares; stout above her sex; and worthy to have found in the world all things better than shee did, except her Parents and Husband. Her onely fault was that, which would have made up other Ladyes praises, too much courage; which befell her with the name of Talbot. But whilst her onely courage haled her on to journeys above her sexe and force (having seen Flanders, France, and Italy, accompanied by her noble Husband, and a hansome traine)[.] In her returne back; like a tall ship, comeing laden home and fraughted with precious acquisitions of mind, she sunck almost in the haven, and alas! Dyed.[31]

Lassels lays the blame for Lady Catherine's overabundance of courage with her family: she is descended from war heroes. In an effort to construct his own authoritative persona as a traveler by "profession," Lassels praises Lady Catherine as a sort of patron saint of travel. Though the text of *Voyage of Italy* is largely based on Lassels account of Lady Catherine's travels, here the determined and even "zealous" desire to travel that enabled Lady Catherine and all her "hansome traine," including Lassels, to go on tour has disappeared. Lassels's role as tutor is transformed into that of a casual acquaintance who "had the honour to see her often in her Travels," and Lady Catherine's role as author of her own travels becomes "an honorable mention" in "mine," Lassels's own, travels. Lassels acknowledges more specifically that Lady Catherine's tour was genuine, resulting in Ulysses-like "precious acquisitions of mind." In the same breath, however, the passage reinforces the popular belief that travel is inappropriate or impossible for women by suggesting that Lady Catherine's "courage haled her on to journeys above her sexe."

The description of her return home as a tragic near miss, a ship sinking "almost in the haven," is borrowed from the Whetenall manuscript. Lady Catherine's travels are cut short in this dramatic way, and this becomes the occasion for Lassels to borrow the paradox that is the Santa Casa on the move in order to cast his patroness in the most positive light. Despite her willful pursuit of travel, her eagerness to move away from home instead of toward it, it is Lady Catherine's very absence from home or her failure to return home that draws pilgrims and tourists alike to note her passing and reflect upon her virtues. Her departure from the familiar understanding of the domestic sphere warrants a revision of that understanding rather than a condemnation of her behavior. Far from a moral failing, then, her adventures or misadventures are made, by Lassels hand, miraculous.

Notes

1. Catherine Talbot, second daughter of the tenth earl of Shrewsbury (Chaney, *Grand Tour*, 371n108). While very little biographical information is available, Edward Chaney provides the best summary, see Chaney, *Grand Tour*. Additional details appear in Bishop, "Thomas Whetenhall." Catherine Talbot apparently came to Ghent to the monastery of "Bernardines of Oosterloe" in 1648 to study French. She met Thomas Whetenhall in Ghent later that year (Lassels, Brussels, fol. 42v).
2. The little group included "their Brother Mr John Whetenhall, Mr Lascells, her woman Mrs Mary Sanders, and his honest man Dick Cuff" (Lassels, Brussels, fol. 44r).
3. Chaney traces the genealogy of the several manuscript versions that predate Lassels's 1670 printed work, *Voyage of Italy*, see Chaney, *Grand Tour*.
4. Lassels, *Voyage of Italy*, a1v. This manuscript has received very little critical attention. Chaney offers the most substantial treatment, see Chaney, *Grand Tour*. See also Games, *Web of Empire*, 35–38; Claydon, *Europe*, 13–14; Chaney, "Richard Lassels"; and Letts, "Contributions." Claydon reviews the rapid "canonization" of *Voyage of Italy* in the late seventeenth century (*Europe*, 14–18).
5. Scholarly work on the history and architecture of the shrine and on images of the Madonna di Loreto is expansive. For a recent art historical

treatment of the Madonna di Loreto focusing on the concept of the home in transit, see Nagel and Wood, *Anachronic Renaissance*, 195–217. Ruben Espinosa's essay in this volume offers an extended treatment of the shrine and of the figure of the black Madonna.

6. On the *ars apodemica* tradition, see Carey, "Travel"; and Stagl, "Methodising."
7. Moryson, *Itinerary*, Ddd6v. On the history of educational travel, see Warneke, *Images*; Chaney, *Evolution*; and Parks, "Travel."
8. On travel licenses, see Warneke, "Coastal 'Hedge.'"
9. Larkin and Hughes, *Stuart Royal Proclamations*, 1:147–48.
10. Larkin and Hughes, eds., *Stuart Royal Proclamations*, 1:147–48. For the statute, see Tomlins, *Statutes of the Realm*, 4:1021, I James I, c. 4, s. vii.
11. Lincolnshire Archives, 10-ANC/Lot 350. Lord Willoughby's passport explicitly names the goal of "better improvement in foreign experience," and limits his travel to three years. Some passports, however, offer no particular justification for travel, instead dictating the length of the stay, the size of the accompanying party, the amount of money and goods allowed the traveler, the types of people and places they could visit, and the penalties to be exacted for disregarding these strictures. Passports provide tantalizing evidence of the travels of women, but are often opaque. A 1667 travel license made out for Richard, Lord Lumley, for example, permits him to travel with a large company including "his Mother, his Brother his two sisters, & Twelve servants" but provides little insight into the experiences of the women (P.R.O. S.P. 44. Entry Book 25, fols. 34v–35r, reproduced in Chaney, *Grand Tour*, 254–55).
12. Moryson, *Itinerary*, Ddd6. Thomas Palmer's table of the kinds and objectives of travel and travelers appears just after the dedicatory epistle.
13. Palmer, *An Essay*, Dr.
14. Lassels, *Voyage of Italy*, a3v–a4.
15. Lassels, *Voyage of Italy*, a3v.
16. Drawn from Homer's *Odyssey*, the phrase is ubiquitous in travel advice throughout the seventeenth century.
17. Moryson, *Itinerary*, Eeev.
18. Campbell, *Witness*, 5.
19. Parenthetical references for "The Voyage" are to the copy of the Lassels manuscript held in the British Library. References to the slightly expanded copy held in the Bibliothèque royale de Belgique include the location, Brussels.
20. Pridgeon's diary ends in 1649, but Willoughby's tour continued for several years, taking him into Italy. The diary may be continued in a

manuscript held in the Lincolnshire Archives, "The Lord Willoughby's voyage from Blois into Italy in 1650" covering the period 1650-52 (10ANC/* Lot 353). This later diary, also written in the third person, mentions Lord Willoughby's visit to Loreto and sight of the Santa Casa.
21. Pridgeon, "Diary," 418.
22. Raymond, *Il Mercurio Italico*, 271.
23. Lithgow, *A most delectable*, cv-c2.
24. For a succinct description of the history and architecture with detailed illustrations, see Ingersoll, "House of the Virgin."
25. Bishop, "Thomas Whetenhall," 46-47.
26. Proverbs 31:14.
27. Lord Balvaird, a Scottish aristocrat, attempted to hire Lassels as a guide himself, but Lassels was already engaged by another family. Balvaird commissioned the written guide as a substitute (Chaney, *Grand Tour*, 98-99).
28. Chaney, *Grand Tour*, 217.
29. Chaney, *Grand Tour*, 218.
30. In 1705, Charles Talbot, the twelfth earl of Shrewsbury visited Padua and wrote in his own travel diary of viewing the sepulcher: "Mr. How and Mr. Con[sul], and West and I went to see where my aunt Cath[e]rine Whetnal lies buried here [at Padua], who died July 1650; it is in St. Thomas of Canterbury's, a church of the Oratorians; she has a very honourable and ample epitaph upon her gravestone, which lies in the middle of the church, composed I believe by her husband" (Chaney, *Grand Tour*, 376n136).
31. Lassels, *Voyage of Italy*, Ttr-v.

Bibliography

Bishop, Edmund. "Thomas Whetenhall of East Peckham, Kent." *Downside Review* 15 (1896): 29-48.

Campbell, Mary. *The Witness and the Other World: Exotic European Travel Writing, 400-1600*. Ithaca NY: Cornell University Press, 1988.

Carey, Daniel. "Travel, Identity and Cultural Difference, 1580-1700." In *Cross-Cultural Travel*, edited by Jane Conroy, 39-47. New York: Peter Lang, 2003.

Chaney, Edward. *Evolution of the Grand Tour: Anglo-Italian Cultural Relations Since the Renaissance*. London: Frank Cass, 1998.

———. *The Grand Tour and the Great Rebellion: Richard Lassels and "The Voyage of Italy" in the Seventeenth Century*. Geneva: Slatkine, 1985.

———. "Richard Lassels (1603-1668) and his European travels, with special reference to the manuscript account of the voyage of the Lady Catherine Whetenhall from Brussels into Italy in the holy yeare 1650." MPhil diss., University of London (The Warburg Institute), 1977.

Claydon, Tony. *Europe and the Making of England, 1660-1760*. Cambridge: Cambridge University Press, 2007.
Games, Alison. *The Web of Empire: English Cosmopolitans in an Age of Expansion, 1560-1660*. Oxford: Oxford University Press, 2008.
Ingersoll, Richard. "House of the Virgin." *Architecture* 90, no. 11 (2001): 93-97.
Larkin, James, and Paul Hughes, eds. *Stuart Royal Proclamations*. Vol. 1. Oxford: Clarendon, 1973-83. 2 vols.
Lassels, Richard. *The Voyage of Italy*. London, 1670.
———. "The Voyage of the Lady Catherine Whetenall from Brussells into Italy." Add. ms. 4217. British Library, London.
———. "The Voyage of the Lady Catherine Whetenhall Into Italy in the Holy Year." Ms. 7119. Bibliothèque royale de Belgique, Brussels.
Lithgow, William. *A most delectable and true discourse*. London, 1616.
Letts, Malcolm. "Contributions to the History of European Travel III: Lady Catherine Whetenall." *Notes and Queries* s12-1, no. 8 (1916): 141-44.
Lincolnshire Archives. Lincoln.
Moryson, Fynes. *An Itinerary*. London, 1617.
Nagel, Alexander, and Christopher Wood. *Anachronic Renaissance*. Brooklyn: Zone, 2010.
Palmer, Thomas. *An essay of the meanes how to make our trauailes*. London, 1606.
Parks, George Bruner. "Travel as Education." In *Seventeenth Century: Studies in the History of English Thought*, edited by R. F. Jones, 264-90. Stanford: Stanford University Press, 1951.
Pridgeon, John. "Diary, by John Pridgeon, of Lord Willoughby's travels in France." *H.M.C, Ancaster MSS* (1907): 418-24.
Raymond, John. *Il Mercurio Italico: A Voyage made through Italy*. London, 1648.
Stagl, Justin. "The Methodising of Travel in the Sixteenth Century: A Tale of Three Cities." In *Facing Each Other: The World's Perception of Europe and Europe's Perception of the World*, edited by Anthony Pagden, 303-38. Burlington VT: Ashgate, 2000.
Tomlins, T. E., ed. *Statutes of the Realm*. Vol. 4, 1547-1624. London, 1819. 11 vols.
Warneke, Sara. "A Coastal 'Hedge of Laws': Passport Control in Early Modern England." In *Studies in Western Traditions*. Bendigo, AU: School of Arts, La Trobe University, 1996.
———. *Images of the Educational Traveller in Early Modern England*. Leiden: Brill, 1994.

7

Advance and Retreat
Reading English Colonial Choreographies of Pocahontas

ELISA OH

> Some say this dance is common in the Canary Isles. Others . . . maintain that it derives from a ballet composed for a masquerade in which the dancers were dressed as kings and queens of Mauretania, or else like savages in feathers dyed to many a hue. This is how the canary is danced. A young man takes a damsel and . . . they dance together to the far end of the hall. This done, he withdraws to the place from whence he started, continuing the while to gaze at the damsel; then he regains her side anew and performs certain passages after which he withdraws again. The damsel now advances, does likewise before him and then withdraws to her former place, and they both continue to sally and retreat as many times as the variety of passages permits. And take note that these passages are gay but nevertheless strange and fantastic with a strong barbaric flavour. You will learn them from those who are practised in them and you can invent new ones for yourself.
>
> —Thoinot Arbeau, *Orchesography* (1589)

This dance manual's description of the canary, a European courtly dance also popular in England in the late sixteenth century, revels in the dancers' mimesis of exoticized encounters with colonial others: its choreography prescribes that, beginning with the men, the dancers take turns advancing to and retreating from their partners across the dance floor and that their movements embody an Other who is, as Arbeau remarks, "strange and fantastic with a strong barbaric flavour."[1] This French dance historian's professed uncertainty about the origin of the dance produces a transatlantic slippage from the otherness of the Canary Islands to Mauritania to "savages in feathers" in the

Americas.² Not only is it startling to see Europeans constructing their own identity and discourses of courtly grace by acting intentionally "barbaric" in the codified ritual of social dancing, but this dance and conduct manual also surprisingly instructs the dancers to "invent" new barbaric gestures and "passages" in the dance as they go along.³ I take this instruction for Europeans to invent dance choreographies of foreign, racialized others for the consumption of other Europeans as an indication of the ideological work being done in many early modern travel narratives and, more specifically, in accounts of the English establishment of the Virginia colony in the early seventeenth century.

This essay traces the English-authored "choreographies" of racialized and gendered otherness written for the Powhatan woman we know by the name of Pocahontas.⁴ For my purposes here, I use the term *choreography* as a metaphor for the culturally inflected representation and interpretation of literal physical movement through space. Therefore, English choreography of Pocahontas orders her movements, connects them with plausible narrative explanations for an English observer, and names their imagined patterns as mercy, affection, or animosity. John Smith, Ralph Hamor, Samuel Purchas, and John Rolfe, among others, are the first generation to construct not only the meanings of Pocahontas's words but also the significance of her movements through social and geographical spaces. Though in a traditional European kinetic "vocabulary" of confrontations between two hostile groups, *advancing* represents masculine aggression and *retreat* represents a feminized defeat or surrender, English colonial texts characterize Pocahontas's advances toward Englishmen as gestures of a subordinate's friendship, compassion, and aid and her retreats as unsettling signs of independence, rejection, and threat.

Pocahontas helped to build a tenuous political bridge between the English colonizers and her people, especially through her marriage to John Rolfe and her 1616–17 voyage with him and their infant son to the Jacobean court to gain investors for the flagging Virginia Company. Though she never produced her own written narrative, attention to early English texts' choreography of her movements reveals the multiple roles and subject positions into which a colonialist ideology sought to interpellate her: 1) compassionate peacemaker and savior of male English life from violence; 2) generous benefactor and useful pawn to save male English lives from hunger; 3) Christian convert and wife who has internalized patriarchal ideologies of her natural subordination to God and husband; and 4) allegorical "masquer" at court in London in a propaganda performance in which she represented the companionate though unequal political "marriage" between masculine English colonists and feminized American Indians. However, her moving body's trajectories both reproduce *and* reject the discourses that construct her as an eager, loving colonial subject and legitimizing symbol of English colonial wish fulfillment. Occasional discrepancies, particularly Smith's description of her unwelcoming reencounter with him in London, disrupt the coherence of Pocahontas's reported motions and attributed motives because her advances and retreats no longer fit seamlessly into the supportive, subordinate roles assigned to her.

Individual agency expressed through physical movements comprises an integral part of the colonialist myth English writers constructed about Pocahontas. Literary critics and historians have noted how this self-interested mythmaking continued from the seventeenth century through the present day and how it moved from English texts to be woven into (Anglo) America's origin stories about itself.[5] I propose that the English-authored choreography of her bodily movements constitutes another example of what Karen Robertson has called "the various transformational processes performed on Pocahontas to enable her to attend James I's court."[6] A critical reading of these colonial texts must therefore demystify their naturalization of her movements and problematize the knowability of her motives. My interpretive goal is to parse the ways in which a colonial quest for land ownership and political power over its inhabitants informs the discursive representation of literal physical motions.

Physical movements provide a persuasive set of signifiers to which spectators can attribute genuine, transparent, universally legible intention and emotion. In English travel narratives like John Smith's, descriptions of gestures and bodily movement are often used to portray the otherwise inaccessible and unfathomable subjectivity of the indigenous Other. Since the body's movements are nonverbal, they can sustain the illusion of transcending language barriers and lend apparent authenticity to the motivations constructed in and through those very motions. Peter Erickson and Kim F. Hall recently called for scholars of early modern racial formation to "insist that race, as an ideology that organizes human difference and power, is always protean and sticky, attaching to a range of ideologies, narratives, and vocabularies in ways both familiar and strange."[7] In this case, English ideologies of colonial, class, and gender hierarchies, as well as Christian vocabularies of virtue and vice, are mapped onto Pocahontas's physical movements, making the accounts of those movements seem all the more recognizable and normative for the English audiences who read them. Without doubt, Pocahontas's movements of "sally and retreat" in relation to the English colonists corresponded to a constellation of meanings specific to her Algonquian-speaking tribe's culture such as virtue, pragmatism, strength, weakness, courage, love, compromise, and duty, among others.[8]

In the wake of the Virginia colony's increasingly divisive leadership conflicts, a massacre of almost 350 colonists in 1622, and a severe winter of mass starvation in 1623–24, Smith published *The generall historie of Virginia* (1624) to raise English confidence and investment in this colonial project.[9] However, in retelling several episodes from his rougher, briefer description of 1608, *A true relation of such occurences and accidents of note, as hath hapned in Virginia*, Smith added in references to "Emperour" Powhatan's favorite daughter, Pocahontas, in order to dramatize acts of spontaneous generosity and compassion from a charismatic Native American woman.[10] The key episode in the story of Pocahontas focuses on her apparent rescue of John Smith from execution at the hands of her father and his warriors, and in it her physical movements are discursively choreographed to express self-motivated protection for this Englishman. Smith describes her intervention in what he claims was a threat to his life during his captivity by the Powhatan Indians: "Having feasted him after their best barbarous manner they could, a long consultation was held, but the conclusion was, two great stones were brought before Powhatan: then as many as could layd hands on him, dragged him to them, and thereon laid his head, and being ready with their clubs, to beate out his braines, Pocahontas the Kings dearest daughter, when no intreaty could prevaile, got his head in her armes, and laid her owne upon his to save him from death: whereat the Emperour was contented he should live."[11] Today many critics read this episode as Smith's misunderstanding of a ceremonial "death" and adoption into the tribe, especially since he was soon afterwards told by Powhatan that "now they were friends . . . and [he would] for ever esteeme him as his sonne Nantaquoud."[12] However, Smith's narration asserts that Pocahontas's actions represent a mercy that counters and then neutralizes the imminent threat of warriors violently brandishing their clubs above his head.

Smith's *Generall Historie* also includes a letter of introduction he wrote on Pocahontas's behalf to Queen Anna when the Rolfe family traveled to London in 1616. In it, he retells this episode, but this version emphasizes Pocahontas's risk more than his own, dramatically claiming that "she hazarded the beating out of her owne braines to save mine, and not onely that, but so prevailed with her father, that I was safely conducted to James towne."[13] Though Pocahontas was then only a child of about ten or twelve, Smith's narrative choreographs for her an impulsive movement to represent a self-sacrificing motive to shield him, and this dramatic advance toward him characterizes her as a rescuing intercessor who successfully opposes the hostility of her nation's men.[14]

This ethos of Pocahontas's reportedly spontaneous, heroic protection of Smith and his men emerges again in his description of how she later saved him from her father's intended treachery. As in the earlier rescue episode, Smith represents her movement as the transparent expression of an actively compassionate and independently motivated subjectivity:

> Powhatan . . . all this time was making ready his forces to surprise the house and him [Smith] at supper. Notwithstanding the eternall all-seeing God did prevent him, and by a strange meanes. For Pocahontas his dearest jewell and daughter, in that darke night came through the irksome woods, and told our Captaine great cheare should be sent us by and by: but Powhatan . . . would after come

> kill us all, if they that brought it could not kill us with our owne weapons when we were at supper. Therefore if we would live shee wished us presently to bee gone. Such things as shee delighted in, he would have given her: but with the teares running downe her cheekes, shee said shee durst not be seene to have any: for if Powhatan should know it, she were but dead, and so shee ranne away by her selfe as she came.[15]

Not only is "the eternall all-seeing God" protecting the Englishmen, but yet again Pocahontas is represented as God's "instrument" for preserving the colony. Her movement toward Smith through the "irksome" forest foregrounds her resolve and strength, while her decision to risk her father's displeasure or death highlights her bravery. She apparently chooses loyalty to Smith over loyalty to her own father, hence the "strangeness" or irony of her actions of betraying Powhatan's plans to ambush and kill Smith. Her refusal to accept any repayment not only suggests intelligence in concealing her secret and selfless charity, but it also fits into a narrative of a self-sacrificing servant protecting her master for love and not money.

Smith further develops his ideological choreography of Pocahontas's movements when she becomes an interpreter and peacemaker in his account of "A Virginia Mask" or "Mascarado" entertainment presented to him in 1608 by thirty young women, including Pocahontas. Here Smith casts her as the trusted ambassador who calms the Englishmen's fears of an impressive vocalization in the woods before the entertainment: "In a fayr plaine field they made a fire, before which, he sitting upon a mat, suddainly amongst the woods was heard such a hydeous noise and shreeking, that the English betooke themselves to their armes, and seized on two or three old men by them, supposing Powhatan with all his power was come to surprise them. But presently Pocahontas came, willing him to kill her if any hurt were intended."[16] Her confidence as a member of both groups means she can safely approach the four English colonists, who have grabbed old men to hold hostage, kill, or use for shields in the attack they fear is falling upon them. The status and credit she has with Smith also means she can use her own life as a means of negotiation, as when she ostensibly swears he may kill her if she is deceiving him about the "entertainment" he is about to receive.

In his description of the following "mascarado," Smith grants himself kingly status and makes the advances of the dancing women the vehicle of a colonial nightmare-turned-wish-fulfillment fantasy. Whereas his initial interpretation of the event expects the masculine martial advances of "Powhatan with all his power," Pocahontas's reassuring feminine advance transforms the encounter into an ideal one for the Englishmen: the women approach instead to offer honor, hospitality, and pleasing spectacles. Smith's widely circulated description of this event echoes the qualities of English court masques, particularly Ben Jonson's *The Masque of Blackness*, which had been performed in the Jacobean court on January 6, 1605, the year before Smith embarked for Virginia. Pocahontas's actual travel trajectory in 1616 from a potential colony to London and her outward performance of assimilation and obeisance before James I's court parallel those of the fictional Daughters of Niger in *Blackness*. Smith plays the part of the masque's sovereign king-observer whom the dancing women seek to please while affirming his authority.[17] "Pocahontas and her women entertained Captaine Smith," just as Queen Anna entertained King James I with her women courtiers in annual masque performances.[18] Also like contemporary Jacobean courtiers, Pocahontas and the other women performed sustained dancing for "neare an hour" in a large, single-gender group, and Smith describes the thirty female performers as being more naked than usual, as they "came naked out of the woods, onely covered behind and before with a few greene leaves."[19] Furthermore, their bodies were elaborately painted, as were the noblewomen masquers in *The Masque of Blackness*.[20]

After rhetorically elevating himself to the status of a preeminent monarch, Smith subordinates and delegitimizes the women's performance by using European vocabularies of sin and feminine disorder. Calling the performance "an anticke" categorizes it as a fool's or devil-worshipping heathen's performance in Smith's imagination; he interprets the women's dance as embodying the inverse of European court-dance codes in which rigid bodily discipline and geometric formations represented orderly Christian virtues: "These fiends with most hellish shouts and cryes, rushing from among the trees, cast themselves in a ring about the fire, singing and dauncing with most excellent ill varietie, oft falling into their infernall passions."[21] His terms "A Virginia Maske" and "Mascarado" indicate some kind of literal disguising of the face and body and the impersonation of allegorical figures, as a European audience member would understand it.[22] Once he realizes that the show is to entertain him, he emphasizes his enjoyment of it while maintaining that its "most excellent ill varietie" does not meet with his aesthetic approval.

Once Smith's narrative has reestablished the "proper" gender and ethnic hierarchy being signified by the women's initially threatening advance toward him, he choreographs their bodies in a performance of sexualized service. The women's dancing is followed by a kind of orgy of eroticized adulation, in which the "Nymphes more tormented him then [sic] ever, with crowding, pressing, and hanging about him, most tediously crying, Love you not me? love you not me?"[23] In this scene of himself being surrounded by young Indian women begging repetitively for his love, Smith's text presents an allegory of the most ideal devotion an English colonist could wish for in the indigenous American attitudes he encountered in Virginia. He does not mention whether or not he engaged in sexual contact with any of the young women, but his retelling of this encounter represents the women as being the initiators, supplicants, the ones who advance and beg for his attention, rather than the other way around in a traditional European pattern of male approach and solicitation for sexual favors from more passive women.

With similar self-interest, Smith's account of Pocahontas's involuntary captivity continues to portray Pocahontas as a savior of English lives and a loving, easily assimilated colonial subject. When "shee her selfe was taken prisoner, being so detained neere two yeeres longer, the Colonie *by that meanes* was relieved, peace concluded."[24] During this time of being held hostage due to food, prisoner, and trade negotiations, she converted to Christianity and, with Powhatan's permission, married John Rolfe, thereby inaugurating a season of "friendly trade and commerce" with her people.[25] In his letter to Queen Anna, Smith praises her successful assimilation to English beliefs and customs:

"Lady Rebecca, alias Pocahontas, daughter to Powhatan, by the diligent care of Master John Rolfe her husband and his friends, was taught to speake such English as might well bee understood, well instructed in Christianitie, and was become very formall and civill after our English manner; shee had also by him a childe which she loved most dearely."[26] Even when Pocahontas's literal (physical) trajectory in Smith's travel narrative moves her into the heart of the English colony by way of treachery and kidnapping, Smith choreographs this move from one society to another by justifying it as a successful conversion of a heathen into Christianity and a racialized upward mobility of American Indian into a "civilized" English identity.

Smith's colonial choreography or process of ideological invention appears in his letter's speculative proliferation of possible motivations for Pocahontas's movements to aid the English. Though he asserts that her "compassionate pitifull heart . . . gave me much cause to respect her," he raises other possible motivations for her motions on their behalf: "This [food] reliefe, most gracious Queene, was commonly brought us by this Lady Pocahontas, notwithstanding all these passages when inconstant Fortune turned our peace to warre, this tender Virgin would still not spare to dare to visit us, and by her our jarres have beene oft appeased, and our wants still supplyed; were it the policie of her father thus to imploy her, or the ordinance of God thus to make her his instrument, or her extraordinarie affection to our Nation, I know not."[27] Smith introduces three explanations for Pocahontas's allegiance to them: a Machiavellian "policie" of Powhatan, use as a divine instrument of God, or her own autonomous, subjective "extraordinary affection" for Englishmen. Performing his own version of the cultural work Arbeau prescribed for the European canary dancers — to invent new strange and barbaric "passages" across the dance floor — Smith choreographs Pocahontas's "barbarous" motions of apparent love for the English colonists by constructing multiple plausible narrative explanations for them.

Pocahontas's travel to London with her husband and baby raises necessary questions of voluntary and involuntary travel for early modern indigenous people who voyaged to Europe. Scholars like Jace Weaver and Coll Thrush have brought valuable attention to the long history of kidnapped and enslaved Native Americans being brought in ships back to Europe, beginning with the Vikings in 1009.[28] Weaver retraces the trajectory of the Native Americans known as Tisquantum or Squanto and his four fellow captives who were taken by trickery in 1605 to Plymouth England, interrogated by Sir Fernando Gorges and Sir John Popham about their land and people, trained as interpreters, and sent back aboard subsequent ships bent on expanding the English colonial presence in North America.[29] In contrast, of his own will, Powhatan's "personal ambassador" Namontack sailed to London in 1608 and returned to report on it to Powhatan.[30] Somewhere in between these two precursors is Pocahontas's obscured degree of willingness to travel to England. As a woman whose words on the subject were not set down in the English archives, her level of acceptance about embarking on this trip remains "covered" by her husband's patriarchal prerogative; that is, her volition in making this journey is hidden in the same way that, when she married, she became a "femme covert," whose legal identity was incorporated into her husband's.[31] However, Natalie Zemon Davis reminds us of the spectrum of "interactions to look for in the colonial encounter other than the necessary but overpolarized twosome of 'domination' and 'resistance,'" and she urges us to "attribute the capacity for choice to Indians as to Europeans."[32] Although Pocahontas was not enslaved or kidnapped, she was still not entirely free in her choice to travel from her homeland due to her status as an English wife.

Though Pocahontas did not have a formal audience with the king or queen while she was in London, she did meet them, and she was entertained by the Lord Bishop of London, as Samuel Purchas records, "with festivall state and pompe, beyond what I have seene in his great hospitalitie afforded to other Ladies."[33] She was also invited to attend the Twelfth Night court masque by Ben Jonson, *A Vision of Delight* (1617). Her attendance at the masque draws our attention to the hybridity of her identity: like the masquers, she too was dressed in an elaborate costume and was moving and being moved through careful choreographies intended to celebrate English sovereign authority over her. John Chamberlain commented in a January 1617 letter to Dudley Carleton that both she and her father's counselor, Uttamatomakkin, "hath ben with the King and graciously used, and both she and her assistant well placed at the maske. She is on her return (though sore against her will) yf the wind wold come about to send them away."[34] Though it is unlikely that Chamberlain could be accurately informed about her feelings about sailing home, his remark that she was "well-placed" at the masque constitutes a piece of tangible evidence of her importance within the intricate competing hierarchies of the Jacobean court.

Alienating Pocahontas, the Virginia Colony's best diplomatic connection to the powerful Powhatan, came with tangible risks. John Smith's letter to Queen Anna represents Pocahontas as a wholly unique civilized and assimilated "Salvage" whom English monarchs would be wise to befriend to protect future colonial endeavors. Smith writes that "at last rejecting [Pocahontas's] barbarous condition, [she] was maried to an English Gentleman . . . [and is] the first Christian ever of that Nation, the first Virginian ever spake English, or had a childe in mariage by an Englishman."[35] This unique status of belonging to both worlds, according to Smith, gives the English sovereign a potent opportunity to cultivate a productive relationship with a pivotal Native American or to make an enemy of her and, by extension, her people: "if she should not be well received, seeing this Kingdome may rightly have a Kingdome by her meanes; her present love to us and Christianitie, might turne to such scorne and furie, as to divert all this good to the worst of evill."[36] This threat of animosity had profound implications for the fragile English colony in Virginia.

Despite Smith's insistent choreography of her motions and motivations, Pocahontas did not perform all the "movements" prescribed for her by the English. Smith's letter to Queen Anna arguing for a strategically gracious reception of Pocahontas at court immediately precedes Smith's uncharacteristically uncertain description of Pocahontas's silence and withdrawal from him when he met her during her visit to London. Her literal physical retreat from Smith introduces the possibility that her personal rejection would translate to political hostility from her nation. As he writes, "After a modest salutation, without any word, she turned about, obscured her face, as not seeming well contented; and in that humour her husband, with divers others, we all left her two or three houres, repenting my selfe to have writ she could speake English."[37] Smith's initial reading of her silent turning away and covering her face with a discontented demeanor is unsympathetic and self-centered: rather than consider the complexity of her perspective or the possibility of her anger towards him, he worries that her presumed inability to speak English will damage his reputation as an authoritative reporter on the New World in his published writings. However, her reported words reinforce Smith's own warning that her "love" might turn into "scorne and furie."

Smith recounts that the two argue about cultural difference and their social intimacy, distance, and trust, but the subtext is the uncertain future of Powhatan-English relations in Virginia:

> But not long after, she began to talke, and remembred mee well what courtesies shee had done: saying, You did promise Powhatan what was yours should bee his, and he the like to you; you called him father being in his land a stranger, and by the same reason so much I doe you: which though I would have excused, I durst not allow of that title, because she was a Kings daughter; with a well set countenance she said, Were you not afraid to come into my fathers Countrie, and caused feare in him and all his people (but mee) and feare you here I should call you father; I tell you then I will, and you shall call mee childe, and so I will bee for ever your Countrieman. They did tell us alwaies you were dead, and I knew no other till I came to Plimoth; yet Powhatan did command Uttamatomakkin to seeke you, and know the truth, because your Countriemen will lie much."[38]

Smith reports that she insists on calling him "father," which would put her in an intimate and yet subordinate relationship to him, but that he refuses this familiar appellation based on a claim of her higher status as a "Kings daughter." Rhetorically, she renders them equals by evoking their unique mutual experiences as a foreigner in the other's homeland.

However, as soon as she claims she "will bee for ever your Countrieman," she retreats emotionally and makes a political threat when she says "*your* Countriemen will lie much," as is vindicated by her false news of Smith's death and her father's general mistrust of Englishmen's words. This statement of moral condemnation establishes her independence from Smith rather than reproducing his previous construction of her as an adoring subordinate. Furthermore, it raises the disturbing possibility of a political withdrawal of peaceful cooperation and trade by her father and the Powhatan Confederacy's large network that surrounded Jamestown. Whereas in the earlier episodes—the "execution" ritual, the warning of Powhatan's treachery, and the "mask"—Smith represents Pocahontas's advances toward him and other Englishmen as impulsive, risky generosity toward them, her cold demeanor and physical retreat from him in London reverses that kinetic allegory of reaching out to him and his people in compassion, protection, and friendship. In this way, her retreat punctures the myth of her willing subordination to his needs and the myth of her untroubled assimilation into "Englishness."

For an English colonist writing of this new colony between 1605 and 1625, advancing toward a foreign settlement did not necessarily sustain the connotations of masculine aggression, dominance, or superiority. In fact, advancing to the domain of the other culture is also represented as a sign of weakness and dependence. John Rolfe wrote a letter to James I while in London 1616–17 as part of his propaganda campaign to attract investors to the Virginia Company, and as evidence of the colony's newly improved fortunes, he cites a reversal of the initial pattern of advances and retreats between the English and the Native Americans. When threatened with starvation in the early years, the English were forced to approach them: "And whereas heretofore we were constrayned yearelie to goe to the Indians and intreate them to sell vs Corne, w[hi]ch made them esteeme verie basely of vs, Now the case is altered, they seeke to vs, come to our Townes, sell their skins from their Shoulders, w[hi]ch is their best gann[. . .]enth to buy Corne, yea some of their pettie king[es] have this last yeare borrowed 4[00] or 500 bushell[es] of wheate, for payment whereof this harvest they haue mortgaged their Whole Countries some of them not much less in quantitie than a Shire in England."[39] Here English colonial identity is deeply invested in reversing the English need to go to the Powhatans, to be the ones who beg for trade and food. Rolfe's proof of the colony's success is his claim that now this advancing movement is performed by the Powhatans, who come to the English to trade for their desirable goods. This English-authored choreography depicts advancing as a sign of disempowerment and supplication for charity or disadvantageous bargains.

In her disillusioned retreat from Smith, Pocahontas thus refuses that attractive role of colonial subject Smith has assigned her: the one who advances to help him on terms advantageous to him. In addition, Smith notes that Pocahontas's retreat means he has no choice but to go away and be the one to approach her again later. Rolfe's propaganda letter to the king shows how Englishmen's advances toward Native Americans because they want or need something are deeply fraught with fears of disempowerment. If the entire Powhatan Confederacy takes offense and retreats politically from the English colony, as Pocahontas does from Smith in London, withdrawing from the peace and trade established by her marriage to Rolfe, then Jamestown will fail. Such a failure would make it much less possible for the English apologists and promoters of the colony to choreograph or "invent new barbaric passages" that give coherent explanation to the motions and motives of America's indigenes. An indigenous woman's travel and travail is thus central to this story.

Notes

1. Arbeau, *Orchesography*, 179–80.
2. Thoinot Arbeau, the pen name of Jehan Tabourot (1519–95), recorded descriptions of many early modern dances along with the appropriate music and commentary on etiquette. Howard, *Politics*, posits that, in the absence of English dance treatises before 1651, "English references to dancing confirm the adoption of French and Italian styles, and support the relevance of Continental manuals" to English practices (6; cf. Shakespeare, *All's Well That Ends Well*, 2.1.74).
3. Howard notes, *Politics*, that "[i]n most social dances, the couple moved in unison around the hall or danced together in place, but in the *canary*, they repeatedly mimed the moment of encounter . . . mediating event and fantasy to reenact, and simultaneously deny, an imperial narrative" (114).

4. "Pocahontas," no doubt an anglicized attempt to reproduce a Powhatan name, remains the most commonly accessible reference we have for an individual who had the given name Amonute and also apparently revealed her "secret" name, Matoaka, upon her baptism and renaming as Rebecca, later to become Lady Rebecca Rolfe. For details, see Rountree, *Pocahontas*, 37–38; for Algonquin linguistic associations with her names, see Allen, *Pocahontas*, 254–57.
5. Townsend notes how "[w]ith one accord, all these storytellers [of the myth of Pocahontas] subverted her life to satisfy their own need to believe that the Indians loved and admired them (or their cultural forebears) without resentments, without guile" (*Pocahontas*, xi). Tilton traces the evolution of Pocahontas's story in American discourse from the eighteenth through the twentieth centuries and the ways her words of rebuke to Smith in London "like her actions elsewhere, are formulated to serve those telling her story" (*Pocahontas*, 186).
6. Robertson, "Pocahontas," 558.
7. Erickson and Hall, "'New Scholarly Song,'" 12.
8. See Rountree, *Pocahontas*, and Allen, *Pocahontas*, who read the English accounts of Jamestown through the lens of a Native American perspective, undercutting myriad cultural assumptions that the Englishmen make about Pocahontas and her people.
9. For more historical contextualization of Smith's publications, see the introductory material from Barbour in Smith, *Complete Works*, 2:27–32; Barbour, *Pocahontas*; Barbour, *Three Worlds*; Olson-Smith, "Captain John Smith," 47–67; and Emerson, *Captain John Smith*.
10. See Barbour's introduction to this text's complicated publication history in Smith, *Complete Works*, 1:5–22. Critics differ on why Smith did not mention Pocahontas's most memorable actions until the later version: it is possible that they were edited out of his 1608 text without his permission, that he partly or entirely fabricated these episodes, or that he did not deem them significant until 1624.
11. Smith, *Complete Works*, 2:151.
12. Smith, *Complete Works*, 2:151. See Rountree's astute questioning of Smith's key details in this episode, including Pocahontas's participation in it (*Pocahontas*, 67–85); for an interpretation of it as a "mock execution and salvation, in token of adoption into Powhatan's tribe" ceremony, see Barbour, *Pocahontas*, 23–35. Lemay argues against many critics of Smith's veracity to assert that Pocahontas actually did save Smith's life in the "ritual of death, sponsorship, and rebirth [that] is typical of adoption into an Indian tribe" (*Did Pocahontas?*, 63).

13. Smith, *Complete Works*, 2:259.
14. Allen, *Pocahontas*, reads this "rescue" episode from the Algonquin worldview as a ritual rite of rebirth in which Pocahontas played the central powerful role of the "Beloved Woman," the one who confers the "Gift of Life and Death" (51).
15. Smith, *Complete Works*, 2:198–99.
16. Smith, *Complete Works*, 2:182–83.
17. See Orgel (*Jonsonian Masque* and *Illusion of Power*) for the argument that the masque performance depends upon the monarch's gaze.
18. Smith, *Complete Works*, 2:182. Many scholars credit Queen Anna with using these annual masques to do far more significant cultural work than mere "entertainment": see Andrea, "Black Skin"; McManus, *Women on the Renaissance Stage*; Barroll, *Anna of Denmark*; and Knowles, "'To Enlight the Darksome Night.'"
19. Smith, *Complete Works*, 2:183.
20. On the ancient and early modern resonances of painted and natural skin blackness in *Masque of Blackness*, see Smith, *Race and Rhetoric*, 45–58, 69–71, and Iyengar, *Shades of Difference*, 80–86. On the early modern theatrical "prosthetics of race" and the ideological work of "blackening," see Smith, "White Skin, Black Masks."
21. Smith, *Complete Works*, 2:183.
22. Smith, *Complete Works*, 2:182–83.
23. Smith, *Complete Works*, 2:183.
24. Smith, *Complete Works*, 2:259 (my emphasis).
25. Smith, *Complete Works*, 2:246.
26. Smith, *Complete Works*, 2:258.
27. Smith, *Complete Works*, 2:258–59.
28. See also Weaver, *Red Atlantic*; Warren, *New England Bound*; Vaughan, *Transatlantic Encounters*; Taylor, *Buying Whiteness*; and Foreman, *Indians Abroad* on early modern Native Americans who were coerced or misled into taking transatlantic voyages before, during, and after Pocahontas's lifetime.
29. Weaver, *Red Atlantic*, 57–60.
30. Weaver, *Red Atlantic*, 146.
31. Bunker summarizes the legal effects of marriage for a woman: "Upon marriage, a single woman, *femme sole*, became a *femme covert*, 'coverture' being the term established for the husband and wife as one person in law: during the marriage the woman's legal existence was suspended, and she was consolidated into that of her husband and his protection" (*Marriage and Land Law*, 227).

32. Davis, "Iroquois Women," 243.
33. Purchas, *Hakluytus Posthumus*, 4:1774.
34. Chamberlain, *Letters*, 2:50.
35. Smith, *Complete Works*, 2:259–60.
36. Smith, *Complete Works*, 2:260.
37. Smith, *Complete Works*, 2:261.
38. Smith, *Complete Works*, 2:261.
39. Rolfe, Letter to King James, 4v–5r.

Bibliography

Allen, Paula Gunn. *Pocahontas: Medicine Woman, Spy, Entrepreneur, Diplomat*. New York: Harper Collins, 2004.

Andrea, Bernadette. "Black Skin, the Queen's Masques: Africanist Ambivalence and Feminine Author(ity) in the Masques of *Blackness* and *Beauty*." *English Literary Renaissance* 29, no. 3 (1999): 246–81.

Arbeau, Thoinot. *Orchesography*. Translated by Mary Stewart Evans. New York: Dover, 1967.

Barbour, Philip. *Pocahontas and Her World*. Boston: Houghton Mifflin, 1970.

———. *The Three Worlds of Captain John Smith*. Boston: Houghton Mifflin, 1964.

Barroll, Leeds. *Anna of Denmark, Queen of England*. Philadelphia: University of Pennsylvania Press, 2001.

Bunker, Nancy Mohrlock. *Marriage and Land Law in Shakespeare and Middleton*. Madison NJ: Fairleigh Dickinson University Press, 2014.

Chamberlain, John. *Letters of John Chamberlain*, edited by Norman Egbert McClure. Vol. 2. Philadelphia: American Philosophical Society, 1939.

Davis, Natalie Zemon. "Iroquois Women, European Women." In *Women, "Race," and Writing in the Early Modern Period*, edited by Margo Hendricks and Patricia Parker, 243–58. London: Routledge, 1994.

Emerson, Everett. *Captain John Smith*. New York: Twayne, 1993.

Erickson, Peter, and Kim F. Hall. "'A New Scholarly Song': Rereading Early Modern Race." *Shakespeare Quarterly* 67, no. 1 (2016): 1–13.

Foreman, Carolyn Thomas. *Indians Abroad, 1493–1938*. Norman: University of Oklahoma Press, 1943.

Hamor, Ralph. *A True Discovrse on the Present Estate of Virginia*. London, 1615.

Howard, Skyles. *The Politics of Courtly Dancing in Early Modern England*. Amherst: University of Massachusetts Press, 1998.

Iyengar, Sujata. *Shades of Difference: Mythologies of Skin Color in Early Modern England*. Philadelphia: University of Pennsylvania Press, 2005.

Knowles, James. "'To Enlight the Darksome Night, Pale Cinthia Doth Arise': Anna of Denmark, Elizabeth I, and the Images of Royalty." In *Women and*

Culture at the Courts of the Stuart Queens, edited by Clare McManus, 21–48. New York: Palgrave Macmillan, 2003.

Lemay, J. A. Leo. *Did Pocahontas Save Captain John Smith?* Athens: University of Georgia Press, 1992.

McManus, Clare. *Women on the Renaissance Stage: Anna of Denmark and Female Masquing in the Stuart Court.* Manchester: Manchester University Press, 2002.

Olson-Smith, Steven. "Captain John Smith." In *The Oxford Handbook of Early American Literature*, edited by Kevin Hayes, 47–67. Oxford: Oxford University Press, 2008.

Orgel, Stephen. *The Illusion of Power: Political Theater in the English Renaissance.* Berkeley: University of California Press, 1975.

———. *The Jonsonian Masque.* Cambridge: Harvard University Press, 1965.

Purchas, Samuel. *Pvrchas his Pilgrimage.* London, 1614.

———. *Hakluytus Posthumus, or Purchas His Pilgrimes*, 4 vols. London, 1625.

Ralegh, Sir Walter. *The Discovery of Guiana*, edited by Benjamin Schmidt. Boston: Bedford/St. Martin's, 2008.

Robertson, Karen. "Pocahontas at the Masque." *Signs: A Journal of Women in Culture and Society* 21, no. 3 (1996): 551–83.

Rolfe, John. Letter to King James I, ca. 1617, British Library Royal MS 18 A XI, 4r.

Rountree, Helen. *Pocahontas, Powhatan, Opechancanough: Three Indian Lives Changed by Jamestown.* Charlottesville: University of Virginia Press, 2005.

Shakespeare, William. *The Riverside Shakespeare.* Boston: Houghton Mifflin, 1974.

Smith, Ian. *Race and Rhetoric in the Renaissance: Barbarian Errors.* New York: Palgrave Macmillan, 2009.

———. "White Skin, Black Masks: Racial Cross-Dressing on the Early Modern Stage." *Renaissance Drama* 32 (2003): 33–67.

Smith, John. *The Complete Works of Captain John Smith.* 3 vols. Edited by Philip Barbour. Chapel Hill: University of North Carolina Press, 1986.

Strachey, William. *The Histoire of Travaile into Virginia Britania.* Edited by R. H. Major. London: Hakluyt Society, 1849.

Taylor, Gary. *Buying Whiteness: Race, Culture, and Identity from Columbus to Hip-Hop.* New York: Palgrave Macmillan, 2003.

Thrush, Coll. *Indigenous London: Native Travelers at the Heart of Empire.* New Haven: Yale University Press, 2016.

Tilton, Robert. *Pocahontas: The Evolution of an American Narrative.* Cambridge: Cambridge University Press, 1994.

Townsend, Camilla. *Pocahontas and the Powhatan Dilemma.* New York: Hill and Wang, 2004.

Vaughan, Alden. *Transatlantic Encounters: American Indians in Britain, 1500–1776*. Cambridge: Cambridge University Press, 2006.

Warren, Wendy. *New England Bound: Slavery and Colonization in Early America*. New York: Liveright Publishing, 2016.

Weaver, Jace. *The Red Atlantic: American Indigenes and the Making of the Modern World, 1000–1927*. Chapel Hill: University of North Carolina Press, 2014.

Fig. 1. Sandro Botticelli, *Venus and Mars*, ca. 1485. (Courtesy of the National Gallery, London)

Fig. 2. The Santa Casa and Madonna di Loreto, *The history of our B. Lady of Loreto*. Saint-Omer, 1608. (Courtesy of the Harry Ransom Center, University of Texas at Austin)

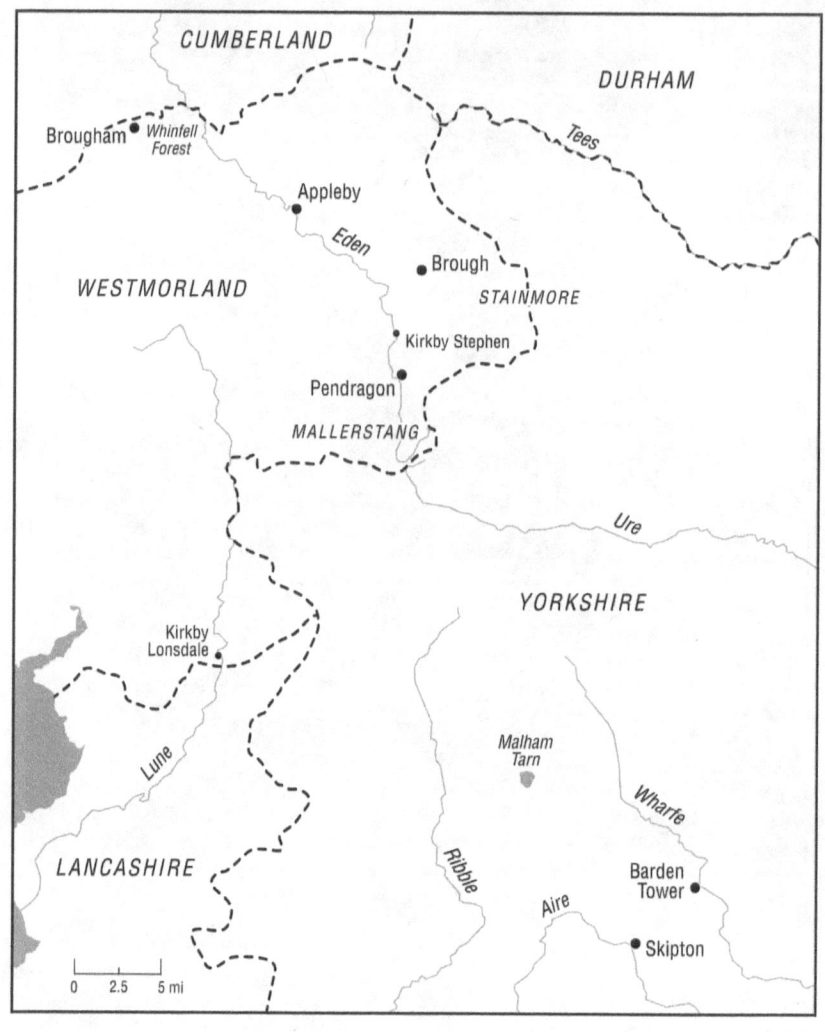

Fig. 3. Map depicting the lands and properties of Lady Anne Clifford's inheritance in northern England. (Map by Erin Greb, 2017)

Fig. 4. Map of England depicting Lady Anne Clifford's many residences and properties. (Map by Erin Greb, 2017)

Fig. 5. Natural history cabinet. Ferrante Imperato, *Dell'historia naturale*,

Naples, 1599. (Courtesy of Getty Research Institute)

8

Lady Anne Clifford's Way and Aristocratic Women's Travel

LAURA WILLIAMSON AMBROSE

Despite decades of uncertainty stemming from legal battles over an extensive land inheritance, Lady Anne Clifford (1590–1676) left a lasting and layered cultural legacy: literary, historical, artistic, architectural, and geographic. She was a prolific self-documenter, writing, dictating, and commissioning annual summaries (1603, 1650–75), diaries (1616–19), *The Great Picture* portrait (1646), a formal autobiography (1652), the "Day Book" diary (1676), and the *Great Books of Record*, an impressive three-volume collection of evidence in support of her family's dynastic lineage.[1] Clifford is also one of the era's greatest landowners, eventually inheriting and restoring five castles and a tower in Westmoreland and Yorkshire Counties after they had been heavily damaged during the Civil War: Brougham, Appleby, Brough, Pendragon, Skipton, and Barden Tower (fig. 3). Her decades in the great country houses of Knole House in Kent (with her first husband, Richard Sackville) and Wilton House in Wiltshire (with her second husband, Philip Herbert) extended Clifford's geographic reach south to London and its environs (fig. 4). Collectively, then, Clifford's vast network of estates and extensive archive produced an impressive and wide-reaching footprint, one that impressed itself upon both the landscape and the literary output of seventeenth-century England.

But it is to contemporary footprints that I would like to turn. An official walking route in northwestern England—aptly titled "Lady Anne's Way"—covers more than one hundred miles, connecting Clifford's various estates and monuments from Skipton in the south to Brougham in the north.[2] By its very name, Lady Anne's Way calls up an early modern lexicon whereby "way" designated a specific kind of thoroughfare as well as a general trajectory through space.[3] Of course, promises to follow in Clifford's "footsteps" are laden with anachronisms, the most obvious of which is mode of transport. As an aristocratic woman, Clifford almost certainly never walked the length of this route, electing instead to travel by horse litter or her "coach and six [horses]" in the company of a dozen or more servants. Nonetheless, the connection to Clifford's lived experience with Lady Anne's Way is more than a marketing ploy. It is, in fact, steeped in layers of material and historical reality. Despite the centuries that divide this walking path from Clifford's own progresses, the modern-day pilgrimage to Penrith draws directly from key aspects of her life and writing, reminding us that Lady Anne Clifford was, as I will argue, one of the seventeenth century's most significant female travelers and travel writers. Clifford did not simply own these properties: she visited them regularly, passing through the countryside an average of every few months for more than twenty-five years between the ages of sixty and eighty-six.

This article looks to these paths, to Lady Anne's seventeenth-century "way" with two purposes in mind: first, the *way* or the road emphasizes spatial practice over place (that which is en route rather than in situ); and, second, it surfaces the discursive patterns that are distinct to each of her texts, each *way* Clifford records, represents, and remembers mobility throughout her life. Doing so, I propose, helps diversify the story we tell of early modern female travelers, one which often recycles narratives of stasis, reading sixteenth- and seventeenth-century women as immobile and confined to the domestic sphere as a result of political, social, or religious restrictions.[4] This essay provides one counternarrative to women's relationships to mobility in the early modern period by examining Clifford's own patterns of mobility and writing throughout her life. Both forms of travel and forms of travel writing, I suggest, tell us about the manner in which she and, by extension, other aristocratic women made meaning of their movements through space in the seventeenth century. For Clifford, the decision to move or not to move became both a literal and a symbolic mechanism for exercising autonomy. It was how she had—and made—her way.

Lady Anne Clifford's early years were spent close to court. Her father, George Clifford, third Earl of Cumberland, was a well-known privateer and adventurer and a high-ranking favorite of Queen Elizabeth I. Her mother, Countess Margaret Russell Clifford, also had strong ties to the Elizabethan court, as her father was one of the queen's privy councilors. In 1605 however, Lady Anne's father died, leaving everything to his brother rather than his only living child, Anne. In response, her mother, highly intelligent and of a "most brave spirit," began building a case for her daughter's inheritance.[5] For the next thirty-eight years, Lady Anne was embroiled in legal suits, subjected to intimidation tactics from countless officials (including King James I), and involved in many disagreements with both her first husband, Richard Sackville (third Earl of Dorset; married in 1609, died in 1624) and her second, Philip Herbert (fourth Earl of Pembroke; married in 1630, died in 1650).[6] Through all of this—including the birth of five children (only two of whom survived) and after outliving both husbands—Clifford stayed her course and eventually acquired the rights to her lands in the north after her male cousin, Henry Clifford, died in 1643, leaving her the only surviving heir at the age of fifty-three.

Six years later, in the summer of 1649, with the Civil War still raging and only six months after the beheading of King Charles I, Clifford was finally able to leave the safety of London for her beloved northern estates, never again to see London or her second husband (who died shortly after her departure). In an entry for 1649, she briefly remarks on the journey that took her more than two hundred miles in just a week,

> by easy journeys on ye road I came to Skypton ye 18th day of ye month [of July] into my Castle there. . . . About ye 28th of ye month I went into ye decayed Tower at Barden, it being ye 1st time I was ever in ye Tower; and so I continued to lye in Skypton till ye 7th of ye month following. . . . So the 8th day of August in 1649 I came into Appleby Castle ye most aunciest seat of myne inheritance, and lay in my own chamber there.[7]

In a characteristic mode for Clifford—one I will examine in greater detail below—she systematically lists three of her six key properties as well as how long she stays at each site in a kind of spatial and temporal gathering in (three properties, eight months) as if to highlight her rightful place in both space and time, situated firmly and proudly as she is in her "aunciett seat of . . . inheritance." Absent of any chorographical, geographical, or even experiential detail, Clifford nonetheless imbues this journey—or, rather, this series of journeys—with a sense of purpose with a gloss at the conclusion of the passage, "So various are ye pilgrimages of this human life." While the line is clearly meant to give shape and significance to her journeys in the north, it also alludes to the six decades that preceded her journey: years rife with the sort of struggle and mobility emblematic of a pilgrimage. Clifford's life was, from beginning to end, infused with great periods of movement and stasis, habitation and circulation.

We know this, of course, because Clifford wrote, referenced, and dictated documents throughout her adult life, leaving a wealth of material, including letters, genealogical histories, records of ownership, and, of course, tomes of life writing. As Katherine Acheson has pointed out, scholars working on Clifford's life writing in particular have erroneously grouped these documents together as "diaries."[8] Acheson has attempted to correct for this homogenization, most notably in the distinctions she draws in titling the 1603 text a "memoir" and the 1616–19 documents "diaries": the "memoir" accounts for the year in summary, while the diaries seem to capture a day, still not in real time but certainly closer to it.[9] Acheson also rightly surmises that the diaries were most likely not written with the intention of public viewing and functioned instead as a sort of resource for Clifford's annual summaries, a point which is supported by the fact that marginalia in the diaries offer addenda (rather than commentary) to the original record.[10] The yearly summaries of her later years (1650–75) appear in the three-volume *Great Books of Record* along with the formal autobiography of 1652 (covering conception to 1643 in a more narrative style than her other "public" works of life writing) and the detailed 1676 "Day Book" diary, which was transcribed by

Clifford's secretary during her last months.¹¹ Jessica Malay has recently pointed out how closely Clifford worked with this *Great Books* project, annotating documents and guiding her scribes as she reviewed their transcriptions of various genealogical, antiquarian, and legal texts.¹² Despite such direct involvement and oversight, Clifford's own hand is conspicuously absent from her life writing: the 1603 and 1616–19 texts are eighteenth- and nineteenth-century transcriptions, and the 1652, 1650–75, and 1676 texts held in the *Great Books*, while contemporary to Clifford's own life, contain records in several different hands (either from dictation or transcription).

This brief overview of Clifford's corpus highlights, among other things, three important facts. First, Clifford's documents are part of a network of texts, few of which were designed as self-standing records; instead one set of documents might serve as a resource for another as a memory aid, a record of an event, or even a draft. Recognizing this intertextuality might help explain, for example, the remarkable dominance or absence of certain details in one set of records as compared to another. Why, for example, does travel fade into the background of her autobiography but become the modus operandi of each annual summary for the last twenty-five years of her life, even in periods where she was writing in both forms? Second, Clifford's patterns of record and use of particular textual forms occur throughout her life, not as a sudden burst of scholarly energy before or after the age of sixty. Third, the trouble with the term "diary" that Acheson and others have noted is similar, I would suggest, to the issues raised by the phrase "travel writing." If we look to Clifford's texts for accounts of discovery, adventure, or even local flora, fauna, and architectural wonders, the record is silent. With an Elizabethan privateer as a father and a mother who invested in both the East India Company and the Virginia Company, Clifford was certainly no stranger to narratives of foreign travel and accounts of voyaging. But her particular domestic experiences of travel required a different set of tropes, textual forms, and discourses. How, then, might we examine Clifford's systematic, ritualistic, and domestic perambulations as *travel*?

It is this last question that gives shape to my critical approach, as I read Clifford's corpus as an extensive collection of travel records rather than through the lens of biography, antiquarian studies, and architectural or legal history. In the scholarship on Clifford, the first few decades of her life and the texts associated with that era—her annual summary of 1603, diaries of 1616–19, the triptych portrait of 1646, and the autobiography of 1652—have garnered a great deal of attention, containing, as they do, references to her legal battles, the deaths of her parents, the births and deaths of her children, her tumultuous marriages, interactions with monarchs, personal and emotional struggles, illness, visits to famous aristocratic families, and political events. Self-fashioning, political agency, legal discourse, and gender, have, understandably served as the focal points in these studies.[13] By contrast, scholarship on architecture, space, and the relationship between Clifford's discursive and built projects tend to cohere around her years in the north (1649–76), where both her textual output and her lived experience draw more attention to mobility and the built environment.[14] This is by no means a steadfast division, nor is it one I would necessarily critique. But this trend is noteworthy for the ways it unintentionally reinforces ideas about travel, gender, and writing—as if Clifford did not *really* travel until she covered great distances over rough terrain after 1649. With the exception of Stephanie Elsky's nuanced examination of Clifford's habit of walking during her time at Knole House, mobility is generally the focus of Clifford's *later* writings. This, I would argue, is largely the product of a tendency to distinguish between modes of mobility, to separate acts of walking or coach riding (particularly on one's own estate and by women especially) from acts of travel.

Further inscribing this scholarly focus is Clifford's habit of mobility or, perhaps more important still, her habit of recording that mobility in those later years when she repeats the various legs of her progresses between estates over and over and *over*. As Anne M. Myers points out, "Many critics have understandably found such passages inhospitable to interpretation, and indeed after reading a year or two of the diary it is difficult not to skip over them in search of something more sensational, or at least less soporific."[15] I concur, or, rather, I sympathize. But, like Myers and Megan Matchinske, both of whom recognize the value of that which lurks beneath such seemingly tiresome repetition,

I read this recurrence as a central paradigm of Clifford's travel record, one which yokes mobility and geographic space to memory. In what follows, and in an effort to link Clifford's early experiences of travel with her later processions between her estates, I will focus on two aspects of her mobility: first, the relationship between movement, stasis, and agency between 1603 and 1649, and, second, Clifford's unique use of verbal mapping and its connection to memory from 1650 to 1676.

Moving Her Way: 1603–49

Long before her life was marked by regular circuits between her northern estates, Clifford's youth swirled with movement. In large part, this mobility was a feature of her aristocratic upbringing. Her 1603 account brims with references to a thirteen-year-old's journeys to and from court, visits to relatives, or stopovers at the homes of high-standing acquaintances as she, her parents, and hundreds of others attended the newly appointed King James I and Queen Anne on their progresses. For example, when her aunt of Warwick desires to meet Queen Anne in an effort to garner favor as the new queen travels south from Scotland in the summer of 1603, Clifford and her mother follow her to Coventry, though a bit later:

> My mother and I should have gone with them, but that her horses, which she borrowed of Mr Elmers . . . were not ready; yet I went the same night and overtook my aunt at Tyttenhanger, my Lady Blount's house, where my mother came the next day to me about noon, my aunt being gone. Then my mother and I went on our journey to overtake her, and killed three horses that day of extreme of heat and came to Wrest, my Lord of Kent's, where we found the doors shut and none in the house but one servant who only had the keys of the hall, so that we were enforced to lie in the hall all night, till towards morning at which time came a man and let us into the higher rooms, where we slept three or four hours. This morning we hasted away betimes and came that night to Rockingham Castle where we overtook my aunt of Warwick and her company.[16]

From the standpoint of an itinerary, Clifford and her mother journey more than ninety miles north, making just two stops at "Tyttenhanger" and "my Lord of Kent's"—indeed, should this trip have taken place forty-seven years later, Clifford's record of it may have been limited to those details alone. Here though, we are privy to so much more: the dependence on and practice of borrowing horses for each leg of a journey (since even a horse could only travel twenty to thirty miles a day and often needed to be rested for twenty four hours before embarking again); the earnestness with which these women move, such that they "killed three horses that day of extreme heat" in their determination to "overtake" her aunt; and an arrival so late they were forced to "lie in the hall all night" and set off the next morning with only "three or four hours" sleep. Clifford, even at a young age, was no stranger to covering significant distances in a day's journey and to recording such a feat with marked nonchalance.

If this earliest record of 1603 reminds us of the ubiquity of aristocratic domestic mobility in Clifford's youth, her diaries from 1616–19 introduce a new element, one that alters both the course and the frequency with which she travels: her husband, Richard Sackville. This first marriage, although not an entirely unhappy one, was troubled by Sackville's gambling, affairs, and heated disagreements over her northern inheritance.[17] When one reads the diaries with travel in mind, a pattern emerges in which Clifford's movements—or lack thereof—serve as a barometer for her agency. One of the clearest examples of this occurs between March and June of 1616. The story runs thus: in exchange for agreeing to discuss the issue of her inheritance with her mother, she was "given leave" to embark on a journey to visit her at Brougham Castle (fig. 4). The journey north from February 21 to March 1 was arduous, involving a coach that nearly toppled over (it needed to be carried down a hill) and a horse that fell off a bridge into the river.[18] Only one month later, angered by her refusal to agree to terms of her inheritance that would benefit him, Sackville sent for his servants, demanding they leave Clifford at her mother's and return south without her, if need be. After "two nights [in which] my mother and I lay together and had much talk about this business" and despite multiple efforts to "entreat them [the servants] to stay," Clifford acquiesced to her husband's will and went "after my folks in my Lady's coach, she bringing me a quarter of a mile in the way where she and I had a heavy and grievous parting. Most part of the way I did rid[e] on horseback behind Mr Hodgson."[19] This abrupt, upsetting departure marks the last time—and the last place—Clifford saw her mother, a fact she memorializes with the installation of the Countess's Pillar in 1654, a monument and memory that I will examine in more detail below.

What is notable in this account is the way in which Clifford's grief is grafted onto mobility and onto her inability to regulate that mobility. This is not simply a symbolic or retrospective representation of grief as is the case in an account of the event from 1652: "I took my last leave of my dear and blessed mother with many tears and much sorrow to us both . . . after which time she and I never saw one another . . . for then I went . . . towards London and so to Knole House in Kent . . . to my first and then only child, the Lady Margaret, and her father."[20] Indeed, much of this summative reflection from 1652 follows the exact itinerary from the 1616 diary (the stop in London before Knole, the date of arrival, the initial sight of her daughter), but it diverges from the original by substituting the real reason for Clifford's grief—being physically wrenched away by her husband—with "tears and much sorrow" that seem more symbolic than particular.[21] If Clifford's later account of this event in her autobiography downplays both her mobility and her husband's role in this sorrow, it is for strategic reasons: this document was to serve as a record of her family's dynasty, and Sackville was part of that history. The diary account of a twenty-six-year-old woman, however, provides crucial insight into the reality of Clifford's life on the ground: her battles for agency were quite literally exercised over geographic terrain.

If the tumult of this period is both exacerbated and reflected by journeys that were both initiated and terminated entirely by her husband, then Clifford's periods of stasis, too, speak volumes as indicators of her struggle. As Elsky and Susan Wiseman have pointed out, these periods also generate new practices of spatial and political agency.[22] In other words, if Sackville enacted his control over expansive geographic range, Clifford mastered more localized maneuvers. Early on, Lady Anne's lack of mobility and isolation seem oppressive and bleak, in direct contrast to the sense of connectedness she seems to achieve "abroad" (a word she uses to describe any movement outside the interior of the home on walks or visits). For example, after returning from her northern journey to see her mother, Clifford is both strikingly isolated—Sackville has, in retaliation, sent her daughter away—and stationary, as she has elected to stay in the country "being condemned by most folks because I would not consent to the agreements, so I may truly say I am like an owl in the desert."[23] Her stasis is especially pronounced as she continues to account for the journeys of those around her (a habit she maintains throughout her later writings): visits, departures, returns, and journeys by coach, barge, or horse. Three years later, though, this stasis takes on a different tone. From October 1619 to March 1620, Clifford refuses to leave her chamber, a decision that, at least initially, stems from an illness related to pregnancy, but eventually the isolation carries the air of decisiveness: "my Lord came and supped with me in my chamber . . . for I determined to keep my chamber and did not so much as go over the threshold of the door."[24] This shift from a sense of helpless isolation to intentional stasis is evident at earlier points as well when she reflects that "though I kept my chamber altogether, yet methinks the time is not so tedious to me as when I used to be abroad."[25] Clifford's resolve and ability to hold steadfast within the interior of her chamber parallels her determination to hold onto her estates. Refusing to move, it seems, is as compelling a choice as moving at all, whether throughout the countryside or in the gardens of her estate.

Clifford's power to recast her social and physical isolation is especially pronounced in the years between 1642 and 1649, when she was forced to stay inside Baynard Castle in London for a period of "6 yeares & 9 monthes, which was ye longest time I continued to lye in all my life, the Civill Warres being then very hot in England."[26] As a Royalist, these were especially tumultuous times for Clifford, and she relied on the protection and cover provided by her second husband Philip Herbert and his support of the Parliamentarian cause.[27] The extremes of this existence—with its juxtaposition of privilege and lack of power, activity and isolation—is captured in Clifford's autobiography when she reflects on her marital years: "the marble pillars of Knole in Kent and Wilton in Wiltshire were to me often times but the gay arbour of anguish.... I lived in both these my lords' great families as the river of Roan or Rodamus runs through the lake of Geneva, without mingling any part of its streams with that lake; for I gave myself wholly to retiredness, as much as I could, in both those great families, and made good books and virtuous thoughts my companions."[28] Clifford articulates a sense of entrapment through both architectural and geographic terms: she is surrounded by built pillars and a lake. Unable to engage the body, she engages the mind in "retiredness" and "virtuous thoughts," all through a metaphor of movement in the flowing river. Given such isolation within Baynard, it is not surprising that, despite calling the castle her "refuge," Clifford fled its walls at her first opportunity in 1649, setting a firm course north toward her inheritance and toward what was to be her most mobile period yet.

Mapping Her Way: 1650–1676

Clifford's journeys to and from her northern estates beg comparison to two forms of ceremonial movement: perambulations and progresses. Indeed, one of Clifford's first items of business once she settled at Skipton in 1650 was "in Causeing the Boundaries to be ridden" and then again a year later in 1651, but this time farther north at Appleby: "about this Aprill and May in one thousand six hundred fiftie and one were the Bounderyes ridden for mee in my Landes here in Westmerland."[29] This, of course, was a longstanding tradition in which village or parish elite physically walked or rode the perimeter of a piece of property as a means of affirming and reinscribing boundaries in the landscape and in the collective memory. Elsky has argued, too, that these perambulations might in fact be directly born of Clifford's familiarity with common law and its emphasis on habitual custom, whether in walking through space or engaging in repetitive writing practices—both of which Clifford exercises.[30] Nonetheless, the vast majority of Clifford's habitual movements are not peripheral but rather transversal: they are not about "bounds" at all. Instead, Clifford's journeys proceed *through* her land with particular destinations in mind and along repeated routes.

Accompanied by servants and welcomed by neighbors as she processed through towns and into castles, Clifford's movements also echo the royal summer progresses of the Elizabethan and Jacobean monarchs: in 1668, "The 26th of June in this yeare ... did I remove from thence in my Horslitter, (my women riding in my Coach drawn with six Horses, and my Menservants on horseback)," and in 1670, "I came safe and well I thank God into my Castle of Brougham in the same Countie about 3 a clock in the afternoon, and bin accompanied hither by severall of the Gentrys of this Countie and my Neighbours and Tenants."[31] Records from an account book in 1665 indicate that she had four wagons, more than thirty carts, horses, and twenty-one cartloads of goods.[32] And, of course, like the processing sovereigns who inhabited great estates as *owners* not as guests, Clifford was no guest on these journeys, a point reiterated in the litany of possessive pronouns and references to "mine" inheritance. There are some notable differences, though. Absent here are the great entertainments that punctuate the legs of a monarch's journey. Moreover, Clifford's choice of language sets her practice apart: she insists on referring to these habitual journeys as "removes." While the term is not entirely unique in the lexicon of departures and returns in the seventeenth century, its usage in texts of travel is less common.[33] Others — relatives, visitors, important political figures — take journeys; Clifford embarks on *removes*. She reserves this term to describe *her way* of moving, a way that downplays actual spatial practice in favor of location and duration. Even as the very word invokes movement (re-move), it seems to prioritize the nodal points of a journey (to remove something or someone from *here* to *there*). This term, I would argue, is consistent with Clifford's overall way of writing travel, one which reads like punctuated points on a map rather than a narrative of travel.

What of these verbal maps? What exactly are Clifford's habits of writing travel? For one, they are highly repetitive. Each of the twenty-six annual summaries contains not one but several accounts of removes. For the year 1654, she provides details for three distinct removes, each of which is then followed by more entries accounting for noteworthy events, visits from family, births, baptisms, etc. In other words, the entries proceed both *in* order — "And the eighth day of this month" followed by "For the ninth day of this month"—and *out* of order—"I now continued to lye in the Round Roome... till the second day of August" followed by "The twentie sixte day of May."[34] Matchinske has noted this disorienting organizational paradigm as well as the use of a repetitive diurnal form in Clifford's travelogue, one she sees as "accomodat[ing] Clifford's obsessive need for serial justification," even as it "does not embrace time as sequence, as one thing after another."[35] I would add that while the texts may not employ a strictly diurnal logic, they exhibit a deep investment in sequence, albeit one that gives equal weight to spatial and temporal logics. In other words, it is not so much that Clifford's summaries proceed without time as a structuring mechanism, but they do so only after incorporating *geographic* order. In what follows, I have recast the annual summary of 1654 in terms of a calendar adding monthly headings and omitting all details not concerning her removes):

> *March 18* [entries omitted]
> *April 11–August 2:* "I removed from Brougham Castle in Westmerland, and lay by the way att Kirkby Lonsdale, and came the next day to Skipton, to lye there againe in it after I had layne in Westmerland without removing out of that Countie, for a yeare and four months. And soe I now continue to lye in the Round Roome whereof I used to lye, till the second day of August following that I came back again into Westemerland."
> *May 26, June 5, 8, 9, 22, July 5, August 2* [entries omitted]
> *August 2 (with a flashback to April 12)–August 25:* "I and my family removed from my house and Castle of Skipton in Craven into Kirkby Lonsdale where I lay in the Inne there all night, and the next day (being the third) I came into Appleby Castle in Westmerland after I had layne there in Skipton Castle from the twelfth day of Aprill last till now. And I continued to lie in Appleby Castle till the five and twentieth of this month, that I removed to Brougham Castle."
> *August 12* [entries omitted]
> *August 25–January 8, 1655:* "I removed from Appleby Castle with my familie into my Castle of Brougham in Westmerland, where I

now cotinewed to lye till the eight of January following, when I removed from thence back againe to Appleby Castle."
September 2, 17 [entries omitted]³⁶

If one looks to the first date in the sequence, particularly for the three removes (April 11, August 2, August 25), the entire year proceeds in perfect chronological order, March to September, 1 to 30. However, the travel passages themselves diverge from this logic, incorporating time past and time future—where a reference to August occurs in the account for April, for example—in an effort to locate Clifford first and foremost in space. Time loops in these instances, bending and folding in on itself to enclose a particular geographic location. With each of these accounts, Clifford marks her "way" by superimposing diurnal sequencing with the spatial logic of an itinerary, resembling a thread that occasionally loops back before once again straightening. Temporal digressions are incorporated into the master diurnal order. In other words, it is not as if temporal logic is abandoned for these journeys; Clifford takes great care to include the length of time of each stay ("till the eight of January following"). Instead, she integrates the two systems, moving between a spatial, itinerant logic and a diurnal one. These removes function, I would argue, as spatial memory markers, small clues or discursive headings that seem to say, *for everything that follows until next January, picture this castle, this chamber, this landscape.* Mobility, then, becomes the primary means through which Clifford organizes and remembers her life.

As Clifford's early years make evident, mobility is not simply experienced on the road. According to Elizabeth Chew, Clifford used movement through the interior spaces of her restored castles to emphasize "her attainment of the spatial position of the owner of the central apartment."³⁷ These records of interior mobility also capture the connection *between* internal and external spaces. In 1671 Clifford provides a highly detailed itinerary of her movements within the castle:

did I go for a little while out of it into the Roome adjoining, being the middle Roome in ye great Pagan Tower . . . and so came into my owne Chamber again, where, after a short stay I went from thence about 11 a clock of the same day through the little Passage Roome and the Painted Chamber and the Hall down into ye garden for a while, and from thence back into ye Court of ye Castle, where I took my Horslitter in which I ridd by ye pillar that I erected in memory of my last parting there with my Blessed Mother, and so through part of Whinfield Park to Julian Bower; and from thence out of ye Park I went over Eden Bridge and through the Townes of Temple Sowerby, Kirbythure and Crackenthorp, and down the Step Stones and over Appleby Bridge and near ye Church, and through Appleby Towne I came safe and well (I thank God) into my Castle of Appleby . . . about 4 a clock in the afternoon."[38]

This is not only the performative, ceremonial spatial practice of household status. It is also an account of *wandering*—between rooms, to the garden, back to the "Court of ye Castle." Indeed, the remove itself begins in these interior chambers not outside in her "Horslitter." In other words, Clifford intentionally links her experience wandering between castle rooms with the more official embarkation of her entourage outside the castle gate. All stages, all spaces, and all practices of mobility register as equally significant and, perhaps most compellingly, connected in an overall spatial system.

Clifford's emphasis on her many removes and the detail she provides regarding the various interior and exterior legs of her journey reminds us of two facts: first, that the buildings were intricately connected to the surrounding landscape, and, second, that these linkages were forged through spatial practice. The Countess's Pillar, referenced in the aforementioned remove for 1671, serves as a case in point. The pillar was commissioned in 1654 by Clifford in memory of her "last parting" with her mother some thirty-eight years earlier. Incorporated as the monument was into the landscape (just one quarter mile south of Brougham castle on her regular route toward Whinfield Forest), the Countess's Pillar, I would suggest, functioned not simply as a monument to her mother but as a way for Clifford to literally and figuratively shape her own relationship with Brougham Castle. It served as a kind of signpost not only to the castle itself, but, more importantly, to the *significance* of the castle for Clifford in particular. Alice Friedman has argued that the pillar "celebrates matrilineal dynasty and the deeply felt relationship of mother and daughter."[39] Why was the significance of this relationship somehow best captured in this precise geographical *location*? Why not commission a memorial in the interior space of Brougham where she so often refers to the chamber where "her Blessed mother died"? The answer, I propose, lies in the history of an event that transpired on the roadside in April 1616.

As I have explored above, Clifford's final departure from her mother was devastating not simply because her mother died one month later but because the farewell was precipitated by a retaliatory evacuation: Clifford's first husband forced her to leave, denying her autonomy of movement. In repeatedly listing the pillar in her accounts of the procession south ("I ridd by ye pillar"),[40] Clifford effectively rewrites an experience of powerlessness with one of agency—of *being* removed to embarking *on* a remove. She buries the original memory beneath layers of new spatial acts and textual references. In her removes, Clifford uses both her acts of travel—riding past the Countess's Pillar on her journey—and the repetitive practice of writing—listing the same landmarks as she records her journey—to rewrite a memory of spatial helplessness and loss with spatial agency and memorialization. She becomes, this time quite literally, a "restorer of paths"—to her castles and her past.

What I have tried to demonstrate here is the importance of contextualizing Clifford's annual accounts of 1650–75 with her earlier patterns of movement and record keeping. Doing so, I believe, reveals several things: first, movement serves as a consistent but dynamic thematic that Clifford deploys throughout her life's writings in a variety of nuanced ways (riding, walking, stasis, procession); second, comparing how Clifford writes and conceptualizes her mobility in 1603 and 1616 with the methodical geo-temporal approach of 1650–75 helps us understand the particular "way" of writing travel that she developed over eighty years, not simply as a method that emerges after she arrives north. Finally, travel and travel writing, particularly in the latter third of Clifford's life, afforded Clifford an opportunity to reshape public perceptions of her agency, ancestry, and legacy. But they also enabled something much simpler and more profound. These records of removes helped her remember. By 1676 Clifford was confined to her chamber, unable to embark on the same journeys that had so characterized much of her more than eight decades of life. The final diary, recorded by a personal secretary, is riddled with references to remembering. In one of her last entries from just two days before she died, Clifford's last thoughts reiterate the themes she spent so many years reinscribing in the pages of her many volumes: "I remembered how this day was 60 years [since] I and my blessed Mother... give in our answer in writing that we would not stand to the Award... concerning the lands of mine inheritance, which did spin out a great deal of trouble for us, yet God turned it out to the best."[41] As this record demonstrates, Clifford continued to move freely in these last months, though in time rather than space, finding comfort in the fact that all "turned out to the best," Lady Anne's way.

Notes

1. On the *Great Books*, see Malay, "Constructing." For an overview of these texts, see Acheson, *Memoir*, 9, and for editions of the 1603, 1616–19, and 1652 texts. For the 1650–75 and 1676 texts, see D. J. H. Clifford, *Diaries*.
2. See Gordon, *Lady Anne's Way*.
3. See Brayshay, *Land Travel*.
4. Key exceptions to this trend include Andrea, "Missionary Position"; Fumerton, *Unsettled*; and McRae, *Literature and Domestic Travel*. Also see Patricia Akhimie's essay in this volume on Lady Catherine Whetenall and "educational travel" as a male enterprise.
5. Acheson, *Memoir*, 222.
6. For analysis of her legal maneuvers and political agency, see Wiseman, "Knowing Her Place." Also see Elsky, "Common-Law Mind."
7. D. J. H. Clifford, *Diaries*, 103. Hereafter, all citations from 1650 to 1676 will be drawn from this text.
8. The term "diary" risks anachronistic associations with secrecy and private emotional outpouring, none of which is characteristic of the seventeenth-century form. As a form of autobiographical writing, the diary itself is in the process of emergence, most recognizably in the diaries of Samuel Pepys.
9. "Memoir," too, seems wrong as a term since it suggests collective reminiscing and an effort toward cohesion, more akin to Clifford's own formal

autobiography in the *Great Books*. In summarizing a single year, the 1603 text resembles the more narrowly focused annual accounts of 1650–75. It seems likely that Clifford drafted the 1603 text from earlier, more diurnal and informal diaries (perhaps like the 1616–19 records), much like she does in a more systematic way in the last decades of her life. The difference in tone (here, informal; in 1650, more restrained and practiced), I would attribute to the passage of time and to opportunities to practice her craft. As such, I will refer to the 1603 text as an annual summary.

10. Acheson, *Memoir*, 37.
11. Acheson points out that the *Life of Me* was written not for the "public at large, but [for] her family, descendants, and others within her circle of influence" (*Memoir*, 217).
12. See Malay, "Constructing."
13. See Friedman, "Constructing an Identity"; Lamb, "Agency of the Split Subject"; Wilcox, "Anne Clifford and Samuel Pepys"; Wiseman, "Knowing Her Place."
14. Chew, "Si(gh)ting"; Malay, "Like a Queen"; Matchinske, "Serial Identity"; and Myers, "Construction Sites."
15. Myers, "Construction Sites," 583.
16. Acheson, *Memoir*, 49.
17. See Acheson, *Memoir*, 23–24, especially, for Sackville's relationship with Mathew Caldicot and for Margaret Russell's critique of Sackville.
18. Acheson, *Memoir*, 73.
19. Acheson, *Memoir*, 75.
20. D. J. H. Clifford, *Diaries*, 228.
21. The immediacy of the diary entries of March, April, and May of 1616 are supported by the fact that Margaret Russell's death on May 24, 1616, is not referenced on the main diary page until May 29 (Acheson, *Memoir*, 87). The precise time of death—"Upon the 24th, being Friday, between the hours of six and seven at night"—is included later as marginalia across from where it might have been inserted in real time.
22. On Clifford's use of the chamber as a metaphoric battleground for the real issues over land inheritance beyond the country estate, see Wiseman, "Knowing Her Place." On Clifford's habits of walking in the estate gardens, see Elsky, "Common-Law Mind."
23. Acheson, *Memoir*, 83.
24. Acheson, *Memoir*, 189.
25. Acheson, *Memoir*, 187.
26. D. J. H. Clifford, *Diaries*, 100.
27. On this tumultuous period, see Spence, *Lady Anne Clifford*, 96–113.

28. Acheson, *Memoir*, 225.
29. D. J. H. Clifford, *Diaries*, 115–16.
30. Elsky, "Common-Law Mind," 524.
31. D. J. H. Clifford, *Diaries*, 194, 214.
32. Chew, "Si(gh)ting," 172.
33. The *Oxford English Dictionary* includes as its third definition for the word's usage as a noun, "The action of moving away or *to* another place, esp. a new place of residence; withdrawal, departure; an instance of this" ("remove, n.3a"). Most famously, Mary Rowlandson uses "remove" in her captivity narrative of 1682 ("A True History") as an organizing principle for her text and a term which emphasizes her lack of agency as a captive—she was herself *removed*, made prisoner. I thank Patricia Akhimie for drawing my attention to this connection.
34. D. J. H. Clifford, *Diaries*, 126.
35. Matchinske, "Serial Identity," 68.
36. D. J. H. Clifford, *Diaries*, 126–28.
37. Chew, "Si(gh)ting," 174.
38. D. J. H. Clifford, *Diaries*, 218.
39. Friedman, "Constructing an Identity," 372.
40. On the significance of Julian Bower, see Hickey, "Roger de Clifford."
41. D. J. H. Clifford, *Diaries*, 280.

Bibliography

Acheson, Katherine, ed. *The Memoir of 1603 and the Diary of 1616–1619*. Peterborough ON: Broadview, 2007.

Andrea, Bernadette. "The Missionary Position: Seventeenth-Century Quaker Women and Global Gender Politics." *In-Between: Essays & Studies in Literary Criticism* 11, no. 1 (2002): 71–87.

Brayshay, Mark. *Land Travel and Communications in Tudor and Stuart England: Achieving a Joined-up Realm*. Liverpool: Liverpool University Press, 2014.

Chew, Elizabeth. "Si(gh)ting the Mistress of the House: Anne Clifford and Architectural Space." In *Women as Sites of Culture: Women's Roles in Cultural Formation from the Renaissance to the Twentieth Century*, edited by Susan Shifrin, 167–82. Burlington VT: Ashgate, 2002.

Clifford, D. J. H. *The Diaries of Lady Anne Clifford*. Stroud, UK: History Press, 2009.

Elsky, Stephanie. "Lady Anne Clifford's Common-Law Mind," *Studies in Philology* 111, no. 3 (2014): 521–46.

Friedman, Alice. "Constructing an Identity in Prose, Plaster, and Paint: Lady Anne Clifford as Writer and Patron of the Arts." In *Albion's Classicism: The*

Visual Arts in Britain, 1550–1660, edited by Lucy Gent, 359–76. New Haven: Yale University Press, 1995.

Fumerton, Patricia. *Unsettled: The Culture of Mobility and the Working Poor in Early Modern England*. Chicago: University of Chicago Press, 2006.

Gordon, Sheila. *Lady Anne's Way*. Saltaire UK: Hillside, 1995.

Hickey, Julia. "Roger de Clifford—the Second Lord Clifford." *The History Jar*. https://thehistoryjar.com/tag/julians-bower/. Accessed November 2, 2016.

Johnson, Matthew. *Behind the Castle Gate: From the Middle Ages to the Renaissance*. London: Routledge, 2002.

"Lady Anne's Way," *Contour Walking Holidays*. https://www.contours.co.uk/walking-holidays/lady-annes-way.php. Accessed January 2, 2017.

Lamb, Mary Ellen. "The Agency of the Split Subject: Lady Anne Clifford and the Uses of Reading." *English Literary Renaissance* 22, no. 3 (1992): 347–68.

Malay, Jessica. "Constructing a Narrative of Time and Place: Anne Clifford's Great Books of Record." *Review of English Studies* 66, no. 277 (2015): 859–75.

———. "Like a Queen: The Influence of the Elizabethan Court on the Structure of Female-Centered Households in the Early Modern Period." In *Tudor Court Culture*, edited by Anna Riehl and Thomas Betteridge, 93–113. Selinsgrove PA: Susquehanna University Press, 2010.

Matchinske, Megan. "Serial Identity: History, Gender, and Form in the Diary Writing of Lady Anne Clifford." In *Genre and Women's Life Writing in Early Modern England*, edited by Michelle M. Dowd, Julie A. Eckerle, and Laura Knoppers, 65–80. Burlington VT: Ashgate: 2007.

McRae, Andrew. *Literature and Domestic Travel in Early Modern England*. Cambridge: Cambridge University Press, 2009.

Myers, Anne M. "Construction Sites: The Architecture of Anne Clifford's Diaries." *English Literary History* 73, no.3 (2006): 581–600.

"remove, n.3a." *Oxford English Dictionary* Online. Oxford University Press, December 2016.

Rowlandson, Mary. "A True History of the Captivity and Restoration of Mrs. Mary Rowlandson." In *Journeys in New Worlds: Early American Women's Narratives*, edited by Amy Schrager Lang, 27–65. Madison: University of Wisconsin Press, 1990.

Spence, Richard T. *Lady Anne Clifford*. Stroud: Sutton, 1997.

Wilcox, Helen. "Anne Clifford and Samuel Pepys: Diaries and Homes." *Home Cultures* 6, no. 2 (2009): 149–62.

Wiseman, Susan. "Knowing Her Place: Anne Clifford and the Politics of Retreat." In *Textures of Renaissance Knowledge*, edited by Philippa Berry and Margaret Trudeau-Clayton, 199–221. Manchester: Manchester University Press, 2003.

PART 2

Early Modern Women and the Globe

Gendered Travel on the English Stage

9

Mapping Women

Place Names and a Woman's Place

LAURA AYDELOTTE

In the opening speech of Shakespeare's *Antony and Cleopatra* the character Philo describes the play's titular couple as they approach:

> Look where they come
> Take but good note, and you shall see in him
> The triple pillar of the world transformed
> Into a strumpet's fool. Behold and see. (1.1.11–14)[1]

The lines stem from the well-worn lineage, from Dido and Aeneas on, of powerful men defined as those who own the world, or have the potential to do so, and powerful women defined as the temptresses who get in the way of that man's conquest and mastery of the world. A few lines later, in playful repartee with her lover, Cleopatra says "I'll set a bourn how far to be beloved" (1.1.17), and Antony responds: "Then must thou needs find out new heaven, new Earth" (1.1.18). Couched within the language of romance, the lines also present the question of how far a woman may set her "bourne." What are the limits of the territory she may claim as her own? Antony's response cuts two ways. It suggests that Cleopatra holds sway over all the world and more, but it could also be read to imply that she can never truly have power over the earth's territories in the way he, the "triple pillar of the world" can, that she must seek new heaven, new earth, the territories of love and imagination, to hold real power (1.1.12).

Within the world of Shakespeare's plays one answer to the question of the "bourne" or boundary of a character's worldly influence lies in the language that character wields.² As the chorus in *Henry V* states clearly, it is the voicing of place names that makes them exist within the world of the theater (1.1.1-35). England, Agincourt, Egypt, or Rome all exist as they are spoken by the actors on the stage. For the characters within the drama, speaking the names of places often indicates their involvement in world affairs and their power in the world. Tracing the way male and female characters employ geographic names can help indicate the boundaries of their power within the world of the plays they inhabit.

The chapter that follows is part of a larger experiment that seeks to explore the significance of geographic names in Shakespeare. The aim of the digital project, Shakespeare on the Map, is to identify and map all the place names in the text of Shakespeare's plays. While print resources exist that have identified place names mentioned in Shakespeare's works, there is not currently a comprehensive digital resource for both searching and visualizing the places that appear in the texts of the plays and poems.³ The Shakespeare on the Map project will both add geographic encoding to the existing TEI markup of the Folger Digital Texts editions of the plays, and produce maps that enable viewers to see all the locations in the plays.

The present chapter comes out of the initial work of identifying place names in six plays — *A Midsummer Night's Dream, Othello, Henry IV, Parts 1 and 2, Henry V,* and *Antony and Cleopatra* — in preparation for the TEI encoding of locations for those plays. My approach has been to record place names in three different categories. The first is place names that refer to the scene where action is taking place in the play at the point when the word appears in the text. The second is references to places other than where the action is currently taking place. The third comprises place names used adjectively or primarily as a means of modifying or describing a person or thing: for example, an Ethiop, a French gown, or the Queen of Egypt. While they may not be mappable, I also include imaginary place names and place names, like the Amazon, that are ambiguously defined or liminal territory between actual locations and imagined lands.⁴

I am using this preliminary gathering of place names to look at the way women do or do not relate to the geographic locations that appear in the text of each play and to explore the potential for a future complete data set for the locations in all the plays that would shed light on the relationship between place and gender in Shakespeare. As John Gillies notes at the start of his study, *Shakespeare and the Geography of Difference*, earlier critical views of Shakespeare's geographic imagination as one primarily bounded by Europe have been supplanted in recent decades by an interest in the global aspects of Shakespeare's plays and what they can tell us about attitudes toward people and places outside of the European sphere in Shakespeare's work.[5] Such interests have intersected with studies of gender that have examined topics ranging from the depictions of fictional women who are "other" than European by nation or race, to the tales and fictions produced about foreign women encountered in travel, to the role of the female body as a symbolic geographic figure across literary and cartographic traditions.[6] There are, however, questions to be asked about how women characters within the plays relate to the specifics of geography and place. What are the patterns in the places women speak about, the places they pass through, the places they are figuratively and metaphorically identified with?

The initial data set of place names used here begins to suggest some new ways of looking at the intersections of gender and geography in Shakespeare. A comparison of the tragedy *Othello* with the comedy *A Midsummer Night's Dream* presents a chiastic pattern related to the romantic ups and downs of each play. While Titania is more likely to speak about place when estranged from Oberon at the start of *A Midsummer Night's Dream* than after the pair reconcile at the end, the opposite is true of Desdemona and Othello as their relationship goes from good to bad, suggesting parallels between the power dynamics of romantic relationships and a woman's relationship to geography. A comparison of the way place names are used within the historically inspired worlds of the last three plays of the Henriad and in *Antony and Cleopatra* suggests an even more complex relationship between political power and place.

Barbary and the Moor in Othello

One of the first things that becomes apparent when tracking the place names in Shakespeare is how often they aren't there. Many passages that deal with travel or geography use general terms that evoke far off places or even a nebulous sense of the world as a whole. This is true of Othello's speech about how he wooed Desdemona (1.3.149–96) in which he alludes to "a traveler's history" (1.3.161) to "rough quarries, rocks and hills" (1.3.174) and to "Anthropophagi" (1.3.167), but never to an identifiable place. The speech notably introduces Desdemona's desires in Othello's voice, and as critics have pointed out, this creates a tension between her passive role as listener and a potentially threatening role of a person who desires, whose ears "devour up" his "discourse" (1.3.151). As Harry Berger puts it, "his language represents him representing her (to himself) as half the wooer. It already glances at the pornographic fantasy Iago will concoct later."[7]

The fact that Othello is representing Desdemona to both others and to himself may help explain the lack of geographic specificity in the description of travel in his speech. The conversations bookending the portion of act 1, scene 3 focused on Desdemona's elopement with Othello are about the present wars and the need for Othello to travel in his capacity as general. These lines are filled with clearly identifiable allusions to Cyprus, Turkey, the Ottoman Empire, and more. As one goes down the list of place names in order of appearance in the play these places associated with Othello's travels in the world appear as easily mappable locations, whereas the description of Desdemona's travel is unmappable, empirically absent. Othello describes Desdemona as wishing "that heaven had made her such a man" (1.3.164), a simultaneous expression of her desire for him and her desire to be him. Yet his description of her interest in his travel either fails to imagine or nervously evades a representation of Desdemona as someone who might realistically play the role of "such a man" who travels to real places in the real world on important errands. He provides an account of a woman who can project herself into his experience in a vague, fantastical way among the anthropophagi, but not as someone who imagines herself traveling to Cyprus or Turkey.

The place-related word Desdemona speaks the most is "Moor" in reference to Othello. It is also the most used place term in the play, appearing ninety-two times. Ambiguous enough to be impossible to pinpoint precisely on a map, but identifiable enough to be able to chart possible geographic regions it may refer to, the term *Moor*, like Othello himself, encompasses a difficult to define middle ground of otherness, what Ania Loomba refers to as a "complicated crux of contemporary beliefs about black people and Muslims."[8] All but one of the geographically associated words Desdemona speaks in the play are either the term *Moor*, connecting her to other regions through her husband's identity, or two references to Cyprus and to Venice that pragmatically refer to the places where she currently is or is from.

The one notable departure from this pattern occurs in the "Willow Song" scene in act 4, scene 3, with Desdemona's two references to the maid "Barbary" (4.3.28 and 4.3.35). As Patricia Parker has demonstrated, the name is a multivalent one. It could be at once a reference to exotic locales, imagining a woman whose name, like the constant references to Othello as "Moor," ties her to a foreign identity along the Barbary coast. "Barbary" could also connote someone outside social boundaries, a barbarian, or, in the case of a woman, a harlot.[9] If Desdemona was defined by Othello at the start of the play as wishing to be a man like him, enchanted by the idea that an identification with him could lead to travel and adventure, her identification with "poor Barbary" at the end of the play reframes her travel imagination. Now exotic otherness is named in the person of a woman like herself and the name of a woman that suggests sexual transgression. Just as Othello ends the play with the memorable comparison of himself with his former enemy, the "circumcised Turk," Desdemona's concluding speeches about Barbary suggest that both of them have shifted to focus on outside places. As Iago stirs Othello's self-consciousness about his identity as outsider, and as he and Desdemona become increasingly estranged, each concludes in a self-comparison with Barbary maid or circumcised Turk, traveling outside themselves and away from one another.

A Midsummer Night's Dream *and International Faeries*

In contrast with Desdemona's comparative lack of association with specific place names, the character of Titania in A *Midsummer Night's Dream* enters the play by referring to a number of different places and to her own travel. For the first act of the play the vast majority of the allusions to place are to the setting of the play itself, Athens.[10] Puck then introduces India into the play's vocabulary at the same time as he introduces Titania, the queen of fairyland, describing how she has kidnapped a "changling boy" from an "Indian King" (2.1.22). A little later in the same scene Titania is the one to allude to both Oberon's recent travel from the "steppes of India" (2.1.71) and to her own time abroad in the "spiced Indian air" (2.1.124). Margo Hendricks, interested in the reasons Shakespeare might specify India as the place of origin for the changeling boy, suggests, among other things, that it was a place associated in the early modern period with "the commodified space of a radicalized feminine eroticism that . . . paradoxically excited and threatens the masculinity of European travelers."[11] Titania is not Indian herself but represents herself as a traveler to the region who shares a bond with a woman there, the mother of the Indian boy.

The fact that she does represent herself and her travels in this scene stands in contrast to Othello's representation of Desdemona as potential traveler absent of any particular destination. Titania is conspicuously the one who specifies other place names in the early part of the play. She is, for example, the first one in the play to directly identify Hippolyta as an Amazon, introducing another exotic location into the play's vocabulary, and another place associated with licentious women. Indeed, Loomba has suggested that one of the many real world locations historically identified with the legendary Amazons is India.[12] Whether this indicates that Titania's speech alludes to an eastern territory of empowered women that she and Hippolyta both share, or whether the territories are intended to be distinct realms of foreign female experience, the striking thing is that Titania is the one in control of naming the places that both she and Oberon travel to and from. His own fictional origins are in India, but he is not the one to allude to the place in the first part of the play.[13] Similarly, Titania is the one who makes all the references to their, presumably mutual home, "Fairyland." In the opening acts she demonstrates symbolic command of territory through her possession of the Indian boy and verbal command of the places she names.

It is, significantly, at the moment that Oberon has sealed his victory over Titania and is on his way to claim the changeling that he first refers specifically to the "Indian boy" (3.2.396). He only specifies the place of the changeling boy's origins when his own victory is assured, and Titania does not specifically allude to a place name or to her own travel for the remainder of the play. Near the conclusion, Oberon describes the two of them circumnavigating the globe:

> Trip we after night's shade.
> We the globe can compass soon
> Swifter than the wand'ring moon. (4.1.100–102)

A play that began rooted in Titania's verbal mastery over the local habitations of the fairy couple, ends with Oberon in control of their travels together. It is the only mention of the word "globe" in the play, and it suggests Oberon's ability to co-opt his wife's traveling ways to his own mastery over the world as a part of a power couple. If Desdemona moves away from her husband and toward an identification of herself with distant places, then Titania's move by contrast is away from an ability to voice the names of places in the world, but toward travel in tandem with her husband's movements.

A Place in History

A very different paradigm from either *Othello* or *A Midsummer Night's Dream* is offered by the set of place names used in a sample group of Shakespeare's history plays: *Henry IV, Parts 1* and *2* and *Henry V*. The first thing apparent when looking at gender and place name in these plays is just what one might expect. The small number of significant women characters means that there are likewise a small number of place names associated with women. Similarly unsurprising is the fact that the place names within these history plays are overwhelmingly focused within Britain.

Henry IV, Parts 1 and *2* and *Henry V* provide examples of two modes in which place names are commonly introduced in these plays. The first is that many place names mentioned within these works are also the names of men within the play. Hence, Westmoreland, Northumberland, York, and other historical characters represent both a person and a place, titles that make apparent the power of a place name to indicate the power of the man who bears it over the territory itself.

The second is that place names often occur in scenes in which military campaigns or political divisions of power are being discussed. This is demonstrated, for example, in the map scene in *Henry IV, Part 1* in which Hotspur, Mortimer, and Glendower plot how they will divide the kingdom amongst themselves. For example, Mortimer proposes,

> The Archdeacon hath divided it
> Into three limits very equally:
> England, from Trent and Severn hitherto,
> By south and east is to my part assigned;
> All westward, Wales beyond the Severn shore,
> And all the fertile land within that bound
> To Owen Glendower; and, dear coz to you
> The remnant northward lying off from Trent.
> And our indentures tripartite are drawn,
> Which being sealèd interchangeably—
> A business that this night may execute—
> Tomorrow, cousin Percy, you and I
> And my good Lord of Worcester will set forth
> To meet your father and the Scottish power,
> As is appointed us, at Shrewsbury. (3.1.75–89)

The speech becomes the opportunity for Mortimer to list locations in England and Wales, to evoke Scotland and Shrewsbury and, in naming these places, to express the power over physical territory that he and others are asserting. Hotspur's responses, quibbling over how the map is divided, are in turn statements about the boundaries of his power and that of others.

Dialogue in scenes like these is rhetorically aimed at introducing place names and associating them with the power, or potential power, of key players. As Richard Helgerson has observed, the presentation of maps in scenes like the one in *Henry IV, Part 1*, or the similar scene in *King Lear* when Lear divides his kingdom, present an image of the land and territories to the audience of the play independent from the symbolic presentation of a ruler in an image like a portrait of Elizabeth I. Helgerson suggests that "[m]aps thus opened up a conceptual gap between the land and its ruler."[14] In this reading the image of the map on stage allows the audience members not only to imagine the geography of their nation, but to reimagine a gap in connection between land and ruler. Similarly, the rhetoric of place in the map scene in *Henry IV, Part 1* presents to the audience both an account of a set of places and the ability to imagine the gap between that land and the powers that currently hold it. It is in part from the ability of the audience to imagine both the land and the potential for the connection between the land and different characters within the play that the drama of the narrative unfolds. The question of who can name and claim places drives the political story.

When the way place names are employed by the men in the *Henry IV* and *Henry V* plays is compared with the use of place names by women in those plays, it demonstrates a difference in the way women relate to place and power in the plays. Of the female characters, the woman who mentions the most places is Mistress Quickly, and her vocabulary of place correlates with her role as innkeeper. She mentions Eastcheap and London a few times, reflecting the local domain of her house of hospitality. By contrast, the other places she names are some of the farthest flung of the plays. Mistress Quickly mentions some of the only places outside England or France, including the price of "holland" linen (1H4 3.3.76) or to the consumption of "too much canaries" (2H4 2.4.27), referring to wine. Her conversations about linens and wine, the domestic goods that are a part of her professional role as hostess, also indicate the way in which the household goods that are a part of her business tie in with international trade. Similarly, her allusion to the "Whore of Babylon" in her malapropism filled eulogy of Falstaff in *Henry V* introduces one of the farthest flung locations mentioned in the play (2.3.39). The mention of Babylon occurs within a context that, again, ties the foreign with the commercial domestic sphere that Mistress Quickly inhabits. The associations of both herself and Falstaff with the prostitute Doll Tearsheet and various bawdy activities are, in this instance, not only elevated to the level of biblical allusion, but also become an allusion to the far-off land of Babylon. If other characters in the play allude to locations in Britain and France as a way of expressing or speculating about their territorial powers, Mistress Quickly expresses the relatively minor economic powers of the very local and the mundane activities of herself and her friends to tie her indirectly with foreign lands.

The other women in the *Henry IV* and *Henry V* plays conspicuously only mention place names that relate to territories aristocratic men acquired through marriage and specifically through the wife's dowry. When Lady Percy complains that she hears her husband, in his sleep, "murmur tales of iron wars" (*1H4* 2.3.50), and that "[s]ome heavy business hath my lord in hand, / And I must know it, else he loves me not" (*1H4* 2.3.66–67), she is expressing her lack of ability to precisely describe the political struggle with which he is engaged. In contrast to the dialogue between Hotspur, Mortimer, and Glendower in act 3, scene 1, filled with talk of the places they intend to conquer and divide, Lady Percy does not know the places to name, the specifics to bring into the conversation. Excluded from such conversations, she knows there is "some heavy business . . . in hand" but lacks knowledge of the specifics of the political affairs, such as the names of the places in play.

The only two place names that Lady Percy speaks in the course of the plays are when she mentions England while eulogizing her husband in *Henry IV, Part 2* (2.3.20), and in *Henry IV, Part 1* when she tells her husband, "Lie still, you thief, and hear the lady sing in Welsh" (3.1.243). The scene, which revolves around the fact that Lady Percy's brother, Mortimer, cannot understand his wife, who speaks only in Welsh, anticipates the scene between Henry V and Catherine de Valois ("Katherine" or "Kate" in the play) at the end of *Henry V*, which similarly revolves around the English king's attempt to communicate with his French bride. Predictably, Katherine only refers to two place names: France and England, most often adjectively, as she compares the French and English tongues and customs. In both cases, Lady Percy and Katherine as women are able to speak of place within a marital context. Lady Percy may not be privy to the "heavy business" discussed by the men in the play, but she can voice her understanding of the marital politics that have brought her Welsh sister-in-law into the family. When Katherine is selected to be the English king's consort, the ability to "speak your England" becomes a necessary part of her sphere of knowledge and her vocabulary.

Even as the men clearly retain the worldly power in both these scenes, the women who have traveled from Wales or France as the instruments of political alliances also pose a problem for the men in their lives. More than one critic has pointed out that there is a tension between the mastery that the men in the plays hold over these women and the extent to which, both historically and within Shakespeare's fiction, they depend upon the women's lines as the means to consolidate their power.[15] The women in these scenes also have an upper hand in knowing a language the men do not, something which causes men in both scenes to defensively position themselves as rough, plain speakers.[16] The women also have the advantage of, for once, being brought into the geo-political conversation. Lady Percy does not know how to talk to her husband about the places he and others plan to conquer on the battlefield, but she, like other women, does know about the politics of marriage. Urging her husband to "hear the Welsh woman sing," she both urges him to listen to a woman's voice and demonstrates her own attempt to engage with the politics of the play.

Egypt and Cleopatra

In contrast to the aristocratic women in the history plays, *Antony and Cleopatra* presents a play centered on the romantic relationship of a woman with political power of her own. Predictably, the place mentioned most in *Antony and Cleopatra* is Egypt. The word "Egypt" occurs forty-three times, with over sixty-five references to Egypt as a place when including the words "Egyptian," "Nile," and "Alexandria." It is also a word used in very particular ways to refer to both the country and to Cleopatra herself. As I noted earlier, one way that place names appear in the English history plays is in the titles and names of characters like Westmoreland, York, and others. In *Antony and Cleopatra*, Cleopatra is referred to by her title as queen, but her power as ruler over her country is often expressed by referring to her person as "Egypt." This becomes the occasion for some interesting slippage between Cleopatra as a woman and Egypt as a place. For example, after Antony has heard about the death of Fulvia, Cleopatra says, "I prithee turn aside and weep for her / Then bid adieu to me, and say the tears / Belong to Egypt" (1.3.92–94). The lines suggest that Antony will hypocritically shed tears for his dead wife and then repurpose those same tears to show his sadness at parting with Cleopatra, Egypt's queen. Yet the line also evokes tears at leaving Egypt the place, referencing Antony's impending departure. The conflation between Cleopatra and her country at this juncture suggests the way she subtly combines the seductions of herself as a woman and the seduction of the power over the land she controls.

This expression of the queen's two bodies is used multiple times throughout the play. Early in the play Cleopatra refers to herself as Egypt as a way of signaling her power, both with Antony and with others, as in the scene when she tells the Eunuch, Mardian, "'Tis well for thee / That, being unseminared, thy freer thoughts / May not fly forth of Egypt," noting that he can escape neither Egypt the country nor her service (1.5.13–14). Later in the play the term becomes one of reproach and then regret. After the failure at Actium, Antony chides Cleopatra: "Egypt, thou knew'st too well / My heart was to thy rudder tied by th' strings, / And thou shouldst tow me after," blaming her as both the woman he can't resist and an inept commander in chief of her country's forces (3.12.60–62). A few lines later, she presages her death along with the conquering of her country when she sends a messenger to tell Caesar "from his all-obeying breath I hear / The doom of Egypt" (3.13.94–95).

And, of course, in his death scene Antony twice repeats the line "I am dying, Egypt, dying" as he bids his last farewell to both the woman and the place that have consumed him throughout the play (4.15.22, 48). Of the twenty-seven places Cleopatra names, eighteen relate to Egypt and seven refer to Rome or Italy. Only two outliers refer to other places.[17] To a certain extent this is true of Antony's use of place names as well. Of thirty-seven places he refers to, seventeen are to places associated with Egypt, while ten are to Rome or Italy. This indicates the extent to which he is, indeed "tethered" to Cleopatra, his thoughts and speech revolving around her and her land.

However, Antony has a greater geographic range in his vocabulary than Cleopatra, much of this coming from scenes in which he is discussing military tactics: for example, in act 3, scene 7, when, anticipating the coming battle, Cleopatra speaks in broad terms, "Sink Rome, and their tongues rot / That speak against us! A charge we bear i' th' war" (3.7.19–20) while Antony talks logistics: "Is it not strange, Canidius, / That from Tarentum and Brundusium / He could so quickly cut the Ionian Sea / And take in Toryne?—You have heard on 't, sweet?" (3.7.26–29). Thus, despite her indisputable power as queen of Egypt, Cleopatra is presented rhetorically in this scene not unlike Lady Percy in *Henry IV, Part 1*. Just as Lady Percy refers to "some heavy business" that her husband has, Cleopatra somewhat vaguely refers to "[a] charge we bear i' th' war." The queen of Egypt is, of course, much more involved in the affairs at hand, but she does not speak in specific terms about the movements of the enemy through different locations as Antony does. In this way she is rhetorically presented as less knowledgeable and less competent than the men around her.

It is, however, neither Antony nor Cleopatra who has command over the greatest diversity of place names in the play, but Caesar. Of the thirty-nine places he names, only twelve are related to Egypt and Rome. In the scene preceding the one just cited, in which Antony speaks a little of the movement of the enemy, and Cleopatra not at all, Caesar presents a clear and detailed view of who he will be fighting and where they come from:

> He hath given his empire
> Up to a whore, who now are levying
> The kings o' th' Earth for war. He hath assembled
> Bocchus, the King of Libya; Archelaus
> Of Cappadocia; Philadelphos, King
> Of Paphlagonia; the Thracian king, Adallas;
> King Manchus of Arabia; King of Pont;
> Herod of Jewry; Mithridates, King
> Of Comagen; Polemon and Amyntas,
> The Kings of Mede and Lycaonia
> With a more larger list of scepters. (3.7.76–86)

Caesar's rhetorical command of those places presents a man with considerable knowledge and interest in the workings of the world at large. This is true of his pattern of referring to place names throughout the play. It is even Caesar, rather than Antony himself, who speaks of Antony's past adventures when he was "beaten from Modena" (1.4.66) and "didst eat strange flesh" in the "Alps" (1.4.76–77), co-opting with his speech the places where Antony has traveled and the deeds he has done. Caesar is presented as the character in the play with the most astute knowledge and awareness of place and of the tactics and politics needed to make territories his own.

Cleopatra is, in many ways very different from the women in the other plays we have looked at in this chapter. She is tied, powerfully, to a nation as its ruler, and she strongly asserts and uses her role not just as woman but as "Egypt" throughout the play. In her romantic relationship with Antony it is he who bends to Egypt, both the person and the place, and it is her country which appears most in his dialogue. She forges an alliance with Rome and with Antony, but on her terms, not as a woman being married off for political purposes. Yet, despite all this, she is not presented as having the same kind of geographic knowledge and scope as Caesar or Antony. As a queen, the leader of a country, it would be easy to imagine ways in which her character could have been given lines demonstrating a larger understanding of the geo-political scene, but instead her speech is mostly restricted to talk of Egypt and Rome. Even as a woman leader, it is beyond her bourne to speak beyond the boundaries of her own realm, or the realm she is tied to via her lover, Antony.

I began this essay by asking what the bourne of a woman's geographic power and influence is in Shakespeare's plays. By looking at the way place names appear in six of the plays, we have begun to see some examples of the possibilities and limits of women's relationships to place in early modern drama. However, these observations constitute a beginning to thinking about the role of particular geographic place names in relationship to Shakespeare's women. A future, comprehensive data set of place names across the corpus will provide the grounds for exploring how larger patterns in the way the geographic place names in the text of the plays intersect with gender, race, class, and other identities represented by characters within the plays. These initial observations also indicate where future fruitful research work might be done in probing what the places they speak about can tell us about the spheres of knowledge and influence that women characters inhabit and raise questions about how Shakespeare's fictions intersect with the experience of historical women. The depictions of Desdemona's longing to travel with her husband and Titania's independent Indian wanderings suggest radical new ways women might begin to imagine themselves as travelers through the fiction of theater. The Holland linens and Canary wines of Mistress Quickly's household suggest ways we might start to understand domestic economic connections between London women and the larger world. At the same time, the presentation of aristocratic and powerful women from Lady Percy to Cleopatra as having a very limited range of place names in their vocabulary provides a fictional account of women in the political sphere as less aware, knowledgeable, and savvy than their male counterparts, restricting the boundaries at which women might imagine themselves exercising power in and over the world. The map of the geographic vocabulary of Shakespeare's women is also a map of a woman's place in the world of his plays, and of the image those plays project for the place of women in history.

Notes

1. All citations from Shakespeare's plays are from the Folger Digital Texts edition, *Shakespeare's Plays, Sonnets and Poems*.
2. Literally, "A boundary (between fields, etc.). *Obs.*" See OED, s.v., "bourne | bourn, *n.*2."
3. Most recently see, Davis, *Dictionary*.
4. This initial list of place names is based, in part, on the list of nouns in Shakespeare's plays compiled by Martin Mueller and Michael Poston in connection with the Folger Digital Texts project at the Folger Shakespeare Library.
5. Gillies, *Shakespeare*, 1–2. Gillies specifically cites Rogers as an earlier view of Shakespearean geography that neglected giving attention to the global "others" appearing in the plays. See Rogers' chapter, "Voyages and Exploration," in *Shakespeare's England* 1:170–72.
6. Suranyi, *Genius*; Hall, *Things of Darkness*; Albano, "Visible Bodies."
7. Berger, "Acts of Silence," 24. Newman *Fashioning Femininity*, similarly discusses the threatening nature of Desdemona's "greedy ear," which "devours" Othello's speech, and the threatening nature of a sexual subject who hears and desires (85).
8. Loomba, *Shakespeare*, 91–111.
9. Parker, "Barbers and Barbary," 208.
10. One exception is a series of jokes about "French crowns" by the mechanicals (MND 1.2.91–93). The other is a brief allusion by Hermia to "Carthage" and the "Trojan" Aeneas when teasing Lysander about "all the vows that men have ever broke / (In number more than ever women spoke)" (1.1.176–77), making the first allusion to travel in foreign lands to Dido, the Queen of Carthage.
11. Hendricks, "'Obscured by dreams,'" 18. Loomba, in "Great Indian," similarly cites historical travel accounts, suggesting that early modern westerners perceived Indian women as having "uncontrollable sexual appetites" and engaging in unusually unbridled licentious behavior.
12. Loomba, "Great Indian," 173.
13. See Hendricks, "Obscured by dreams," 46, and my own piece on the faerie king's origins in the romance, *Huon de Bordeaux*: Aydelotte, "'A Local Habitation and a Name.'"
14. Helgerson, *Forms of Nationhood*, 114.
15. See Simmons, "Masculine Negotiations"; Abate, "'Once more'"; Howard and Rackin, *Engendering a Nation*.
16. See Abate, "'Once more,'" for a nuanced examination of the ways in which she sees Katherine using the language barrier and other factors to her

advantage in this scene. See also Steinsaltz, "Politics of French Language," who brings up the point that it seems odd a medieval English king would not have known French well and investigates the many ways in which this and other scenes play into the nationalism of Shakespeare's own time.

17. Cleopatra refers to an occasion when she first seduced Antony and "wore his sword Philippian" (2.5.27), and she refers to "the boar of Thessaly" in describing Antony's anger following Actium (4.13.2).

Bibliography

Abate, Corinne. "'Once more unto the breach': Katharine's Victory in *Henry V*." *Early Theatre* 4, no. 1 (2001): 73–85.

Albano, Catarina. "Visible Bodies: Cartography and Anatomy." In *Literature, Mapping and the Politics of Space in Early Modern Britain*, edited by Andrew Gordon and Bernhard Klein, 89–106. Cambridge: Cambridge University Press, 2001.

Aydelotte, Laura. "'A Local Habitation and a Name': The Origins of Shakespeare's Oberon." *Shakespeare Survey* 65 (2012): 1–11.

Berger, Harry. "Acts of Silence, Acts of Speech: How to Do Things with Othello and Desdemona." *Renaissance Drama* 33 (2004): 3–35.

Davis, J. Madison, ed. *The Shakespeare Name and Place Dictionary*. 2009. Reprint, New York: Routledge, 2012.

Gillies, John. *Shakespeare and the Geography of Difference*. Cambridge: Cambridge University Press, 1994.

Hall, Kim. *Things of Darkness: Economies of Race and Gender in Early Modern England*. Ithaca NY: Cornell University Press, 1995.

Helgerson, Richard. *Forms of Nationhood: The Elizabethan Writing of England*. Chicago: University of Chicago Press, 1992.

Hendricks, Margo. "'Obscured by dreams': Race, Empire and A Midsummer Night's Dream." *Shakespeare Quarterly* 47, no. 1 (1996): 37–60.

Howard, Jean, and Phyllis Rackin. *Engendering a Nation: A Feminist Account of Shakespeare's English Histories*. London: Routledge, 1997.

Loomba, Ania. "The Great Indian Vanishing Trick—Colonialism, Property, and the Family in *A Midsummer Night's Dream*." In *A Feminist Companion to Shakespeare*, edited by Dympna Callaghan, 163–87. Oxford: Blackwell, 2000.

———. *Shakespeare, Race, and Colonialism*. Oxford: Oxford University Press, 2002.

Newman, Karen. *Fashioning Femininity and English Renaissance Drama*. Chicago: University of Chicago Press, 1991.

Parker, Patricia. "Barbers and Barbary: Early Modern Cultural Semantics." *Renaissance Drama* 33 (2004): 201–44.

Rogers, J. D. *Shakespeare's England: An Account of the Life and Manners of His Age*. Vol. 1. Oxford: Clarendon Press, 1932.
Shakespeare on the Map, edited by Laura Aydelotte. http://www.shakespearemap.org/.
Shakespeare's Plays from Folger Digital Texts, edited by Barbara Mowat, Paul Werstine, Michael Poston, and Rebecca Niles. Folger Shakespeare Library. www.folgerdigitaltexts.org. Accessed on December 10, 2016.
Simmons, J. L. "Masculine Negotiations in Shakespeare's History Plays: Hal, Hotspur, and Mortimer." *Shakespeare Quarterly* 44, no. 4 (1993): 440–63.
Steinsaltz, David. "The Politics of French Language in Shakespeare's History Plays." *Studies in English Literature, 1500–1900* 42, no. 2 (2002): 317–34.
Suranyi, Anna. *The Genius of the English Nation: Travel Writing and National Identity in Early Modern England*. Newark: University of Delaware Press, 2008.

10

Eroticizing Women's Travel

Desdemona and the Desire for Adventure in Othello

STEPHANIE CHAMBERLAIN

Early in Shakespeare's *Othello*, Othello recounts Desdemona's rapt obsession with his travel narratives, of one whose "greedy ear [would] / Devour up my discourse" (1.3.148–49).[1] While he reads Desdemona's response to his "disastrous chances" (1.3.133) as one of pity, it is likewise evident that his narratives stir desire within her. While she clearly admires the spirit that enables Othello's heroic bravado, Desdemona likewise betrays a longing to travel the "brave new world" that his narratives describe.

Desdemona's fascination with the strange and marvelous world Othello describes locates her text within the early modern travel narrative, where exotic images of the cultural Other incited both fascination and fear. Adventure experienced vicariously through Othello's marvelous narratives, I argue, arouses Desdemona's desire to embrace such wonders for herself. The way in which we read her arousal, however, becomes important to an understanding of not only her relationship with Othello, but also how such desire is rendered within in the play. While the text is overlaid with strong cultural caveats that rehearse the dangers of women failing to adhere to patriarchal protections, we may also glimpse the allure such travel must have held for women. For Desdemona travel constitutes a wholly erotic desire, not for the black male body, as might be reflected in a colonialist reading of the play, but for the strange and wondrous world beyond Venice. Such experience, however, comes at a cost as patriarchal forces recast Desdemona's desire. Iago fashions her as a whore—one who, like Bianca, would sell her body to satisfy her desire; Brabanzio views her as charmed and seduced by a sexualized Muslim world; and Othello willfully misreads her desire as damning evidence of marital infidelity. Collectively, patriarchal forces within the play recast a woman's desire for travel as one for as sexual adventure.

As the play opens, Othello has just clandestinely married Desdemona, an event that Iago manipulates in his evolving plot to destroy the general. Crudely delivering the news of a daughter's elopement to her sleep-dazed father—"Even now, now, very now, an old black ram / Is tupping your white ewe" (1.1.88–89)—the ensign uses calculated vulgarity to incite the senator's rage. Iago fabricates a graphic image of a bestialized sexuality, suggesting that Brabanzio "will have [his] daughter / covered with a Barbary horse" (1.1.112–13) or that Desdemona "and the / Moor are now making the beast with two backs" (1.1.117–18), introducing religious as well as racial bias. The animal/human coupling that Iago so vividly sketches resembles, in fact, one of the monstrous creatures found in Ambroise Paré's *On Monsters and Marvels* (1573). Paré, who was chief surgeon to the French kings Charles IX and Henri III, depicts the coalescence of creature and human as the result of what he calls the "mingling of seed."[2] He notes: "There are monsters that are born with a form that is half-animal and the other [half] human, or retaining everything [about them] from animals, which are produced by sodomists and atheists who 'join together' and break out of their bounds—unnaturally—with animals, and from this are born several hideous monsters that bring great shame to those who look at them or speak of them."[3] Paré's account clearly evinces xenophobia: his monsters are the bizarre result of sexualized contact with the "sodomists and atheists" of non-European alterity. European writers applied both slurs to Moors of the Islamic Barbary Coast, who were often depicted as sexually licentious. As Ania Loomba notes, colonialist Europeans applied racialized attributes to the non-European Other including "sexual promiscuity, bestiality, primitivism, innocence and irrationality."[4] In this vein, Iago's bestialized depiction of Othello and Desdemona's union portrays a woman literally being consumed by a dark and dirty beast in an unnatural sexual act.

Iago's racist vulgarity elicits a similar response from Brabanzio, who declares that "a maiden never bold" (1.3.94) would never willingly choose to "run from her guardage to the sooty bosom" of "a creature" such as

Othello (1.2.71). Brabanzio's charges are, in many respects, puzzling given his purported fondness for the general, whom he often invited to dinner. What Othello's liberties and Desdemona's choice uncover is the Venetian senator's underlying bias. It may be, as Imtiaz Habib argues, that Brabanzio as well as the other Venetian senators never, in fact, see Othello as anything other than an alien—useful when the state is threatened, but otherwise marginalized.[5] Brabanzio declares that "the Moor" used "spells and medicines bought of mountebanks" on the unsuspecting Venetian woman (1.3.61). From his arguably distraught perspective, this is the only conceivable explanation for why his daughter would marry a cultural outsider. The representation of seduction through the use of magic and potions is later employed in the handkerchief scenes as well, where Othello's first gift to Desdemona, given by an Egyptian "charmer" (3.4.55), woven by "a sibyl" (3.4.68) with "magic in the web of it" (3.4.67) is declared to have the potential to ensure or destroy a husband's love.

Hence, Brabanzio's charge and the play's support of cultural stereotypes portray Othello's Muslim world as a place of mystery and seduction, as possessing a siren-like quality that could lure an unsuspecting Venetian to her doom. This world has analogues in early modern accounts of both European men and women "turning Turk" after being seduced by an alluring Islamic world.[6] Nabil Matar notes that "the dangerous encounter with the religious Other—the Muslim . . . threatened Christian belief by enticing hundreds of men and women to Islam and making them renounce their allegiance to God and monarch."[7] In the case of women, as Carmen Nocentelli observes, "'to turn Turk' might mean not only to convert to Islam but also 'to become a whore' or 'to commit adultery.'"[8] While, as Daniel Vitkus notes, Othello is "a 'purified' and Christianized Moor, converted to whiteness, washed clean by the waters of baptism," he remains nonetheless an outsider who seduces a nobly born Venetian woman.[9] As Habib suggests, Othello's "unnatural" marriage to Desdemona represents a clear "social danger to the state": the actions of a "black alien" seeking "legal access not only to permanent Venetian residency but also to political power."[10] As mentioned above, from Brabanzio's distraught perspective, only charms or spells could have accomplished such a feat. Iago and Brabanzio are not, of course, the only patriarchal figures within the play to reconfigure the nature of Desdemona's desire. Reading her response from a Christianized perspective, Othello declares that Desdemona takes pity on him for the pains he has experienced during the course of his travels. As he notes, "she loved me for the dangers I had passed, / And I loved her that she did pity them" (1.3.166–67). Pity is rendered here as Christian virtue, a submissive response to the sufferings of another individual. Stephen Greenblatt argues that Othello's "identity depends upon . . . an embrace and perpetual reiteration of the norms of another culture. It is this dependence that gives Othello, the warrior and alien, a relation to Christian values that is the existential equivalent of a religious vocation."[11] As an outsider converted to Christianity, Othello lacks the critical acumen to make Desdemona capable of a nuanced response to his tales. She may well take pity on him, but she is also subject to needs and desires that transcend the perimeters of a narrowly defined Christian virtue.

Othello's account, however, reveals the nature and source of Desdemona's attraction to his narratives. When brought before the Duke on charges that he used magic and charms to seduce her, Othello recounts:

> I spoke of most disastrous chances,
> Of moving accidents by flood and field,
> Of hair-breadth scapes i' th' imminent deadly breach,
> Of being taken by the insolent foe
> And sold to slavery, of my redemption thence,
> And portance in my traveller's history,
> Wherein of antres vast and deserts idle,
> Rough quarries, rocks, and hills whose heads touch heaven,
> It was my hint to speak. Such was my process,
> And of the cannibals that each other eat,
> The Anthropophagi, and men whose heads
> Do grow beneath their shoulders. (1.3.133–44)

Othello's "traveller's history" constitutes for Desdemona a cornucopia of what David McInnis has called "mind-travelling."[12] As Thomas Elyot describes in *The Boke Named the Governour* (1531), "What pleasure is it in one houre, to beholde those realms, cities, sees, ryvers, and mountaynes uneth [scarcely] in an olde mannes life can not be iournaide and pursued; what incredible delite is take[n] in beholding the diversities of people, beasts, foules, fishes, trees, frutes, and herbes."¹³ Indeed, Othello's travel narratives constitute a virtual curiosity cabinet of exotic objects over which to marvel. Early modern curiosity cabinets often housed wonders of the world, including birds, sea creatures, and other oddities found within nature. Ferrante Imperato's *Dell'historia naturale* (1599) is representative (fig. 5). The small room depicted in Imperato's sketch contains numerous artifacts from an exotic world and is an obvious source of fascination to those gathered within it.

Othello's travel narratives touch upon everything from his stint as prisoner, presumably in the hands of the Ottoman Turk, "the insolent foe," to the vast, barren, and strange lands he has traversed, to the seemingly bizarre cultures he has encountered. The cannibals or the anthropophagi, in particular, come to characterize the exoticism of a world Desdemona knows only through Othello's mesmerizing language. Men consuming other men: strange but wondrous creatures whose bodies are monstrously rearranged. Even while Othello relates his tales of wonder, Desdemona is pulled away by "house affairs" (1.3.146) to which she reluctantly attends. That she is drawn to the world outside her protected sphere, however, becomes readily apparent for, as Othello notes, "she'd come again, and with greedy ear / Devour up my discourse" (1.3.148–49).

From Othello's perspective, his appeal to Desdemona lies in her sympathies for him. Yet, the language he uses to describe her attraction speaks of appetite, for it is a "greedy ear" that "devour[s] up [his] discourse": a sexualized ear that eagerly receives his travel narration. Desdemona clearly cannot get enough of his tales of adventure. Emily Bartels suggests that "when Othello wants to exonerate himself from charges of bewitching Desdemona, he writes her into his narrative of exoticism, portraying her as a vicarious adventurer, hungry to hear of his 'disastrous chances' (I.iii.134) and frustrated by 'house affairs' (I.iii.147)."¹⁴ Yet, Desdemona is clearly not weak spirited, nor is Othel-

Io's storytelling just a means to get her out of the kitchen, so to speak. His tales instead arouse Desdemona's desire for adventure of her own. This is evident when, as Othello further relates,

> My story being done,
> She gave me for my pains a world of kisses,
> She swore in faith 'twas strange, 'twas passing strange,
> 'Twas pitiful, 'twas wondrous pitiful.
> She wished she had not heard it, yet she wished
> That heaven had made her such a man. (1.3.157–62)

While he reads her response as one of pity—"She gave me for my pains a world of kisses"—I read arousal. Indeed, there is an almost orgasmic rhythm in lines punctuated by kisses. Her reported language is breathy, repeated again and again until an aroused Desdemona arrives at her wish "that heaven had made her such a man." I think it important to note that Desdemona's decidedly erotic desire here is not for Othello's battered, bruised, or sexualized body, but rather for the travel his marvelous narratives have awakened. While their exchange here is undeniably sexualized, the climax she reaches is a realization that she wishes "that heaven had made her such a man" so that she could experience firsthand Othello's wondrous adventures. His concluding argument to the Duke, "this only is the witchcraft I have used" (1.3.168), is in many respects ironic for his tales of wonder and adventure constitute a kind of witchcraft for Desdemona: his marvelous narratives are every bit a drug to one who has been restricted to the domestic sphere. Indeed, it is the strange, man-eating world that Desdemona very much desires to experience.

The imminent Ottoman threat against Cyprus opens the door for Desdemona's own travel narrative as well as her misrepresented desire. When he learns that he "must away tonight" (1.3.276), Othello requests "fit disposition for my wife, / Due reverence of place and exhibition, / With such accommodation and besort / As levels with her breeding" (1.3.234–37). His initial request seems to acknowledge the unsuitability of Cyprus for Desdemona. Such "disposition" is clearly not on a ship engaged in battle against the Turks; nor does Cyprus seem an especially appropriate place for the nobly born Desdemona. The Duke's suggestion—"Why, at her father's!" (1.3.238)—seems, in fact, the best one. From the play's patriarchal perspective, there really is no other place suitable for the general's wife. That this suggestion proves unacceptable either to Brabanzio or Othello is not difficult to understand given residual tensions surrounding the marriage. From Brabanzio's vantage point, a Moor has seized his daughter, and as her father he is "done" with her (1.3.188). Othello does not disagree. Desdemona is now his, having transferred her allegiance from father to husband. Yet, neither one proposes she join the general as he journeys toward battle with the Turks. Othello, in fact, represents war as a "flinty and steel couch" (1.3.228) that may suit his hardened disposition, but not his wife's.

It is Desdemona herself who proposes that she be allowed to travel with her husband as he battles the Turks. As she argues,

> If I be left behind,
> A moth of peace, and he go to the war,
> The rites for why I love him are bereft me,
> And I a heavy interim shall support
> By his dear absence. Let me go with him. (1.3.254–58)

In many respects, her argument is conventional, that of a wife who does not want to be separated from her husband. After all, they have barely traded vows. Desdemona's fear of separation echoes, in fact, that of early modern wives left behind as their husbands departed on uncertain trading ventures. Such ventures often proved extremely difficult on the families of men engaged in trade who had to endure long periods of separation with the very real possibility that husbands, fathers, and sons might not return. As Bernard Capp notes, many an early modern marriage "ended in limbo, with a man going to sea, to the wars, or to seek work, and simply failing to return."[15]

Such uncertainty regarding the fate of missing spouses finds its way into *The Lawes Resolutions of Womens Rights* (1632), which defines the legal rights of women as maids, wives, and widows under English common law. In regard to missing husbands, the *Lawes* states that:

It falleth out not seldome, the one of them which are married to be taken captive, or otherwise so deteined, that it is uncertaine if he live or no. Therefore because it is in some sort dangerous to expect long the incertaine returne of an absent yoake-fellow, here the Civill Law did ordaine, that after a husband had beene gone five yeares, and nothing knowne whether he lived or no, the wife might marry againe, and so might the husband, that had expected his wife, &c. But the Common Law commandeth simply to forbeare marriage till the death of him or her that is missing be certainely knowne.[16]

This legal opinion must have proven small comfort to wives of missing travelers. Not only is there clear disparity between civil and common laws regarding remarriage—five years or never if the fate of the missing remains unknown—but the *Lawes* says virtually nothing about the separation issue.

Indeed, what the resolution fails to address is the emotional and physical privation wives of missing husbands must have experienced. Ann Christensen examines the many domestic dramas from the early modern period that address the unmet desires of "unpartnered wives."[17] As she notes, "beneath all the limitations caused by the absence of husbands is the extreme fragility of women's reputations."[18] There is, in other words, the expectation, real or purported, that wives of missing husbands will seek sexual satisfaction elsewhere. Not only were such women left virtual widows by their missing husbands, but they often had to contend with charges of sexual infidelity.

The "heavy interim" Desdemona will suffer with the "dear absence" of her husband would indeed be difficult, both emotionally and sexually. A 1624 broadside poignantly captures the dual turmoil experienced during such travel-related separations:

> All the tedious long Night
> In close Prison I lye,
> But methinks I behold
> My dear love lying by:

> In the midst of my pains,
> This doth still give me ease,
> That is pleasant to me
> Which some call a Disease.[19]

The speaker exudes a kind of wistfulness in this decidedly sexualized account of the travails of separation. It is during "tedious long Night" that the absence of a loved one becomes most painful. The husband's imaginary presence provides some "ease." Does this "prisoner" satisfy herself as well as her imagination to provide some relief for the anguish she is feeling? Does this ballad inscribe a guilty masturbatory pleasure to which this wife resorts during the long and torturous absence from her husband? Desdemona's privation could well be considered sexual as well as emotional since the "profit's yet to come 'tween" Desdemona and her husband (2.3.10).

At the same time, Desdemona's urgent request reveals a greater unmet desire: the desire to experience the adventures that caused her to fall in love with Othello in the first place. As she argues, "the rites for why I love him are bereft me" (1.3.254). Ronald Boling suggests that Desdemona "would seem to be abandoning the privileges of Venice, where her own life narrative is already scripted, to enter, as it were, Othello's narrative, to dwell in his heroic aura, to witness his legend in the making."[20] Yet, this reading merely reinforces a patriarchal view that a wife lives through her husband. Arguably, Desdemona could better "dwell in his heroic aura" surrounded by the privileges and protections afforded in Venice if this is all she desires. She clearly wants more. What draws Desdemona to Othello is the life he has led and the adventures he has experienced. Take that away and "the rites [i.e., reasons] for why [she] love[s] him are bereft." She thus seizes an opportunity to experience such adventure through him, no longer vicariously through his wondrous tales, but as Othello's "fair warrior" and as his equal (2.1.178).

That Desdemona's request is readily granted by the Duke is equally surprising given the purpose of the travel. He dismisses the matter with the remark: "be it as you shall privately determine, / Either for her stay or going" (1.3.274–75). Arguably the imminent attack by the

Turks drives this deference. Yet, if the Turks represent a grave and urgent threat to Cyprus, why would the general's wife be allowed to accompany him into a battle setting? When East India Company captain William Keeling requested permission to take his wife Anne on a trading venture in 1615, his request was denied by company officials who worried that a woman might prove a distraction not only to her husband, but also to the other men onboard.[21] Othello clearly anticipates objections from the Duke. After Desdemona pleads her case, Othello unexpectedly makes a similar appeal:

> Let her have your voice.
> Vouch with me heaven, I therefor beg it not
> To please the palate of my appetite,
> Nor to comply with heat—the young affects
> In me defunct—and proper satisfaction,
> But to be free and bounteous to *her mind*;
> And heaven defend your good souls that you think
> I will your serious and great business scant
> When she is with me. (1.3.259–67, my emphasis)

His appeal is both curious and revealing. Denying that his request is motivated by sexual desire, Othello gestures to Desdemona's needs; his request is made to comfort her "mind," not "to please the palate of [his] appetite." That he even brings up his sexual desires, however, is curious. One could argue that sex is very much on his mind, and he fears this will trouble the Duke as well. Othello's assurance that Desdemona's presence will in no way interfere with the "serious and great business" he is charged with overseeing makes him sound a bit like Captain Keeling. The general really doth protest too much! Desdemona could well become a distraction to Othello as he carries out this critical military engagement.

What is equally revealing is Othello's presentation of Desdemona. By referencing her mind, he likewise calls attention to her desires. Yet, in linking her to his physical needs, Othello misreads the nature of her desire, effectively reducing Desdemona to a sexualized object whose siren-like appeal threatens his libido. Importantly, it is this sexualized Desdemona, one that Othello creates through his own desire, who sets in motion the tragedy that ensues: her desire for travel within the strange and wondrous world he has known is reconfigured as desire for sexual adventure beyond the bounds of matrimony.

For Desdemona, travel to the island outpost of Cyprus results in a deadly metamorphosis. Through Iago's machinations, she devolves from chaste and loving wife to a "cunning whore of Venice" (4.2.93). While Iago authors Desdemona's mutation, this tragedy arguably would not have occurred had she never traveled from Venice. How is he able to manipulate such an outrageous narrative? Bartels suggests that Cyprus is an unfortunate location for Desdemona, given that it is "the locus of Venus and very wanton women in classical and other contemporary accounts—a dangerous place for a new wife to be on both accounts."[22] Once in Cyprus, Desdemona is labelled a "strumpet" (5.2.86), one who will "betray more men" (5.2.6). Yet, while an outpost, Cyprus is relatively staid. The Turks have threatened it, but they do not occupy it. When the drunken brawl breaks out on the streets, Othello angrily denounces it as "barbarous" (2.3.155) and the resulting discord "frights the isle / From her propriety" (2.3.158–59). Moreover, Desdemona is in the company of her husband. She is not one of the "idle" women transported to the Jamestown colony in the early 1620s to stabilize male settlers, an action Fiona McNeill describes as "an investment, or in early modern terms, an 'adventure' in the potential labor of the bodies of prostitutes and female vagrants."[23] Nonetheless, Desdemona's desire places her in a similar dilemma. With more than a little help from Iago, she is recast as a kind of Bianca: "a hussy that sells"—or in Desdemona's case, indulges—"her desires" (4.1.92).

Bianca proves, in fact, an important point of comparison when assessing Desdemona's altered representation in Cyprus. That Bianca is a courtesan, we know, but is she a permanent resident of Cyprus—one of the island's "working ladies" who greet the conquering warriors upon their arrival—or does she follow Cassio from Venice? Nicholas de Nicolay's travel narrative records numerous encounters with loose and lascivious women within the Mediterranean, suggesting that "the Ilands and Coastes of the Sea Mediterane, [are] given all to whoredome, sodometries, theft, and all other most detestable vices."[24] When greeting her for the first time, Cassio says: "I' faith, sweet love, I was coming to your house" (3.4.166). That Bianca has a house would seem to suggest that she is a resident of the island. Yet, Cassio is also described as having "lodging" on Cyprus (3.4.167). While "lodging" is arguably different from "house," it is by no means certain that Bianca permanently resides on the island. While time is somewhat indeterminate in the text, it is apparent that the two have known each other for a while. Moreover, Bianca is clearly impatient with Cassio's recent delay in visiting her: "What, keep a week away? Seven days and nights, / Eight-score-eight hours, and lovers' absent hours / More tedious than the dial eightscore times!" (3.4.168–70). Has Cassio traveled to the island before? Based on Iago's dismissive assessment of Cassio's battle experience, it seems unlikely that the Florentine knows her from previous military action. Moreover, Bianca's name, meaning "white," is Italian in origin. Based upon this textual evidence, it appears likely that Bianca knows Cassio from Venice and travels to Cyprus to be with him. Such movement would, in fact, not be inconsistent with that of early modern courtesans, who as Margaret Rosenthal and Duncan Salkeld have observed, possessed a degree of freedom not typically afforded to wives. Elizabeth Mazzola argues that "Bianca's agency . . . comes from being able to move so freely, and her movements allow her to challenge official notions of identity, place, and propriety."[25] Ironically, Mazzola could be describing Desdemona as well, whose travel from Venice to Cyprus challenges accepted notions of propriety for wives.

Within Cyprus, Desdemona almost immediately becomes associated with Bianca. Through Iago's misrepresentation, Bianca and Desdemona are also made to share a real, as well as purported sexual, relationship with Cassio. When Cassio asks his lover to copy the embroidery of the trifle he so admires—Desdemona's misplaced handkerchief—Bianca charges that it is "some token from a newer friend" (3.4.176). Clearly, Desdemona travels to Cyprus with her husband, not in expectation of meeting with a lover. As woman traveler, however, she is made guilty by association. Of course, if we view Bianca as traveler, who, like Desdemona, journeys to Cyprus in search of "adventure," the distinctions become even more blurred.

It may in fact be the nature of adventure itself that proves so detrimental to women's travel in *Othello*. From Desdemona's perspective, travel constitutes adventure. She will enter Othello's world of wondrous tales to experience "as a man" what the world has to offer. This objective is consistent with what the *Oxford English Dictionary* defines as "an extraordinary thing or event; a wonder; a marvel." While Othello's stories tell of danger and "hair-breadth scapes," she feels no fear. Yet, according to the OED, "adventure" in its verbal form also means, "to risk oneself." Indeed, travel with her husband does not protect Desdemona from the abusive perceptions of the play's patriarchal world, for Othello ultimately comes to embody those abuses as the result of his cultural Otherness: regressing to what he always already is. As Vitkus observes, "the play seems to prove the ancient proverb 'abluis Aethiopem, quid frustra,' as the Moor shows his true color—demonic black, burnt by hellfire and cursed by God."[26]

For Desdemona, danger lies not simply in cannibals or anthropophagi or barren crags that could dash a ship, but in a vicious patriarchal world that recasts a woman's desire for travel as one for adventure of a sexual nature: the journey itself becoming a metaphor for the female body opened up to common use. Boling argues that Othello "looses his worst brutality to force corruption upon her to overpower her will with his, to compel her to be as degenerate as he imagines her."[27] Yet, Desdemona is arguably doomed the moment she seizes the opportunity to go with Othello. When she enters into Othello's travel narratives with all their attendant dangers and intrigue, a role is subsequently constructed for her that reflects those narratives. Desdemona becomes the loose woman, "the cunning whore of Venice," a Bianca if you will, not because of any illicit sexual behavior on her part, but because within the play's patriarchal narrative this becomes the only role available to her. Through Iago's misogyny—indeed, through the play's patriarchy as a whole—Desdemona's desire is rewritten as part of the erotic and exotic world of Othello's travel narratives.

Notes

1. All quotations are from Shakespeare, *The Norton Shakespeare*.
2. Paré, *On Monsters*, 67.
3. Paré, *On Monsters*, 67.
4. Loomba, *Colonialism/Postcolonialism*, 107. Vitkus, *Turning Turk*, challenges a purely colonialist reading of late sixteenth- and seventeenth-century writings, suggesting that "from a vantage point of awe and deference (and sometimes envy), English writers began to gather knowledge about the Mediterranean world from a position of inferiority, not power, and so a Saidian 'orientalist discourse' based on power and the control of knowledge was not possible" (31).
5. Habib, "Black Alien," discusses the critically discussed possibility that the Duke summons one Marcus Luccicos before sending for Othello (1.3.44). As he notes, "from Venice's perspective, a presumably Christian Luccicos would have been a perfectly trustworthy choice as overall military leader, with the alien but usefully experienced Othello being a backup choice or a supplementary one" (149).
6. For accounts on "turning Turk," see Vitkus, *Turning Turk*; Matar, *Turks, Moors and Englishmen*; and Vitkus, *Piracy, Slavery, and Redemption*.
7. Matar, *Britain and Barbary*, 78.
8. Nocentelli, *Empires of Love*, 131.
9. Vitkus, *Turning Turk*, 91.
10. Greenblatt, *Self-Fashioning*, 245.
11. Habib, "Black Alien," 148.
12. See McInnis, *Mind-Travelling*.
13. Elyot quoted in McInnis, *Mind-Travelling*, 30.
14. Bartels, "Strategies of Submission," 424.
15. Capp, "Bigamous Marriage," 537.
16. T. E., *Lawes Resolutions*, 66.
17. Christensen, *Separation Scenes*, 12.
18. Christensen, *Separation Scenes*, 198.
19. *The Algerian Slaves Releasement or, The Unchangeable Boat-Swain* (London, 1624), quoted in Matar, *Britain and Barbary*, 79.
20. Boling, "Desdemona's Venetian Agency," 2.
21. See Barbour, "Desdemona and Mrs. Keeling," in this volume.
22. Bartels, "Strategies of Submission," 423.
23. McNeill, *Poor Women*, 182.
24. Nicholas de Nicolay, *The Navigations, Peregrination and Voyages, made into Turkie* (1571), quoted in Stanivukovic, "Cruising the Mediterranean," 66.

25. Mazzola, "Going Rogue," 39.
26. Vitkus, *Turning Turk*, 91.
27. Boling, "Desdemona's Venetian Agency," 18.

Bibliography

Bartels, Emily. "Strategies of Submission: Desdemona, the Duchess, and the Assertion of Desire." *Studies in English Literature* 36 (1996): 417–33.

Boling, Ronald J. "Desdemona's Venetian Agency." *Philological Review* 34, no. 1 (2008): 1–34.

Capp, Bernard. "Bigamous Marriage in Early Modern England." *Historical Journal* 52, no. 3 (2009): 537–56.

Christensen, Ann. *Separation Scenes: Domestic Drama in Early Modern England*. Lincoln: University of Nebraska Press, 2017.

Greenblatt, Stephen. *Renaissance Self-Fashioning: From More to Shakespeare*. 1980. Reprint, Chicago: University of Chicago Press, 2005.

Habib, Imtiaz. "The Black Alien in *Othello*: Beyond the European Immigrant." In *Shakespeare and Immigration*, edited by Ruben Espinosa and David Ruiter, 135–58. London: Routledge, 2014.

Loomba, Ania. *Colonialism/Postcolonialism*. London: Routledge, 1998.

Matar, Nabil. *Britain and Barbary, 1589–1689*. Gainesville: University Press of Florida, 2005.

———. *Turks, Moors, and Englishmen in the Age of Discovery*. New York: Columbia University Press, 1993.

Mazzola, Elizabeth. "Going Rogue: Bianca at Large." *Critical Survey* 27, no. 1 (2015): 36–59.

McInnis, David. *Mind-Travelling and Voyage Drama in Early Modern England*. New York: Palgrave Macmillan, 2013.

McNeill, Fiona. *Poor Women in Shakespeare*. Cambridge: Cambridge University Press, 2007.

Nocentelli, Carmen. *Empires of Love: Europe, Asia, and the Making of the Early Modern Identity*. Philadelphia: University of Pennsylvania Press, 2013.

Paré, Ambroise. *On Monsters and Marvels* (1571). Translated by Janis Pallister. Chicago: University of Chicago Press, 1982.

Rosenthal, Margaret. *The Honest Courtesan: Veronica Franco, Citizen and Writer in Sixteenth-Century Venice*. Chicago: University of Chicago Press, 1992.

Salkeld, Duncan. *Shakespeare among the Courtesans: Prostitution, Literature, and Drama, 1500–1650*. New York: Routledge, 2016.

Shakespeare, William. *The Norton Shakespeare*, edited by Stephen Greenblatt, et al. New York: Norton, 2008.

Stanivukovic, Goran. "Cruising the Mediterranean: Narratives of Sexuality and Geographies in Early Modern English Prose Romances." In *Remapping the Mediterranean World in Early Modern English Writings*, edited by Goran Stanivukovic, 59–74. New York: Palgrave Macmillan, 2007.

T. E. *The Lawes Resolutions of Womens Rights*. 1632. Clark NJ: Lawbook Exchange, 2005.

Vitkus, Daniel, ed. *Piracy, Slavery, and Redemption: Barbary Captivity Narratives from Early Modern England*. New York: Columbia University Press, 2001.

———. *Turning Turk: English Theater and the Multicultural Mediterranean, 1570–1630*. New York: Palgrave Macmillan, 2003.

11

Desdemona's Divided Duty

Gender and Courtesy in Othello

MICHAEL SLATER

> Brabantio. I pray you hear her speak!
> If she confess that she was half the wooer,
> Destruction on my head if my bad blame
> Light on the man! Come hither, gentle mistress,
> Do you perceive in all this noble company
> Where most you owe obedience? (1.3.174–79) [1]

In the patriarchal world of *Othello*, Desdemona marks a site of contest. Suspended between father and husband, Venice and Cyprus, domestic and public, her character is largely a function of place and obedience, and her relation to both is obscure. As her response to her father's question makes clear, Desdemona perceives in herself and her situation a "divided duty." Occupying the space in between, with no clear or obvious position, Desdemona represents, as Dympna Callaghan claims, a tabula rasa, "pure, white, and also blank . . . and since blank, open to any inscription."[2] Throughout the play Desdemona is subjected to many such inscriptions, variously and often conflictingly prescribed by the different masculine perspectives: by her father as the properly submissive daughter (the "maiden never bold"), by Cassio as the ineffable object of a courtly poetic tradition ("One that excels the quirks of blazoning pens"), and by both Iago and her husband as "that cunning whore of Venice" (1.3.95, 2.1.63, 4.2.90).

Such acts of inscription have not been limited to the play. Desdemona has been diversely appropriated by the critical tradition as well, particularly by readings of *Othello* concerned with gender and patriarchy. Whereas some critics regard Desdemona as utterly obedient to the dictates of her patriarchal culture, others find in her character an embodiment of willful subversion. Here, too, Desdemona represents something of a "divided" figure, poised inexplicably between the remarkable agency and self-assertion of the play's early scenes and the absolute obedience and passivity of its closing scenes. For some time now, critics have faced the challenge of reconciling or somehow accounting for Desdemona's divided portrait.

Nevertheless, our impulse to reconcile the play's two visions of Desdemona—the one violently self-assertive, the other disturbingly self-effacing—has too often exaggerated the disparity between her early and late appearances. Following critics such as Irene Dash and Sara Munson Deats, I argue that Desdemona is never as unconventional as she appears.[3] But whereas Dash suggests that we reassess our understanding of Desdemona, who ultimately only transfers obedience from one patriarch to another, I maintain that what is needed is a reassessment of convention. Too often, I think, we have focused on Desdemona's gender while ignoring her class. Her position within the intensely patriarchal world of Venice is certainly constrained because she is a woman, but her status as a member of the aristocracy no less powerfully shapes Desdemona's character. Reading *Othello* through the lens of courtly ideals, I contend, can help us to more fully account for Desdemona's unique journey throughout the play—both her travel within and beyond Venice and ultimately her travail.

A "Maiden Never Bold": Women and the Literature of Conduct

For nearly thirty years, scholarship has tended to locate Shakespeare's female characters—Desdemona included—principally within the context of a domestic discourse: hence, to evaluate them according to a set of prescriptive texts that purport to exemplify the ideal wife and/or daughter. In *Fashioning Femininity*, Karen Newman neatly identifies the essential characteristics of this domestic ideal: "Religious handbooks and sermons, as well as secular works," she notes, "all represent sexual roles in binary terms: men love, women submit; men speak, women are silent; men provide through work outside the home, women are confined to the home."[4] At least since Peter Stallybrass published his foundational essay, "Patriarchal Territories: The Body Enclosed," these traits have come to dominate discussions of gender in the early modern world. As Phyllis Rackin wryly observes, "[r]eminders that women were expected to be chaste, silent, and obedient probably occur more frequently in recent scholarship than they did in the literature of Shakespeare's time."[5]

While conclusions about Desdemona's role in *Othello* have often varied, regarding her either as an exemplar of the domestic ideal or as a challenge to it, the context itself has remained highly consistent. Peter Erickson, for instance, argues that Desdemona attempts, however ineffectually, to escape the "domestic realm" of her father's home through her elopement with Othello; like Dash before him, though, Erickson finds that the play ultimately treats Desdemona as "still only an accomplished housewife."[6] In David Bevington's account, Desdemona succumbs finally at her death to her culture's rampant sexism, "lapsing sadly into the stereotypical role of passive and silent sufferer that the Venetian world expects of women."[7] More strikingly still, Diane Elizabeth Dreher vigorously asserts that Desdemona's "tragic state stems from slavish conformity" to the traditional Renaissance ideal of a wife's relation to her husband, "that of an obedient child."[8] As Othello murders Desdemona, she "becomes the ultimate embodiment of the feminine ideal: silent, cold, and chaste."[9]

Other critics, however, insist that Desdemona stridently subverts such ideals. In Ann Jennalie Cook's insightful analysis, Desdemona remains as courageous and subversive at the play's conclusion as she was at its inception. Her final statement in the play only superficially absolves Othello of responsibility for her murder. More to the point, it reveals her consistently rebellious agency: "if her choice of Othello involves parental defiance or social disgrace or public humiliation or even undeserved death, so be it. She alone, 'Nobody—I myself,' has made the choice, and she alone accepts responsibility for its consequences."[10] Deats, for her part, names more specifically the character of feminine transgression in *Othello*. Desdemona may become stunningly passive at her death, but in her earlier behavior—not unlike Emilia's at the end—she "violates three cardinal rules for the good wife: to be silent, to remain at home, and to obey her husband."[11] Indeed, for Lena Cowen Orlin, Desdemona's speech at court and her subsequent travel both flagrantly challenge the patriarchal order of Venetian society. "Just as Desdemona's relocation to Cyprus is the most unfit of her physical dispositions," she maintains, "so her very request to accompany Othello there is the most troubling—and most portentous—instance of her agency."[12] Given the double failure to remain silent and to remain home, her tragedy seems all but inevitable.

The domestic ideal against which Desdemona is so frequently judged is not difficult to find in early modern handbooks. In fact, its persistence in early modern texts, along with the insistence with which it is expressed, may go a long way to explain the prevalence of this ideal in contemporary criticism. Submission, silence, and confinement certainly appear from a host of authors to have been among the chief virtues of an early modern woman. In his rather colorful injunction against female speech in 1631, for instance, Richard Brathwait advises that "[w]hat is spoken of Maids may be properly applied to all women: They should be seene and not heard.... What restraint is required in respect of the tongue may appear by that ivory guard or garrison by which it is impaled: See, how it is double warded, that it may with more reservancy and better security be restrained!"[13] A woman's mouth, like her body more generally, was to remain steadfastly closed, her tongue locked away behind her ivory teeth. An open mouth or a loose tongue might imply a loose woman, as Barnabe Rich makes clear. In *My Ladies Looking Glasse* (1616), he elaborates more overtly—and apparently with biblical precedent—the deeply entrenched connections between a woman's speech, a woman's travel outside the home, and her sexual promiscuity:

> Salomon thinketh that a good woman should be a home *housewife*, he pointeth her out her houseworke. Shee overseeth the waies of her household ... but *the pathes of a harlot* (he saith) are *moovabl, for now shee is in the house,* now in *the streetes,* now *shee lieth in waite*

in every corner, she is still gadding from place to place, from person to person, from companie to company: from custome to custome, she is ever more wandring: her feet are wandring, her eies are wandring, her wits are wandring . . . *a harlot is full of wordes, she is loude and babbling,* saith Salomon.[14]

The increasing anxiety of Rich's account illustrates how seamlessly a woman's speech and physical mobility could come to signify a dangerous sexuality in the early modern imagination. To travel in such a context was problematic because the boundaries of the home functioned as a protective guard for a woman's chastity.[15]

It seems painfully clear how someone like Brathwait or Rich—indeed, how many of Shakespeare's contemporaries—might have perceived Desdemona. By eloping with Othello, she appears to violate all of these prohibitions in a single gesture. Desdemona escapes what Brabantio calls the "guardage" of her father's home, an act of unprotected and unsanctioned mobility she then defends by means of public speech. In her defense of this initial movement outside the home, moreover, Desdemona proclaims with "downright violence" a further desire to escape Venice by attending her husband to Cyprus. If, as Henry Smith warns in *A Preparative to Marriage* (1591), "a wife should teach her feet, go not beyond the door," Desdemona fails entirely. Measuring her character against this domestic ideal has enabled us to articulate a space for feminine resistance in *Othello*, challenging earlier interpretations that have regarded Desdemona as at best docile and tedious or at worst complicit in her own tragedy.[16] At the same time, though, such readings almost certainly stumble when Desdemona becomes at the end of the play, as Lodovico puts it, "truly, an obedient lady" (4.1.239).

Our frequent attempts to situate *Othello* within a broader context of conduct manuals and marriage tracts have contributed substantially to our understanding of early modern patriarchy and the constraining concepts of gender it entailed. But such attempts also underscore what Carolyn Porter describes as the overarching danger of the New Historicism. In her remarkable essay, "Are We Being Historical Yet?," Porter claims that the chief methodological problem of new historicist scholarship consists "in being limited to one set of discourses—those which form the site of a dominant ideology—and then reifying that limit as if it were coterminous with the limits of discourse in general."[17] As critics we have tended to settle on a particular set of patriarchal norms, implicitly positing a universal and consistent discourse on female subjectivity and behavior. The facts and contexts we emphasize ultimately shape the kinds of narratives we can tell. With Desdemona, as with many of Shakespeare's female characters, that narrative has persistently been one of patriarchal oppression—a narrative that stresses above all chastity, silence, obedience, and confinement.[18]

If this story is the most consistently told, however, it is not the only one we might tell. The ideal of domestic confinement may have been among the most widely articulated in the period, but it does not in itself mark the limits of gender discourse in early modern England. As Ann Rosalind Jones argues, it represents only one element in a more complex discursive system, a particularly "bourgeois" conception of domesticity.[19] Against the bourgeois ideals of conduct books and Protestant marriage manuals, another set of texts, courtesy books, circulated a vastly different conception of the feminine ideal—the court lady. Despite increasing instability among the aristocracy in the late sixteenth and early seventeenth centuries, the ideal of the court lady persisted in the public imagination and discourse. In 1561 for instance, Sir Thomas Hoby produced an English edition of Castiglione's *The Book of the Courtier* (1528), and as late as 1581 George Pettie translated Stefano Guazzo's *Civil Conversation* (1574). The extraordinary popularity of these texts as models of courtly behavior in England has been well documented, the former's influence so pervasive that it became, as one critic puts it, "almost a second bible for English gentlemen."[20]

While much of courtesy literature was directed to the conduct of male courtiers, both Castiglione's *Courtier* and Guazzo's *Civil Conversation* devoted considerable attention to the significance of a female presence at court. In the beginning of the third book of the *Courtier*, for instance, Cesare Gonzaga claims that "there is no Court, however great, that can possess adornment or splendour or gaiety without the presence of women," and as any court is imperfect without women, so too, he continues, is any discussion of the ideal courtier imperfect without an examination of his female counterpart.[21] Just as the ideal courtier represented a model of behavior that solidified class distinction, a code of conduct that allegedly could not be emulated by the lower ranks, the ideal of the court lady distinguished itself from lower-class conceptions of proper female conduct. Her very presence at court was a marker of nobility and already a significant divergence from bourgeois ideals of domestic confinement. And whereas "the bourgeois wife was enjoined to silence," Jones declares, "the court lady was *required* to speak."[22]

Female participants in civil conversation were a central element of courtly entertainment, as Castiglione's courtiers repeatedly insist. Giuliano de' Medici, the Magnifico, advises that

> the lady who is at Court should properly have, before all else, a certain pleasing affability whereby she will know how to entertain graciously every kind of man with charming and honest conversation, suited to the time and the place and the rank of the person with whom she is talking. And her serene and modest behaviour, and the candour that ought to inform all her actions, should be accompanied by a quick and vivacious spirit by which she shows her freedom from boorishness; but with such a virtuous manner that she makes herself thought no less chaste, prudent and benign than she is pleasing, witty, and discreet.[23]

The court lady, like the courtier, is valued for her pleasing and witty contributions to discussion, but she must also maintain with utmost rigor the appearance of her chastity and prudence. She must "observe a certain difficult mean," appearing amiable, but not too amiable.[24] "Rather than prohibiting amorous repartee to women," Jones explains that "the courtly code elicited it from them. To paraphrase Foucault, the court lady had to speak of sex; she had to speak in public, and in a manner determined by the divisions between licit and illicit pleasure. She performed a generalized erotic function directly opposed to the silent fidelity demanded of the private woman."[25] In her attempt to manage the boundary between licit and illicit, the court lady faced two opposing challenges—to appear neither excessively sexual nor excessively reserved, for both could signify indecency:

> Nor in her desire to be thought chaste and virtuous, should she appear withdrawn or run off if she dislikes the company she finds herself in or thinks the conversation improper. For it might easily be thought that she was pretending to be straight-laced simply to hide something she feared others could find out about her; and in any case, unsociable manners are always deplorable. Nor again, in order to prove herself free and easy, should she talk immodestly or practice a certain unrestrained and excessive familiarity or the kind of behaviour that leads people to suppose of her what is perhaps untrue.[26]

Despite the overt sexual function she served, the courtly code fixated upon a woman's chastity as obsessively as the domestic code. Both attempted to discipline rigidly female sexuality and desire, but women were offered by each wildly different strategies for representing their chaste demeanor. Whereas the bourgeois wife was admonished to remain silent and to confine herself within the home, the court lady was instructed to speak, and to do so in public.

To "Lie by an Emperor's Side": Desdemona's Place at Court

Given the presence of a courtly discourse that expressed a distinctly aristocratic ideal, it seems somewhat surprising that critics would locate Desdemona so consistently within the context of bourgeois gender ideology. As the daughter of a Venetian senator that "hath in his effect a voice potential / As double as the Duke's," Desdemona clearly belongs to a noble family (1.2.13–14). When Othello is informed that he must journey to Cyprus, he requests that the Duke allow some "fit disposition" for his wife, such as "levels with her breeding," and Desdemona is routinely described as "fair," "gentle" and "noble," all markers of class status (1.3.235, 238). Even as Iago aims to erode Othello's confidence in Desdemona's love by indicating that she married outside "her own clime, complexion, *and degree*," moreover, Othello initially insists that he is every bit her equal—not just in clime or complexion, but especially in degree (3.3.234). As Rebecca Olson points out, Othello originally seems more concerned that his station, not his race, may prove worrisome for his new father-in-law. "Let him do his spite," Othello boasts as he considers the possibility that Brabantio may challenge his marriage, confident that both his social position and accomplishments will be sufficient to ensure the match:

> My services which I have done the Signory
> Shall out-tongue his complaints. 'Tis yet to know—
> Which, when I know that boasting is an honour,
> I shall promulgate—I fetch my life and being
> From men of royal siege. (1.2.17–22)

What stands out to Othello, at least prior to Iago's insinuations, is not so much that Desdemona is white and he black, but that she is of the highest social standing. In defending the legitimacy of his marriage, he claims to have been bred, like her, "from men of royal siege." While critical discussions have tended to focus more on racial and gender differences, the play seems from the very beginning to be as invested in distinctions of class and status.

When critics note that Desdemona's speech before the court, particularly her frank assessment of her own involvement in the marriage and her request to accompany Othello to Cyprus, brazenly challenges the patriarchal norms of her culture, they ultimately overlook the importance of social rank. Speaking in such a context may have been deemed inappropriate for some women, but for a court lady it was expected. In fact, Desdemona is openly invited to speak multiple times throughout the scene. When the Duke says to her, "What would you, Desdemona," he asks that she speak her will (1.3.245). Her father, too, when she first arrives on stage, asks that Desdemona speak. "I pray you, hear her speak," he says to the court, and though he may be dissatisfied with her response, Desdemona's statement proves sufficient to assert her agency, to demonstrate, as Brabantio has it, that she was "half the wooer" (1.3.174–75). Unlike Emilia at the end of the play, Desdemona does not speak out of turn; not once enjoined to silence, her speech does not appear to threaten the patriarchal order of the play.

If Desdemona's social status and her accompanying license to speak are beyond question, certain elements of the play still seem to indicate that she functions within the parameters of domestic ideology. In his discussion of wooing Desdemona in act 1, for instance, Othello alludes in passing to her domestic responsibilities within the confines of Brabantio's household. Relating to the court, as he often did in Brabantio's home, fantastic tales of cannibals and "men whose heads / Do grow beneath their shoulders," Othello claims,

> This to hear
> Would Desdemona seriously incline;
> But still the *house affairs* would draw her thence,
> Which *ever as she could with haste dispatch*
> She'd come again, and with greedy ear
> Devour up my discourse. (1.3.144–50; italics mine)

In her incisive reading of these lines, Orlin suggests that Desdemona's house-affairs establish her "place" within a patriarchal social structure. "This passage," she explains, "establishes a telling dichotomy between, on the one hand, Othello's stories of sieges and monsters and, on the other, Desdemona's duties in managing Brabantio's wifeless household. The house exerts a socializing force that 'ever' and 'again' she attempts to frustrate, but her responsibilities repeatedly 'draw her' away from Othello."[27] The socializing force of the house is certainly not without significance, but there is no indication that Desdemona's duties are those of the bourgeois daughter or wife; her "house-affairs," as Orlin recognizes, almost certainly signify management of Brabantio's home, not her own domestic labor. Nor, for that matter, are domestic responsibilities antithetical to the aristocratic ideal of the court lady. In addition to her courtly virtues, Cesare Gonzaga explains that the court lady should have also "the qualities that are common to all kinds of women, such as goodness and discretion, the ability to take good care . . . of her husband's belongings and house and children, and the virtues belonging to a good mother."[28]

Although she has a domestic role in *Othello*, Desdemona's character is by no means restricted exclusively to the domestic sphere. For while Othello acknowledges the social force exerted on Desdemona by her father's house, he also obliquely describes the courtly education she received under her father's care: "'Tis not to make me jealous / To say my wife is fair, feeds well, loves company, / Is free of speech, sings, plays, and dances well," a catalogue of traits that mirrors almost identically the "more worldly education" Guazzo claims is necessary for a "girl who is to go to court" (3.3.186–88). As Guazzo continues to explain, the court lady will need to "write, to discourse, to sing, to play on Instruments, to daunce, and to be able to perform all that which belongeth to a Courtier to doe."²⁹ In our attempt to understand the patriarchal structures that frame the world of the play, we cannot overemphasize the importance of Desdemona's education. Education is telling because it had, as Guazzo recognized, pragmatic significance: "At this day," he claims, "the manner of bringing up [daughters] is so different, I say not of one Countrey from another, yea but of one Countye, and of one Citie, that a manne can set downe no certaine determinate rule of it."³⁰ Because of intense class and regional variation in the codes of conduct regulating female behavior, Guazzo argues that a girl's education should vary to suit the style of life she will lead. A woman who is to maintain a life of silent confinement has no need of the education Desdemona apparently received. She was taught to sing, to play instruments, to dance, and to engage in witty discourse because it was expected she would entertain at court.

In her many appearances throughout the play, Desdemona frequently exhibits the characteristics that stem from her courtly education. To begin with, we actually hear her sing in act 4, and given its underlying circumstances, we might safely assume the "willow song" to be an especially poignant performance. Indeed, even at the height of his madness, Othello himself testifies to the bewitching charm of Desdemona's voice. "Hang her," he says, as he plots her murder, "I do but say what she is: so delicate with / her needle, an admirable musician—O, she will sing the / savageness out of a bear—of so high and plenteous wit and invention" (4.1.181–84). In addition to her unparalleled talents as a musician and singer, Othello catalogues a range of other notably aristocratic qualities: her delicacy with needlework, for instance, and most importantly her "high" wit and invention. She is for Othello a paragon of courtly virtue—a woman fit for a king, not a general. Her status and skill are such that "[s]he might lie by an emperor's side," as he all too anxiously acknowledges (4.1.178).[31]

Of all her courtly gifts, though, perhaps none is more conspicuous than Desdemona's rhetorical proficiency. She dexterously navigates a perilous situation at court, expressing in the same breath both deference and defiance toward her father. Even more strikingly, she speaks openly about her own desire and sexual appetite, but always with the careful euphemism of a court lady. When Brabantio seeks to determine if she was "half the wooer," he significantly underestimates not only Desdemona's agency, but her subtlety and sophistication in courtship, too. Othello, in his attempt to court Desdemona, tells her the story of his life:

> My story being done
> She gave me for my pains a world of sighs:
> She swore, in faith 'twas strange, 'twas passing strange,
> 'Twas pitiful, 'twas wondrous pitiful!'
> She wished she had not heard it, yet she wished
> That heaven had made her such a man. (1.3.158–63)

Her response, in addition to miming the postures of a Petrarchan lover, reveals simultaneously her admiration and pity for Othello, her appetite for adventure, and her sexual desire. There is nothing especially immodest here: on the surface, Desdemona merely relates her wish that she too could have been made such a man, that she too might have experienced such a "pilgrimage" (1.3.153). When she travels to Cyprus not long after, it is in part the fulfillment of this wish. But beneath the surface, Desdemona expresses an entirely different desire. Her longing to be transformed into a man like Othello pales before her more salient—if only because more realistic—desire to *have* a man like Othello. She wishes, that is, that "heaven had made [for] her such a man," an implication she reinforces by suggesting that any potential suitor need only be taught Othello's story. Desdemona proves to be as aggressive in the courtship as Othello, if not more so (half the wooer, indeed). She speaks here and elsewhere about sex, as Jones indicates the court lady must. But she deftly manages in her speech to be suggestive without being explicit, respecting the crucial boundary between licit and illicit.

Even as Desdemona's loquaciousness and physical motions violate central tenets of the domestic ideal, they nonetheless conform to both the ideals and the realities of early modern court ladies, at least as far as we know them. Beyond her penchant for cunning speech and amorous conversation, Desdemona's courtliness extends also to her physical "disposition," the various places that, as Othello has it, "level[s] with her breeding" (1.3.238). Her travel to Cyprus may have been somewhat exceptional even for a court lady, but Desdemona's general mobility outside her father's home was not remotely atypical. Aristocratic women in England often exercised considerable authority and agency over themselves and others. As Phyllis Rackin claims, they "managed great estates and wielded economic power comparable to that of the head of a large modern corporation."[32] Travel was often a practical reality of their lives. In fact, as Diana Henderson argues, "[s]ome aristocratic women . . . managed to avoid being confined to any of their numerous homes, much less 'the' home."[33] We know from various accounts that women of many social stations traveled outside the home regularly, as Patricia Akhimie and Laura Williamson Ambrose document in their contributions to this collection. For aristocratic women in particular, such travel was vitally important not only for the maintenance of scattered estates, but also for the upkeep of significant social networks. The household accounts of Lady Anne Lestrange, for example, demonstrate that while she herself rarely left the vicinity of her primary residence in Norfolk, she routinely entertained a host of aristocratic female visitors—Lady Elizabeth Woodhouse, Margaret Lestrange (her aunt), Lady Elizabeth Robsart, Anne Shelton (Anne Boleyn's first cousin), Elizabeth Boleyn (Ann's mother), Catherine Hastings, Lady Catherine Lovell, Anne Lovell, Lady Bedingfield, and Mary Mordaunt all among her frequent guests.[34] Sometimes they appear to have traveled with their husbands, often without them.

For an actual court lady like Eleanor, the Countess of Rutland, travel was an even more common aspect of social life. In *English Aristocratic Women, 1450-1550*, Barbara Harris details Lady Rutland's "peripatetic existence" and "itinerant lifestyle." She "traveled regularly between the court; the Rutland's main residence at Belvoir Castle, Lincolnshire; their London mansion at Holywell; and their manor at Endfield, Middlesex, just outside of the city."[35] A life at the center of court was hardly governed by the dictates of domesticity. The critical commonplace that "[w]oman's place was within doors, her business domestic," while questionable more generally, certainly does not apply to a character like Desdemona.[36] Tellingly, we seem to have been more concerned that Desdemona has violated a central rule in her travel than are the patriarchs of the play, not one of whom registers even the slightest apprehension at the prospect that she might follow Othello to Cyprus. To be sure, Brabantio and Roderigo and Iago all voice concern over her elopement, a different instance of her agency. But nobody challenges her request to leave Venice. Othello immediately lends his own consent, seeking only to reassure the court that she shall not prove a distraction to his duties. Such assurances made, the Duke responds to Desdemona's request quite simply: "Let it be so" (1.3.285). Her travel, in and of itself, is not what leads to Desdemona's troubles. But her status as a court lady, which enables that travel, does offer Iago a powerful tool for his machinations.

That "Cunning Whore of Venice": The Dangers of Courtliness

If the court lady ideally enjoyed a wider range of freedoms than her domestic counterpart, those freedoms were not without risk. Her chastity, too, was of the utmost concern, and motion and speech could still be linked with sexual promiscuity. In Brabantio's painfully naive vision, Desdemona was to remain "[a] *maiden* never bold, / Of spirit so *still* and *quiet* that her motion / Blushed at herself" (1.3.95-97; emphasis mine). Even for his aristocratic daughter, Brabantio appears to prize immobility and silence, qualities he clearly takes to be signs of innocence and chastity. The differences between domestic and courtly ideals, though great, were not absolute. Ideals of appropriate feminine behavior, as we might expect, could be messy and uncertain. The most progressive of Castiglione's courtiers still recognize that a woman's speech might pose distinct dangers. Her task was challenging: to appear in her speech and manner both chaste and prudent even as she was also pleasing and witty. She had to "observe a certain difficult mean, composed as it were of contrasting qualities, and take care not to stray beyond certain fixed limits."[37] Her speech was expected, but not thereby free from scrutiny. Likewise, her travel beyond the protective boundary of the home allows room for suspicion and jealousy that a life of confinement would seem largely to foreclose.

For Desdemona, these dangers finally prove tragic. The plot to unhinge Othello can succeed only to the degree that his wife behaves as a typical court lady, as Iago plainly admits in act 2. His chief strategy to manipulate Othello entails refashioning the dictates of courtesy into an impression of lechery. As Cassio and Desdemona exchange pleasantries in Cyprus, Iago, standing aside, takes us into his confidence:

> He takes her by the palm—ay, well said, whisper!—with as little a web as this will I ensnare as great a fly as Cassio.—Ay, smile upon her, do! I will gyve thee in thine own courtship.—You say true, 'tis so indeed.—If such tricks as these strip you of your lieutenantry, it had been better you had not kissed your three fingers so oft, which now again you are most apt to play the sir in.—Very good, will kissed, and excellent courtesy! 'Tis so indeed. (2.1.165–73)

Considering that Iago's displeasure and vindictiveness stem at least partly from his inferior social and military position, despite his allegedly superior merits, his obsession with courtesy as the mechanism for revenge is especially fitting. His plan is laden with snide references to the conventions and ambitions of the social elite. Cassio is apt "to play the sir," to assume the standard graces of nobility. Touching hands, kissing fingers, doting smiles, excessive praise, and witty banter—these are the signs of an "excellent courtesy," but they are also the signs, as

Iago knows, of "courtship." The etymological link between "courtesy" (2.1.172) and "courtship" (2.1.168), which can signify both courtly behavior and romantic flirtation, underscores just how seamlessly the former can bleed into the latter. Iago is without question a cunning foe, but his task is by no means Herculean.

As the play proceeds, we witness Iago's strategy in action on multiple occasions. Before convincing Othello of Desdemona's infidelity, Iago first takes aim at a more gullible mark. Like Othello, Roderigo idolizes Desdemona. And like Othello, he is initially unwilling to believe her susceptible to extramarital seduction. When Iago implies that Desdemona's nature will "compel her to some second choice," Roderigo vigorously objects: "I cannot believe that in her: she's full of most / blest condition" (2.1.228, 2.1.242–43). Iago thus finds in Roderigo a prime surrogate to test his plot.

> IAGO. Blest fig's end! The wine she drinks is made of grapes.
> If she had been blest, she would never have loved the
> Moor. Blest pudding! Didst thou not see her paddle with
> the palm of his hand? Didst not mark that?
> RODERIGO. Yes, that I did—but that was but courtesy.
> IAGO. Lechery, by this hand!—an index and obscure
> prologue to the history of lust and foul thoughts. They
> met so near with the lips that their breaths embraced
> together. Villainous thoughts, Rodergio! (2.1.244–52)

Iago attempts primarily to diminish Desdemona's status in the eyes of the men who adore her. Reversing the transmutation by which grapes become wine, he hopes to demystify the court lady by revealing her baser parts—her lust, her foul thoughts, her sinful breath. Roderigo's idealistic description of Desdemona as "blest" mutates, at the hands of Iago, into a shockingly bawdy, basely sexual innuendo. "Blest fig's end!" is doubly suggestive: while "end" is not uncommonly glossed as "genitalia," Michael Neill notes that *fica*, or "fig," could also refer to "a woman's quaint," a crude reduction of Desdemona to her sexual parts.[38] The divine associations of "blest," not unlike the divine associations of wine, are degraded to mundane materiality. Herein lies the essence of Iago's scheme. As he points out the paddling of palms, Roderigo calls it what it is. "That was but courtesy," he insists, but under pressure of Iago's quasi-alchemical wit, courtesy devolves. "Lechery, by this hand!"

The same tactic can be uncovered in Iago's interactions with Othello. In the moments Othello most emphasizes Desdemona's courtly nature, Iago strikes. At the outset of act 4, just as he settles increasingly upon the idea of murder, for instance, Othello laments the future loss of a wife so "delicate," delineating her many courtly skills: needlework, music, singing, wit, and invention. "She's the worse for all this," Iago declares, to which Othello offers his hearty—and yet still qualified—assent:

> OTHELLO. O, a thousand thousand times! And then of so gentle a condition—
> IAGO. Ay, too gentle.
> OTHELLO. Nay, that's certain. (4.1.186–89)

Iago's "too gentle" speaks volumes, a double entendre that, as Rebecca Olson claims, thoroughly conflates Desdemona's social standing, her gentility, with her alleged promiscuity, her pliability.[39] She too easily grants her suitors' "favors," Iago implies.

The more fully Desdemona adheres to the social codes of court, the more susceptible she becomes to Iago's trap. This, I think, is the root of her tragedy. Her suits on behalf of Cassio to restore his social standing are perfectly in keeping with the court lady's role; predictably, they serve only to further estrange her from Othello, who now sees his wife's courteous preferment only through the prism of her devious sexuality. The point is not that Desdemona defies convention at the beginning of the play only to succumb to it so completely at her death. Desdemona was never quite as unconventional as she seemed, if only we apply the appropriate conventions. This does not make her any less remarkable, however. She is not tragically punished for flouting the oppressive codes of her patriarchal culture. Instead, and I think all the more tragically, she is punished for living up to them. She was charged to live according to an ideal "composed as it were of contrasting qualities." Her status demanded that she appear vivacious and seductive, but that she not "be seen to be seduced," as Jones reminds us.[40] Her death is thus the product of an attempt not to escape the constraints of domesticity, but to embody the virtues of a discourse deeply ambivalent in its demands—to embody, that is, her "divided duty."

Notes

1. All references to the play are to the Oxford World Classics *Othello*, edited by Michael Neill.
2. Callaghan, *Woman and Gender*, 78.
3. Situating Desdemona within conventional discourses surrounding marriage, Dash argues that the play merely has Desdemona transfer obedience from one patriarch (her father) to another (her husband) (*Wooing*, 119).
4. Newman, *Fashioning Femininity*, 19.
5. Rackin, *Shakespeare and Women*, 11.
6. Erickson, *Patriarchal Structures*, 93.
7. Bevington, introduction to *Othello*, 1121.
8. Dreher, *Domination and Defiance*, 92.
9. Dreher, *Domination and Defiance*, 95.
10. Cook, "The Design of Desdemona," 193.
11. Deats, "'Truly, an Obedient Lady,'" 249. See also Deats, "'Erring Barbarian,'" where she asserts that Desdemona "challenges all feminine ideals of the period" (204).
12. Orlin, "Desdemona's Disposition," 178.
13. Brathwaite, *English Gentlewoman*, 64, 88.
14. Rich, *My Ladies Looking Glasse*, 43–44. For additional conduct books prescribing such characteristics, see John Dod and Robert Cleaver's *A Godly Form of Household Government* (1621) and William Whately's *A Bride-Bush* (1617).
15. See also Smith, *Preparative to Marriage*: "Paul biddeth Titus to exhort women that they be chaste, and keeping at home: presently after chaste, he sayeth, keeping at home, as though home were chastity's keeper" (F6r–F7r).
16. For earlier critical accounts, see the characterization of "Othello critics" and "Iago critics" in Neely, "Women and Men."
17. Porter, "Are We Being Historical Yet?," and Wayne, "Historical Differences."
18. Orlin writes that "[l]iterary historians have so often repeated the mantra that women were enjoined . . . to be chaste, silent, and obedient; have so often described the spatial restrictions on women; and have so often 'explained' playtexts in terms taken from the most conservative literatures

of their time that the reigning orthodoxy of historiography has become that of patriarchal ideology. I and perhaps others have been seduced by the mere effort of research into thinking these prescriptions were culturally operative in a way that they cannot have been in many women's daily lives" ("Case for Anecdotalism," 75).

19. Jones, "Nets and Bridles," 40.
20. Simon, *Education and Society*, 340.
21. Castiglione, *Courtier*, 210.
22. Jones, "Nets and Bridles," 40.
23. Castiglione, *Courtier*, 212.
24. Castiglione, *Courtier*, 212.
25. Jones, "Nets and Bridles," 43–44.
26. Castiglione, *Courtier*, 212.
27. Orlin, "Desdemona's Disposition," 174–75.
28. Castiglione, *Courtier*, 212.
29. Guazzo, *Civil Conversation*, 78.
30. Guazzo, *Civil Conversation*, 74.
31. For an alternative treatment of Desdemona's social status, particularly the relation between her role as heir to Brabantio and the notion of jealousy, see Olson, "'Too Gentle,'" 20.
32. Rackin, *Shakespeare and Women*, 7.
33. Henderson, "Theater and Domestic Culture," 192.
34. Harris, *English Aristocratic Women*, 68.
35. Harris, *English Aristocratic Women*, 69–70.
36. Keeble, *Cultural Identity*, 186.
37. Castiglione, *Courtier*, 212.
38. Neill, *Othello*, 23n315.
39. Olson, "'Too Gentle,'" 20.
40. Jones, "Nets and Bridles," 45.

Bibliography

Bevington, David. Introduction to *Othello*. *The Complete Works of Shakespeare*, edited by David Bevington. New York: Harper Collins, 1992.

Brathwaite, Richard. *The English Gentlewoman*. London, 1631.

Callaghan, Dympna. *Woman and Gender in Renaissance Tragedy*. Atlantic Highlands NJ: Humanities Press International, 1989.

Castiglione, Baldesar. *The Book of the Courtier*. Translated by George Bull. London: Penguin, 1976.

Cook, Ann Jennalie. "The Design of Desdemona: Doubt Raised and Resolved." *Shakespeare Studies* 13 (1980): 187–96.

Dash, Irene. *Wooing, Wedding, and Power*. New York: Columbia University Press, 1981.

Deats, Sara Munson. "The 'Erring Barbarian' and the 'Maiden Never Bold': Racist and Sexist Representations in *Othello*." In *Women, Violence, and English Renaissance Literature*, edited by Linda Woodbridge and Sharon Beehler, 189–215. Tempe AZ: ACMRS, 2003.

———. "'Truly, an Obedient Lady': Desdemona, Emilia, and the Doctrine of Obedience in *Othello*." In *Othello: New Critical Essays*, edited by Philp Kolin and Francis Kuhn, 233–54. New York: Routledge, 2002.

Cleaver, Robert, and John Dod. *A Godly Form of Household Government*. London, 1621.

Dreher, Dianne Elizabeth. *Domination and Defiance: Fathers and Daughters in Shakespeare*. Lexington: University Press of Kentucky, 1986.

Erickson, Peter. *Patriarchal Structures in Shakespeare's Drama*. Berkeley: University of California Press, 1985.

Guazzo, Stephano. *The Civil Conversation*. London, 1581.

Harris, Barbara. *English Aristocratic Women, 1450–1550*. Oxford: Oxford University Press, 2002.

Henderson, Diana E. "The Theater and Domestic Culture." In *A New History of Early English Drama*, edited by John D. Cox and David Scott Kastan, 173–94. New York: Columbia University Press, 1997.

Jones, Ann Rosalind. "Nets and Bridles: Early Modern Conduct Books and Sixteenth-Century Women's Lyrics." In *The Ideology of Conduct*, edited by Nancy Armstrong and Leonard Tennenhouse, 39–72. New York: Methuen, 1987.

Keeble, N. H. *The Cultural Identity of Seventeenth-Century Woman*. New York: Routledge, 1994.

Neely, Carol Thomas. "Women and Men in Othello: 'What should such a fool / Do with so good a woman?'" *Shakespeare Studies* 10 (1977): 133–58.

Neill, Michael. Introduction and notes to *Othello*. Oxford: Oxford University Press, 2006.

Newman, Karen. *Fashioning Femininity and English Renaissance Drama*. Chicago: University of Chicago Press, 1991.

Olson, Rebecca. "'Too Gentle': Jealousy and Class in *Othello*." *The Journal for Early Modern Cultural Studies* 15, no. 1 (2015): 3–25.

Orlin, Lena Cowen. "A Case for Anecdotalism in Women's History." *English Literary Renaissance* 31, no. 1 (2001): 52–77.

———. "Desdemona's Disposition." In *Shakespearean Tragedy and Gender*, edited by Shirley Nelson Garner and Madelon Sprengnether, 84–110. Bloomington: Indiana University Press, 1996.

Porter, Carolyn. "Are We Being Historical Yet?" *South Atlantic Quarterly* 87 (1988): 743–86.

Rackin, Phyllis. *Shakespeare and Women*. Oxford: Oxford University Press, 2005.

Rich, Barnabe. *My Ladies Looking Glasse*. London, 1616.

Shakespeare, William. *Othello*. Edited by Michael Neill. Oxford: Oxford University Press, 2006.

Simon, Joan. *Education and Society in Tudor England*. Cambridge: Cambridge University Press, 1966.

Smith, Henry. *A Preparative to Marriage*. London, 1591.

Wayne, Valerie. "Historical Differences: Misogyny and *Othello*." In *The Matter of Difference: Materialist Feminist Criticism of Shakespeare*, edited by Valerie Wayne, 153–79. Ithaca NY: Cornell University Press, 1991.

Whately, William. *A Bride-Bush*. London, 1617.

12

From Adventure to Danger in the Travels of Desdemona and Miranda

EDER JARAMILLO

In her amazement, Miranda emphasizes the power of a "tale" that can "cure deafness" as she is captivated by the story Prospero tells about her own travels across the Mediterranean: "Your tale, sir, would cure deafness" (*Tmp.* 1.2.106),[1] she reassures her father. As was often the case for early modern women whose travels were largely reduced and even omitted by the renditions of male narrators, Miranda's journey is subject to the power of Prospero's tale. Most of her travel experiences are carefully crafted—indeed, reconstructed in her memory—into a peculiar narrative controlled by Prospero's narration of the past: too young to remember, Miranda learns that the story of her journey is one of exile, of torments in turbulent seas, and of her subsequent arrival on a remote island. Perhaps the most glaring detail from Miranda's travels is her experience on the island where she is met with another form of danger embodied in her cross-cultural encounter and subsequent interactions with Caliban.

For modern audiences and critics, the story of Miranda as a traveler plays a smaller, if at all significant, role in the ways we understand her plot. Were it not for Prospero's tale of their shared past, we might be more inclined to associate Miranda with the island natives. But for early modern audiences, the brief reference to Miranda's identity as a traveler carried greater significance: it signaled a set of texts about early modern women and the prospect of travels that prime the way her story is understood in the ensuing plot. The dangers of Miranda's cross-cultural encounter with Caliban, for example, recall other instances where the prospect of women's travel is portrayed by the apparent threat to their sexuality. This essay considers the ways Shakespeare and his audiences could expand on Miranda's travels and experience her story more vividly by drawing from any number of texts within the larger context of voyages and exploration.

The brief reference to Miranda's travels is particularly suitable for this mode of analysis given the intertextual nature of Shakespeare's dramatic text. In her intertextual reading of *The Tempest*, Barbara Mowat points to the literary effect of the play in connection with the active role of the audience: "whether through actual quotations within the dialogue or through less obtrusive echoes," Mowat maintains, "the books in *The Tempest* leave traces that weave themselves in our minds into an intricate intertextual mélange."[2] Other critics such as Barbara Fuchs consider the intertextuality of *The Tempest* in overlapping imperial contexts where colonialist ideologies are "quoted" from one contact zone to the next.[3] The term intertextual, as I shall argue, suggests a broad scope of analysis that considers various kinds of texts. As I shall further elaborate, the broader contextual approach and the more specific and traditional context of early modern books come alive on the English stage, which had itself established a community of interwoven texts in the form of performance, what William N. West refers to as "intertheatricality."[4]

The Tempest features, as it were, a storm of texts that Shakespeare keenly represents in the reference to Prospero's books. This essay accordingly examines the ways Miranda's story is "quoted" from performances where women's fascination for the prospect of travels is also restricted by portrayals of danger in cross-cultural encounters. In Shakespeare's *Othello*, for example, Desdemona's fascination with "the Moor" and his adventures as a traveler result in their elopement, which is later characterized by Iago as a form of ravishment by a racialized "other." In a series of parallels between *The Tempest* and *Othello*, I show how patriarchal anxieties over women's desires for travel meld with other concerns such as colonialist ideologies in the form of the common trope of land as a woman awaiting ravishment, manifested through attraction and vulnerability to a ravishing "other." As the fascination for non-European cultures and peoples that characterizes Desdemona's desire for travels superimposes Miranda's, I illustrate an intertextual process wherein women's attractions for travels and adventure are overwritten by the dangers that the sexual threats of non-European cultures are designed to represent.

"Knowing I loved my books": Prospero's Books and Shakespeare's Intertextuality

As glossed above, in the opening scene on the island, Shakespeare's *Tempest* presents a telling dynamic between Prospero's storytelling and Miranda's attentive listening: theater in early modern England seen as a community where travels are not only staged, but also experienced by its performers and audiences. A popular genre at the time, travel writing quickly found other avenues to circulate through the streets of London besides the print culture of books and pamphlets. In this opening scene on the island, Shakespeare captures these mediums of dissemination and their interconnections: a story of two exiles on the stage, performed in the oral tradition with the peculiar presence of books (i.e., Prospero's) in the background. Prospero's narration of the past engages in a rather complex and fundamental intertextual moment in the play. Indeed, even as criticism of *The Tempest* has generated some interest in reading the play intertextually, we have scarcely considered intertextuality as a fundamental component in the craft of Shakespeare's dramatic text.

Prospero's obsession with his books signals a nod to the play's inherent intertextuality, as it also speaks to the effect that texts had on early modern English culture. As Prospero tells Miranda, he "loved" his books to such an extent that in their haste to escape Antonio's murderous plot, he had Gonzalo equip him with the "volumes" he prized "above [his] dukedom" (1.2.166–67). Indeed, Prospero lost his dukedom to Antonio while he read in seclusion, and even then he was unwilling to part ways with those books that traveled with him into exile. Prospero's reading habits, while not explicitly described, can be inferred from the reading practices of the time. In his extensive study of the reading practices of grammar schools in Tudor England, namely those influenced by Erasmian humanist principles, Eugene R. Kintgen illustrates the act of reading as part of a writing process that treats any given text as "radically intertextual."[5] Students of grammar schools read a specific passage in a text through stages, including engaging "the nexus of a rich intertextuality" that prompted readers to consider echoes of earlier works in the passage. A final rereading then focused on, in Kintgen words, "the philosophy or moral implications of the passage, conceived in terms of the set topics of a commonplace book."[6]

In Prospero's fondness for reading, Shakespeare also suggests the value of books as essential to travels as reflected in broader culture of early modern voyages in print. As Mary C. Fuller has shown, navigational and commercial writing provided the groundwork that allowed Englishmen to travel to faraway places as the printed text allowed them to transform what they saw into valuable information, as well as reinforce their difference from new surroundings.[7] As a literary device that signals the intertextuality of *The Tempest*, Prospero's books represent a collection of texts that includes travel accounts with the knowledge to help the voyager assess and understand his and Miranda's experience on a remote island. In the tradition of humanist practice, Prospero may skim his books for accounts of women's travels that can help him construe and construct Miranda's experience as a traveler.

From a broader standpoint, Prospero's books also represent the texts familiar to Shakespeare's England, especially texts from which audiences could readily draw in order to understand brief and allusive episodes such as Miranda's encounter with Caliban. While texts about travels and cultural clashes with the world at large may have circulated in print form, the English stage was just as powerful a place for their dissemination. In his analysis of post-Armada Hispanophobia in England, Eric Griffin points to how "the nexus of English print and theatrical culture contributed a new form of participatory community, where variously invested 'publics' could gather to witness multiple personal and collective social anxieties, aspirations, and resistances."[8] Griffin reminds us that we don't always appreciate a direct connection between the writings of English pamphleteers and the playwrights who draw from typologies of, in this case, the Spanish Black Legend.

The transmission of printed texts in the culture at large is thus often lost in the process of dissemination, as seen in Shakespeare's *Othello* when a puzzled Brabantio desperately searches for a reasonable explanation to Desdemona's elopement: "Have you not read, Roderigo," Brabantio anxiously inquires, "Of some such thing?" (1.1.171–72). Brabantio's uncertainty is peculiar as he wonders whether his knowledge—in this case, of charms used to seduce innocent maids—came from a text he read. Surely he has "read" about these charms—or else, where has he seen or heard about them? His remarks echo what audiences familiar with Shakespeare's plays may have recalled from the opening scene in *A Midsummer Night's Dream*, where Egeus takes his complaint to the Duke of Athens, Theseus, that the Athenian youth Lysander used similar charms in order to "bewitch'd the bosom of my child," Hermia (1.1.27). Egeus's claim is echoed in *Othello* by Brabantio's ensuing actions at court, where he pleads his case before the Duke of Venice that his daughter has also been deceived by similar "witchcraft" (1.3.65).

The parallels I attempt to draw here are characteristic of what William N. West defines in intertheatricality as "recalling or re-enacting that is neither wholly allusive nor wholly citational, in the sense that it does not primarily point towards a single past performance, much less an original one."[9] Indeed, the network that theater companies in the late sixteenth- and early seventeenth-century England had established between playwrights, players, and playgoers allowed for dramatic productions to capitalize on the familiarity of a variety of tropes and themes. Within this theater culture, a number of these devices were associated with one another, and such was the case with the prospect of women's travels. For both Egeus and Brabantio, the elopement of daughters becomes a form of travel and a threat to patriarchal authority: hence, Brabantio's anxious cry after he discovers Desdemona's flight: "Fathers," Brabantio laments, "from hence trust not your daughters' minds / By what you see them act" (1.1.168–69). In turn, Brabantio's call of distrust to all fathers echoes across London's theater communities.

West further maintains that "intertheatrical moments in early modern plays call on their audiences to witness for them, making the audiences, as it were, responsible for elaborations or explanations that the play omits."[10] As Prospero's tale references his daughter's travels, audiences may indeed elaborate on Miranda's journey and consider her interactions with Caliban in relation to previously staged cross-cultural encounters. For Prospero, Brabantio's call to all fathers has a peculiar ring: the anxiety over a daughter's elopement portrayed in the context of sexual threat of a racialized "other." What gets lost, however, is that Desdemona's interactions with Othello prior to their elopement constitute a cross-cultural encounter linked to the prospect of travels. Thus, her exchange with Othello deserves further consideration as a text among Prospero's books and a "quotation" to Miranda's experience with Caliban.

Miranda's travels and subsequent encounter with Caliban must also be considered within the framework of what Fuchs refers to as a process of "quotations" that "naturalizes expansion by bringing newly 'discovered' lands and people under the conceptual domain of the already known."[11] Fuchs contextually illustrates European anxieties over a ravishing menace as seen in the increasing concerns for European sovereignty given the presence of the Ottoman Empire and the threat of Islamic Mediterranean expansion in the early seventeenth century. Both Desdemona's and Miranda's travels form part of this broader scope of multiple imperial contexts: what Ania Loomba's recent "inter-imperial" reading of *The Tempest* sees as the "interconnections between encounters with non-Europeans in different parts of the world."[12] Further, both Desdemona's and Miranda's cross-cultural encounters are influenced by what Fuchs calls a "strategy for containing the role of Islam in the play," the same strategy that also "recall[s] the more common gendered colonialist trope of ravishing a newly discovered land."[13] In the case of Prospero's colonialist discourse, however, my application of Fuchs's method suggests that it benefits from a similar process of "quotation" where Caliban's attempt on Miranda draws from previous examples, such as when the "other" represents a sexual threat in the form of invasion.

Fuchs notably alludes to Louis Montrose and the trope of gendering land as woman that he examines in his influential essay on the language of gender.[14] Recent criticism has contested the Montrose model of the masculine colonizer figure in ways that further reveal the nuances of these gender dynamics. Kristen G. Brookes, for instance, considers "a feminine version of 'writing that conquers'" to show that it "both serves as an alternative to 'the' eroticized colonial encounter that has come to dominate contemporary thinking and poses a challenge to recent arguments suggesting that the identification of Elizabeth's body and the 'island' of England limited the queen's imperial sexual agency to her ability to defend and contain herself."[15] In the context of England's expansionist visions in Ireland and the New World, Brookes points out that while Englishmen were much at ease with the "aliens and alien lands" they targeted, they "dreaded the damage that might be done by 'incorporate' aliens."[16] Brookes points to these anxieties that merely "haunt the margins of texts of travel and colonization and tend to be voiced openly only in fictional texts, such as Shakespearean plays."[17] As I elaborate in the following sections, both *Othello* and *The Tempest* play on these anxieties through the themes of women and the dangers of their respective travels.

"Devour up my discourse": Desdemona's "greedy ear" and the Tragic Attraction of Adventurous Travels

As the opening act of *Othello* centers on Desdemona's elopement with "the Moor," her tragedy constitutes a theatrical reference where the dangers of a woman's travels are dramatized through her encounter with the ravishing "other." Desdemona's fascination with travel gets lost as her story is also told by another male voice. Before her actual flight with Othello and subsequent journey to Cyprus, her elopement is prompted by her attraction to Othello and the exotic adventures of his "traveler's history" (1.3.140).[18] Indeed, Desdemona's peculiar intrigue for Othello's tale is such that, in Othello's words, "[s]he'd come again, and with a greedy ear / Devour up my discourse" (1.3.150–51). The fascination Desdemona shows for Othello as well as the content of his accounts is one that Othello views as the motive for her love for him. But, as Othello also points out, she loved him "for the dangers [he] had passed" (1.3.168). Othello's adventures represent the prospect of travels, and Desdemona experiences these journeys vicariously. Her cross-cultural encounter with Othello takes place the moment his tale transports her beyond the Venetian realm she is confined to; through his "traveler's history" Desdemona travels to various contexts where she may imagine the different cultures and peoples such as "the Cannibals" and "[t]he anthropophagi" (1.3.144–45).

Patricia Parker has explored the curiosity that travel narratives prompted in early modern readers, especially from reports of the "monstrous" found in exotic peoples, alien cultures, and non-normative sexualities.[19] In Othello's narrative, however, the potential encounter with "the Cannibals" and other peoples does not explicitly represent the threat of sexual ravishment (1.3.144). It is only after Desdemona's elopement with Othello that her travels are construed as a theft by a ravishing "other." Indeed, it is a commonly made point that Iago's description of "the Moor" conveys images of this ravishing "other," which alerts Brabantio that "an old black ram / Is tupping" his "white ewe" (1.1.90–91).

Iago's depiction of "the Moor" both conveys a sexualized threat invading the home of a Venetian senator, and slowly takes the focus away from Desdemona's sense of adventure. Desdemona's desire to travel is further restrained when the play merges the narrative of Othello's domestic invasion with the ensuing news of the encroaching Turkish fleet. Here, Shakespeare deploys common gender discourses that conflate woman and land to further dramatize concerns of invasion: schematically, Othello's alleged abduction of Desdemona is conflated with matters of state in the subplot of the Turks threatening to invade Venetian territories. As the action of the play moves inside the Venetian court, Othello's trial for his theft of Desdemona must also be considered in light of the Ottoman threat. The third scene thus opens with a tone of distrust conveyed by the Venetian officials who carefully monitor the path of the Turkish fleet: "We must not think the Turk is so unskillful," warns the senator, "To leave that latest which concerns him first" (1.328–29). The concerns voiced by the Venetian senator are in response to the news from a sailor that "[t]he Turkish preparation makes for Rhodes" instead of Cyprus, as the Venetians had earlier suspected (1.3.15). This distrust points to what the senator continually refers to as a singular entity in "the Turk," which calls attention to the intercultural tensions Othello must overcome in his trial. As Daniel

Vitkus and other critics suggest, the moral, sexual, and religious anxieties that the Ottoman threat evoked also prompted Christians to demonize representations of "the Turk."[20]

Although "the Turk" and "the Moor" historically represent two different entities, the play aligns Othello with the Ottoman threat and conflates them both as an invasive foe. While Othello is seen as invading Brabantio's home to steal away Desdemona, "the Turk" threatens to penetrate Venetian territories: both Desdemona and Cyprus must be protected from the threat of invasion and ravishment; both Othello and "the Turk" must be contained. Desdemona's eventual journey to Cyprus becomes her ultimate form of exposure to the threat of the ravishing other, and her tragic ending is thus closely associated with her desires to travel which emerged through her cross-cultural encounter with "the Moor."

"How came we ashore?": "Providence divine" in Miranda's Travels

As with Desdemona in *Othello*, in the opening act of *The Tempest* Miranda reveals her intrigue (intensified by Prospero withholding the tale) for the story of her exile and the subsequent travels that led them "ashore" (1.2.159). Their arrival on this remote island was, as Prospero claims, "[b]y Providence divine," a form of foresight that is conspicuously tied with Prospero's recollection of the past (1.2.159). Prospero, for example, had the foresight to prevent a predicament like Brabantio's of losing a daughter to an undesired non-European suitor. Although Miranda is fascinated by Prospero's story of her travels, she does not share the intrigue for other non-European cultures that Desdemona finds captivating in Othello's travels. In what Fuchs calls colonial "quotations," Desdemona's tragic travel story represents a theatrical reference that resonates with Prospero's own concerns with Miranda's journey and encounter with the "other": "The equation between prior and ongoing colonial encounters [which] may be achieved by literal textual quotation of authorities, by referring to the colonialist's own previous experiences in another territory, or by reading a newly discovered culture as another manifestation of one already othered."[21] While Prospero reads "a newly discovered culture" in Caliban, Desdemona's interactions with Othello—the "manifestation of one already othered"—impact the way Prospero responds to Miranda's contact with Caliban.

Since their arrival on the island, Prospero became Miranda's devoted "schoolmaster" (1.2.172); Miranda's actions are hence an extension of Prospero's teachings, which are in turn influenced by his books. The prudent tutor teaches his pupil to view Caliban as, in Miranda's words, a "villain" whom she does "not love to look on" (1.2.312–13). The sentiment is reminiscent of Brabantio's unwillingness to believe that Desdemona could "fall in love with what she feared to look on!" (1.3.99). Indeed, Prospero's initial perception of Caliban recalls a figure like "the Moor," and their subsequent relationship follows the pattern of how Othello became a sexual threat to Desdemona. Similar to Brabantio, who was once a generous host to Othello, Prospero claims to have "lodged" Caliban in his home (1.2.349). Here, Prospero perceives Caliban's intentions toward Miranda in much the same way Brabantio viewed Othello's, which Brabantio eventually condemns. Hence, the famous claim of a hospitality that lasted until Caliban, to use Prospero's words, "didst seek to violate / The honour of my child" (1.2.350–51).

Miranda's rendition of her interactions with Caliban is also reminiscent of the ways Othello describes his relation with Desdemona. Miranda's claims to have "pitied" Caliban (1.2.352), similar to how Othello describes Desdemona as one who "loved me for the dangers I had passed / And I loved her that she did pity them" (1.3.168–69). Perhaps while recognizing that Miranda "pitied" him, Caliban was moved to love Miranda. Even as he plots against Prospero, Caliban speaks highly of "[t]he beauty of his daughter," saying that she "surpasses" his mother Sycorax "[a]s great'st does least" (3.2.94–98). But Desdemona's "pity" is in large part prompted by Othello's adventures and the exotic peoples of his travels. Miranda, on the other hand, though she likewise "pitied," could not be moved by a young Caliban who "wouldst gabble like / A thing most brutish" (1.2. 359–60). Caliban's prospects as a suitor are further damaged by the fact that he, unlike Othello whose days of slavery found "redemption thence" (1.3.139), remains a slave and has no "traveler's history" with which to woo Miranda.

Miranda's experiences as a traveler are further limited by Prospero's protective patriarchal discourses, which merge with colonialist ideologies to enable his appropriation of Caliban's island. Because he "wouldst gabble like / A thing most brutish," Miranda's encounter with Caliban becomes a misunderstood interaction that allows Prospero both to perceive and portray a sexual threat who was, as Miranda claims, "[d]eservedly confined into this rock" (1.2.364).[22] According to Caliban's version of their first encounter, he shared with Prospero "all the qualities o' th' isle," including "barren place and fertile" before Prospero expropriated the island (1.2. 340–41). Prospero confined Caliban to the "barren" parts of the island as a result of the latter's attempt to "violate" Miranda's "honour" (1.2.350–51). But Prospero's allegation of the attempted rape, enacting patriarchal colonialist ideology, is in response to Caliban's claims to the island: "This island's mine by Sycorax," he famously disputes (1.2.331). As Prospero's perception and eventual intervention between Miranda's interactions with Caliban would suggest, the fertility of both the island and Miranda become synonymous. In this case, Caliban's knowledge of "the barren place and the fertile" suggests that he, too, recognized Miranda's fertility. So that as Caliban admits his intentions to "people else / This island with Calibans" (1.2.353–54), Prospero's expropriation of the island parallels well with protecting Miranda's "honour" and the fertility of the island. The most prominent feature of Miranda's cross-cultural encounter with a non-European subject is not her efforts to educate Caliban or her inability to understand his language. Miranda avoids the threat of the ravishing "other" thanks to Prospero's foresight and familiarity with colonialist ideology.

In summary, the story of Miranda's travels is one of exile and rough seas as well as a cross-cultural encounter that poses a sexual threat; her eventual return to Italy is contingent on the avoidance of the dangers in her travels and her consequent survival on the island, which culminates in her betrothal to Ferdinand, the heir to the throne of Naples. As I have argued, Miranda's tale of her travels draws substance from Prospero's books, particularly texts where women's travels are subject to male anxieties in both domestic and foreign realms. The intertextuality of *The Tempest*, moreover, draws on all forms of texts, including theatrical references from Shakespeare's oeuvre, to give meaning and enrich the action of the play. Analogously, in *Othello*, Shakespeare's dramatizes the patriarchal anxiety with the sexual threat of the "other" and the broader imperial concerns of Turkish invasion. This conflated threat of sexual invasion portrays Desdemona's desire for adventure and curiosity for exploring non-European cultures and peoples as a form of danger in women's travels. As an intertextual point of reference, Desdemona's tragic travel story informs and affects the way Miranda interacts with and understands Caliban. Like Othello, he is also deemed a sexual threat who evokes anxieties about cross-cultural travel. Ultimately, the fascination that both Desdemona and Miranda show for the prospect of travels illustrates how women's mobility presented opportunities for adventure fraught with danger. Desdemona's intrigue with the dangers of travels centers on a sense of adventure and the desire to interact with other non-European cultures. Miranda's excitement for the story of her journey, on the other hand, is denied the same curiosity for exploration by rendering Desdemona's sense of adventure as another form of danger in women's travels embodied by a non-European other.

Notes

1. All Shakespeare citations (*The Tempest*, *Othello*, and *A Midsummer Night's Dream*) are from *The Norton Shakespeare*. All subsequent citations will appear parenthetically as follow: act. scene. lines (1.2.106).
2. Mowat, "'Knowing,'" 27.
3. Fuchs, "Conquering Islands," 45–46.
4. West, "Intertheatricality," 154–55.
5. Kintgen, *Reading*, 26.
6. Kintgen, *Reading*, 40.
7. Fuller, *Voyages*, 2–3.
8. Griffin, "Copying," 197.
9. West, "Intertheatricality," 155.
10. West, "Intertheatricality," 156.
11. Fuchs, "Conquering Islands," 45.
12. Loomba, "Mediterranean Borderlands," 23.
13. Fuchs, "Conquering Islands," 45.

14. Montrose, "Work of Gender," 177–79.
15. Brookes, "Feminine 'Writing,'" 229.
16. Brookes, "Feminine 'Writing,'" 229.
17. Brookes, "Feminine 'Writing,'" 229.
18. In her chapter in this volume, Stephanie Chamberlain examines more extensively how Desdemona's attraction for adventure motivates her desire to travel. My contribution is to consider colonialism as part of this dynamic using an intertextual analysis.
19. Parker, "Fantasies," 87–89.
20. Vitkus, "Turning Turk," 145.
21. Fuchs, "Conquering Islands," 47.
22. It is worth mentioning here that different editors have often assigned these words and its passage to Prospero, noting that its diction and sentiment seems out of character for Miranda.

Bibliography

Brookes, Kristen. "A Feminine 'Writing that Conquers': Elizabethan Encounters with the New World." *Criticism* 48, no. 1 (2006): 227–62.

Brown, Paul. "'This Thing of Darkness I Acknowledge Mine': *The Tempest* and the Discourse of Colonialism." In *The Tempest: A Case Study in Critical Controversy*, edited by Gerald Graff, 268–92. Boston: Bedford, 2000.

Fuchs, Barbara. "Conquering Islands: Contextualizing *The Tempest*." *Shakespeare Quarterly* 48, no. 1 (1997): 45–62.

Fuchs, Barbara, and Emily Weissbourd, eds. *Representing Imperial Rivalry in the Early Modern Mediterranean*. Toronto: University of Toronto Press, 2015.

Harris, Jonathan Gil. "Rematerializing Shakespeare's Intertheatricality: The Occidental/Oriental Halimpsest." In *Rematerializing Shakespeare: Authority and Representation on the Early Modern English Stage*, edited by Bryan Reynolds and William West, 75–94. New York: Palgrave Macmillan, 2005.

Fuller, Mary. *Voyages in Print: English Travels to America, 1576–1624*. Cambridge: Cambridge University Press, 1995.

Griffin, Eric. "Copying 'the Anti-Spaniard': Post-Armada Hispanophobia and English Renaissance Drama." In Fuchs and Weissbourd, *Representing*, 191–216.

Kintgen, Eugene. *Reading in Tudor England*. Pittsburgh: University of Pittsburgh Press, 1996.

Loomba, Ania. "Mediterranean Borderlands and the Global Early Modern." In Fuchs and Weissbourd, *Representing*, 13–32.

Montrose, Louis. "The Work of Gender in the Discourse of Discovery." In *New World Encounters*, edited by Stephen Greenblatt, 177–217. Berkeley: University of California Press, 1993.

Mowat, Barbara. "'Knowing I Loved My Books': Reading *The Tempest* Intertextually." In *The Tempest and Its Travels*, edited by Peter Hulme and William H. Sherman, 27–36. London: Reaktion, 2000.

Parker, Patricia. "Fantasies of 'Race' and 'Gender': Africa, Othello and Bringing to Light." In *Women, "Race," and Writing in the Early Modern Period*, edited by Margo Hendricks and Patricia Parker, 84–100. London: Routledge, 1994.

Shakespeare, William. *The Norton Shakespeare*, edited by Stephen Greenblatt, et al. 2nd edition New York: Norton, 2008.

Vitkus, Daniel. "Turning Turk in *Othello*: The Conversion and Damnation of the Moor." *Shakespeare Quarterly* 48, no. 2 (1997): 145–76.

West, William N. "Intertheatricality." In *Early Modern Theatricality*, edited by Henry Turner, 151–72. Oxford: Oxford University Press, 2013.

13

Marian Mobility, Black Madonnas, and the Cleopatra Complex

RUBEN ESPINOSA

In his account of his travels through Italy, Michel de Montaigne lingers on his experience visiting the Holy House of Loreto and details the miraculous events and reverential tone that surround this Marian pilgrimage site. Beyond describing the impressive adornments and various riches that travelers leave there, Montaigne shares the story of the preternatural conveyance of the house from Galilee to Slavonia and ultimately to Loreto itself, which, he explains, is written "on large marble tablets" in "Italian, Sclavonic [Slavonic], French, German, and Spanish."[1] The varied translations are a testament to the diversity of travelers who visited Our Lady of Loreto. Focusing on one particular group of visitors, Montaigne writes: "They told me that great crowds of Sclavonians are wont to come here to worship, and moreover, that as soon as they catch sight of the place from their barks at sea they set up a cry, which they let continue in the town itself, with many protestations and promises added, and beg Our Lady to return to their land, pouring out their regrets that they should have given her reason for deserting them; which thing seemed to me very marvelous."[2] The travels surrounding this house register the religious desire for a material Marian connection for many believers, but the mobility behind both the history of the house and the various visitors who journey to see Our Lady of Loreto also registers the cross-cultural energies of this Marian site and the cult of the Virgin Mary itself.[3] Of no small consequence is the fact that the Marian image at this famous pilgrimage site is black.

Our Lady of Loreto's blackness was not necessarily unusual for pre- and early modern renditions of the Virgin Mary, but it does introduce to us a means of considering the versatility of Marian imagery for varied cultures and communities. It also impels us to scrutinize what this blackness meant for early modern English conceptions of Mary's cultural value. It is clear that Marian iconography in pre- and post-Reformation England possessed a distinct currency. In the case of the former, it helped position the cult of the Virgin Mary as one of the most prominent movements in Roman Catholicism.[4] In the case of the latter, it offered fodder for an iconoclastic campaign that sought to eradicate Catholicism in England. Regardless of what side one took in this debate, Marian imagery enkindled a host of possibilities when it came to religious and cultural identity. For an early modern theater that relied on the power of representation, the evocation of Marian iconography allowed dramatists to tap into the vein of these energies, and Shakespeare's drama drew on them in provocative ways.[5]

In part, it is the Virgin Mary's multifaceted nature that positions her as such a powerful figure for early modern dramatists. Her maternal, chaste, intercessory, feminine, and divine potential aroused impassioned reactions in Catholic and anti-Catholic sympathizers alike, and so it comes as no surprise that Marian elements were often employed to make or mar female figures in Shakespeare's drama. But where most of his drama engages Marian elements through characters often identified as "fair" and thus as white—characters such as Portia, Desdemona, Ophelia, Isabella, and Marina, to name a few—Shakespeare's *Antony and Cleopatra* instead uses the "tawny" skinned Cleopatra as a vehicle through whom to evoke a foreign Marian representation, one that calls to mind images of the Black Madonna (1.1.6).[6]

This essay considers the cultural, religious, and racial implications behind the invocation of the Black Madonna in *Antony and Cleopatra* and scrutinizes how the shaping of English religious and national identity along the lines of race and gender was complicated by the influential value of a black, foreign, and mobile Marian figure. Black Madonnas in European and trans-Atlantic settings offer an interesting nexus through which to explore the influence of an archetypal black foreign femininity on perceptions of an English Christian identity that was also increasingly coded as white.[7] Given the absence of power for both women and black people in early modern England, the deployment of black Marian imagery surrounding the arguably black heroine of *Antony and Cleopatra* opens an array of possibilities where perceptions of religious and cultural identity are concerned. Celia Daileader's reading of the "white monopoly on the role" of Cleopatra presents an interesting understanding of the vital nature of Cleopatra's blackness in contemporary performance, but it is not an argument that lingers on early modern views of Cleopatra's character.[8] Employing Daileader's argument about what she terms the "Cleopatra Complex"—that is, the tendency to render Cleopatra white, conflate her authority with sexually seductive power, and position her as superior to the dark-skinned women who surround her—would seem to be at odds with a study that is historically focused; however, by engaging cross-historical energies, we can better understand why the evocation of a Black Madonna in this play matters both then and now. As Dympna Callaghan keenly argues, "All representation is predicated upon the absence of the thing represented, but in the instance of race and gender on the early modern stage, there is a perfect coincidence between social exclusion and exclusion at the level of dramatic representation."[9] The prohibition of all women and black male actors on the English public stage during the late-sixteenth century and into the seventeenth century reflects the dominant perception of their subordinate status. Moreover, while the actor representing foreign bodies on Shakespeare's stage was always white and male, the material representation of blackness—as Ian Smith has deftly argued—introduces a process of imagining and representing the "abject notion of a black man as a thing."[10] The theater, then, perpetuated views of women and black people in early modern society as innately inferior.

Without doubt, the Virgin Mary provoked strong reactions in a post-Reformation society that was being imagined not only as masculine, but also as white.[11] As Dennis Britton argues about the privileging of whiteness in early modern Christian frameworks, "Infidels could be saved in spite of their race, while the children of Christians are saved because of their race."[12] For the English Church, this amounted to a Christian identity "defined mainly by race and lineage."[13] To consider a figure as complex as the Virgin Mary within this racially defined framework is to recognize that the multifaceted manifestations of the Virgin Mary's persona across racial lines situated black Marian images external to England's nascent Protestant identity. As I argue elsewhere, while "the cult of the Virgin Mary in England suffered" as a result of the Protestant Reformation, "her importance remained, because, unlike all worldly females, including Queen Elizabeth herself, the Virgin Mary was alone of all her sex."[14] Her role as Theotokos, or God bearer, preserved her magnitude in pre- and post-Reformation thought, but her potency was regulated. Black Marian images, then, offer an interesting window into the complexities behind the Virgin Mary in the shifting religious atmosphere of Shakespeare's England.

Black Madonnas clearly engage anxieties about Marian influence in the larger Christian community, and they shed light on English attitudes about white supremacy and the way Shakespeare's theater negotiated those attitudes.[15] Despite their darkness, and akin to the dazzling nature of Shakespeare's Cleopatra, Black Madonnas—actual and imagined—offered viewers and travelers a glimpse of the simultaneous magnetism of cross-cultural religious communities and the delimiting nature of an English nation that had foreclosed on the power of the image to organize community. This provocative dynamic finds its way into *Antony and Cleopatra* through its strong heroine who herself draws on powerful Marian iconography and yet does not eschew her sexuality. By deploying Marian elements that are evocative of the Black Madonna via Cleopatra's character, *Antony and Cleopatra* conveys its audience into the vicinity of this foreign, yet familiar, femininity.

Isis and the Intercultural Influence of the Black Madonna

The imagined travels in *Antony and Cleopatra*, and particularly through vicarious contact with Egypt, expose Shakespeare's audience to the foreign femininity of Cleopatra's "infinite variety" (2.2.248). In other words, the cross-directional movement between Rome and Egypt positions Shakespeare's London audience in imagined proximity to Africa and the East. This movement is not unlike Peter Erickson's view of *Othello* as a play that offers a "double migration"; that is, where the characters Othello, the mercenary soldier, and Barbary, the serving maid, migrate to a Venetian society marked as white, and where Shakespeare's London audience is conveyed to Venice and "into the wider geographical space" via the "metatheatrical process."[16] Unlike *Othello*, where the "meeting with Othello is indirect and vicarious, and thus mediated and hedged by various strategies of insulation," *Antony and Cleopatra* transports its audience directly into the space of its other.[17] *Othello*'s audience is given access to Othello within the markedly white borders of Venice and Cyprus, but *Antony and Cleopatra*'s audience is transported into this eastern queen's Egypt. Within her element, Cleoptra's magnetism is undeniable, and given the Marian undertones that surround her in the closing moments of the play—undertones I discuss below—the Virgin Mary's own mobile, foreign, and wide-ranging intercultural appeal is put on full display. Before scrutinizing how Shakespeare's theater draws on this Marian strength, however, it is worthwhile to explore the distinctive nature of the Black Madonna's influential reach.

Montaigne's account of Our Lady of Loreto that I outlined at the onset of this essay is, in many ways, no different than accounts of other Marian pilgrimage sites, featuring rich trimmings, offerings left behind by various travelers, stories of miracles, and a strong reverence for the Virgin Mary. Indeed, in pre-Reformation England, the shrine of Our Lady of Walsingham, originally a copy of the Holy House of Loreto, was incredibly popular and received the most donations after Canterbury.[18] The obvious difference between the two Marian icons is that the image of Our Lady of Loreto is black. For an English culture that valued fairness, the rendering of Our Lady of Walsingham as white would make sense. However, one cannot ignore that the inspiration for England's most popular Marian shrine was a darker, more established, and more globally recognized image of the Virgin Mary.

Black Madonnas like the image of Our Lady of Loreto have a connection both to pre-Christian sensibilities about woman's divinity and to popular beliefs connecting blackness to the earth. Despite church-sanctioned efforts to whiten Marian images "at Lucera, Montenero, Avellino, Chiarmonte Gulfi, and other places," Lucia Birnbaum explains, devotees continue to identify these whitewashed Madonnas as black.[19] The veneration is tied up with traditions of indigenous goddesses in

Europe that merged with surrounding "African, Middle Eastern, and Asian dark goddesses."[20] From this perspective, Black Madonnas held rare value because of their cross-cultural energies.

The influence of pre-Christian goddesses on Black Madonnas is not entirely unique to these darker Marian images, but it is critical. Pre-Christian goddesses influenced the cult of the Virgin Mary at large in various ways, and figures as prominent as Erasmus made note of this.[21] However, the rich potential for "cultural fusion," as Małgorzata Oleszkiewicz-Peralba suggests, sets Black Madonnas apart.[22] While Oleszkiewicz-Peralba traces the cultural energies of the Black Madonna in Europe and Latin America to contemporary times, her attention to the "ethnic mixing" surrounding the sites wherein Black Madonnas thrive presents an entry point to consider how *Antony and Cleopatra* attends to black Marian origins and the potential value of ethnic mixing.[23]

Before turning to *Antony and Cleopatra*, however, I first want to consider the syncretism involved in the formation of the cult of the Virgin Mary, and the Black Madonna in particular. Both Birnbaum and Oleszkiewicz-Peralba point to the cross-cultural encounters that surround most Black Madonnas, but Oleszkiewicz-Peralba specifically examines the process of syncretism behind the Virgin Mary: "During this process different cultures enter into contact with each other, because of either geographical proximity or superimposition by force. In either circumstance, rather than being totally eliminated, one culture becomes blended with the other."[24] The Virgin Mary absorbs attributes of her black predecessors, and some of these include the Russian Mother Moist Earth, the Sumerian Inanna, the Greek Diana/Roman Venus, and—of rather significant importance to this essay—the Egyptian goddess Isis.[25]

From Isis, the Virgin Mary borrows a host of attributes: the image of a mother holding a child (as Isis holds Horus in her lap), the suckling of that child, and sometimes being part of a triune Holy family. In the case of Black Madonnas, these similarities are explicitly pronounced. The Mary-Isis parallels, however, stem beyond iconographic similarities, and encompass the power of multifaceted personas, as Isis's "most distinctive cultic title was 'Isis of the Myriad names.'"[26] Detailing this diverse quality of the cult of Isis in Hellenistic times, Chris Maunder explains how her titles were listed in "shrines across the Roman world; not merely in Egypt, Asia minor and Greece, but also in western inscriptions that show just how far she had traveled: in temple carvings from Cilicia, Latium, Cisalpine Gaul, Dacia, Germany, and northern France. The Oxyrhyncus Litany salutes her as protector of Horus and, accordingly, as 'Mother of the God.'"[27] This latter title bears a striking resemblance to the Virgin Mary's own title as Theotokos, but Maunder makes clear that Isis's influence on this particular title is negligible. The significant correspondence is the degree to which both Isis and the Virgin Mary cross borders and travel to such far-reaching locales.[28]

Although Mary is imagined to absorb many of her powers from female predecessors like Isis, some of these powers, "such as her dominion over life and death, her wisdom, and her sexuality" are lost.[29] To be certain, both Catholics and Protestants emphasized God's sovereignty, but the Virgin Mary's intercessory potential in Catholic thought granted her some influence over God.[30] The issue of sexuality, however, was definitively foreclosed upon, as there was steadfast belief in Mary's perpetual virginity from both Catholic and Protestant perspectives.

The idea of a woman's sexuality and authority often cast the Virgin Mary in a threatening light where reformers were concerned. Specifically, in their castigation of Catholic reverence for Mary, English reformers often diminished the Virgin Mary along gendered lines. Anglican bishop John Jewel, for example, chastises Catholics for "shamelessly call[ing] upon the Blessed Virgin, Christ's mother, to have her remember that she is a mother and to command her Son and to use a mother's authority over him."[31] Jewel finds Mary's maternal influence threatening, but William Crashaw is even more forceful in explicitly connecting Mary's authority to her body: "And beholde, the Jesuits as though the Mother were a woman and the Sonne but an Infant: or as though they had gained mercy by Christ already, and would now see what they could get by the Mother, began to call in question his *merits* and mediation, and the dignity of his *wounds* and sufferings, & at last pronounce that his *wounds* and her paps, his *blood* and her milke, are either all one, or else that the *milke is better*."[32] The imagined blending of Mary's "paps" and Jesus's "blood" effeminizes Christ and diminishes his power.³³ Through this anti-Catholic design, the Virgin Mary is positioned to possess something closer to the subversive, and often destructive, powers of her pre-Christian predecessor goddesses.

This particular attack on the influential nature of the Catholic Virgin Mary seems to reveal quite a bit about the apprehensions that surround feminine and maternal potency at large. The appealing nature of Mary, though, is aligned with a willingness to help rather than a power to do so. As Mary Lefkowitz argues, "Mary was always directly accessible to her worshipers and in sympathy with them. Through her they were able to approach her powerful and distant son, and his even more remote father, much as the mothers and wives of the remote and all-powerful Roman emperors had served as intercessor for their subjects. Thus the cult of the Virgin Mary was a replacement for, rather than a continuation of, the ancient cults of the goddesses."³⁴ This intercessory potential, of course, is precisely what anti-Catholic writers like Jewel and Crashaw resented in Catholic imaginings of the Virgin Mary, but it also gets to the heart of Mary's magnetism.³⁵ She is akin to worldly intercessors and yet possesses a divine persona, one that is acceptable in Christian thought, from Catholic to Anglican, because it is severed from previous goddess cults. And while her influential nature was being marginalized in post-Reformation England, her popularity across cultures hardly suffered. Indeed, although images of the Virgin Mary were absent in Shakespeare's England, her central role in Christian thought was on firm footing. Shakespeare's theater often drew on this lingering popularity and made the most of Mary's enduring magnetism.

Where energies of the Black Madonna are concerned, however, Mary's blackness — to draw on Callaghan's attention to racialized attitudes about Shakespeare's theater — would have, unequivocally, "marked sheer difference" for the English.³⁶ Race and gender work to situate Black Madonnas in opposition to the masculinist and Anglocentric sensibilities that were defining early modern England. By absorbing the strengths of predecessor goddesses like Isis, Black Madonnas work both within and without a Christian framework to offer symbolic intercultural connections that position these Marian images as mediators for societal contradictions. They are at once similar and yet strange, and so register an accessible and acceptable image of devotion while retaining powerful elements of forbidden pre-Christian goddesses. Because Marian iconography had been proscribed and shattered in Shakespeare's England, the evocation of a Marian image—one that was black, no less—would register something forbidden, but it would also point directly to the powerful nature of the Black Madonna's influence in organizing community within the greater, intercultural Christian world. England's insularity and fraught relationship with this larger community positioned them as outliers, and this made the pervasive influence of Black Madonnas all the more engrossing.

Hardly existing as the mere other within the play, Cleopatra holds her audience's fascination in the way, as one might imagine, an image of a black Virgin Mary might have for European travelers who were both accustomed to viewing and venerating white versions of the Virgin Mary. *Antony and Cleopatra* employs the multivalent energies of Marian imagery in constructing Cleopatra's near-divine persona, and this bolsters her seductive power over her audience in Egypt and in Shakespeare's theater.

Arousing Fear and Desire: Race, Religion, and Cleopatra as Black Madonna

Elsewhere, I have argued that *Antony and Cleopatra* draws on Marian iconography through the most unlikely of characters and does so to infuse the theater with a divine feminine power that was no longer available in Protestant England.[37] Two moments, in particular, align Cleopatra with Marian iconography: when she holds dying Antony in her arms in a move reminiscent of the pietà, and when she holds the asp at her breast, an image that evokes the Madonna and child.[38] Because both moments are associated with monuments—Antony is in her arms as she sits on an actual monument (4.15.9), and shortly before holding the asp to her breast, like a "baby... That sucks the nurse asleep" (5.2.305–6), she remarks, "Now from head to foot / I am marble-constant" (5.2.237–38)—the play seems to be mindful of the lasting power of Marian iconography that was no longer part of the visual landscape in post-Reformation England. To consider Cleopatra's black skin, however, is to recognize an even more provocative facet of that iconography.

As Queen of Egypt, Cleopatra functions as a representation of Egypt for both the Romans in the play and for an audience who imagines the travels and the foreignness of that land. In direct juxtaposition to Rome's masculine leanings, Egypt is cast in a feminine light because, as Laura Levine argues, Cleopatra's "effeminizing power" is "diffused onto" the "whole landscape" of Egypt.[39] In this way, the space of the play is dominated by feminine rule that was not altogether foreign for the English. Although Queen Elizabeth's reign had come to an end by the time *Antony and Cleopatra* was staged, the English certainly knew something about being associated with anomalous female sovereignty.

I draw attention to the influence of gender on national identity because I believe it should lead us to consider the influence of race on that very issue.[40] Kim Hall has adeptly drawn attention to the way that whiteness, buried within dominant ideologies, gives us an idea about the way "'race' becomes part of social heritage."[41] From her perspective, "fairness" becomes an "emergent ideology of white supremacy" in Shakespeare's England.[42] The correlation between skin color and country of origin was certainly in place, and this allows us to understand how England's emerging sense of national identity, and its ethnocentrism, was crafted along racial lines, however subtle those lines might appear.[43] Moreover, perceptions of Christian identity for the English, as Britton demonstrates, play an important role in organizing religion via race.[44] As such, the value of whiteness was advanced in both literary and religious realms. Although the Virgin Mary's "fairness" could suggest her virtuous nature, the influence of this term on perceptions of her skin color was, at the very least, conceivable.[45] Was her whiteness taken as a given? If so, how were Black Madonnas understood within societies that viewed whiteness as morally superior?

One common explanation for the darkness of Black Madonnas is that the devotional candles blackened the Marian image.[46] This presents an interesting dynamic as it reveals the desire to see the image representing the Virgin Mary (or, at least, the material used to depict the image) as only artificially black. Like an early modern English actor in blackface, the material beneath the blackness is white. However, as Lisa Hopkins notes, early modern justifications for the darkness of Black Madonnas also relied on the belief that Palestinian women were dark-skinned or that the artists who rendered the Madonna black (in her reading, the "Coptic Christians in Egypt") were themselves dark and thus crafted the icons of the Virgin Mary in their own image.[47] In this scenario, the attempt would be to depict the Virgin Mary authentically. Generalizations surrounding pigmentation aside, representing the Virgin Mary had more to do with the desire for similitude than anything else.

When considered along these lines, Cleopatra's connection to the Virgin Mary offers an interesting view of the play's negotiation of religious symbols, and black Marian iconography in particular, as a means of drawing attention to that which was only available within dramatic imagination or travels to foreign lands. It at once provokes the imagination and underscores the inaccessibility of this type of visual impact in Protestant England. However, this Marian iconographical force remained on the greater global stage, and anti-Catholic polemics often registered unease about the enduring popularity of the Virgin Mary. Jewel, for example, takes to task the ubiquity of the Virgin Mary in the realm of Roman Catholicism: "And where one saint hath images in dyvers places, the same saint hath dyvers names thereof, moste lyke to the Gentiles. When you heare of our lady of Walsingham, our Lady of Ipswich, our Lady of Wylsdon, & such other: what is it but an imitation of the Gentiles idolaters' Diana Agotera, Diana Coriphea, Diana Ephesia & c. Venus Cipria, Venus Paphia, Venus Gnidia. Whereby is evidently meant, that the saint for the image sake, shoulde in those places, yea in the images themselves, have a dwellyng, whiche is the grounde of theire idolatrie."[48] Although Jewel's central move here is to draw a direct line from paganism to Roman Catholicism, the comparison he makes between English manifestations of the Virgin Mary to the multifarious foreign goddesses is a seeming warning to the English that they also might be too close to the pre-Christian, foreign devotees of Mary's predecessors. Establishing difference is critical to underscoring the primacy of English Protestantism, but that which was unfamiliar often aroused interest and not fear.

Imagining Cleopatra, this "Rare Egyptian" (2.2.230), in the way the various characters in the play describe her consequently reveals something both foreign and undeniably alluring. Enobarbus attempts to register Cleopatra's unique beauty to Agrippa, but he cannot quite relate her specific appeal. Instead, he describes, at length, the marvelous ornamentation that surrounds her person:

> The barge she sat in like a burnished throne
> Burned on the water. The poop was beaten gold,
> Purple the sails, and so perfumed that
> The winds were lovesick with them. The oars were silver,
> Which to the tune of flutes kept stroke, and made
> The water which they beat to follow faster,
> As amorous of their strokes. For her own person,
> It beggared all description. She did lie
> In her pavilion—cloth-of-gold, of tissue—
> O'erpicturing that Venus where we see
> The fancy outwork nature. On each side her
> Stood pretty dimpled boys, like smiling Cupids,
> With divers colored fans, whose wind did seem
> To glow the delicate cheeks which they did cool,
> And what they undid did. (2.2.203–17)

The regal nature of this opening is emphasized, as her boat is imagined as a golden throne replete with rich metals and fabrics that create the royal and sensual setting. The visual meets both the olfactory and aural, and all of this ultimately leads to Cleopatra's "own person," which, Enobarbus tells us, defies description. Not coincidentally, she is compared to Venus but is said to surpass that particular goddess. This prominent description of Cleopatra situates her as deific, and it does so by invoking not only the sensual nature of Venus, but also the shrines that pay respect to figures such as Venus and, indeed, the Virgin Mary.

As I suggested via Montaigne's detailed description of the shrine of Our Lady of Loreto above, rich adornments are a staple of Marian pilgrimage sites. However, the influence of such ornamentations on travelers—in the same way that the multilayered trimmings surrounding Cleopatra work to seduce viewers—is rather loaded. For anti-Catholic polemicists, these Marian shrines were clear examples of idolatry and often connected to sexual seduction. Anthony Munday, for example, offers the following description of Our Lady of Loreto's shrine:

> And before her is a great barred Chest of iron, wherein they throwe money to our Lady, by whole goblets full at once: Within this little house, there is an Aultar made right before our Lady, & there is sayd everie day, fortie or fiftie Masses, whereat the people will throng in great heapes, to get into the house, for they thinke them selves happie, if our Lady have once séene them. And all the Church is likewise hung with pictures, Tapers, and waxe Candles, which are the vowes of the Pilgrimes to our Lady. I have heard of some, who by the counsaile of their ghostlie Father, have made money of all their householde stuffe, and have come five or six hundred mile bare foote and bare legged, to give it all to our Lady there: meane while, the holy Father hath had libertie, to play with [the] mans wife, at &c. In all my life I never sawe a place more frequented with people, then this is dayly, onelie for the admirable Miracles [that] be done there.[49]

Here, Munday does not implicate the Virgin Mary as seductive in and of herself, but rather draws attention to the way her popularity is used to exploit believers. First off, priests encourage believers to sell their belonging and undertake the long journey to offer these earnings to Our Lady of Loreto. This, of course, is a perversion of Jesus's teachings where he instructs the rich young man to sell his possessions and give to the poor.[50] What follows in Munday's account is of a more damning nature. He imagines said priest taking advantage of the pilgrim's absence by having "libertie, to play with [the] mans wife."[51] In this careful negotiation of the Virgin Mary's popularity, Munday is able to connect greed, licentious behavior, and seduction to this Marian pilgrimage site without directly addressing Mary's person.

Through both Munday's and Montaigne's accounts, we see how the opulent setting of the Marian shrine of Our Lady of Loreto generates a fervent following and fodder to critique its allure. For critics of the shrine, its seductive nature is deemed dangerous. But narratives that detail the danger and/or seduction of these Marian pilgrimage sites no doubt arouse concurrent interest in and fear of their far-off presence for the English. In a similar vein, Enobarbus's recollection of Cleopatra on her barge as shrine offers an interesting parallel to Mary's own mobility and alluring magnetism. In the case of Cleopatra, the audience is asked to imagine her mesmerizing image as she travels across the Cydnus River, and in the case of the Virgin Mary, believers undertook pilgrimages to far-off locales so as to behold and pay homage to any number of Marian icons. In both cases, viewers and devotees are drawn to move toward that female figure. Enobarbus's detailed report underscores the richness of the setting to register the seductive nature of that image of Cleopatra and works to fascinate his own audience through that description. However, attention to Cleopatra's magnetism stems beyond Enobarbus's oft-cited account and often takes her to task for the ornamentation that surrounds her. Like the Black Madonna at Loreto, Cleopatra's drawing power is sometimes connected to lasciviousness.

Perhaps no description is more provocative when it comes to Cleopatra's connection to Black Madonnas than that which Caesar offers to Maecenas. The Egyptian scene Caesar describes is one laden with images of opulence—a silver stage where Antony and Cleopatra sit on chairs of gold—in a moment when Antony audaciously grants territories and titles to Cleopatra and their "unlawful issue" (3.6.7). Caesar says of Cleopatra and Antony appearing in "th' common showplace where they exercise" (3.6.12):

> His sons he there proclaimed the kings of kings.
> Great Media, Parthia, and Armenia
> He gave to Alexander. To Ptolemy he assigned
> Syria, Cilicia, Phoenicia. She
> In th' habiliments of the goddess Isis
> That day appeared, and oft before gave audience,
> As 'tis reported, so. (3.6.13–19)

In the moment that Cleopatra's power and legacy grow, she is explicitly connected to the goddess Isis. Caesar's anger here stems from the fact not only that Antony is working unilaterally, but also that Cleopatra's heirs are overstepping their rightful bounds. As "kings of kings," the imagined influence they hold is reminiscent of Jesus.[52] This power is excessive, and it recalls the apprehension that reformers like Jewel articulated about Catholic views of Marian influence. More important, perhaps, it anticipates the overpowering iconography that comes at the play's end. When Cleopatra states, "Give me my robe; put on my crown. I have / Immortal longing in me" (5.2.276–77), she is keenly aware of the enduring nature of the image she will leave behind once she places the "baby at [her] breast" (5.2.305). Fusing both Isiac and Marian qualities to render this would-be Black Madonna, Cleopatra's appealing nature is both captivating and threatening within the greater world that surrounds her.

This process of costuming to kindle the imagination about particular iconography is critical to seeing how the play holds power to influence an audience whose vast religious visual heritage had been lost to iconoclasm. The process also calls to mind Daileader's impressive attention to the "Cleopatra Complex" to which I alluded above. Daileader details the consistent desire to imagine the sovereignty of Cleopatra as indicative of a power that is deemed, by many, closer to white than black. For Daileader, this is problematic on multiple fronts. She writes:

> Cleopatra, though unique among Shakespeare's heroines for her regality and the relative dignity of her demise, embodies a stereotype that poses as many problems on feminist as on antiracist grounds. Both the role and its racially whitewashed counterpart in modern Western visual culture translate the *political* power of the historical Egyptian sovereign into sheer, passive sex appeal. When this erotic so-called power is cast as epitomizing white feminine privilege—that is, sustained by, even arguably *produced* by black subservience—the message is doubly damning. Productions wherein Cleopatra's attendants are people of color both eroticize white female aristocratic decadence and expose this decadence, this sensuality, as racially parasitic.[53]

Daileader's attention to the power dynamics at work in adaptations of plays that posit Cleopatra as a white woman surrounded by servants of color is powerful and for me serves to reinforce the need to consider the compelling nature of Cleopatra's blackness. Shakespeare's audience did not witness an Elizabeth Taylor–like actress donning the queen's attire, but rather they saw a young white man in blackface and cross-dressed—the "squeaking" boy actor of Cleopatra's imagination (5.2.218). In Cleopatra's mind, he is not worthy of representing her "greatness" (5.2.218). However, on some level, this is precisely what has happened to representations of Shakespeare's heroine.

Portrayals of Cleopatra's character over time have indeed white-washed her dark skin, and as such the power behind her blackness has been lost. Shakespeare's audience, though, bore witness to this authoritative power rendered as black. And while the translation of Cleopatra's *political* power" into "sex appeal" could certainly be germane to my reading of Cleopatra, I do not see this latter characteristic as altogether passive. In the absence of a "white feminizing privilege," the sexuality of Cleopatra draws on a power that stretches beyond qualities of the Virgin Mary to encompass aspects of Isis, and in the process infuses the view of this would-be Black Madonna with something concurrently familiar and foreign.

Daileader finds fault with the type of "erotic so-called power" that Cleopatra holds, but I find that aspect of her character somewhat more fascinating when considered through the amalgamation of the Virgin Mary and Isis because an image that contains such power overturns the insular perspective of what religious iconography should register. This is not to suggest that Isis was the erotic antithesis to the virginal Mary. Indeed, the myth of Isis stresses her devotion as both wife and mother. Nevertheless, as Michael Carroll argues, "the association of Isis with sexual promiscuity derived from the activities associated with Isiac temples"—activities such as married women who "routinely used these temples to carry on clandestine affairs."[54] Such stories seem to call to mind the kind of promiscuity that Munday associates with the shrine of Our Lady of Loreto, where sexual indiscretions are not an aspect of the Virgin Mary herself per se, but are nonetheless associated with that

Black Madonna. Such stories of sexual transgressions did little to curb the popularity of these figures, though, as their greatness remained in place. By placing sexual promiscuity squarely on Cleopatra's lap while simultaneously deploying Marian and Isiac iconography to define her, Shakespeare capitalizes on the multilayered appeal of the narratives and imagery that rendered some Marian pilgrimage sites so seductive. That Shakespeare's theater evoked such impactful icons despite their erasure within post-Reformation England certainly draws attention to their influential nature. Would a white Madonna afford such possibilities? This, I believe, would be unlikely.

Marian Versatility and La Virgen in the New World

The mobility of Marian images from remote places into the English imagination leaves an impression of the enduring potency of iconography. Without doubt, that same iconography has worked to hold believers in awe across borders and across time around the globe. The Virgin Mary in the early modern world traveled afar and caught the imagination of many, and when race and cross-cultural experiences enter into the picture, her versatility is ever so rich.

To think of the undeniable hold that the Virgen de Guadalupe—whose reputation had reached England long before *Antony and Cleopatra* was staged—has had on the cultural construction of Mexican identity is to recognize that there is no monopoly on race where the Virgin Mary is concerned.[55] In an early recounting of the pilgrimage site of Our Lady of Guadalupe in Mexico, for example, Miles Philips writes:

> The next morning we departed from thence on our journey towards *Mexico*, and so travelled till wee came within two leagues of it, where there was built by the Spaniards a very faire church, called our Ladyes church, in which there is an image of our Lady of silver & gilt, being as high, & as large as a tall woman, in which church, and before this image, there are as many lamps of silver as there be dayes in the yeere, which upon high dayes are all lighted. Whensoever any Spaniards passe by this church, although they be on horse backe, they will alight, and come into the church, and kneele

before thie image, and pray to our Lady to defend them from all evil... which image they call in the Spanish tongue, *Nuestra sennora de Guadalupe*... and they say that our Lady of *Guadalupe* doeth worke a number of miracles. About this Church there is not any towne of Spaniards that is inhabited, but certaine Indians doe dwell there in houses of their own countrey building.[56]

Philips's account provides a snapshot of the way Marian worship transcends borders for the Spanish, who clearly exhibit great reverence for this dark-skinned manifestation of the Virgin Mary. Of more importance, his report notes that the Spanish do not occupy the space surrounding this pilgrimage site, and instead "certaine Indians" live about this particular shrine. It is these Indians, after all, who eventually organize both a community and an identity around this Black Madonna.[57]

While I will not pretend that the dignity afforded to Black Madonnas like Our Lady of Loreto and Our Lady of Guadalupe yields a comparable deference for black and brown bodies, the inherent implications about black, feminine strength are worthy of attention. The Virgin Mary's wide-ranging mobility allows for her own "infinite variety" (2.2.281) to be on display in pilgrimage site after pilgrimage site, only not in Shakespeare's England. It is as if the play, through the *black* Cleopatra, presents the possibility of something imaginative and visually striking even as it stages the sober masculinity of a Roman Empire that England was seeking to emulate. England's ensuing colonial enterprise makes both facets of the play that much more important for us to explore and to seek to understand. Rather importantly, *Antony and Cleopatra* uses blackness to get here and, ostensibly, it illustrates the cross-cultural—perhaps the universal—appeal of Shakespeare's theater; however, one must also acknowledge the limits of this universality by recognizing, as Daileader does, how Cleopatra has been co-opted by white actresses in a way similar to the whitewashing of the Virgin Mary through the proliferation of white depictions of her person. Still, blackness carries with it a unique and substantial worth—like Guadalupe in Mexico, like Isis in anticipation of Mary, or like Cleopatra in owning her black and beautiful strength.

Notes

1. Montaigne, *Journal*, 2:206.
2. Montaigne, *Journal*, 2:206–7.
3. For an incisive reading of the travels surrounding the Santa Casa di Loreto, see Patricia Akhimie's essay in this collection.
4. See Warner, *Alone of All Her Sex*; Pelikan, *Mary Through the Centuries*; Cunneen, *In Search of Mary*; Carroll, *Cult of the Virgin Mary*; and Maunder, *Origins of the Cult*.
5. For readings that attend to Marian connections in Shakespeare and early modern drama, see Buccola and Hopkins, *Marian Moments*; Espinosa, *Masculinity and Marian Efficacy*; and Waller, *Virgin Mary*.
6. All of the characters I list as examples are described as "fair" within their respective plays, and these diverse plays connect the idea of "fairness" and "white beauty" at various moments (e.g., *The Merchant of Venice* 2.4.12–14). For sustained attention to the correlation between fairness and whiteness in Shakespeare, see Hall, "'These bastard signs.'" All references to Shakespeare are taken from the third edition of *The Norton Shakespeare*.
7. For a sharp study on the influence of race on early modern English religious identity, see Britton, *Becoming Christian*.
8. Daileader, "The Cleopatra Complex," 206. Given her Macedonian Greek descent, the issue of Cleopatra's skin color has been a focal point of debates. I align myself with Daileader who looks at the "stupefyingly obvious" solution to the debate: Cleopatra calls herself "black" (208; see *Antony and Cleopatra* 1.5.27–29).
9. Callaghan, *Shakespeare without Women*, 76–77.
10. Smith, "Othello's Black Handkerchief," 23.
11. For attention to masculinity and Protestant identity, see Eire, *War against the Idols*, 315.
12. Britton, *Becoming Christian*, 57.
13. Britton, *Becoming Christian*, 57.
14. Espinosa, *Masculinity and Marian Efficacy*, 27.
15. For a focused exploration of ambivalent views about the Virgin Mary in post-Reformation England, see Espinosa, *Masculinity and Marian Efficacy*. For the formation of English views of white supremacy via early modern poetry, see Hall, "'These bastard signs.'"
16. Erickson, "Race Words," 159–60.
17. Erickson, "Race Words," 160.
18. Morrison, *Women Pilgrims*, 16.
19. Birnbaum, *Black Madonnas*, 3.

20. Birnbaum, *Black Madonnas*, 4.
21. See Warner, *Alone of All Her Sex*, and Cunneen, *In Search of Mary*. For Erasmus, see Espinosa, *Masculinity and Marian Efficacy*, 162.
22. Oleszkiewicz-Peralba, *Black Madonna*, 14.
23. Oleszkiewicz-Peralba, *Black Madonna*, 11.
24. Oleszkiewicz-Peralba, *Black Madonna*, 17–18.
25. Oleszkiewicz-Peralba, *Black Madonna*, 14.
26. Maunder, *Origins of the Cult*, 9.
27. Maunder, *Origins of the Cult*, 9.
28. Maunder tells us that the cult of Isis had "spread all over the ancient world in the centuries shortly before the appearing of Christ" and that she "had become one of the great success stories of the exporting of the Egyptian cults across the Roman Empire" (*Origins of the Cult*, 7). For the proliferation of the cult of the Virgin Mary and pre- and early modern Europe, see Espinosa, *Masculinity and Marian Efficacy*, 2–20.
29. Oleszkiewicz-Peralba, *Black Madonna*, 16. See also, Maunder, *Origins of the Cult*, 12–13.
30. See Espinosa, *Masculinity and Marian Efficacy*, 59–90.
31. Jewel, *An Apology*, 38.
32. Crashaw, *Jesuites Gospel*, E3v. I have normalized the orthography of the following letters throughout this essay: u/v, i/j, and vv/w.
33. See Dolan, *Whores of Babylon*, who argues that the Virgin Mary is not only imagined as a "commanding mother," but also as a "bossy woman" (110).
34. Lefkowitz, "Mary and the Ancient Goddesses," 134.
35. For more on the dynamics surrounding Mary's intercessory potential, see Espinosa, *Masculinity and Marian Efficacy*, 59–90.
36. Callaghan, *Shakespeare without Women*, 79.
37. See Espinosa, *Masculinity and Marian Efficacy*, 149–72.
38. For an interesting reading of Cleopatra "strik[ing] the pose" of the Virgin Mary at the play's end, see King, "Blessed When They Were Riggish," 449.
39. Levine, *Men in Women's Clothing*, 47.
40. See, for example, Macdonald, *Race, Ethnicity, and Power*, who argues that "race and gender were coupled to do the work of a colonizing culture whose assumptions were of necessity not only masculine, but white" (8).
41. Hall, "'These bastard signs,'" 66.
42. Hall, "'These bastard signs,'" 67.
43. Some studies that offer sustained attention to geohumoralism and racial formation in the early modern period include Bovilsky, *Barbarous*

Play; Feerick, *Strangers in Blood*; Iyengar, *Shades of Difference*; Malcolmson, *Studies of Skin Color*; and Floyd-Wilson, *English Ethnicity and Race*.
44. See Britton, *Becoming Christian*, 1–34.
45. In "The Virgins Salutation" within Southwell's *Moeoniae*, Mary's breast is imagined as the place where the "heavens ... incline" (B2v). The salutation reads, "Haile fairest heaven, that heaven and earth do blisse / Where vertues starre Gods sunne of justice is" (B2v). The connection between fairness and virtue is clearly in place, but as Hall argues in regard to lyric poetry, the term "faire," like whiteness, "avoids particularity, and like whiteness, it is represented as 'plain,' obvious, and curiously opaque" ("'These bastard signs,'" 68). How this influenced views of the Virgin Mary remains unclear, but the currency of the term in relation to notions of race is certainly evident.
46. Hopkins, "'Black but Beautiful,'" 78.
47. Hopkins, "'Black but Beautiful,'" 79.
48. Jewel, *Second Tome of Homilies*, G2r.
49. Munday, *English Romayne Lyfe*, P1r–P1v.
50. Matthew 19:21.
51. Munday, *English Romayne Lyfe*, P1v.
52. 1 Timothy 6:15.
53. Daileader, "The Cleopatra Complex," 208.
54. Carroll, *Cult of the Virgin Mary*, 8.
55. Hopkins, "'Black but Beautiful,'" 79.
56. Hakluyt, *Principal Navigations*, Rr3r–Rr3v.
57. For the influence of the Virgen de Guadalupe on Mexican identity, see Pelikan, *Mary through the Centuries*, 180–81.

Bibliography

Birnbaum, Lucia Chiavola. *Black Madonnas: Feminism, Religion, and Politics in Italy*. Boston: Northeastern University Press, 1993.

Bovilsky, Laura. *Barbarous Play: Race on the English Renaissance Stage*. Minneapolis: University of Minnesota Press, 2008.

Britton, Dennis A. *Becoming Christian: Race, Reformation, and Early Modern English Romance*. New York: Fordham University Press, 2014.

Buccola, Regina, and Lisa Hopkins. *Marian Moments in Early Modern British Drama*. Burlington VT: Ashgate, 2007.

Callaghan, Dympna. *Shakespeare without Women: Representing Gender and Race on the Renaissance Stage*. London: Routledge, 2000.

Carroll, Michael P. *The Cult of the Virgin Mary: Psychological Origins*. Princeton: Princeton University Press, 1986.

Crashaw, William. *The Jesuites Gospel*. London, 1610.
Cunneen, Sally. *In Search of Mary: The Woman and the Symbol*. New York: Ballantine, 1996.
Daileader, Celia. "The Cleopatra Complex: White Actresses on the Interracial 'Classic' Stage." In *Colorblind Shakespeare*, edited by Ayanna Thompson, 205–20. New York: Routledge, 2006.
Dolan, Frances E. *Whores of Babylon: Catholicism, Gender, and Seventeenth-Century Print Culture*. Ithaca NY: Cornell University Press, 1999.
Eire, Carlos M. N. *The War against the Idols*. Cambridge: Cambridge University Press, 1986.
Erickson, Peter. "Race Words in *Othello*." In *Shakespeare and Immigration*, edited by Ruben Espinosa and David Ruiter, 159–76. Burlington VT: Ashgate, 2014.
Espinosa, Ruben. *Masculinity and Marian Efficacy in Shakespeare's England*. Burlington VT: Ashgate, 2011.
Feerick, Jean. *Strangers in Blood: Relocating Race in the Renaissance*. Toronto: University of Toronto Press, 2010.
Floyd-Wilson, Mary. *English Ethnicity and Race in Early Modern Drama*. Cambridge: Cambridge University Press, 2006.
Hakluyt, Richard. *The Principal Navigations*. London, 1599.
Hall, Kim. "'These bastard signs of fair': Literary Whiteness in Shakespeare's Sonnets." In *Post-Colonial Shakespeares*, edited by Ania Loomba and Martin Orkin, 64–83. London: Routledge, 2002.
Hopkins, Lisa. "'Black but Beautiful': *Othello* and the Cult of the Black Madonna." *Marian Moments in Early Modern British Drama*, edited by Regina Buccola, 75–86. Burlington VT: Ashgate, 2007.
Iyengar, Sujata. *Shades of Difference: Mythologies of Skin Color in Early Modern England*. Philadelphia: University of Pennsylvania Press, 2004.
Jewel, John. *An Apology for the Church of England*. London, 1564.
———. *The Second Tome of Homilies*. London, 1571.
King, Laura S. "Blessed When They Were Riggish: Shakespeare's Cleopatra and Christianity's Penitent Prostitutes." *Journal of Medieval and Renaissance Studies* 22 (1992): 429–49.
Lefkowitz, Mary. "Mary and the Ancient Goddesses." In *Divine Mirrors: The Virgin Mary in the Visual Arts*, edited by Melissa Katz and Robert Orsi, 133–35. Oxford: Oxford University Press, 2001.
Levine, Laura. *Men in Women's Clothing: Anti-Theatricality and Effeminization, 1579–1642*. Cambridge: Cambridge University Press, 1994.
MacDonald, Joyce Green, ed. *Race, Ethnicity, and Power in the Renaissance*. Madison NJ: Farleigh Dickinson University Press, 1997.

Malcolmson, Cristina. *Studies of Skin Color in the Early Royal Society*. Burlington VT: Ashgate, 2013.

Maunder, Chris. *The Origins of the Cult of the Virgin Mary*. New York: Burns and Oates, 2008.

Montaigne, Michel de. *The Journal of Montaigne's Travels in Italy by Way of Switzerland and Germany*. Vol. 2. London: John Murray, 1903.

Morrison, Susan Signe. *Women Pilgrims in Late Medieval England: Private Piety as Public Performance*. London: Routledge, 2000.

Munday, Anthony. *The English Romayne Lyfe*. London, 1582.

Oleszkiewicz-Peralba, Małgorzata. *The Black Madonna in Latin America and Europe*. Albuquerque: University of New Mexico Press, 2007.

Pelikan, Jaroslav. *Mary through the Centuries*. New Haven: Yale University Press, 1996.

Shakespeare, William. *The Norton Shakespeare*, edited by Stephen Greenblatt, et al. New York: W. W. Norton, 2015.

Smith, Ian. "Othello's Black Handkerchief," *Shakespeare Quarterly* 64, no. 1 (2013): 1–25.

Southwell, Robert. *Moeoniae*. London, 1595.

Waller, Gary. *The Virgin Mary in Late Medieval and Early Modern English Literature and Popular Culture*. Cambridge: Cambridge University Press, 2011.

Warner, Marina. *Alone of All Her Sex: The Myth and the Cult of the Virgin Mary*. New York: Vintage, 1976.

14

Precarious Travail, Gender, and Narration in Shakespeare's *Pericles, Prince of Tyre* and Margaret Cavendish's *The Blazing World*

DYANI JOHNS TAFF

The meaning of the word "travel" intertwined with that of "travail" in the sixteenth and seventeenth centuries. As Daniel Vitkus observes, unlike today's association of travel with "with leisure and pleasure," in the early modern period "the various spellings ('travail,' 'traveyle,' 'travel,' etc.) signified the labor, trouble, discomfort, hardship, and pain associated with travel."[1] Vitkus centers his analysis of Thomas Dekker's *Old Fortunatus* and Shakespeare's *Pericles* on overlaps between two primary sixteenth-century definitions of "travail": "1) hard work or effort in general, [and] 2) the work and effort required to travel from one place to another."[2] In particular, he traces an emergent capitalist reconceptualization of the hazards of travel as necessary for profitable investments.[3] He also notes a third definition of "travail" — "3) the pain and 'labor' of child-birth" — but he passes rapidly over this definition, even when discussing Thaisa's shipboard labor in the beginning of act 3.[4] In what follows, I trace figures of and stories about sea travel that William Shakespeare, in *Pericles, Prince of Tyre* (ca. 1608-9), and Margaret Cavendish, in *The Blazing World* (1666), use to explore the messy, contested relationship between travel and labor, taking as my focus connections between intellectual "travail" and the "travail" of childbirth. Shakespeare repeatedly foregrounds these connections in *Pericles*, narrating Thaisa's shipboard labor and insistently merging the language of childbirth, dramatic production, and sea travel.[5] Figurative and physical childbirth are almost entirely absent from *The Blazing World*, but Cavendish dwells on the precariousness of her narrator's and the Lady-cum-Empress's intellectual, imaginative labor as well as on the her subjects' physical work in manipulating the natural world—particularly the sea—in order to consolidate her power. In both *Pericles* and *The Blazing World*, Shakespeare and Cavendish represent voyages and labors—both authorial and physical—that amplify conflicting ideas about human separation from or interaction with the environment.

In *Pericles*, the maritime environment is unpredictable, violent, and effeminizing; Shakespeare depicts the sea as hazardous for his characters and also represents maritime dangers as analogous to the challenges of theatrical staging and authorship more broadly. In the play, the border between human bodies and the sea is porous, and Shakespeare often represents something like what Stacy Alaimo terms "trans-corporeality": that is, a view of the relationship of the human to the nonhuman that "insists that the human is always the very stuff of the messy, contingent, emergent mix of the material world."[6] Steven Mentz reads the play with a similar concept in mind, seeing the staged shipboard storm in act 3, scene 1, as "direct[ing] the play's attention ... to the entanglement of human bodies with rough water."[7] He also argues that Marina's birth at sea governs her interactions with both the human and nonhuman world: "so much of Marina remains in the water. Her birth at sea and (supposed) death on the beach tie her to the unending struggle of the roiling waters encroaching on the shore."[8] My focus on Thaisa's travel and travail reveals that Shakespeare's exploration of trans-corporeality results in a repeated staging of precarity, both in the danger of sea travel and in the danger of failed narrations and theatrical productions. Gower's narrations in *Pericles* draw our attention to the convenience of the storms that wash characters up on just the right shores, sundering and bringing them together at the opportune narrative moments. The staged sea reminds us that those characters' movements are *staged* and that their "entanglement ... with rough water" serves the design of the playwright, actors, and production. The characters' lives are endangered through their encounters with the sea, *and* staging the sea and narrating sea travel is itself precarious and unpredictable.

Cavendish's sea is also violent and unpredictable, but in *The Blazing World* she invests in representing the sea—as well as other parts of the environment—not as enmeshed with human (or animal-men) bodies but rather as a useful, manipulable element, dominated by the Empress's initiatives.[9] Amy Boesky argues that Cavendish—through the Empress's actions and interactions with the Duchess of Newcastle—claims the imagination as a locus for power, restoration, and violence, but simultaneously recognizes the Blazing World as a "toy," and her mental authority as trivial or fleeting.[10] Cavendish's intellectual labor, while powerful in a sense, is also vulnerable to claims of impotency or smallness in that it is not a labor that matters (or that creates *matter*). Few critics have examined Cavendish's representation of the ocean and travel as it contributes to Cavendish's conflicted portrayal of imaginative labor.[11] I focus on the Lady's hazardous journey to the Blazing World, on the Lady-cum-Empress's staging of a performance of her power, and on the narrator's strategic representation of these maritime events. These scenes foreground Cavendish's anxiety about the value of imaginative intellectual labor that appears enmeshed with anxiety about the construction and destruction of boundaries between bodies and the world. Cavendish's narrator, like Gower in Shakespeare's play, uses the precarious relationship between humans and the sea to remind us of the precariousness of performance. In revealing to readers the operations by which the Empress and her subjects create an oceanic stage and by detailing the science and dramaturgy they use to set the Empress up as a magical, Christ-like figure, Cavendish calls attention to her character's manipulation of nonhuman objects and environments. She recalls the nonhuman forces that enabled the Lady's travel to the Blazing World to become the Empress and invites us to see the enmeshment of an agential environment with the Empress's and her subjects' bodies even as the Empress and the Duchess at times deny that connection.

Female travelers such as Thaisa and the Empress embark either as a result of or in spite of maritime hazards such as piracy, storms, and so on. Once they are on board, though, they often disrupt binaries such as male/female and human/nonhuman that writers use to structure narrative and figurative elements of their texts.[12] As Karen Lawrence asserts, some "examples of women's travel writing... remap (and destabilize) femininity in relation to the poles of travel/home, other/self and foreign/domestic."[13] Lawrence usefully traces gender in "the journey plot" and in theorizations about travel, revealing a "certain blindness to the role of gender" even in texts—by both men and women—that overtly challenge representations of women as Penelope (at home or a figure for home itself) and men as Odysseus (abroad, transformed through contact with the foreign).[14] Thaisa and the Empress, traveling and travailing in the multiple senses of those words, simultaneously control and are shaped by not only the events of their voyages but also the maritime environments through which they travel. They are enmeshed in a fluctuating power relationship with their male counterparts and with the environment itself.

Gender and Temperature

It is perhaps unsurprising that, given the gender-specific dangers of sea travel, women brave enough to venture to sea and strong enough to survive those dangers might be described as possessing qualities usually coded male. Both Thaisa and the Lady (who becomes the Empress) survive harrowing sea voyages, and both are described as having unusually or unexpectedly warm bodies. In contrast to the cold, wet sea—associated with humoral theories about femaleness—Thaisa and the Lady are hot and dry enough to survive the storms through which they pass, and their bodies are presented as humorally masculinized.[15] But both women also have an ambiguous power relationship with the environment through which they travel, underscoring Gail Kern Paster's observation that "if the insubstantial margins of the humoral body open that body to the world, the cultural meaning of that openness remains indeterminate."[16] A "porous and permeable" boundary between body and environment undermines depictions of travel that rely on crucially nonpermeable ships. Thaisa and the Lady trouble the narrative of a male hero who conquers the environment-as-obstacle in the quest for commercial or exploratory profit. Their encounters with the maritime environment destabilize both the male/female binary and notions of human authority over the nonhuman world.

Representations of Thaisa's agency fluctuate in the play. She actively chooses to travel with Pericles, but subsequently becomes — temporarily — a dead body, and then a body figured as passive treasure that belongs to Pericles.[17] Gower describes Thaisa as powerful in her decision to accompany Pericles when he is recalled to Tyre: "[Pericles's] queen, with child, makes her desire — / Which who shall cross? — along to go" (3 Chor. 40–41).[18] He implies that neither Pericles nor Simonides has the power to controvert Thaisa's "desire." The storm robs her of this strength; it induces early labor, and her subsequent seeming death prompts Pericles to imagine her decomposition at sea: she shall be "scarcely coffined, in the ooze / Where... // the belching whale / And humming water must o'erwhelm" her body, which will end "[l]ying with simple shells" (3.1.65–69). Pericles imagines her body disintegrating and merging with the cold, wet depths of the ocean. Her body, in Pericles's imaginative grief, becomes so feminized that it no longer maintains human form. But Thaisa's sea burial is not final and her undersea decomposition does not come to pass. Pericles's sailors apparently have very thoroughly "caulked and bitumed" the "chest" into which they put Thaisa (3.1.75–76). They judiciously preserve the boundary between sea and body, working against the forces of the storm, the ocean, and death itself that seek to render the body and the environment entirely unified. When her coffin, still sealed, washes up in Ephesus, Cerimon exclaims,

> What e'er it be,
> 'Tis wondrous heavy. Wrench it open straight.
> If the sea's stomach be o'ercharged with gold,
> 'Tis a good constraint of Fortune it belches upon us.
> (3.2.61–64).

Cerimon's speculations highlight the constellation of words — coffin, coffer, casket, chest, etc. — that blend containers for treasure with containers for dead bodies. He does discover actual treasure in Thaisa's coffin — placed in the chest by Pericles as a "fee" (3.2.85) for anyone "Who finds her... [to] give her burying" (3.2.83) — but his words additionally invite the audience to compare Thaisa herself to "gold."[19] He positions Thaisa as valuable property that Pericles has lost as a result of the capricious, dangerous nature of economic, political, marital, or other ventures by sea. Thaisa at this moment has become entirely inert, exhibiting no agency, and borne on the waves to those who watch the shipwreck from the beach, hoping for monetary bounty to be "belche[d] upon" the shore.

And yet, in seeming death and resurrection, Thaisa has more power over human and nonhuman elements in the play than a view of her as passive property might afford. As Pericles holds the infant Marina and mourns for Thaisa, one of his sailors shouts, "Sir, your queen must overboard. The sea works high, the wind is loud, and will not lie till the ship be cleared of the dead" (3.1.51–53). Pericles responds, "That's your superstition" (3.1.54), calling the sailor out for a specious belief, but the sailor persists, and Pericles yields, telling him to do "[a]s [he] think[s] meet" (3.1.59). As a presumed-dead body, and indeed as a female body dead or alive, the sailors believe that Thaisa has the power to keep the storm going if she remains aboard or to abate it if they throw her into the sea. Though Pericles's remark invites us to question the validity of the sailors' "custom" and belief (3.1.56), the storm does in fact end when they cast Thaisa's coffin overboard, and Pericles, Marina, and the crew survive to sail on to Tarsus. Although Thaisa is not conscious, Shakespeare suggests that her body has the power to quell the storm and save the ship. It would appear that, though the sailors effectively seal her body into the coffin, they cannot entirely control the boundary between her body and the oceanic environment. They persist in their belief, even after sealing her body in a smaller vessel, that Thaisa's body will have an effect on the storm. Furthermore, in contrast to Pericles's earlier immersion in the ocean and arrival on shore as "[a] man thronged up with cold" (2.1.76)—deeply wet and cold, and thereby humorally feminized—Thaisa washes up "warm": as Cerimon examines her, he says,

> This queen will live. Nature awakes a warm breath
> out of her. . . .
> See how she gins to blow
> Into life's flower again. (3.2.105–8)

"Nature" here reverses humoral ideas about gender and body temperature. In comparing Thaisa to a flower (as well as to treasure), Cerimon uses metaphors often reserved for describing women.[20] But her "warm[th]" after exiting the cold sea bespeaks a more complicated understanding of Thaisa's gender and of her relationship to the environment. She is female, but "warm." She has been submerged—thrown overboard, imagined as becoming a part of the whales and corals—but has not touched the depths of the sea at all. She controls her travel and the maritime environment: she chose to sail with Pericles, and she perhaps stops the storm. But she has also lost control: the sailors and the sea dictate her travels, and the storm induces her labor and initiates the events that separate her from Marina. Her body and her actions evince qualities coded both male and female and bespeak both power and powerlessness, challenging the male/female and human/nonhuman binaries that the play itself often seeks to reinforce.

The Lady in the beginning of Cavendish's *The Blazing World* exhibits, like Thaisa, extraordinary body heat that saves her from a nearly fatal sea voyage. After she is abducted by a "Merchant" who had fallen "extreamly in Love" with her, the Lady survives the "double cold" at the joined poles of her "Native world" and the Blazing World "by the light of her Beauty, the heat of her Youth, and Protection of the Gods," while the Merchant and his crew of fellow abductors freeze to death.[21] Line Cottegnies reads this episode as "[g]iving the lie to the Galenic view of woman as colder than man" because "the heroine does not freeze, and survives the whole crew."[22] But Cavendish's presentation of the Lady's physiology as partially responsible for her survival—along with her beauty and the favor of the "Gods"—does more than cheekily negate contemporary medical theories. It also describes a mobile sharing of power among male, female, and supernatural agents and a fluid conception of gender. The Lady's boat moves "as if it had been guided by some Experienced Pilot, and skillful Mariner," pushed by the "violent motions of the wind" (154). The Lady has the "favor of the Gods" (154), but that divine influence shares control over the vessel with the power of the wind, the lightness of the boat, and perhaps the flowing of the water's currents. Cavendish, like Shakespeare, employs the convenient romance trope of the ship blown off course in order to move her main character into the other "World" that will be her narrative's main focus. She takes the opportunity of the trope not to confirm ultimate divine control over the natural world but instead to ruminate on the multiple and conflicting natural powers that appear capable of joining with or moving against divine impulsion and human initiative. Though the Lady certainly avoids freezing or being shipwrecked because of divine "favor" and the "Protection of the Gods," Cavendish first remarks on "the light of her Beauty" and "the heat of her Youth," allowing readers, at least momentarily, to consider the Lady's bodily fortitude—the "heat" that makes her humorally manly and therefore strong enough to survive temperatures that freeze lesser men—independent of divine intervention.

When she enters the Blazing World, the Lady becomes a traveler, a colonizer, and a romance hero, gleefully shattering English cultural norms that—as Lawrence has shown—often assigned these roles to men.[23] At least partially because of her "heat" and "beauty," she handily becomes Empress and converts all of the inhabitants of the Blazing World to Christianity "without inforcement or blood-shed," but rather "by gentle perswasions" (193). In part 2, returning to the world from which she was abducted, the Empress uses power that, in contrast, requires violent "inforcement" and "blood-shed" to subdue those who threaten her country's monarch. She fluctuates between displaying qualities coded female, such as her inspiring chastity and "beauty," and qualities coded male, such as her sometimes violent, strategic maneuvers for power and her ability to control all "Trade and Traffick" in the world and "force" any people she encounters "to submit as well as the rest of the World had done" (241).[24] The Empress's power also, crucially, comes from her investigations of the Blazing World's geology and biology, and of the animal-men's technological innovations. The Worm-men locate and mine "a great quantity of the fire-stone, whose property . . . is, that it burns so long as it is wet" to bring as ammunition for the Empress's war (234). The Giants create proto-submarines that convey the Empress and her subjects to her native world. The Fish-men tow the submarines that convey the fire-stones to the enemy's ships and set fire to them. Although the Empress does reject some scientific instruments—such as telescopes, which she "Command[s her Bearmen] to break" after they produce debate about the nature of the heavens (170)—Anne Thell contends that Cavendish endorses the scientific power of imagination.[25] Thell argues that, alongside her portrayal of the animal-men's explorations and inventions, "the concept of travel allows Cavendish to dramatize the propulsion and the reach of imaginative thought."[26] And yet, despite this "reach," Cavendish's narrator, the Empress, and the Duchess gloss over the painful labor of physical, not imaginative, travel. Their manipulations of the sea, of the "fire-stones" that her animal-men locate, and of other environments and objects enable the Empress to easily obtain absolute power, eliding the labor of the Empress's subjects as well as the hardships of travel and war.

Pericles, like the Empress, is a "colonizer" who through "protracted travels ... attempts to expand his sway,"[27] and Shakespeare portrays him as "an elite, masculine adventurer."[28] As Michelle Dowd argues, the play uses the "adventurer narrative as a formal means of reestablishing male control and imposing order on the text's wide ranging effects."[29] At the same time, according to Dowd, the narrative "resolution" in the play is "a process of struggle" that "makes visible alternative narratives of lineage and gendered authority."[30] Pericles is both the strong, male romance hero and the character through whom we see fissures in the play's "conservative" emphasis on Pericles's successful restoration of his patrilineal line.[31] Because Shakespeare repeatedly foregrounds the connection between travel and travail—physical labor and childbirth—Pericles's adventures destabilize the very masculinity that his "elite" travels confirm or bolster. In act 5, for example, when Pericles speaks with Marina, attempting to recognize her and to discuss his painful maritime adventures, he exclaims, "I am great with woe, and shall deliver weeping" (5.1.120). He, like Thaisa, "delivers" in a cold, wet, salty environment, and his metaphorical—and perhaps also physical—tears blur the boundary between his body and the ocean.[32] He insulates himself from the sea in his ship and survives his encounter with the waves; his role as adventurer pits him against the hazardous sea, and he prevails. But salt water within his body undermines the antagonistic relationship between adventurer and environment that often characterizes romance narratives. Examining the link between portrayals of incest in *Pericles* and the complex relationship between Mary and Christ, Ruben Espinosa contends that in this scene Pericles's "self-description is anchored in a maternal identity.... Pericles aligns himself with a feminine source of compassion; he wants to feel [Marina's] pain, and perhaps this is a way for him to cope with his own suffering."[33] Espinosa sees Pericles as "re-fashion[ing] his gendered identity" here, his articulation of a "Marian" relationship with Marina as rendering "the difference between 'man' and 'girl' immaterial."[34] Pericles figures his body as feminine and his suffering as a form of childbirth. In doing so, he not only troubles gender binaries but also emphasizes the porous boundary between his skin (or his maritime vessel) and the sea.

Stage as Sea, Sea as Stage

Travel in *Pericles* and *The Blazing World* is sometimes abortive, always difficult (even when described as easy), and often associated with fluid conceptions of gender and with figurative and physical birth. When these texts turn self-reflexively to consider performance and literary production, both Cavendish and Shakespeare use the language of precarious sea travel to do so, perhaps finding the associations with difficulty and fluidity apt for revealing anxieties about what an author or actor is capable of creating within an audience's mind. The staged sea and the sea used as a stage make this anxiety central and glaring. As the Chorus in Thomas Heywood's *A Fair Maid of the West, Part One*, remarks, "Our stage can so lamely express a sea," for such an expression requires the imaginative help and good will of the audience, never a surety.[35] Many companies, Shakespeare's included, chose to convey shipwreck and maritime adventures through choruses or by having characters relate what they saw or experienced off stage. The sea itself was also often figured in plays, prose fictions, and sea manuals as a stage. Dan Brayton remarks that "the frontispiece from *The Mariners Mirrour*, a compendium of essential technical information for navigators [in its] composition... suggests the metaphor of the sea as a stage, with mariners as actors in a *naumachia*, or nautical drama, and a group of cartographers assembled around a blank globe as playwrights of a sort."[36] Shakespeare and Cavendish are interested in the imaginative rewards of representing the stage as a sea and the sea as a stage, but they also commit to revealing the failings of that representation, failings that reveal the sea's fluidity, unpredictability, and porousness as troublingly analogous to the stages on which actors and characters perform.

As we have seen, critics often pass over Thaisa's labor and childbirth at sea relatively quickly. Vitkus, for example, focuses on the way that Cerimon's "careful labor and skill" in reviving Thaisa illuminate the "play['s] combin[ation of] romantic, fateful wandering with real-world scenes of lower-class labor on the sea-shore and in the brothel" (240).[37] But Thaisa, as much as Cerimon, is a traveler and travailer, enduring fear and danger in order to travel and also working hard to birth a child. When Gower describes Thaisa's travel and labor at sea, he solicits the audience's participation. For Dowd, "Gower's [narrative] interventions . . . illuminate the dramaturgical strategies through which patrilineal order gets restored in the play, a process of consolidation and control that resituates the text's disjointed episodes within a larger narrative of teleological momentum" (185).[38] Gower's appeals to the audience's imagination certainly present the play's bids for patrilineal control, but they also reveal the ever-present possibility that the audience will not participate, that the gaps between scenes will not be effectively filled, and that the performance will fail. Gower briefly describes Pericles and Thaisa's marriage and Marina's conception, and then addresses the audience:

> Be attent,
> And time that is so briefly spent
> with your fine fancies quaintly eche. (3 Chor. 11–13)

Gower suggests that we might "eche"—fill or increase—the narrative gap between conception and Thaisa's swollen belly in the dumb show with our "fine fancies" in parallel to the way that the "loss of maidenhead" (3 Chor. 10), and presumably Pericles's seed, has "A babe . . . molded" (3 Chor. 11) in Thaisa's womb. When Pericles and Thaisa's ship is assailed by a storm, Gower again asks the audience to augment his narration:

> In your imagination hold
> This stage the ship, upon whose deck
> The sea-tossed Pericles appears to speake. (3 Chor. 58–60)

Gower asks us not only to fill in the details of the scene that Shakespeare—in this play—has decided not to represent on stage, but also to "hold" a stage as ship within our minds. His words, and subsequently those of the other actors, populate or fill our minds as Thaisa's child filled her belly. Gower constructs the fantasy of the sea voyage, but he also calls our attention to that construction and to the potential failure of his plea for us to use our "imagination[s]." It remains entirely possible, despite the playwright's and actors' best efforts, that the stage will, in fact, "lamely express a sea." Early modern understandings of pregnancy and the doubts surrounding conception are important to this representation of failure; as a woman's body was supposed to be a vessel for the man's seed, so the performance relies on the audience's ability to be a vessel for the playwright's, the actors', and the characters' creative production. How much agency the woman or audience as vessel has in the creative venture is disputed. Gower's narration highlights the theatrical, narrative labor of representing maritime travel. He reveals conflicted motivations: on the one hand, he shores up the control of the human over the maritime environment, of the powerful over the powerless, and of the artistic creator over the audience. On the other, he explores fissures in those hierarchies and systems of control.

Cavendish's narrator, like Gower, engages in revealing the precariousness of the relationship of the actor or author to the audience, but where Gower focuses on metaphors of pregnancy and travel, Cavendish's narrator by turns glosses over and reveals the labor and destruction involved in consolidating absolute authority, even of the imaginative variety. As Boesky asserts, "It is true that women in the Blazing-world are able to borrow the role of monarch. But monarchy is a contested institution for Cavendish, a performance at times powerful, at others a mere toy."[39] Cavendish's conflicted portrayal of the Empress's power, as Boesky argues, defines imaginative, intellectual labor as both powerful and powerless. In Cavendish's representation of the Empress's interactions with the natural world, she moves to paint the environment as a tool or as material that is malleable and available to human initiatives. But Cavendish's narrator also shows the Empress hiding the scientific, practical sources of her power and staging an elaborate performance on the backs of her Fish-men designed to inspire terror and awe.[40] Her carefully staged public appearance in her own world reminds her in-text audience of "the time of Judgment, or the Last Day was come" because of the flaming fire-stones that she uses on her clothing and her stage (236). In order to inform her countrymen of her plans for action, she appears before them "with Garments made of the Star-stone, and was born or supported above the Water, upon the Fish-mens heads and backs, so that she seemed to walk upon the face of the Water" (237). To her audience, the Empress is miraculously supported by the water's surface, and they later remark with awe that she has "so great a power . . . to walk upon the waters" (242). The Empress recalls Christ and derives "power" from her apparent ability to keep her body above the waves; that is, her separation of her body from the sea enables her to manipulate her audience. During this performance, the Empress also remains, importantly, apart from the audience, "at such a distance where her voice might be generally heard, by reason she would not have that of her Accoustrements any thing else should be perceived, but the splendor thereof" (237). It is imperative that her countrymen not see the device by which she appears in Christ-like "splendor" and thereby discover the trick or — to use Boesky's language, "toy" — she uses to control them. She relies on theatrical techniques both to get their attention and to cement her religious, political, and economic power over her native world and the maritime environment.

The Empress takes great pains to avoid revealing the theatrical staging of her performance to her audience, engaging in a concerted effort to police the boundary between her body and the sea. Yet Cavendish's narrator makes the reader privy to the details of that staging, drawing attention to the constructed, precarious nature of the body/sea and performer/audience boundaries and to the collective labor necessary to set up and maintain the Empress's absolute power. Cottegnies asserts that this "episode . . . deconstructs a 'miracle' by showing it is an illusion contrived through artificial means."⁴¹ But by inviting us backstage, Cavendish's narrator highlights both the hard labor of the Fish-men that subtends—physically and figuratively—the Empress's conquest of her world and also the labor of the narrator herself in masking and negating the dangers of the maritime environment—storms, currents, winds, etc.—that could easily destroy the performance and the Empress's power. By performing the role of a divine Angel of God's "Judgment" or of Christ himself (236), the Empress can implicitly claim that her scorched-earth tactics are divinely justified and necessary to root out the "enemies" of her countrymen (in effect, *her* chosen people). Yet because we see the Empress and her subjects constructing this performance, the text also invites us to question the validity of divine justifications for violence. Cavendish's narrator, in the epilogue to the reader, strategically forgets the violence of part 2. The narrator boasts that her creation of the Blazing World "was more easily and suddenly effected, then the Conquests of the two famous Monarchs of the World, *Alexander* and *Caesar*: Neither have I made such disturbances, and caused so many dissolutions of particulars, otherwise named deaths, as they did; for I have destroyed but some few men in a little Boat" (251). Her creation and ascent to absolute control of the "*Blazing-world*, a Peaceable World" is indeed effected "easily" and without violence (251). But, as Boesky argues, "[w]itty as [the narrator's] disclaimer is meant to be, she reminds her readers in this way that the imagination can be as harmful a place as any . . . Cavendish in her utopia starts a fire and then denies it."⁴² The narrator's assertion pointedly ignores the massive, destructive violence that the Empress inflicts on her native world in part 2. The deconstruction of the "miracle"—to return to Cottegnies's language—of walking on water and the narrator's disavowal of the violence of conquest underscore the idea that the dream of conquering or converting people to Christianity "without inforcement or blood-shed" but rather "by gentle perswasions" is just that: a naive dream (193).

Both Cavendish and Shakespeare construct and deconstruct boundaries between purportedly masculine and feminine bodies and behaviors and between the human and the nonhuman world. The Empress, Thaisa, and Pericles travel and travail, laboring to physically and imaginatively produce new beings and new worlds, but the narrators in these texts pull back the curtain that obscures the work of travel and performance. That work often depends on a firm boundary between humans and the world: the vessel, whether ship or audience member, must be seaworthy to survive. Yet these texts reveal that boundary to be tenuous at best. They prompt us to see the labor of a narrator as precarious travail that depends on the work of agents beyond the authors' and actors' control, and they invite us to view gender and human/nonhuman binaries as constructed, not given. These binaries, my reading of maritime voyages suggests, are necessitated or called into play by discourses seeking to define human gender and the human relationship to the environment through patriarchal, hierarchical structures. Human and nonhuman agents in Shakespeare's and Cavendish's texts upend these schemas of control, revealing anxiety both about gendered definitions of the human and about the role of texts in reifying those definitions.

Notes

1. Vitkus, "Labor and Travel," 229–30.
2. Vitkus, "Labor and Travel," 229. Vitkus cites *The Oxford English Dictionary*, "travail, *n.*" I. 1–4, and "travail, *v.*," I. 1–2, as his source for all three definitions of "travail."
3. Vitkus, "Labor and Travel," 228–31.
4. Vitkus, "Labor and Travel," 229. Many critics refer to Thaisa's childbirth only in passing or in the service of an argument about Marina or Pericles if they refer to her at all: for example, Brayton, *Shakespeare's Ocean*; Dowd, *Dynamics of Inheritance*; Espinosa, *Masculinity*; and Hall, "'[B]orn at Sea.'"
5. For an excellent discussion of the *Pericles* authorship debate, see Mowat and Werstine's introduction and notes to the *Folger Shakespeare Library* edition. I refer to William Shakespeare as the author of the play throughout for the sake of simplicity but wish to acknowledge George Wilkins and indeed the rest of Shakespeare's acting company as possible collaborators.
6. Alaimo, *Bodily Natures*, 11.
7. Mentz, *At the Bottom*, 81.
8. Mentz, *At the Bottom*, 77.
9. Cavendish's utopia begins with the abduction and dangerous maritime journey of the Lady to a "new world"; there, the Lady marries the Emperor—becoming the Empress—and conducts scientific and philosoph-

ical explorations of the Blazing World. In her explorations, she converses with spirits, eventually asking them to send her the soul of a writer to be her scribe and to aid her in writing a "Cabbala" (208). The spirits send her the soul of the Duchess of Newcastle, who is a representation of the historical Margaret Cavendish, Duchess of Newcastle, in the style of Thomas More's depiction of himself in *Utopia*. The soul of the Duchess invites the Empress's soul to her own world to meet the Duke and go to the theater, among other adventures. The Duchess's soul also serves the Empress in an advisory capacity in the end of book 1 and throughout book 2.

10. Boesky, *Founding Fictions*, 117, 121, 127.
11. Scholarship on *The Blazing World* has primarily focused on Cavendish's relationship to the Royal Society and her engagement with contemporary scientific debates, her use of the utopian genre, and her royalist leanings as a shaping force in her fiction: for example, Cottegnies, "Utopia"; Fletcher, "Irregular Aesthetic"; Gallagher, "Embracing the Absolute"; and Holmesland, *Utopian Negotiation*.
12. On gender and violence in early modern voyages, see Tucker, "She Would Rather Perish."
13. Lawrence, *Penelope Voyages*, xiii.
14. Lawrence, *Penelope Voyages*, 1, 11.
15. On gender and temperature in humoral and Galenic theory, see Greenblatt, *Renaissance Self-Fashioning*, 66–93.
16. Paster, *Body Embarrassed*, 13.
17. Dowd in *Dynamics of Inheritance* argues that, "[a]lthough the lineage at Pentapolis is eventually redeemed by the play's romance structure and its ultimate privileging of reunion over loss, Thaisa's temporary disappearance [to Ephesus] stages a compensatory turn to physical seclusion as one response to the socioeconomic mutability that the heiress represents" (179). Hall, "'[B]orn at Sea'" gives a suggestive reading of Marina's and Pericles's giving and withholding of Thaisa's name in 5.1 as crucial to these characters' reunion and the resolution of the play (12–13).
18. Further references to the play will appear in text using act, scene, and line numbers from the Folger Shakespeare Library's *Pericles, Prince of Tyre*, edited by Barbara A. Mowat and Paul Werstine.
19. See Espinosa, *Masculinity*, especially 163–66, for a discussion of Thaisa as likened in this scene to a Marian icon.
20. For just one of many early modern examples, see Spenser, *Amoretti*, 15.
21. Cavendish, *Blazing World*, 154. Further references to the narrative will appear in text using page numbers from this edition, edited by Sylvia Bowerbank and Sara Mendelson.

22. Cottegnies, "Utopia," 74.
23. Lawrence makes a related point about another of Cavendish's texts, "Assaulted and Pursued Chastity," which features the adventures of the aptly named Travalia (*Penelope Voyages*, 49).
24. See Cottegnies, "Utopia," 77–79, 83–87, for a discussion of religion in *The Blazing World*.
25. Thell, "'[A]s Lightly,'" 21.
26. Thell, "'[A]s Lightly,'" 22. See also Cottegnies, "Utopia," 88–91, on the smashing of scientific instruments in *The Blazing World* and on Cavendish's attention to Bacon's *New Atlantis* in her critique of experimentalism and the Royal Society. On Cavendish and Hooke's *Micrographia*, see Pearl, *Utopian Geographies*, 50–51.
27. Mentz, *At the Bottom*, 71.
28. Dowd, *Dynamics of Inheritance*, 192.
29. Dowd, *Dynamics of Inheritance*, 193.
30. Dowd, *Dynamics of Inheritance*, 208.
31. Dowd, *Dynamics of Inheritance*, 206.
32. For a reading of Othello's tears as "unman[ning]" him and of the maritime resonances of weeping, see Mentz, *At the Bottom*, especially 19–33.
33. Espinosa, *Masculinity*, 164. See also Espinosa's chapter in this volume, "Marian Mobility, Black Madonnas, and the Cleopatra Complex."
34. Espinosa, *Masculinity*, 166. Espinosa references Pericles's claim (5.1.154–57) that Marina's suffering, like his own, can alter or complicate her gender.
35. Heywood, *Fair Maid*, 4.5.1. This remark from the Chorus—perhaps a joke at *The Tempest*'s expense—is in tension with the many scenes in *Fair Maid* that *do* represent action on board ships at sea. For a further discussion of Heywood's play, see Gaywyn Moore's chapter in this volume, "English Women, Romance, and Global Travel."
36. Brayton, *Shakespeare's Ocean*, 2.
37. Vitkus, "Labor and Travel," 240.
38. Dowd, *Dynamics of Inheritance*, 185.
39. Boesky, *Founding Fictions*, 127.
40. On staging in *The Blazing World*, see Cottegnies, "Utopia," 86, 163, and Tomlinson, "'My Brain the Stage.'"
41. Cottegnies, "Utopia," 86.
42. Boesky, *Founding Fictions*, 140.

Bibliography

Alaimo, Stacy. *Bodily Natures: Science, Environment, and the Material Self.* Bloomington: Indiana University Press, 2010.

Boesky, Amy. *Founding Fictions: Utopias in Early Modern England*. Athens: University of Georgia Press, 1996.

Brayton, Dan. *Shakespeare's Ocean: An Ecocritical Exploration*. Charlottesville: University of Virginia Press, 2012.

Cavendish, Margaret. *The Description of a New World, Called the Blazing World*. In *Paper Bodies: A Margaret Cavendish Reader*, edited by Sylvia Bowerbank and Sara Mendelson, 151–251. Orchard Park NY: Broadview, 2000.

Cottegnies, Line. "Utopia, Millenarianism, and the Baconian Programme of Margaret Cavendish's *The Blazing World* (1666)." In *New Worlds Reflected: Travel and Utopia in the Early Modern Period*, edited by Chloë Houston and Andrew Hadfield, 71–91. Burlington VT: Ashgate, 2010.

Dowd, Michelle M. *The Dynamics of Inheritance on the Shakespearean Stage*. Cambridge: Cambridge University Press, 2015.

Espinosa, Ruben. *Masculinity and Marian Efficacy in Shakespeare's England*. Burlington VT: Ashgate, 2011.

Fletcher, Angus. "The Irregular Aesthetic of *The Blazing-World*." *Studies in English Literature* 47, no. 1 (2007): 123–41.

Gallagher, Catherine. "Embracing the Absolute: Margaret Cavendish and the Politics of the Female Subject in Seventeenth-Century England." In *Early Women Writers, 1600–1720*, edited by Anita Pacheco, 133–45. London: Longman, 1998.

Greenblatt, Stephen. *Renaissance Self-Fashioning*. 2nd edition. Chicago: University of Chicago, 2005.

Hall, Mark Webster. "'[B]orn at Sea, Buried at Tarsus,/And Found at Sea Again': Pericles and Liminal Form." *Journal of Language, Literature and Culture* 60, no. 1 (2013): 3–15.

Heywood, Thomas. *The Fair Maid of the West, Parts I and II*, edited by Robert Turner. Regents Renaissance Drama. Lincoln: University of Nebraska Press, 1967.

Holmesland, Oddvar. *Utopian Negotiation: Aphra Behn and Margaret Cavendish*. Syracuse: Syracuse University Press, 2013.

Lawrence, Karen R. *Penelope Voyages: Women and Travel in the British Literary Tradition*. Ithaca NY: Cornell University Press, 1994.

Mentz, Steve. *At the Bottom of Shakespeare's Ocean*. New York: Continuum, 2009.

Paster, Gail Kern. *The Body Embarrassed: Drama and the Disciplines of Shame in Early Modern England*. Ithaca NY: Cornell University Press, 1993.

Pearl, Jason H. *Utopian Geographies and the Early English Novel*. Charlottesville: University of Virginia Press, 2014.

Shakespeare, William. *Pericles, Prince of Tyre*, edited by Barbara A. Mowat and Paul Werstine. Folger Shakespeare Library. New York: Simon and Schuster, 2005.

Spenser, Edmund. *Edmund Spenser's Amoretti and Epithalamion*. Edited by Kenneth Larsen. Tempe AZ: Medieval and Renaissance Texts and Studies, 1997.

Thell, Anne M. "'[A]s Lightly as Two Thoughts': Motion, Materialism, and Cavendish's *Blazing World*." *Configurations: A Journal of Literature, Science, and Technology* 23, no. 1 (2015): 1–33.

Tomlinson, Sophie. "'My Brain the Stage': Margaret Cavendish and the Fantasy of Female Performance." In *Women, Texts, Histories, 1575-1760*, edited by Claire Brant and Diane Purkiss, 134–63. New York: Routledge, 1992.

Tucker, Judith E. "She Would Rather Perish: Piracy and Gendered Violence in the Mediterranean." *Journal of Middle East Women's Studies* 10, no. 3 (2014): 8–39.

Vitkus, Daniel. "Labor and Travel on the Early Modern Stage: Representing the Travail of Travel in Dekker's *Old Fortunatus* and Shakespeare's *Pericles*." In *Working Subjects in Early Modern English Drama*, edited by Michelle M. Dowd, Natasha Korda, and Jean E. Howard, 225–42. Burlington VT: Ashgate, 2011.

15

Traveling Companions

Shakespeare's As You Like It *and the Book of Ruth*

SUZANNE TARTAMELLA

One of the paradigmatic accounts of female companionate travel is the Book of Ruth, which describes a Moabite widow so devoted to her mother-in-law Naomi that she decides to leave behind her own family—and her religion—to journey into a strange land. There the two women contrive to unite Ruth to a kind, wealthy farmer named Boaz, who gives Ruth marital satisfaction and security. Their union produces an impressive genealogy that includes Jesse, David, and (eventually) Jesus. Along with this broad biblical significance, the story's romantic plot and sympathetic characters have ensured its position among the most beloved books of the Old Testament.[1] Yet the work has made surprisingly few *direct* inroads in early English literature. A handful of extant sixteenth- and seventeenth-century commentaries, along with an anonymous poetic retelling entitled *Ruth Revived* (1639), explore this biblical text, but meaningful references appear only sparingly in the best-known literature of the period.[2] On this short list is Shakespeare. His account of female travel in *As You Like It* (1598) inspires an allusion to Ruth at a crucial moment in the play: when Celia decides to leave her father and the court to follow her exiled cousin Rosalind into the Forest of Arden. This essay argues that the Book of Ruth not only serves as a source for the play, but also helps frame its exploration of female identity, alienation, and adaptability. More broadly, the play's biblical backdrop clarifies the role of female travelers in effecting cultural change and, in the process, highlights an essential strangeness at the heart of domestic Christian identity.

Like so many of Shakespeare's plays, *As You Like It* is a deep chamber of literary resonances, harking back to Virgil's bucolic poetry (the *Eclogues* and *Georgics*) and Ovid's *Metamorphoses* and echoing themes and characters found in Ludovico Ariosto's *Orlando Furioso*, Sir Philip Sidney's *Old Arcadia*, and Edmund Spenser's *The Shepheardes Calender*. The play derives its central story and characters, however, from Thomas Lodge's *Rosalynd* (1590). In his dedicatory epistle, Lodge claims he composed the prose romance while traveling to the Azores and the Canary Islands and considers it "rough, as hatched in the storms of the ocean, and feathered in the surges of many perilous seas."[3] Yet the resulting story, despite what Lodge insists, is quite eloquent and refined. Although more violent in sections than *As You Like It*, *Rosalynd* is filled with well-crafted love sonnets and songs; moving explorations of selfhood, fortune, and nature; debates about the merits of courtly life versus country living; and insightful meditations on the plight of women—all of which we see in Shakespeare's play.

Shakespeare's adaptation also preserves *Rosalynd*'s multivalent attention to travel, recalling contemporary as well as classical accounts of dangerous and life-changing expeditions, including Sir Walter Raleigh's mythologized voyage to Guiana in 1595.[4] Juliet Dusinberre observes, however, that *As You Like It* (and, by extension, *Rosalynd*) is not just about secular travel but also religious pilgrimage, which implies "weary spirits" as well as "weary legs."[5] "If the play were first performed on Shrove Tuesday," Dusinberre posits, "the Forest could have acquired for the Elizabethans the associations of the veritable 'desert' in which Christ's temptations were played out during his forty-day fast."[6] Given the depth and agility of their biblical understanding, Elizabethan audiences would have also discovered associations with the Book of Ruth, which offers typological and familial links to people and events in the New Testament. Indeed, the modifications Shakespeare makes to Lodge's work show evidence that he was doing more than interpolating allusions to Ruth; he was deliberately borrowing some of the biblical story's language to help frame his own.[7]

Passages in *As You Like It* directly recall key moments in the Old Testament story: particularly, Ruth and Naomi's departure for Bethlehem and, later, the pastoral setting in which Ruth successfully courts Boaz. Neither of these allusions appears explicitly in Lodge's romance, even though his plot allows for these connections. Evoking (perhaps indirectly) the biblical story's representation of female loyalty but not its precise language, Lodge describes Alinda (Celia) as loving Rosalynd "more than herself" and protesting to her usurping father that, because they "have two bodies and one soul," she must be "co-partner" of Rosalynd's "hard fortunes" and so "participate in exile."[8] While these declarations easily earn Alinda the sentence of banishment, Shakespeare's Celia is less successful in securing this fate and thus better primed to undertake the sort of willful defiance exhibited by Ruth. After her father twice calls her a "fool" for attempting to solicit banishment,[9] an impassioned Celia takes matters into her own hands, privately informing Rosalind that she is, in fact, in exile along with her cousin:

> No, hath not? Rosalind lacks then the love
> Which teacheth thee that thou and I am one.
> Shall we be sundered? Shall we part, sweet girl?
> No, let my father seek another heir!
> Therefore devise with me how we may fly,
> Whither to go and what to bear with us,
> And do not seek to take your change upon you
> To bear your griefs yourself and leave me out.
> For by this heaven, now at our sorrows pale,
> Say what thou canst, I'll go along with thee. (1.3.93–102)

Banishing Rosalind logically implies that Celia, too, is banished because they are "one" and cannot be separated—physically or emotionally. This moment echoes Ruth's boldly moving declaration to Naomi: "Intreat me not to leave thee, nor to departe from thee: for whither thou goest, I wil go: and where thou dwellest, I will dwel: thy people *shalbe* my people, and thy God my God."[10] Harkening to her cousin, Rosalind also adopts Ruth's language—in a probable attempt to refute Celia's earlier charge that she "lacks . . . love" — and immediately accepts her cousin's sacrifice, saying, "Why, wither shall we go?" (1.3.103).

With this question, Shakespeare challenges us to seek, not a stable one-to-one correspondence between *As You Like It* and the Book of Ruth, but rather a broader intertextual relationship. Act 2, in fact, shows Orlando asking his trusty servant Adam, "Why wither . . . wouldst thou have me go?" (2.3.29), and Adam professing, "I will follow thee / To the last gasp with truth and loyalty" (2.3.69–70). Then, later in the play, it is the lovesick shepherd Silvius who recalls Ruth's labor in Boaz's field when he tells his beloved Phoebe,

> So holy and so perfect is my love,
> And I in such a poverty of grace,
> That I shall think it a most plenteous crop
> To *glean* the broken ears after the man
> That the main harvest reaps. Loose now and then
> A scattered smile, and that I'll live upon. (3.5.100–105, emphasis added)

The word *glean* does not appear in Lodge's romance, but it does in the Book of Ruth when the young widow is described "glean[ing] in [the] field after the reapers," "gather[ing] eares of corne" in hopes of finding "favour" in Boaz's "sight" (2:2–3). Briefly commenting on this scene in the play, Russell Fraser argues that the reference to Ruth, a "sad tale with a happy ending," reinforces the shepherd's reward for his dogged devotion to his beloved.[11] Dusinberre, too, notes this and the earlier allusions to Ruth in her edition of the play. Yet most scholars have ignored these connections — and none has examined at length the influence of Ruth on *As You Like It* or on any other Renaissance work. Even Hannibal Hamlin's impressive study, *The Bible in Shakespeare*, takes as its premise the centrality of the Bible in early modern culture, cataloguing the numerous biblical allusions across Shakespeare's oeuvre and exploring the significance of some of those allusions in chapter-length essays. Hamlin records the references in *As You Like It* to Adam, the Psalms, Job, and the Prodigal Son.[12] But he curiously ignores Ruth.

One reason for this omission is the fact that the Ruth references are ostensibly subtler than representations of the Prodigal Son, to take one example. Yet Shakespeare's use of Ruth to adapt Lodge's story deserves our attention, and it behooves us to investigate what the period would have thought about this biblical text, why Shakespeare chose to use it, and how it informs our understanding of *As You Like It*.[13] Sixteenth- and seventeenth-century commentaries on the Book of Ruth provide insight into various approaches English pastors would have taken in their Sunday sermons, including those Shakespeare himself may have heard. Those exegeses emphasize the titular heroine's "true affection and constant resolution," directed not only to Naomi but also to the inchoate Christian faith and its "true God."[14] They also cite Boaz's marriage to Ruth as establishing an essential genealogy in salvation history and providing, more generally, a model for sacred unions based on public affirmation of nuptials, commitment to bearing children, and the willingness of women to leave their old lives behind and "bee in the house with the husband."[15] Finally, they reinforce how God's power in "lift[ing] upp . . . the basest of the people"—in this case the Moabites—foretells his exaltation of the Gentiles.[16] Corroborating this latter interpretation, the argument printed at the beginning of the 1560 Geneva version of the Book of Ruth explains that her status as a "Moabite of base condicion [condition], and a stranger from the people of God" is God's way of "declaring unto us thereby that the Gentiles shulde be sanctified by him and [j]oyned with his people, and that there shulde be but one shepefolde, and one shepherde."[17] The story of the Moabites, in other words, is the story of Christianity as it traveled outside the borders of Israel.

Beyond, however, invoking a broader redemptive narrative, the Book of Ruth is a human story of transformation and second chances. It describes two women making their way in the world after suffering incredible emotional defeat. The anonymous *Ruth Revived*, although printed several decades after Shakespeare composed *As You Like It*, elucidates this biblical book's potential as a literary adaptation and helps explain Shakespeare's own attraction to it. The author (who refers to him- or herself in the dedicatory epistle as S.R.) frames the work as an epic poem, complete with epic similes and an invocation to a muse, the "flowre of Jesse" and "greatest Saviour of the meanest men." Tellingly, S.R. begins the Virgilian-inspired work, saying, "I Sing the praise of Moabs choisest flowre, / The fairest blossome in that foulest bowre; / The poorest widdow, and the richest wife," thus reminding us to situate the muse Christ within the lineage of Ruth and Naomi.[18] Most of the remaining poem, however, elaborates on the very human interactions recounted in the Book of Ruth. Embellishing on the emotions of its principal people, S.R. provides long lamentations spoken by Naomi and Elimelech (Naomi's husband and Boaz's kinsman), a protracted description of Ruth's "constancy" and "noble grace," and a detailed depiction of Boaz's immediate attraction to Ruth, who inspires "[s]ome secret symptoms of some future good" to "boyle" in his "blood."[19]

S.R. delineates three distinct settings for this family drama: Moab, Bethlehem, and Boaz's barley fields. This allows a strategic separation of the pastoral world inhabited by Boaz from *both* famine-stricken Bethlehem (now an "unholy holy land") and "filthy" Moab, populated by idolatrous descendants of Lot's incestuous liaison with one of his daughters.[20] The author narrates how Naomi and Ruth must navigate between these locations, both physically and intellectually. Departing from Moab, the women become "[m]anlesse" pilgrims ready to take on the "[s]tormes" that can "swell abroad," affording little protection to female exiles venturing in from a strange land.[21] Once settled in Naomi's homeland, the women embark on another kind of journey, one that will secure their life and livelihood in Bethlehem: finding a husband for Ruth. Here S.R. emphasizes not only the courtship plan outlined in the Bible, but also the intellectual preparation for that undertaking. The author describes, for example, how Ruth's

>tender mother in her carefull minde
>Casts many a project, until one she finde.
>The project found the secrets of her heart
>To her deer daughter straight she doth impart.[22]

This passage reinforces the agency the women assume at almost every stage of the story, reminding us that if the biblical narrative contains the material for an epic, its crafty heroes are female.

Ruth Revived helps illuminate why Shakespeare was drawn to the Book of Ruth in adapting Lodge's story for the Elizabethan stage: it contains strong female characters braving the hazards of pilgrimage and exerting control over the practice of courtship. Although not explicitly framed as an epic, *As You Like It* gives us something of a diffused epic romance, replete with questing and crafty characters, mythically inflected scenes, and softened versions of "such epic themes as empire building and global Christian conversion."[23] Within a structure built on the conversion of antagonists and the reestablishment of a civil society is a broadscale, gendered tension between two kinds of heroes: Orlando, the heir of Ariosto, who engages in a Petrarchan quest for his beloved Rosalind, and the wily, conniving heroines whose own escapades allow them the freedom to thwart, undermine, and educate that hero. Indeed, because *As You Like It* centers on the travels and travails of two intelligent women, it foregrounds some of the same complications involved in crafting a female epic hero. In her book *Penelope Voyages*, Karen R. Lawrence observes that the dutiful wife of Odysseus has long "serve[d] as the symbolic embodiment of home" and that the archetypal "plot of the male journey depends on keeping woman in her place."[24] But if "Penelope," as Lawrence proposes, decides to set down her loom and go on an adventure, she automatically "destabilizes" all kinds of "borders," effectively "break[ing] the law of boundaries."[25] Defying social expectations, a traveling woman also presents a *rhetorical* conundrum in that she wanders a landscape traditionally construed as feminine as a voyager traditionally represented as male.[26] Shakespeare attempts to scale this polarity by dressing his star female in male garb and calling her Ganymede, yet all the while reminding us of her feminine identity: "Do you not know I am a woman?" Rosalind tells Celia, "When I think, I must speak" (3.2.242–43).

Hence, the Book of Ruth—a fascinating, if anomalous, feminine interlude in the patriarchal narrative of the Old Testament—constitutes valuable background for *As You Like It*. Similar to the author of *Ruth*

Revived, Shakespeare saw in Ruth's story an inversion of the conventional (epic) narrative of male travel and nurtured a kinship with his own story of Rosalind and Celia. More than that, he recognized that the Book of Ruth completes a series of biblical allusions in *As You Like It* that begin with Adam (the first name mentioned in the play) and culminate in the Prodigal Son.[27] In this sweeping story of fall and redemption—of exile and return—exist the linchpins for such a tale: the wandering women whose courage in the face of adversity helps ensure the progression of that salvation narrative. Just as Naomi and Ruth contrive a union with Boaz (whose progeny include King David and then Jesus), so Rosalind and Celia orchestrate a series of marriages that lead to a happy resolution and a return to a court free of the major problems it possesses at the outset.

Rosalind and Celia's journey begins, however, with their leaving the court fearful of their vulnerable state and fully aware of their disrupted senses of self. As Rosalind laments, "Alas, what danger will it be to us, / Maids as we are, to travel forth so far!" (1.3.105–6). Outside the protection of the court and headed into a land that deems them strangers, the women decide to disguise themselves—Rosalind as a boy named Ganymede and Celia as the aptly named Aliena (1.3.122–25). More than a response to their new environment, these names symbolize the fluidity of identity, the ways in which exile and altered circumstances have potential to transform us. Celia's choice of the name "Aliena" to denote her self-imposed state is somewhat akin to Naomi's selection of "Mara" to reflect what she perceives to be her fallen condition upon her departure from Moab: "Call me not Naomi," she tells Ruth, "*but* call me Mara: for the Almightie hathe given me muche bitternes. I we[n]t out ful, & ... [the] Lord hath caused me to returne empty: why call ye me Naomi, se[e]ing the Lord hath hu[m]bled me, & the Almighty hathe broght me unto adversitie" (1:20–21). Although Ruth does not alter her name, the text's repeated references to her identity as a Moabite call attention to her changing *function* and *defiance* of her native status. Eventually, she proves herself capable—in spite of her birth—of assimilating into the culture of the Israelites such that she becomes "like Ra[c]hel and like Leah, which twaine did buyld the house of Israel"

(4:11). In *Ruth Revived*, S.R. implies that she is primed to do so through her sacrificial devotion to Naomi, insisting that Ruth's "resolution" and "courage stout" were "not bred in Moabs land," but rather "graffed in by great Jehovahs hand. / Who put the scion in will blesse the fruit, / And make it sound as loud as Davids lute."[28]

Shakespeare's play also dramatizes the ways in which identity is shaped by our social and physical environments, in moments of spiritual awakening, and, of course, through art. In their new roles in the Forest of Arden, Rosalind and Celia—who each at different points reflect aspects of both Ruth *and* Naomi—play devoted siblings (brother and sister) overseeing a land that was hitherto alien to their full understanding, a land that probably used to be cultivated *for* them and without their knowledge. But Rosalind goes further, playing not only a male agricultural manager but also modified versions of her natural self—first, a stern educator debunking myths about Petrarchan love and, finally, a matchmaking "magician, most profound in his art" (5.2.59–60). The women's status as travelers allows this flexibility of outward expression even as it nurtures concomitant changes in their inward response to the environment. This is consistent with what scholars have long recognized in travel literature: adventurers journeying not merely into the world but "into the self."[29] Like the Book of Ruth, *As You Like It* demonstrates the inextricable relationship between movement across space and transformation within the wandering individual.

Yet the nature of that space in *As You Like It*—particularly the qualities of Arden—has stimulated a great deal of critical debate. The play's motley assortment of literary sources has led some scholars to explore its archetypal "green world" qualities, others to consider whether Shakespeare meant to locate Arden in France or midland England, and still others to compare the play's pastoral setting to Utopias, classical Arcadia, the New World, and biblical Eden.[30] Most people, though, recognize that the world of Arden is not altogether golden or green or Edenic. In fact, one of the most famous speeches in the play—Duke Senior's utopian description of the forest—derives its power from his ability to reinterpret his surroundings, to "translate the stubbornness of fortune / Into so quiet and so sweet a style" (2.1.19–20). Willfully idealistic, Duke Senior avers:

> Are not these woods
> More free from peril than the envious court?
> Here feel we not the penalty of Adam,
> The seasons' difference—as the icy fang
> And churlish chiding of the winter's wind,
> Which when it bites and blows upon my body
> Even till I shrink with cold, I smile and say:
> "This is no flattery. These are counsellors
> That feelingly persuade me what I am."
> Sweet are the uses of adversity,
> Which, like the toad, ugly and venomous,
> Wears yet a precious jewel in his head;
> And this our life, exempt from public haunt,
> Finds tongues in trees, books in the running brooks,
> Sermons in stones, and good everything. (2.1.3–17)

If the duke is successful in transmuting "the stubbornness of fortune" into ubiquitous good, he does so through rhetorical comparison. The Forest of Arden is not "free from peril" or devoid of all bitterness; rather, its "exempt[ion] from public haunt" renders it merely better than the alternative. The duke himself later admits, "True is it that we have seen better days, / And have with holy bell been knolled to church, / And sat at good men's feasts" (2.7.121–23). This last observation is telling, for one of the principle difficulties experienced by characters in the play is hunger. Orlando enters this scene carrying a nearly expired Adam, weak from lack of food; a few scenes earlier, Rosalind and Celia go in search of something to eat, with Celia complaining that she "faint[s] almost to death" (2.4.62). Almost every character becomes, one way or another, a touchstone for illuminating the problems of the forest: Jaques criticizes the court foresters for slaughtering deer for food; the rustics struggle with enclosure difficulties and engage in romantic tiffs; and Orlando saves his brother Oliver from a "hungry lioness" (4.3.125) after Oliver is nearly poisoned by a "green and gilded snake" (4.3.107). Arden's green and gold evidently come with significant risk.

This is not to say, however, that Arden lacks spiritual vitality. On the contrary, it is brimming with it, and Duke Senior is perhaps correct in observing the peculiar power emanating from trees, brooks, and stones. Characters simply change for the better in the forest. Helga L. Duncan "read[s] Shakespeare's treatment of Arden as a comment on a [post-Reformation] religious conflict that has dislocated the sacred and as part of Shakespeare's attempt to recover and reimagine the place of the sacred."[31] Duncan accordingly argues that Duke Senior's imperviousness to the "penalty of Adam" (2.1.5) and his insistence that "Arden is also a kind of Promised Land" scales important events in the Bible; his speech, that is, "traces the spatial imagination of the Judeo-Christian tradition, situated between the protracted wanderings of Exodus and the founding of the Kingdom of Israel."[32] Crucial for Duncan's argument are the play's multiple references to "desert," which denotes the absence of people but connotes the mystical, biblical dry lands. Rosalind and Oliver at different points in the play call Arden a "desert place" (2.4.71, 4.3.140), and Orlando uses the word twice, first in conversation with Duke Senior when he compares Arden to a "desert inaccessible" (2.7.111) and again in one of his maudlin poems (3.2.122). These allusions reinforce, Duncan contends, the play's "hagiographic wilderness spaces" outside which Rosalind—settling with Celia in a more tempered bucolic sheepcote—"serves as a gatekeeper, facilitator, and mediator."[33] Living "[a]t the fringes of utopian Arden," Rosalind and Celia negotiate between the uncivilized wildness of the forest and the established civilization of the court.[34] Their actions help nurture that reinvented sacred space.

Duncan's analysis supports the Book of Ruth as a source for *As You Like It*. For one, the whole story of Ruth and Naomi stands in that liminal space "between the protracted wanderings of Exodus and the founding of the Kingdom of Israel": in other words, between the exile of the Jews and the establishment of a kingdom ruled by Ruth's great-grandson, David. However, insofar as David's kingdom is merely a forerunner of Christ's, then that "settled spiritual community" to which Duncan refers could also be the Christian Church, dependent as well on the clever machinations of Ruth and Naomi, who like Rosalind operate as "gatekeeper[s], facilitator[s], and mediator[s]."[35] Narrowing our scope, we can see other correlations between the play and the Book of Ruth, since it focuses on two women moving between Moab and Bethlehem and operating successfully "at the fringes" in Boaz's barley fields. As places of famine and loss, Moab and Bethlehem together help underscore the extreme wildness of Arden's deepest recesses and a fallen court waiting for redemption.

Of course, the male protagonists of these stories—Boaz and Orlando—seem at first glance to have little in common. Boaz is older, wiser, and more established than Orlando, who begins the play lamenting his brother Oliver's betrayal of their father's dying wishes and his subversion of his status as a gentleman (1.1.1–23). Kept "rustically at home" (1.1.7) and living in "servitude" (1.1.22), Orlando must undergo an education, changing, Marjorie Garber observes, from "an infatuated youth to a man who knows the real nature of love, from a boy who pins poems on trees to a man whose love token is a 'bloody napkin.'"[36] Still, this lusty youth shares with Boaz a few commonalities that Shakespeare perhaps had in mind when he crafted the play. Both men are virtuous characters essentially exiled into a pastoral setting. Less violent and more innocent than his counterpart in Lodge (Rosader), Orlando heeds the recommendation of his servant Adam and quietly submits to the vicissitudes of nature in order to save his own life (2.3.56–68). In an interpretation of Boaz's situation and character—one perhaps shared by Shakespeare—the author of *Ruth Revived* remarks, "In Bethlehem Boaz could no longer stay: / To field he comes about the heat of day. / The masters pray'r with servants labour suits: / His painfull workmen kindly he salutes."[37] While Boaz leaves the city of Bethlehem in response to famine and economic strife, Orlando (whose name suggests "land" as well as recalls the epic figure from Ariosto) absconds into the country after encountering life-threatening domestic and political turmoil at court.

Living in situations that seem to have chosen them, Orlando and Boaz must negotiate issues of legal custom and social status. In the process, they learn more about the world and their function within it. Orlando must defer to a malicious older brother, battle his stunted education and experience, and learn how to love and court a woman properly. Like Orlando, Boaz quickly falls in love with the heroine of the story but earns her love only after a poignant demonstration of selfless integrity. Choosing loosely to follow levirate custom (strictly speaking, a man's marriage to his brother's widow), Boaz first offers Ruth to a closer family relation—another *go'el*, or "kinsman-redeemer." Although scholars debate why the anonymous kinsman agrees to redeem Naomi's property but balks at marrying her daughter-in-law, they also suggest that Boaz ultimately gets what he wants: a chance to offer *himself* as Ruth's *go'el*.[38] Orlando, similarly, pays lip service (as it were) to the pedagogical goals Rosalind articulates at the outset—to "wash" his "liver as clean as a sound sheep's heart, that there shall not be one spot of love in't" (3.2.404–6)—and is rewarded with her love in the denouement. Ultimately, a happy recompense for both men depends on altered perspectives. Just as Orlando must learn to see past his Petrarchan idealization of Rosalind to engage her as she really is, so Boaz comes to appreciate Ruth as more than a Moabite. Boaz's implied assent to the Elders' description of Ruth standing alongside Leah and Rachel to help "buyld the house of Israel" transcends his initial kindness to her as an outsider (4:11); it reflects his willingness to see Ruth as an insider after all.

Perhaps the most significant point of connection between Orlando and Boaz is the fact that they are successfully courted, and ultimately transformed, by women whose actions upend feminine stereotypes. The women achieve this through a series of theatrical posturing. In *As You Like It*, Rosalind assumes a centrality that transcends her representation in Lodge's narrative.[39] She also possesses more depth. In Orlando's absence, she convincingly fights her "deep . . . love" and spends time "sigh[ing]" in "shadow[s]" (4.1.202–4). In his presence, she remains fully accoutered as a boy, speaking dismissively of love as "merely a madness" (3.2.384) and steering Orlando away from Petrarchan idolatry in order to "cure" him (3.2.403–8). Rosalind operates as both feminist and antifeminist in her approach, exerting power over Orlando in order to invite him to imagine a jealous wife who will be "more clamorous than a parrot against rain" (4.1.141) and who possesses an ability (reminiscent of Chaucer's Wife of Bath) to "make her fault her husband's occasion" (4.1.163). Rosalind's hyperbolic "misuse" of the female sex counterbalances Orlando's wild misrepresentation of real love (4.1.189). But she ultimately nurtures within him not a negative portrait of Rosalind or women generally but rather a realistic perception, one that will allow him fully to connect with another person. In one of the most significant parts of their exchange, she tests Orlando's willingness to break from Petrarchan solipsism and unrequited desire by enacting a mock marriage (4.1.117–35). Once Orlando's subsequent physical injury, sustained by a lioness, fully eradicates his self-indulgent love wounds, he is ready to marry Rosalind for real, having learned to access the less familiar parts of himself: restraint, self-sacrifice, and forgiveness.[40] Rosalind controls every stage of this delightful courtship—from its exploratory beginnings to its culmination at the altar.

That Rosalind manages all of this outside the confines of her home environment echoes what happens in the Book of Ruth, which also narrates a female-driven courtship in foreign terrain. Soon after the widows arrive in Bethlehem, Ruth decides to spend time gleaning in Boaz's barley fields with the express intention of gaining his courtesy and esteem. Having attracted Boaz's notice because of her outsider status and received assurances that he will protect her nonetheless, Ruth boldly tells him, "Let me finde favour in thy sight, my lord: for [thou] hast co[m]forted me, and spoken comfortably unto thy maid, thogh I be not like to one of thy maids" (2:13). In the second stage of their courtship, Ruth follows Naomi's instructions to dress appropriately for the occasion—cleansing and anointing her body with perfume before participating in a mock marital union of her own. Like Rosalind, Ruth essentially proposes marriage, offering herself to Boaz in order to force a response.[41] "And when he [Boaz] shal slepe," Naomi tells her daughter-in-law, "marke the place where he layeth him downe, & go, and uncover the place of his fete [feet], and lay thee downe, & he shal tel thee what [you] shalt do" (3:4). Similar to Orlando's "education," this intimate encounter tests Boaz's virtue, integrity, and adherence to social decorum—including whether he can temper his desire. Indeed, each stage of the courtship gives Boaz another opportunity to prove his value to Ruth and to learn to see her as a marriageable insider.

Despite each work's movement toward marriage, however, the resolution of *As You Like It* seems to differ from the Book of Ruth on an important point: the return. The end of the play describes most of the characters' departure for the court, hopeful for a better society. In the biblical text, Naomi returns to her homeland whereas Ruth (of course) does not. Yet Northrop Frye, in his essay "The Bride from the Strange Land," argues that Ruth, too, "is returning to her appropriate place" and that the work in general constitutes a "microcosm... of the entire story of exile, return, and redemption that the Bible is telling." Insofar as Ruth the Moabite is related to Abraham through Lot, she is an hereditary insider; this fact undergirds Frye's comparison of her to the "Israelites leaving Egypt for the Promised Land."[42] But within this cultural cohesion resonates an implied insularity. To become a transformed and transformative Gentile, one must already be grafted on to the Jewish olive tree, even if only spiritually.[43] To quote again the words of S.R., Ruth's "resolution" and "courage stout" were "not bred in Moabs land," but rather "graffed in by great Jehovahs hand."[44] By virtue of both her genealogy and her unique birth, Ruth was a natural Israelite even before she converted.

This insular perspective also characterizes *As You Like It*. Tracing the "process of provincialization" evident in Shakespeare's adaptation of Lodge's *Rosalynd*, Leah S. Marcus argues that the play's "emptying out of Lodge's Islamic motifs," its excision of "most of the geographically specific references that locate *Rosalynde* securely in France," and its tendency to privilege "inland" breeding all point to a critique of travel and cosmopolitanism.[45] For Marcus, that critique is constituted in the figure of Jacques, the male global "traveler/colonizer [who] represents a threat of contamination."[46] In contrast, Rosalind, Marcus contends, is the play's most important "figure of the anti-conquest," an "ambassador-at-large whose loveliness and moral worth can be disseminated via language rather than by travel."[47] Although Marcus downplays the fact that Rosalind and Celia also travel (encountering in their short journey challenges related to food and lodging), her interpretation is in keeping with Ruth's own "inland" migration from Moab to Bethlehem, her courtship of Boaz through meaningful words and gestures, and the ease with which she assimilates into her new life.

Ultimately, the Book of Ruth enriches our understanding of the complexities of female travel and identity in *As You Like It*. On the one hand, Shakespeare seems to naturalize the biblical story, using it to promote the kind of "inland" (in a religious sense, Judeo-Christian) preferences suggested by Marcus and consistent with contemporary attitudes toward foreigners and women. That task was perhaps not a difficult one given that the Book of Ruth—despite a likely composition date of more than two thousand years prior to *As You Like It*—shares a comparable historical environment. Both periods were concerned with the "influence of foreigners" and the ethics of how to respond to them.[48] In an observation that could also characterize the context of Ruth, Eric Griffin writes, "English citizens [of the early modern period] were discomfited by the presence of 'strangers' in their midst, even when they understood why they ought to be offering support."[49] That both works examine this issue, at least in part, through their female travelers reveals an inherent correspondence between foreigners and women: the domestic "other" whose constancy and relative immobility were needed to placate anxieties about feminine recalcitrance and help maintain a nation's stable sense of itself. In this context, the Book of Ruth seems to reinforce in *As You Like It* the notion that female travel has its limits in that the female protagonists' efforts at initiating courtship still uphold the patriarchal status quo, and their identities are simultaneously fluid in their expression but fixed in their essence. To borrow the well-known aphorism from Pindar, all characters "become what they are" before they decide to return home.

On the other hand, the biblical text also offered Shakespeare a more radical scenario. For even if Ruth is a genealogical insider, she is also a foreigner who travels into Israel from a strange land. To reiterate the argument in the Geneva Bible, Ruth is a "Moabite of base condicion, and a stranger from the people of God." Her assimilation (with the help of Naomi) into the culture of the Israelites utterly transforms its history. From this perspective, the power that Rosalind and Celia wield in their play illuminates the impact of female travelers on their society, regardless of how limited their movements. Part of that feminine power involves not merely disrupting that stable domestic center but inviting characters to access the alien parts of their own natures before they assume their "natural" place in the world.[50] As the self-proclaimed "magician" of the play who "can do strange things" (5.2.58), the apparent conjurer of the marriage god Hymen, and the speaker of the epilogue, Rosalind assumes such "strange" authority that she seems to oversee even those radical character transformations outside her purview; she becomes, in effect, an extension of strange-making Arden itself.[51] We see an analogous interpretation of Ruth's role in the second part of the Geneva Bible's argument. Extending her significance to encompass the Gentile readership, the argument aligns Ruth-the-Moabite with future Christians who would "be sanctified by" God "and [j]oyned with his people [the Jews] . . . that there shulde be but one shepefolde, and one shepherde." To be a Christian, this passage suggests, is to come to terms not only with one's assimilation into a new society, but also one's status as a Moabite—one's inherent, and inherited, foreignness. A comparatively secular version of this central message is enacted in *As You Like It*, with both works suggesting that fully *accepting* those terms of inheritance could very well mean behaving more graciously toward female travelers.

Notes

1. The Book of Ruth appears between the Song of Songs and Lamentations in the Hebrew Ketuvim. By resituating the book between Judges and 1 Samuel, Christian compilers emphasized the historicity of the text and its genealogical progression culminating in Jesus of the New Testament. See Hubbard, *Book of Ruth*, 4–7; Wojcik, "Improvising," 145.
2. Those references nonetheless show a culture sensitive to the story's paradigmatic features. See, for example, "Sonnet 9" in *Annotated Milton*, 30. Also Bunyan, *Pilgrim's Progress*, 195.
3. Lodge, *Rosalynd*, 24. See also Gaywyn Moore's essay in this volume on the impact of voyages to the Azores on English drama in the period.
4. See Hopkins, "Orlando"; Dusinberre, Introduction, 90–95.
5. Dusinberre, Introduction, 96.

6. Dusinberre, Introduction, 96.
7. For an essay on how Shakespeare expands Rosalind's role in his adaptation of Lodge, see Berry, "Rosalynde."
8. Lodge, *Rosalynd*, 44–45.
9. Shakespeare, *As You Like It*, edited by Juliet Dusinberre, 1.3.77–84. Subsequent references to the play will appear parenthetically in the text.
10. *Geneva Bible*, Ruth 1:16. Subsequent biblical references will appear parenthetically in the text.
11. Fraser, "Shakespeare's Book of Genesis," 125.
12. Hamlin, *Bible in Shakespeare*, 54, 151–54.
13. For a similar methodology on a different play and biblical book, see Hamlin's chapter on *King Lear* and Job in *Bible in Shakespeare*, 305–33.
14. Bernard, *Ruths Recompence*, 97. Lavater, *The book of Ruth*, 43. For an essay on how *Ruths Recompense* helps illuminate early modern attitudes toward the Book of Ruth, see McAlister, "Interpretation."
15. Parsons, *Boaz and Ruth Blessed*, 21.
16. Lavater, *The book of Ruth*, page number illegible.
17. *Geneva Bible*.
18. S.R., *Ruth Revived*, A3.
19. S.R., *Ruth Revived*, 11, 12, 16.
20. S.R., *Ruth Revived*, 2–3.
21. S.R., *Ruth Revived*, 8–9.
22. S.R., *Ruth Revived*, 22–23.
23. Cavanagh, "Romancing," 20. Cavanagh is discussing epic themes generally.
24. Lawrence, *Penelope Voyages*, 1.
25. Lawrence, *Penelope Voyages*, 10.
26. Lawrence argues that this woman becomes both a "traveler and signatory of the [travel-writing] discourse" (*Penelope Voyages*, 27). See also Marcus, "Anti-Conquest," 181; Raman, *Renaissance Literature*, 142–51.
27. For an analysis of Adam and the Prodigal Son, see Hamlin, *Bible in Shakespeare*, 152–54.
28. S.R., *Ruth Revived*, 13.
29. Youngs, *Travel Writing*, 102.
30. For discussions of Arden, see Barber, *Shakespeare's Festive Comedy*, 252–71; Frye, *Anatomy of Criticism*, 182–84; Dusinberre, Introduction, 79–106; Hopkins, "Orlando"; and Enos, "Catholic Exiles." This list is much abbreviated.
31. Duncan, "'Here at the Fringe,'" 127.
32. Duncan, "'Here at the Fringe,'" 129–30.
33. Duncan, "'Here at the Fringe,'" 136, 133.

34. Duncan, "'Here at the Fringe,'" 133. Duncan makes use of Dubrow, "Fringe Benefits," 67–69.
35. Duncan, "'Here at the Fringe,'" 129–30.
36. Garber, "Education of Orlando," 106.
37. S.R., *Ruth Revived*, 15.
38. For two accounts of these intricate customs, see Hubbard, *Book of Ruth*, 48–63, and Wojcik, "Improvising."
39. See Beckman, "The Figure of Rosalind"; Berry, "Rosalynde"; and Kinney, "Feigning."
40. Garber, "Education of Orlando," 108–9.
41. See Hubbard, *Book of Ruth*, 51; and Wojcik, "Improvising," 151.
42. Frye, "Bride," 59.
43. For a fascinating discussion of such grafting in early modern theology, see Freinkel, *Reading Shakespeare's Will*, 115–236.
44. S.R., *Ruth Revived*, 13.
45. Marcus, "Anti-Conquest," 171.
46. Marcus, "Anti-Conquest," 173.
47. Marcus, "Anti-Conquest," 192.
48. Hubbard, *Book of Ruth*, 39–46.
49. Griffin, "Shakespeare," 14.
50. For an analysis of how discourses of femininity in Shakespeare's *Henry VIII* are construed as "internalized outsideness" showing Britain as "foreign to itself," see Andrea, "'A noble troop of strangers,'" 92, 94.
51. For a discussion of this function, see Beckman, "The Figure of Rosalind," and Kinney, "Feigning." Berry, too, argues that Rosalind "becomes in a sense a figure for the playwright himself, a character whose consciousness extends beyond the boundaries of the drama" ("Rosalynde," 43).

Bibliography

Andrea, Bernadette. "'A noble troop of strangers': Masques of Blackness in Shakespeare's *Henry VIII*." In *Shakespeare and Immigration*, edited by Ruben Espinosa and David Ruiter, 91–111. Farnham UK: Ashgate, 2014.

Barber, C. L. *Shakespeare's Festive Comedy: A Study of Dramatic Form and Its Relation to Social Custom*. Princeton: Princeton University Press, 1959.

Beckman, Margaret Boerner. "The Figure of Rosalind in *As You Like It*." *Shakespeare Quarterly* 29, no. 1 (1978): 44–51.

Bernard, Richard. *Ruths Recompense: Or A Commentarie Vpon The Booke of Rvth*. London, 1628.

Berry, Edward I. "Rosalynde and Rosalind." *Shakespeare Quarterly* 31, no. 1 (1980): 42–52.

Bunyan, John. *The Pilgrim's Progress*. Edited by W. R. Owens. Oxford: Oxford University Press, 2008.

Cavanagh, Sheila. "Romancing the Epic: Lady Mary Wroth's *Urania* and Literary Traditions." In *Approaches to the Anglo and American Female Epic, 1621–1982*, edited by Bernard Schweizer, 19–36. Aldershot UK: Ashgate, 2006.

Dubrow, Heather. "Fringe Benefits: Rosalind and the Purlieux of the Forest." *Notes and Queries* 53, no. 1 (2006): 67–69.

Duncan, Helga L. "'Here at the Fringe of the Forest': Staging Sacred Space in *As You Like It*." *Journal of Medieval and Early Modern Studies* 43, no. 1 (2013): 121–44.

Dusinberre, Juliet. Introduction to *As You Like It* by William Shakespeare. Edited by Juliet Dusinberre. London: Arden, 2006.

Enos, Carol. "Catholic Exiles in Flanders and *As You Like It*; or What If You Don't Like It At All?" In *Theatre and Religion: Lancastrian Shakespeare*, edited by Richard Dutton, Alison Findlay, and Richard Wilson, 130–42. Manchester: Manchester University Press, 2003.

Fraser, Russell. "Shakespeare's Book of Genesis." *Comparative Drama* 25, no. 2 (1991): 121–28.

Freinkel, Lisa. *Reading Shakespeare's Will: The Theology of Figure from Augustine to the Sonnets*. New York: Columbia University Press, 2002.

Frye, Northrop. *Anatomy of Criticism*. Princeton: Princeton University Press, 1957.

———. "The Bride from the Strange Land." In *The Eternal Act of Creation: Essays, 1979–1990*, 50–61. Edited by Robert Denham. Bloomington: Indiana University Press, 1993.

Garber, Marjorie. "The Education of Orlando." In *Comedy from Shakespeare to Sheridan: Change and Continuity in the English and European Dramatic Tradition*, edited by A. R. Braunmuller and J. C. Bulman, 102–12. Newark: University of Delaware Press, 1986.

The Geneva Bible: A Facsimile of the 1560 Edition. Introduced by Lloyd Berry. Rev. ed. 1969. Reprint, Peabody MA: Hendrickson Publishers, 2012.

Griffin, Eric. "Shakespeare, Marlowe, and the Stranger Crisis of the Early 1590s." In *Shakespeare and Immigration*, edited by Ruben Espinosa and David Ruiter, 13–36. Farnham UK: Ashgate, 2014.

Hamlin, Hannibal. *The Bible in Shakespeare*. Oxford: Oxford University Press, 2013.

Hopkins, Lisa. "Orlando and the Golden World: The Old World and the New in *As You Like It*." *Early Modern Literary Studies* 8 (2002): 2.1–21.

Hubbard, Robert, Jr. *The Book of Ruth*. Grand Rapids MI: William Eerdmans, 1988.

Kinney, Clare R. "Feigning Female Faining: Spenser, Lodge, Shakespeare, and Rosalind." *Modern Philology* 95, no. 3 (1998): 291–315.

Lavater, Ludwig. *The book of Ruth expounded in twenty eight sermons*. London, 1586.

Lawrence, Karen. *Penelope Voyages: Women and Travel in the British Literary Tradition*. Ithaca NY: Cornell University Press, 1994.

Lodge, Thomas. *Rosalynd*. Edited by Brian Nellist. Staffordshire UK: Keele University Press, 1995.

Marcus, Leah. "Anti-Conquest and *As You Like It*." *Shakespeare Studies* 42 (2014): 170–95.

McAlister, Arlene. "The Interpretation of the Book of Ruth in Richard Bernard's *Ruths Recompense*." *Seventeenth Century* 30, no. 1 (2015): 33–54.

Milton, John. *The Annotated Milton: Complete English Poems*. Edited by Burton Raffel. New York: Bantam, 1999.

Parsons, Bartholomew. *Boaz and Ruth Blessed*. London, 1633.

Raman, Shankar. *Renaissance Literature and Postcolonial Studies*. Edinburgh: Edinburgh University Press, 2011.

S.R. *Ruth Revived*. Oxford, 1639.

Shakespeare, William. *As You Like It*. Edited by Juliet Dusinberre. London: Arden, 2006.

Wojcik, Jan. "Improvising Rules in the Book of Ruth." PMLA 100, no. 2 (1985): 145–53.

Youngs, Tim. *The Cambridge Introduction to Travel Writing*. Cambridge: Cambridge University Press, 2013.

16

English Women, Romance, and Global Travel in Thomas Heywood's *The Fair Maid of the West, Part 1*

GAYWYN MOORE

Written around 1600, probably while Queen Elizabeth still lived, Thomas Heywood's *The Fair Maid of the West, Part 1*'s central action takes place in and around the ill-fated 1597 "Islands Voyage" to the Azores, and the play integrates the miscommunications and later rivalry between the two admirals, Robert Devereux, Earl of Essex and Sir Walter Raleigh.[1] The goals of the expedition, an Anglo-Dutch venture, were to destroy the Spanish fleet, assumed to be a new Armada assembling to attack England, in the Spanish port of Ferrol. Next, the navy planned to sail to the island of Terceira to take control of the Azores where they would loot treasure-laden Spanish ships traveling from the Americas. This project was doomed from the start. Conceived in mid-April, the combined Dutch-English fleet lost ships, men, and money because of weather, dysentery, miscommunication, and dissention among the admirals. A much-diminished fleet finally arrived at Ferrol at the end of August, only to abandon this integral piece of the mission as impossible. In September, the divided fleet sailed to the Azorean island of Fayal, where additional miscommunication allowed the Spanish fleet to sail past without opposition. Between attempts to capture the islands and the Spanish, many sailors and privateers died. October found the largely bankrupt English fleet limping home and the new Spanish Armada bearing down on England. History repeated itself and both fleets were scattered by storms.[2] Spain retook the Azores soon after and held them until 1642. The Azores themselves lacked stable ownership, having been settled by the Portuguese, conquered and used as a base of operations for Spanish fleets during Philip II of Spain's consolidation of both crowns, and unsuccessfully attacked by the French and English.³ Further, the Azores provided a popular location for pirates to prey on ships traveling from and to everywhere. According to Christopher Ebert, the Atlantic Islands (including the Azores) also provided informants for markets and trading routes as well as destinations for a global trading economy, thus effectively evading whatever nation happened to claim their loyalty at that moment.⁴

Despite the rather spectacular failure of the Islands Voyage, Heywood's play makes the island setting and the military actions surrounding the voyage central to its plot. All of the principal characters must travel to the Azores before taking up new lives in foreign lands. The destination of the Azores signals more than historical specificity, and more than a romantic and exotic island adventure; the Azores were, and remained well into the twentieth century, a major port of call for ships (and later aircraft) traveling from all over the world. This destination represents the crossroads of the world's trade routes, a legacy still visible in the architectural materials and foliage of the islands, which astonish with their far-flung origins.⁵ As the crossroads to the world, the Azores become an emblem for the expanding global economy of the early modern period and, at least in Heywood's play, a location that expands what it means to be English, offering a kind of global citizenship to the principle characters in the play. This new global citizenship includes Atlantic trade routes and the Americas, stretching the standard romance geography beyond the Mediterranean. Within the play, the Azores function as a kind of philosopher's stone, converting landed wealth into the liquid assets gained at sea, transforming English nationalism to global citizenship, and translating the traveling woman romance into a high-seas adventure.

The Fair Maid of the West, Part 1, fuses classical romance with New World exploration, ultimately disassembling the questing, cross-dressing female knight narrative and, simultaneously, expanding the geography of the romance to Atlantic trade routes. Bess Bridges, the fair maid in *Part 1*, combines romantic heroine with contemporary world travel. In the balance of this chapter, I argue that Heywood's play dismantles the image of the woman traveler provided within the romantic quest narrative and establishes an alternative defined by constant travel and global citizenship. Bess's character introduces, and then disrupts, established Mediterranean romance narrative restrictions of the woman traveler. Further, Bess expands the genre geographically by incorporating contemporary sea travel, particularly the seafaring industry of port towns like Plymouth and Fowey, and Atlantic–New World engagement through the Azores setting and active piracy.

Seafaring Economies

Sea travel was a dangerous and miserable enterprise in the late sixteenth century. In fact, the historical backdrop to Heywood's play, the Islands Voyage, presents a particularly grim image of the privateering enterprise. The military venture was costly in funds and lives, and many of the participants had been pressed into service, a common practice. Patricia Furmerton's careful reconstruction of the early modern English seafarer underscores the poverty and insecurity attached to this profession for both the sailors and their landlocked loved ones: "Given the huge and growing demand for manpower to service the navy, merchant shipping, and privateering expeditions, it is no wonder that seamen were drawn widely from the vast sector of the laboring poor."[6] Vagrants, unskilled laborers—and on merchant/pirate vessels, foreigners—made up the bulk of the laborers.[7] Many were pressed or sold into service; others were paid small sums to take the place of wealthier men. Many poor also chose to sign on to a naval or merchant vessel for the small initial fee, room and board, and the opportunities for wealth sea voyages promised.[8]

Counter to the financial realities of sea travel, *The Fair Maid of the West, Part 1* is a play awash in gold. If we follow the money, we can see that it all arrives at the Azores, where it transforms into new opportunities and New World wealth. The play begins with two captains and a gentleman discussing the popularity of the imminent Islands Voyage, which draws rich gallants "trick'd in scarf and feather" (1.1.13) from all over England who "are all on fire / To purchase from the Spaniard" (1.1.7–8).[9] Purchase, in this case, means steal through state-sanctioned piracy. The streets of Plymouth "Glister with gold" (1.1.12), and we soon witness evidence of this largess when the love-struck Spencer presses upon Bess one hundred pounds for safekeeping. For comparison purposes, a household servant could earn between two to five pounds a year in 1600, and the minimum yearly income required for knighthood was thirty pounds.[10] The money in this play, both the abundance in the port towns and the gentleman Spencer's wealth, is a particularly unrealistic fantasy and unusual in a privateer. More typical is his duel in which he kills another tavern customer, becomes a criminal, and flees the country by way of the Islands Voyage. His much-discussed excessive wealth funds Bess's quest to follow him to the Azores and provides the play's audience with a money trail to follow as Spencer systematically divests himself of his wealth, transforming from a rich privateer and romantic lover to impoverished ex-patriot and, humorously, the play's damsel in distress.

Before the duel, we hear the motivations of Spencer and his companion, Goodlack, for partaking in this dubious venture. The wealthy Spencer claims honor as his goal, "The great lord general [Essex] drew me hither first, / No hope of gain or spoil" (1.2.11–12). In contrast, the penniless Goodlack enlists as a hired sword to "seek abroad for pillage" (1.2.8). The play offers little difference between chivalry and piracy except personal motive. Barbara Fuchs argues that the difference between these labels is merely "the *performance* of legitimacy" and that the shift from privateer to pirate to *renagado* represents "a trajectory of increasing independence of the subject vis-à-vis the English state."[11] State-sanctioned piracy comes and goes; the pirates remain. Further, the state cannot effectively withdraw approval once given, blurring the distinction between privateer and pirate. Spencer initially performs as a privateer; his need to run from the law undermines his legitimacy. In contrast, many of the other characters in *The Fair Maid of the West, Part 1* bluntly identify as pirates, including Bess. State-sanctioned piracy invites a permanent instability into terms intended to confer legitimacy to shady mercantile and naval enterprises; further, the very unstable origins of sailors as vagrants, criminals, and landless wanderers, often free of personal obligations and material possessions, add to the instability of the profession and perceived instability of the seaman: "Displaced but housed, enslaved but free, alienated but communal, objects of capitalism but subjects of resistance, nationalistic but revolutionary—such was the conflicting character of the growing body of seaman wage laborers in the seventeenth century."[12] Add to this the fluid identity of the Azores, and we can see that the background of the Islands Voyage becomes integral in destabilizing both English identity and the romance genre within the play. Thus, the Islands Voyage, which includes English, Dutch, and Spanish military occupation of the Portuguese Azores, state-sanctioned piracy, unsanctioned piracy, and mercantile ventures, provide a destination where one can, or perhaps must, embody multiple titles, nations, and goals.

Spencer divests himself of his wealth over the course of the Islands Voyage. First, he wills an initial one hundred pounds to Bess should he die as a result of his military service. Before fleeing justice, Spencer leaves Bess his trunks, with all the money and material possessions therein, as well as a Cornish tavern in Foy.[13] Thus, he leaves the country with only the gold he carries, Bess's promise of constancy and virtue, and his annual income from an unknown source. He leaves behind the physical manifestation of his wealth—trunks and commercial property. Mortally injured trying to halt a brawl between two English captains, Spencer makes a final bequest: he leaves Bess five hundred pounds a year, divides the rest of his wealth among friends, and reserves "a bare 100 pounds / To see me honestly and well interr'd" (2.2.77–78).[14] At this point in the play, Spencer languishes at Fayal having given away all but the last one hundred pounds of his English money (still a small fortune). When he unexpectedly survives, he releases his last monetary connection to England by donating his funeral funds to another man named Spencer who has died in the skirmish with the Spanish. Thus, his last purchase is a plot of land in the Azores, effectively severing ties with England's wealth. While a funeral plot hardly constitutes land ownership, the plot becomes a contested site for national identity within the play and ultimately frees both of the lovers from their last ties to England and the romance genre. Spencer leaves the Azores penniless, landless, and legally dead—free from all ties to England, even his own name and identity. Bess leaves Spencerless, her quest vanishing with Spencer's body.

Seafaring Women and Cross-Dressing Heroines

Women sailors or passengers at the time of Heywood's play were uncommon. Within a few short years, the purpose of travel would "shift from male-dominated exploration and fortune seeking to permanent settlement, [and] women joined the migrations to North America in numbers," but the Islands Voyage places this play, and its plot, at a time when sea travel for women was both unusual and fraught with danger.[15] John C. Appleby emphasizes the masculine culture of sea travel, particularly piracy: "[Seafaring] held little opportunity or appeal for women. They were out of place at sea, straying into a shifting frontier which was also a heavily gendered zone of labor, travel and trade, war, and depredation. Neither an extension nor a mirror of the land, the seafaring world developed its own culture which denied or precluded a female presence."[16] Seafaring women faced captivity, slavery, and enforced marriage as passengers or the rare sailor aboard captured vessels, and this danger (as in other modes of travel where these dangers existed) served to actively discourage sea travel for women.[17] Pressures from the domestic culture also discouraged travel. The virtuous woman stays at home: "a woman who strays from home is one who errs, in every sense of the word. . . . For a woman to travel, then, is for her to jeopardize her virtue."[18] One more deterrent for sea travel existed: women were thought to be bad luck on board a ship and refused passage.[19]

However, women did support the infrastructure of sea voyage, including piracy, in the capacities of wife, port worker (which could include inn employees, fencers of goods, and prostitutes—not mutually exclusive jobs), and even raiders for short-term piracy such as river raids. *The Fair Maid of the West, Part 1* begins in Plymouth where the Islands Voyage consolidates ships and men. Bess serves ale to these future privateers/pirates at a local inn. Heywood immediately immerses the characters in the world of sea travel, and while Bess remains land bound for a third of the play, her activities wholly support a seafaring economy, first at Portsmouth, and later at Foy where she (bankrolled by Spencer's legacy) owns and runs a tavern before purchasing her ship.

Bess distinguishes herself as both part of the seafaring economy and as a potential romance heroine by her employment and virtue. With few exceptions, romance heroines brave the dangers of traveling for love, questing to find, rescue, or revenge lost lovers or parents, usually disguised as either a knight or a page.[20] In any of these cases, the traveling woman risks discovery, ravishment, or loss of her chaste reputation. Bess is both the questing virgin following her lover and the revenging spouse seeking her husband's killers (the Spanish), providing her a double layer of chastity with which to defend her virtue. Romance heroines rarely turn a profit on the side.

Although Bess's quest for profit threatens her virtue, it underscores her immersion in the seafaring economy. Valerie Forman links the expanding global economy and trade of the late sixteenth and early seventeenth century and new or hybrid dramatic genres, much as we see happening in *The Fair Maid of the West, Part 1*: "economic change could and did stimulate the production of new dramatic genres, and . . . the drama participated in developing new economic theories that enabled overseas trade and investment."[21] Thus, the combining of commerce and romance serves as a response to, and potential augmentation of, economic changes in early modern society.

Bess accordingly establishes herself as both an economic agent and a romance heroine, and the play immediately launches the audience into the inherent conflict between woman laborer and chaste traveling heroine. The play begins with two captains determining to dine at Bess's tavern because it has the "best wench":

> Bess Bridges; she's the flower
> Of Plymouth held. The Castle needs no bush;
> Her beauty draws to them more gallant customers
> Than all the signs i'th' town else. (1.1.19–22)

While the language here is approving, Bess's role as advertising for the tavern, and as the main draw for the customers, threatens her reputation. One captain insists she is honest; the other seems astounded at the possibility: "Honest and live there? / What, in a public tavern, where's such confluence / Of lusty and brave gallants? Honest, said you?" (1.1.24–26). Her current job, her "lusty" customers, and her commercial allure all undermine her virtue. While she may not literally be selling herself, it is her *self* that sells.[22] We soon discover that Bess is a tanner's daughter whose father sent her into service after falling on hard times. This biographical detail rings true in a seafaring economy that primarily relies on (or preys on) those too poor to find work elsewhere. The nature of her service—tavern wench pressed into service by a downturn in her family's income—makes her a common feature of a port town and an active part of the supporting infrastructure of a seafaring economy. Her virtue, and her ability to maintain her virtue, makes her uncommon. As a tavern wench, Bess is an unlikely heroine for a romance; as an honest and constant lover, Bess is a perfect heroine for a romance. Her status as a port-town tavern wench remains both a source of tension within the play (Spencer wants to marry her, but her status remains a barrier and has the additional problem of making her virginity and chastity improbable at best) and a source of mobility. Bess already functions as part of the travel industry.

Bess's freedom to travel comes about through a combination of romance genre hoops the character jumps through and seafaring dangers the character resolves in her favor. Her chastity, which comes into question a mere twenty-five lines into the play, provides the most helpful permit to her future mobility. Bess's virtue must be tested multiple times within the play—Spencer's need to frequently assure himself of her honesty becomes rather tiresome, but the combined reputation of popular tavern wench, successful tavern owner, and cross-dressing woman traveler proves difficult to overcome. Hackett points out that the traveling woman heroine in a romance is "morally disruptive in her determination to pursue her own sexual desires. In many cases she assumes male disguise to gain freedom of travel, and this compounds her moral ambiguity.... The efforts that authors make to reassure the reader of the warrior woman's femininity and virtue bespeak the fact that she always inevitably remains unsettlingly aggressive and unfeminine."[23] Thus, the multiple tests of Bess's virtue reinforce both the romance genre in which Bess is the questing lady, and the culture of piracy in which she provides services to sailors of the honest and dishonest kind (again, not mutually exclusive categories). In fact, Bess is a bit of an overachiever where virtue is concerned. As questing virgin and revenging (future) wife, Bess embodies both valued types of female chastity—taking on the wifely chastity so championed by Protestant England in addition to the chastity of the unmarried virgin actively seeking her lover in epic romances.[24] Her bases are covered.

Having fit herself into the role of the romance heroine despite the limitations of her birth and employment, Bess also transforms her seemingly fixed English identity as baseborn to wellborn through a conflation of romance and commerce. Upon hearing that Spencer had indeed remembered her lovingly and left her a significant inheritance, Bess exclaims, "you change my blood" (3.4.82), which marks her extreme surprise and, significantly, suggests a major change in her social status. By receiving a gentleman's inheritance, Bess takes on at least one of the social markings of the wellborn. Changing her blood requires a kind of alchemy; she must transform from a tanner's daughter, the social equivalent of lead, into an eternally faithful lover, which is getting closer to gold. Inheriting the money and trust of a gentleman catalyzes the cascade of transformations that make her "a girl worth gold" by the end of the play. While Spencer slowly distances himself, geographically and financially, from his wellborn English identity, Bess seemingly inherits both before she, too, arrives at the Azores and expands what it means to be English. She sails to the Azores to reclaim Spencer's body and to serve as a "pattern to all maids hereafter / Of constancy in love" (3.4.93-94). As a role model for a romance heroine's "constancy in love," she continues the metamorphosis, and as a woman pirate dressed as a man, she changes her external appearance as well as her internal pedigree.[25]

Bess doubles up on her protection from gendered violence as well. By choosing to cross-dress as a pirate, a captain no less, Bess adopts, and updates, the romance convention of the warrior woman—the questing lady who dresses as a knight to both hide her gender and travel safely in a masculine world. Replacing the female knight with the female pirate effectively adapts an already conflicted symbol of honor—while knights had chivalry and codes of conduct, many a romance knight errant failed to follow those rules. Thus an honorable knight and a dishonorable knight tread the same paths; likewise, the distinction between the honorable privateer (Spencer) and the less-honorable pirate (Goodlack) becomes a matter of self-definition, not behavior, within the play. Bess intentionally chooses title and dress that cross the line of honest and respectable labor (as a cross-dressing pirate) while maintaining her honest and respectable virtue (as a chaste heroine). Choosing to become a pirate captain and ship owner signals the audience that Bess breaks the romance rules. Her own self-definition straddles the line between criminal and honorable, escaping the pattern of romance by embracing the most prominent criminal element of sea travel, and also rejecting the national security England offers the privateer engaged in state-sanctioned piracy.

Not content simply to dress as a man to protect herself on her highseas adventures, Bess proves herself brave and effective with a weapon while collecting a loyal gang of men to sail the ship she purchases and refits as a pirate vessel. Bess meets the threat of male violence with her own cross-dressing male violence. As a tavern owner, Bess experiences sexual harassment in the form of the braggart Roughman who mistreats her servants and sets himself up as the man of her house. Bess dresses like a page with a sword and ambushes her harasser, who confesses to his cowardice and willingly humiliates himself to avoid a fight. Bess introduces herself as her own brother (a typical romance heroine's disguise). Her disguise isn't just about protecting her virtue but also her leadership status as owner and boss, and as with her pirate disguise later, everyone is soon in the know. Roughman meets further humiliation when he tries to spin the encounter with himself as the victor to impress Bess. She reveals herself as the armed page who bested and humiliated him, motivating him to mend his cowardly ways. When she later sells her tavern to purchase a pirate ship, Roughman signs on as her loyal employee. Cross-dressing for Bess functions as a method to control and enact the threat of male violence, not hide from it. Nor does she disguise herself as a man in order to protect her virtue; the crew of her ship provide her with "rich apparel / For man or woman as occasion serves" (4.2.87–88) and thus remain aware of Bess's true gender at all times. Bess's cross-dressing disperses threats of male violence while also adopting them, allowing her freedom to travel.

Her mode of travel engages in a bit of cross-dressing too, which, like her own diversely gendered wardrobe, performs a shifting, and shifty, identity. As with her first job as a barmaid, Bess surrounds herself with a "ging [gang] of lusty lads" (3.4.109), a potential challenge to her chaste reputation that she, and the play, simply ignore. Her purchase of a ship with the money she earns through the sale of her tavern in Foy also signals the last of Spencer's wealth that financially ties the two characters to England. The ship, in a gesture bound to make the modern reader wince, is tarred black and rechristened the *Negro*. Partially, the ship's transformation signals Bess's new occupation as pirate; however, it also employs a kind of cross-dressing like its owner. Here the ship dresses like a foreigner who hails from Africa, perhaps even Barbary where the ship ends up.[26] The ship changes its identity and, as the play progresses, captures gold bound from the Americas to Europe, especially from "the rich Spanish and barbarous Turk" (4.5.8). Bess's successful piracy makes her rich again, but this time her trunks overflow with New World wealth.[27] Her personal transformation mirrors her ship's transformation. Both relinquish their outward English identity and engage exclusively foreign revenues.[28] This story arc takes up the middle of the play, and by the end of it all the English money has been converted into properties that belong to the wealth of the New World rather than the inheritance of the homeland. Spencer's grave and Bess's ship represent the last vestiges of the English pound and highlight respectively the dangers and the promise of privateering and "purchasing" Spanish gold from the Americas.

As the central locus of travel in the play, the Azores function as a kind of reverse money-laundering enterprise, turning respectable wealth into (state sanctioned) ill-gotten gain via piracy funded by New World booty. As funds transmute national identities, so too do the characters, especially the sea traveler Bess, whose gender, national, and genre identities expand throughout the play.

The setting of the Azores completes the transformation, making each lover worthy of the other and redefining an identity more appropriate for a global worldview. As ship and grave converge, our Spencer finds redemption through the other Spencer who died, and the grave itself, as contested burial site for the bodies of English and Spanish combatants, works a kind of physical transformation for Spencer that matches Bess's change of blood. Arriving at Fayal, Bess learns that the body of the man she believes is her Spencer has undergone its own unfortunate metamorphosis. Although Spencer's comrade by the same name was buried under "a goodly monument" (4.4.40), the Spanish who retake Fayal believe the English sailor to have been a heretic and disinter him, reburying him in a field, and then, at the request of the unhappy farmer, moving his body yet again and burning it (4.4.43–51). This transformation from respectfully interred English citizen to heretical ash, while quite unfortunate for the fallen sailor, relieves our Spencer of the last anchor to his English wealth: his last one hundred pounds donated for the funeral monument. The name and body doubling of the two Spencers has already served as a convenient plot device for getting Bess to the Azores; now the mistaken identity serves to finalize the release of her Spencer from his initial sin, murdering his dueling opponent and then fleeing England and the law to avoid the consequences of his actions. Clearly, one Spencer dies so that another might live within the providence of the play; further, it would seem that one dies for the other's sins. Our hero essentially buries his weaker, sinful body, rising from his deathbed penniless but forgiven—and legally dead, so the charges against him presumably no longer exist unless he tries to reinstate his claim to his English inheritance.

The burning of the body in the Azores proves pivotal to the ensuing action. Bess's initial quest, and her reason for turning pirate, is to sail to the Azores, collect Spencer's body and bring him home to bury him, and be buried with him, a rather sad but appropriate quest to seek her lover and remain permanently by his side. Bess had intended to return Spencer's body to England and "erect a tomb / And lasting monument, where when I die / In that same bed of earth and bones may lie" (4.4.12–14). Thus, the obliteration of the body releases both Bess and Spencer from a very permanent final destination in England. A little payback by way of attacking Spanish ships allows for a quest revenge scenario to play out. However, her quest proves impossible once she learns that the body she believes to be her beloved has been cremated. Bess reaches the Azores only to discover her quest has gone up in smoke. Her course shifts from that of an extremely fixed location, a funeral monument for the two lovers, to that of an unfixed location, a ship, constantly in motion. Spencer's funeral pyre literally unmoors Bess.

Traveling beyond the Romance

At this point in the play, Bess lacks a quest, lacks a lover, lacks a husband, and has sufficiently met her revenge goals. She openly cross-dresses and sails with a gang of "lusty lads" while retaining her spotless virtue. The epic romance plot has been subsumed into the seafaring adventure plot. The pirate, a featured plot device in the larger romance genre, replaces the romance heroine, who is now a manless, questless world traveler who goes where she wants: a heroine for the eve of exploration.

The necessity of taking on water leads Bess to her final location in the play, the Barbary Coast. Dressing once again as a woman, word of Bess's beauty reaches the King of Fez, who attempts to pay for Bess's attentions. The play could, at this point, revert to the romance narrative—we are back in the Mediterranean and the situation offers threats to Bess's virtue and potentially her Christianity—all the dangers of sea travel loom. Instead, Bess negotiates with the King of Fez, securing her own safety and her status with the king. The king promises that Bess will "live lady of her free desires" (5.1.28). His wording here suggests that he's hoping she will be free with her desires, but soon Bess reframes her own desires while rejecting the gold the king attempts to buy her with:

> Captain [Goodlack], touch [the gold] not—
> Know, King of Fez, my followers want no gold.
> I only came here to see thee for my pleasure
> And show thee what these say thou never saw'st,
> A woman born in England. (5.1.38–42)

She dresses and travels for her own pleasure, not the king's. Further, this moment exposes the ruse Bess created for negotiating her safety—Goodlack had been acting as the captain and leader of the ship in his diplomatic role; here, Bess reasserts her leadership of the men who follow her, making it clear that she is in charge of herself and of her sailors. Finally, she claims her English identity as something as exotic to the king as he is to her—conflating both the male gaze (she's there to look at him) and the exotic Other (she acknowledges that she is the novelty).[29] Additionally, her phrasing qualifies her English identity as located in the past—her birthplace—suggesting that her current identity might be something different.

The Azores serve as the agent of transformation for the English characters within the play. Bess, an imprecise referent to Queen Elizabeth, allows the queen to recoup her losses through a worthy namesake and state-sanctioned piracy.[30] At the same time, the play's transfer of wealth from England to a global economy via the Azores establishes an English identity that breaks from traditional avenues of inheritance and privilege, and from England. While both characters remain decidedly English, they are no longer beholden to English circulation of wealth or to its definitions of worth. What it means to be English changes—especially as it concerns the accumulation of wealth produced outside of England. Bess's pleasure to see new people and willingness to be seen as foreign novelty in Fez, while refusing any money with strings attached, insists on both her mobility and her new global identity. Both people and goods that move beyond the reach of English law remain English—but also expand the definition of English into something new, an identity based on their global mobility. We are asked to imagine a quintessential Englishness that also includes an unfixed globalized sense of self.

Bess remains mobile, and a pirate captain, even as the play concludes, conventionally enough, with her imminent wedding to Spencer. Her stay in Fez is clearly temporary. The king continues to entice her to stay longer but also acknowledges that when she grows "weary of our sunburnt clime / Thy *Negro* shall be ballast home with gold" (5.2.36–37). Thus Bess has become a terror of the high seas and, more interestingly, a constant traveler. She becomes very much her own woman.[31] For the typical romance heroine, her wandering ends with the completion of her quest—often via marriage, or at least the promise of marriage in the future. While female travel remains essential to the romance genre, it also retains what Hackett describes as moral ambiguity, which "arises directly from her displacement from her proper location, combined with the duplicity of her disguise."[32] Bess, the already morally ambiguous cross-dressing pirate, divests herself of both quest and location, and thus by the end of the play, her proper location is anywhere but England, where her quest, had it been successful, would have ended in a funeral monument.

Through the industry of sea travel, and by overfulfilling, and then dismantling, the rules by which the romance heroine roams, *The Fair Maid of the West, Part 1* subverts the inherent threat of and limitations to female mobility within the romance genre. Instead, the play supplants the romance heroine with a new role model who, by pillaging New World wealth with her upwardly mobile career, mastering the specific seafaring culture of male violence, and dissipating any claim to a proper location, replaces quest with conquest and the courtly knight errant with the tavern wench turned dangerous pirate.

Notes

1. See Turner's introduction to Heywood, *The Fair Maid of the West Parts I and II* for the plays' publication history and plot, ix–xx.
2. Haynes, "Islands Voyage."
3. See James, "French Armada?" for a detailed account.
4. Ebert, "European Competition," 63.
5. The historical capital of the Azores, Angra do Heroismo, is a World Heritage Site.
6. Fumerton, *Unsettled*, 87.
7. Fumerton, *Unsettled*, 92. Ebert argues that foreigners (Portuguese or speakers of Portuguese) familiar with trading routes and also trading markets would have been necessary for other countries to effectively compete with Portugal and later Spain ("European Competition," 64–66). Further, both possibilities of a ship engaged in an English venture with a substantial foreign crew or "an illegal Portuguese venture operating out of England with the support of some English merchants" remain viable (65).

8. See Fumerton, *Unsettled*, 84–107.
9. All parenthetical citations are from Heywood, *The Fair Maid of the West, Parts I and II*, edited by Robert K. Turner, Jr.
10. Greenblatt, "British Money," A36–37.
11. Fuchs, "Faithless Empires," 48, 51.
12. Fumerton, *Unsettled*, 95.
13. The modern Fowey, pronounced "foy," a port town with a reputation for piracy. See Holland, "Dramatic Form," 172.
14. In yet another divestment of Englishness, Fumerton reads this particular irony within the play as undoing "any national unity" through the captains' greed (*Unsettled*, 59). I would add that Spencer's personal redemption through the repetition of his earlier sin, a foolish brawl, by the same witnesses of that brawl, suggest that English gentlemen-privateers fail in their pursuits because they repeat unsuccessful behaviors (and cling to English markers of status and distribution of wealth).
15. Jowitt, "'Her flesh must serve you,'" 95.
16. Appleby, *Women and English Piracy*, 191.
17. For additional information on gendered violence at sea, see Tucker, "She Would Rather Perish."
18. Hackett, "Suffering Saints," 126. See also Holland, "Dramatic Form" for a discussion of journeying while female. He paraphrases Turler's description of woman travelers on the stage in *The Traveiler* as "[t]o be mad or a woman makes travel unsuitable" because travel for women conflates with female desire ("Dramatic Form," 171).
19. Appleby, *Women and English Piracy*, 191. Appleby recounts a report whereby a conversation about women by sailors is credited with calling forth a storm. Even talking about women represented risky behavior. See also Taff, "Precarious Travel," in this volume.
20. Hackett, "Suffering Saints," 126.
21. Forman, *Tragicomic Redemptions*, 2.
22. Sebek in "'Strange Outlandish Wealth'" also makes this connection between the commercial and the sexual, noting that Bess's job, beauty, and gender link "eroto-commercial urges and their tendency toward violence" (187).
23. Hackett, "Suffering Saints," 127.
24. Protestant England did not have a monopoly on wifely chastity, but the play's seemingly blunt references to Spenser's *The Faerie Queene* through the character Bess as an updated Britomart and Queen Elizabeth stand-in who follows her beloved Spencer suggests that the combination of wifely and virginal chastity in Bess has deliberate religious and national referents.

25. Many scholars have commented on the relationship to the plot and popular sea ballads, for instance, Fumerton, *Unsettled*, 135.
26. Fuchs adds that Barbary, home to infamous pirates, creates an unexpected connection between England and Islam—business associates, of sorts ("Faithless Empires," 49–50). Later a conflation of English and Moor occurs as one of Bess's English crew members mishears a word and volunteers to be gilded [enriched] but instead gets gelded [castrated] and dressed as Moorish eunuch.
27. Forman, in *Tragicomic Redemptions*, argues that transformational genres such as tragicomedy depend on profitable transformation—that is, loss (financial, but other losses as well) is transformed into profit or redemption. Bess's sale of her thriving business and purchase of a ship (financially risky, at best) and expanding wealth suggest that travel genres may also engage in profitable transformations (7).
28. Scammell, "Shipowning," 387, underscores the superiority of the English ship and the political and economic support that shipbuilding and ship owning enjoyed in the late sixteenth century. Thus, it is possible to see Bess's disguising and rechristening her ship as a pirate vessel as another instance of English nationalism expanding into a global identity.
29. The reverse—that Bess's female beauty exists to be looked at by the king, and that the king represents the exotic other for the play's London audience—is also true. See Howard, "An English Lass," for distinctions between Moroccan Moors and the "barbarous Turk" as well as the sexual threat of the racial other in Heywood's play (114–15). Holland's "Dramatic Form," 172–73, provides an alternative view of the sexual threat of the exotic other in *The Fair Maid of the West, Part 1*.
30. See Howard, "An English Lass," 101–17, for the connections between Bess Bridges and Elizabeth I. Jowitt, in "Piracy and Politics," 219, discusses Elizabeth I and piracy.
31. Both Fumerton, *Unsettled*, 92–93, and Fuchs, "Faithless Empires," 50–51, emphasize the revolutionary potential of seamen and their profession.
32. Hackett, "Suffering Saints," 139.

Bibliography

Appleby John. *Women and English Piracy, 1540–1720*. Rochester: Boydell Press, 2013.

Ebert, Christopher. "European Competition and Cooperation in Pre-Modern Globalization: 'Portuguese' West and Central Africa, 1500–1600." *African Economic History* 36 (2006): 53–78.

Forman, Valerie. *Tragicomic Redemptions: Global Economics and the Early Modern English Stage*. Philadelphia: University of Pennsylvania Press, 2008.

Fuchs, Barbara. "Faithless Empires: Pirates, Renegadoes, and the English Nation." *English Literary History* 67 (2000): 45–69.

Fumerton, Patricia. *Unsettled: The Culture of Mobility and the Working Poor in Early Modern England*. Chicago: University of Chicago Press, 2006.

Greenblatt, Stephen, ed. "British Money." In *Norton Anthology of English Literature*, vol. B, A36–37. New York: Norton, 2012.

Hackett, Helen. "Suffering Saints or Ladies Errant? Women Who Travel for Love in Renaissance Prose Fiction." *Yearbook of English Studies* 41, no. 1 (2011): 126–40.

Haynes, Allan. "The Islands Voyage, 1597." *History Today* 25, no. 10 (1975): 689–96.

Heywood, Thomas. *The Fair Maid of the West, Parts I and II*. Edited by Robert Turner Jr. Lincoln: University of Nebraska Press, 1967.

Holland, Peter. "The Dramatic Form of Journeys in English Renaissance Drama." In *Travel and Drama in Shakespeare's Time*, edited by Jean-Pierre Maquerlot and Michele Willems, 160–78. Cambridge: Cambridge University Press, 1996.

Howard, Jean. "An English Lass Amid the Moors: Gender, Race, Sexuality, and National Identity in Heywood's *The Fair Maid of the West*." In *Women, Race and Writing in the Early Modern Period*, edited by Margo Hendricks and Patricia Parker, 101–17. New York: Routledge, 1994.

James, Alan. "A French Armada? The Azores Campaigns, 1580–1583." *Historical Journal* 55 (2012): 1–20.

Jowitt, Claire. "'Her flesh must serve you': Gender Commerce and the New World in Fletcher and Massinger's *The Sea Voyage* and Massinger's *The City Madam*." *Parergon* 18, no. 3 (2001): 93–117.

———. "Piracy and Politics in Heywood and Rowley's *Fortune by Land and Sea* (1607–9)." *Renaissance Studies* 16, no. 2 (2002): 217–33.

Scammell, G. V. "Shipowning in the Economy and Politics of Early Modern England." *Historical Journal* 15 (1972): 385–407.

Sebek, Barbara. "'Strange Outlandish Wealth': Transglobal Commerce in *The Merchant's Mappe of Commerce* and *The Fair Maid of the West, Parts I and II*." In *Playing the Globe: Genre and Geography in English Renaissance Drama*, edited by John Gillies and Virginia Mason Vaughan, 177–202. Madison NJ: Farleigh Dickinson University Press, 1989.

Tucker, Judith. "She Would Rather Perish: Piracy and Gendered Violence in the Mediterranean." *Journal of Middle East Women's Studies* 10, no. 3 (2014): 8–39.

Afterword

Looking for the Women in Early Modern Travel Writing

MARY C. FULLER

A colleague once told me a story about visiting a colonial archive in Latin America. She asked for help identifying sources relating to women and was told in response, "There are no women here—only nuns." The negative proved doubly misleading, not only discounting nuns as women, but discouraging exploration of what proved (because she was undeterred) to be rich and numerous sources.[1] This collection of essays finds, recognizes, and scrutinizes a sample of women in the archive of early modern travels, in both historical and fictional texts. Patricia Akhimie and Bernadette Andrea have described some of the obstacles that kept early modern women *from* traveling in the same ways their male counterparts did—barriers that are qualified and localized in some of the essays that follow but nonetheless remained.[2] They have rightly invited us to broaden our optic on what might be considered under the rubric of travel and travel writing: as in, for instance, Laura Williamson Ambrose's discussion of records kept by Lady Anne Clifford of movement around and between the various properties she owned.[3] Yet women remain harder to find than men in this context; in part, to be sure, because overall they simply traveled less, but also because, in many of the places we might look for them, finding the women who *are* there is neither easy nor straightforward.

As a response to the work undertaken by this collection's editors and authors, I wanted to offer some evidence from a key source that has been a focus of my own research and, perhaps more importantly, to reflect on the experience of navigating through the informational architectures in which this evidence was embedded. The case study will be a very particular but equally very important resource for students of early modern travel writing: the documentary collections on English travel published by the editor and geographer Richard Hakluyt in 1589 and 1598–1600 as *Principal Navigations*.[4]

It is tempting to assert, at the outset that there were not really any women in Hakluyt's books—much of his collections draw on a maritime world that, as John Appleby comments, was "a heavily gendered space."[5] Drawing on the memory of reading *Principal Navigations*'s thousands of pages over the last quarter century, I recall no women's names listed among ships' companies on the long voyages in search of a northern passage to China, the small fleets that tried to intercept Spanish treasure ships off the Azores, or even among merchants writing home from Muscovy, Persia, or Benin. And yet, here and there, women can be found in the body text, if not in titles, headings, and lists of names: for example, the "two wenches" observed by the Arctic navigator Stephen Borough accompanying "certaine Lappians" in their boats in the White Sea.[6] Making a positive effort to look for women in *Principal Navigations*, in other words, turns "not any" into "some"; even if these women are unnamed and briefly glimpsed, "some" encourages a harder look even at a well-known and apparently unlikely source because— for scholars as much as archivists—memory is not a trusty witness. Questions like "are there women in *Principal Navigations*?"—ones that run against our own expectations, or against the ways fields, archives, or discourses are shaped—have to be posed deliberately, persistently, and in multiple ways without taking any given "no" as a final answer.

The first and most obvious recourse for testing memory against evidence—or indeed for beginning an initial query—is the simple expedient of searching an index. Indexes, of course, take effort to prepare: Hakluyt provided an index only to *Principall Navigations* (1589), the shorter *first* edition of his great work. There, his "Table alphabeticall, containing a compendious extract, of the principall names and matters comprised in the whole precedent worke," contains this entry for "women": "Women of Arabia, their apparell and ornaments. 232. Women paint their faces in Moscovie. 346. Breasts of women very long. 102. Women deadly and hurtfull in their lookis. 71. The undecent maner of riding used by the women of Moscovie. 409. Women bought and sold, and let out to hire in Persia. 425. The maners of the young women amongst the Savages of America. 530."[7] Even without exploring these references, a few obvious remarks suggest themselves. First, the index notices women who have been observed in distant countries by travelers, rather than women who travel—the "women" of Hakluyt's index are implicitly not English. Second, the index notices women only in the plural, as groups rather than as individuals. Third, women appear by way of cultural norms and general behaviors (mostly ones that appear aberrant in English eyes) rather than as occasioned by any particular action or event. In short, Hakluyt's entry for "women" directs us towards ethnographic observations of a gendered exoticism.

Such observations deserve attention, and memory suggests others of a similar nature that Hakluyt's entry fails to include: for instance, references to the "apparel and ornaments" of African women in an early narrative of travel to "Guinea" in the 1550s.[8] These references and others like them are not all there is, however: the index entry is not comprehensive either in providing *all* the references to women or in providing a representative sample of the *ways* women feature in the text. A cursory examination even of the single index page on which the entry "women" appears turns up several further references of the same kind to foreign women, including "The great Turks yearly charge in his seraglio or court" and "Venetian women exceed in pompous apparel"; multiple references to Queen Elizabeth's diplomatic letters, charters, and other textual interventions, including correspondence with the sultan and "Virginia a part of America so named by the Queens Majesty"; and, finally, a list of the Roanoke colonists, "both men and women." Hakluyt is not altogether reliable as a guide to his own work, at least in response to this particular query.

At least for the 1589 edition of *Principall Navigations*, a thorough *modern* index also exists. Hakluyt's modern indexer, Alison M. Quinn, built on an earlier twentieth-century index to the longer second edition of *Principal Navigations* focused on names, places, and ships, adding a wide array of subject headings.[9] As she wrote of this project, "Some I tried out of curiosity. In what was very much a man's world I wondered what sort of information there was about women."[10] This fruitful question allowed Quinn to expand on Hakluyt's own enumeration of gendered exotica with entries that direct us towards European and Creole women living and traveling alongside men in the new worlds of the Atlantic and Pacific: "wives ... of mine owners in Mexico ... of Spaniards emigrating to the Philippine Islands ... Passengers, in *Our Lady of Pity* ... And Portuguese ships at the River Plate ... From Lisbon to Goa ... In N. Carolina, wives of English colonists."[11] (A further entry, "in Britain, as wives for Norway," leads to an excerpt from William Lambard's *Archaionomia* (1568) that describes medieval Norse invaders as having been, after conversion by King Arthur, "incorporated with us by the receiving of our religion and sacraments, and by taking wives of our nation").[12]

Even with this more attentive eye on the topic, however, to move beyond the general and normative to the particular actions and experiences of women in Hakluyt's documents requires further drilling down. Both Quinn and Hakluyt index a list of "men and women" who traveled to Roanoke Island in 1586 as colonists on a voyage that was the third attempt at founding an English settlement there.[13] This item is itself rich in information, albeit regarding an enterprise that was anomalous among English voyages under Elizabeth. The names of seventeen women can be found on Hakluyt's list; ten have last names corresponding to the names of men on the list, suggesting that these are married couples.[14] Two family names shared by male and female colonists also appear among the nine individuals under the heading of "children and boys" (in fact, all nine appear to be male). We can surmise that at least two families—mother, father, and son—may have been among the colonists. Four other boys share last names with men on the list, suggesting some form of kinship. Finally, the list includes two infants born in "Virginia," as the English named the colony: Virginia Dare, the daughter of Ananias Dare and Eleanor (herself the daughter of the colony's governor John White); and "Harvye," name and gender unrecorded, presumably the child of Dyonis and Marjorie Harvie. Both Eleanor and Marjorie gave birth before White's departure in late August and consequently must have been pregnant when they sailed from England in April. Ananias and Dyonis are respectively third and sixth on a non-alphabetized list of male colonists that begins with John White; Ananias is named elsewhere as "one of the Assistants," and both men (along with White) are named in an indenture between Sir Walter Raleigh on the one hand, and a list of merchants, adventurers, and gentlemen concerned with the Roanoke colony to whom Raleigh assigned rights under his patent.[15] It would thus appear that the two women who traveled while heavily pregnant both belonged to higher-status couples.

These names also allow for a more targeted search of narrative and other documents, places in the text to which neither index points us directly in response to a query about "women." Documents associated with the exploration and attempted colonization of Roanoke yield additional women: some English, some indigenous, mostly unnamed but nonetheless identified as individual agents located in time and space rather than as the broader groups of "typical" women identified by Hakluyt's "Table Alphabeticall." The seventeen English women whom we know were among the colonists appear three times in a narrative of the "Fourth Voyage to Virginia . . . 1587," twice in association with maternity: when "some of our women, and men" eat a Caribbean fruit that causes oral inflammation and swelling, symptoms that then trouble an infant nursing at the breast (764); when Eleanor Dare gives birth to a daughter who "was the first Christian borne in Virginia" and given the new colony's name (768); and finally when White is petitioned by "not onely the Assistants, but divers others, as well women, as men," to return to England for necessary supplies (769), the petitioners offering to sign a document guaranteeing the safety of any possessions White left behind.[16] The resulting instrument "under their handes, and seales" is transcribed in the document, one of the occasional petitions and testimonials in *Principal Navigations* that record the voices of those not otherwise given a hand in generating public narrative.[17] Even though we know the names of the seventeen women who were among the colonists—at least some of which are implied to have been subscribed to the document—they are otherwise largely invisible in this anonymous account.

Attention to the "Fourth voyage" also finds one indigenous woman, as the English planned a raid in darkness on a community they have mistakenly identified as hostile to them. The inhabitants flee, and "it was so darke, that they beeing naked, and their men and women apparelled all so like others, we knewe not but that they were all men: and if that one of them, which was a *Weroans* wife, had not had her childe at her backe, she had beene slaine in steede of a man."[18] This episode of the weroance's wife adds a mote of additional evidence to the impression we might gain from the references to settler women, that while the narrative attends in detail to the decisions and actions of men, women become visible in it primarily in connection with their capacity to birth and nurture children. The confusion here—between friends and enemies, women and men—suggests something else, in addition: that English colonists struggled to decode (and renarrate) a cultural and diplomatic interface that was both largely opaque to them and critical to their survival. In this context of a pressing need for data and uncertainty about what and how it signified, the actions, words, and gestures of indigenous women were at times recorded with far greater attention than those of English women (who were in any case present only on the fourth voyage).[19] Elisa Oh's essay in this volume, on the textual detail of Pocahontas's "advance and retreat" provided by colonists in Jamestown, testifies to the writers' sense that such movements could be made legible. Further representations of indigenous women appear in materials related to the earlier voyage of 1585, including the watercolors of John White and widely disseminated engravings by Theodor de Bry. English women were present on this voyage only symbolically, in the form of a dressed doll that appears twice in de Bry's illustrations: once in the hands of an indigenous girl, drawn in company with her mother, and once—so minute as to be discernible only under high magnification—in the outstretched hand of an Englishman leaning from the bows of his boat towards the island, an image titled "The arrival of the English in Virginia."[20]

The multifaceted quality of the documentary record is surely one of the reasons the Roanoke voyages have attracted so much scholarly (and literary) attention.[21] Yet these materials are not at all typical either of the kinds of experiences documented in Hakluyt's collection or of the documentary record. This is a conjecture: a search of *Principal Navigations* for feminine pronouns would generate hits primarily on ships, with (in declining order), a number for Queen Elizabeth, a small number on other women (named and unnamed), and a small number of figurative uses. The famous cluster of feminine metaphors found in accounts of voyages to Guiana occurs (like the Roanoke materials) in association with the enterprises of Sir Walter Raleigh, who deployed his New World activities as moves within the gendered politics of the Elizabethan court.[22] The Guiana materials are worth exploring: Joyce Lorimer's recent edition of Raleigh's *Discoverie of Guiana* (1596) includes annotations to the manuscript by Sir Robert Cecil, which provide some perspective on how Raleigh's representations of Amazons, for instance, played with one important reader; the edition as a whole provides important evidence of the ways in which exotica like cannibals and men without heads were introduced into firsthand accounts.[23] But Raleigh was unusual; and despite their claims on our attention, Hakluyt's materials on Guiana and Roanoke cannot be relied on as a representative sample of the collection's contents. Although "no" should not be the final answer here either, I *suspect* that searching elsewhere in *Principal Navigations* for feminine metaphors—analogues to Raleigh's famous description of Guiana as "a land that hath yet her maidenhead"—would yield diminishing returns.[24]

Where, or how else, might we then query Hakluyt's collection regarding women before abandoning it to turn to other kinds of sources and other time periods richer in evidence? For a compendium such as *Principal Navigations*, one of the necessary moves for analytic readings is to confer Hakluyt's documents with other print or manuscript versions. Such due diligence can not only clarify authorship (as in the case of Eden's African narratives) and highlight editorial alterations to the text, but also recover information lost or obscured when a portion of text has been extracted from a larger document.[25] Richard Willes's discourse on the Northwest Passage, "Certaine other reasons, or arguments to proove a passage by the Northwest," provides one example of one such extract. Turning to the original in Willes's *History of travayle*

(1577) restores a more expansive treatment of geographic evidence about routes to the Indies and how to assess it, and also leads us to several women whom he believed to have a serious interest in this and other geographical information.

Willes's original makes evident the discourse's origin in a particular situation of address between two individuals, as a document prepared at the request of Anne Russell Dudley, the Countess of Warwick. (The document's internal heading reads, "For M. Captayne Furbishers passage by the Northwest. To the ryght honourable and vertuous Ladie, the Lady Anne, Countesse of Warwyke.")[26] We would not know this from reading *Principal Navigations*. The extract presented by Hakluyt preserves numerous instances of first- and second-person pronouns from the original context of address, but these suggest little (if anything) about any particular "you" or "I": "[Sebastian] Cabota . . . entred personally that straight, . . . as in his owne discourse of navigation *you* may reade. . . . *I* can affirme it to be very possible and most likely. . . . From the North *I* say, continually falleth downe greate abundance of water. . . . Lay *you* now the summe hereof together."[27]

The immediate situational context for Willes's discourse was the search for a northwest passage to Asia and the Pacific that was actually in process at the time of writing; his text is dated March 20, and internal evidence places its composition in the interval between Martin Frobisher's return from his first voyage of exploration in 1576 and departure on his second voyage in 1577. Willes refers to Frobisher as "your Honours servaunt"; the conclusion to his discourse suggests not only that Anne Dudley was Frobisher's patron but also that his own text responds to specific questions she has posed about the enterprise and enjoined him to answer:

> Thus muche, right honorable, my verye good Lady, of your question concernyng your servantes voyage. If not so skylfully as I would, and was desirous fully to do, at the least as I could, & leasure suffered me, for the litle knowledge God hath lent me, yf it be any at all, in Cosmographie and Philosophie, and the small experience I haue in travaile. Chosing rather in the cleare judgement of your

Ho. mynde to appeare rude and ignorant, and so to be seene unto the multitude, then to be founde unthankefull and carelesse in any thing your Ho. shoulde commaunde me.[28]

Not all of Willes's second-person pronouns address Anne Dudley in this quite particular way—some are indeed rhetorical, as when he asks, in his review of possible objections to the alleged passage, "In the Northeast that noble Knyght sir Hugh Willoughby perished for colde: and can *you* then promyse a passenger any better hap by the Northwest?"[29] When Willes invites his addressee to consult particular texts for further information, the gesture of address may be of this general kind, gesturing towards *any* hypothetical reader: "Of a lawe denying all Aliens to enter into *China* . . . shalle *you* reade in the report of *Galeotto Perera.*"[30] Yet prominent among the globes and maps whose evidence he confers is "Sebastian Cabote . . . his table, the which my good Lorde your father hath at Cheynies."[31] (Chenies was the seat of Dudley's father Francis Russell, the Earl of Bedford). Willes appears to refer to Clement Adams's engraving of an earlier world map by Sebastian Cabot, a copy of which also hung "in her majesties privie galerie at Westminster," a map which Dudley, one of Elizabeth's ladies in waiting, would have had many opportunities to observe and examine.[32] These varied examples suggest that, while we can't treat Willes's references as evidence about the countess's reading, we also can't assume that Willes was never, in fact, literally inviting Dudley to consult actual books familiar to her. Another document in the *Historie*—in fact, the introduction to Pereira's treatise on China, translated from Italian and addressed to Anne Dudley's stepsister, Elizabeth Morison—makes allusion specifically to such intellectual interests on the part of a female reader, complimenting the addressee's "good skill both in Cosmographie and in forreine languages."[33]

As with the list of named Roanoke colonists, connecting the Countess of Warwick to Frobisher's voyages suggests a return to Quinn's index, which in turn directs us to an account of the second Frobisher voyage by Dionyse Settle reprinted among Hakluyt's materials on North America. Settle records that on August 3, his company "anchored in a faire harborough named *Anne Warrwickes sound*, unto which is annexed an

Island both named after the Countesse of Warwicke, *Anne Warrwicks sound and Isle.*"[34] Settle's account, and this record of toponyms honoring the Countess of Warwick, might prompt us to pursue our inquiry into other kinds of sources related to the Frobisher voyages, both cartographic and financial.[35] Several maps accompanied George Best's *A true discourse of the late voyages of discoverie* (1578), an overview of the three voyages; one of these represents Frobisher Bay, on the southeastern coast of Baffin Island (then believed by the English to be a passage open at the westward end), and shows not only "Countis of Warrick Ylad" but also a feature named "Countis of Sussex Mynn."[36] Best's map provides the names of *two* women whose involvement with the Northwest Passage can be explored.

A second source, Michael Lok's financial accounts for the Frobisher enterprise, lists among investors the names of Anne Russell Dudley, Countess of Warwick; Frances Sidney Radcliffe, Countess of Sussex; and a third noblewoman, Frances's niece, Mary Sidney Herbert, the Countess of Pembroke.[37] The earls of Warwick, Sussex, and Pembroke were among the largest investors in the enterprise, but Lok's accounts indicate that the three countesses made independent investments in at least the voyage of 1578. Mary's brother Philip was also among the investors, and their father Sir Henry Sidney—Frances's brother—was married to Anne Dudley's aunt. The Arctic navigator Richard Chancellor was a member of their household. The family networks of the three countesses would thus have given them access to the leading edge of thinking about exploration in their time; in turn, they seem to have chosen to become actively involved.[38]

It seems evident that Anne Russell Dudley played a role in these voyages in search of a northwest passage, voyages that were the "big science" of their day.[39] Yet the evidence of her involvement cannot be easily discerned by readers of any single source, and particularly not from the Hakluyt collections in any of their initial *or* modern editions. Willes's discourse, along with the narratives of both Dionyse Settle and George Best, is present in the second edition of *Principal Navigations* (1598-1600), and the MaClehose edition of 1903-5 adds Best's two maps as illustrations, yet the modern index to that edition leads us from "Warwick, Countess of" only to "Anne or Countess of Warwicks Sound and Island, discovered by Frobisher." As filtered through Hakluyt's editing and the MaClehose indexer, Anne Russell Dudley has been dematerialized into newly found land, and persistent effort—along with access to Willes's *Historie*, which lacks a modern edition—is required to assemble the fragments of evidence that reconstitute her as scholar, patroness, and investor.

Another attentive reader of travel writing emerges from Willes's original work: the collection as a whole was dedicated to Bridget Hussey Russell, the Countess of Bedford, Elizabeth Morison's mother and Anne Russell Dudley's stepmother. Willes's dedication pictures the countess as travel reader, but also as traveler. He imagines that she might, in fact, attend to his book *while* traveling on a planned journey with her husband, and as a respite for a mind "traveled with weighty matters, and wearied with great affaires."

> These last doings of R. Eden newly encreased, my first labours in our language, his history & mine of trauel in the west & East Indies, altogeather in one volume, duetifully do I present unto your Honour, . . . most earnestly requesting your good Ladiship, that you will vouchsafe it, & by leysure, in this journey, the whiche my Lorde and you have determined into the west countrey, to let your page reade them over to your Honours recreation. . . . If varietie of matter, occurrents out of forraigne countryes, newes of newe founde landes, the sundry sortes of governement, the different manners & fashions of divers nations, the wonderfull workes of nature, the sightes of straunge trees, fruites, foule, and beastes, the infinite treasure of Pearle, Golde, Silver, & joyes may recreate and delight a mynde travelled in weighty matters, & weeried with great affayres: credit me, good Madam, in listning unto this worke, shall you have recreation.[40]

Willes's dedication suggests that, like her daughter, Elizabeth, whose "skill in Cosmographie" he recognized, the elder countess had some learned interest in geography: she accorded him "the first yeerely pension I ever was assured of in England" at a time when no lecture, stipend or reward was commonly available to support the scholars of a geography whose findings were ever more timely.[41] (Hakluyt's letters to Sir Francis Walsingham, Elizabeth's secretary of state, complained in similar terms about this absence of institutional support and funding.)[42]

Other evidence suggests that the countess may have had had a broader interest in learned books. She appears to have brought to her subsequent marriages the library of her first husband, the humanist and diplomat Sir Richard Morison. Morison's collection was rich in Greek and even Hebrew books, including standard classical texts on cosmography and mathematics as well as the *Decades* of Peter Martyr, the core of Eden's later collection which, in turn, was updated by Willes. Although Morison had initially bequeathed the library to John Hales, a relative by marriage who shared his scholarly interests, his widow interpreted her own legacy of all Morison's "movable goods" to include her late husband's books. A catalogue of the library was later in the possession of her third husband, the Earl of Bedford, suggesting that the books, as well, came with her and that she had not obtained the collection simply for its commercial value.[43]

Like the three countesses who invested in Frobisher's voyage of 1578, Bridget Hussey Russell contributed to the intellectual and practical infrastructure supporting distant travels and navigations of Elizabeth I's reign. She also had her own *history* of travel. During her marriage to Morison, she accompanied her husband on several extended journeys to Europe, both while he attended the peripatetic court of Charles V and, later, when the couple became religious exiles during the reign of Mary Tudor. At least one of her children was born abroad. After her husband's death, Bridget remained in Strasbourg for some period, extending charity to other English refugees and returning only on the accession of Elizabeth.[44]

The geographically inclined Countess of Bedford is even harder to find than her stepdaughter Anne, Countess of Warwick. We will not find her in *Principal Navigations* and would be hard pressed to find her through the standard reference of the *Oxford Dictionary of National Biography*.[45] Once found, her interests are not easily discerned. The entry for

Francis Russell, Earl of Bedford, in a survey of books dedicated to the earl, appears to attribute Willes's "surprising" dedication of his travel collection to Russell, rather than to his wife; both Willes's first name and the title of his book are given incorrectly.[46] (Such mistakes are not infrequent with obscure documents of complex authorship, but they place additional obstacles in the path of tracking down the original source). Yet like Anne Dudley, Bridget Russell seems worth finding: both provide an example of how persistent following of recondite threads can make the invisible visible again.

Richmond Barbour opens the present collection of essays by attending to the character of Desdemona as an analogue to historical women who, like her, petitioned to accompany their husbands overseas. Her character has a second dimension of interest to other essayists: as an eager auditor of Othello's travel stories, stories that conveyed an exotic human geography even while celebrating the experience of a heroic individual traveler. Both aspects of "women and travel" turned up in my search. Attending to Hakluyt's *Principal Navigations* led to the discovery of historical women who, in different ways, "participate[d] in the era's expansionist projects" or were touched by them: two unnamed Laplanders; Eleanor Dare, Margery Harvie, and their fifteen companions; the wife of the Croatoan leader; Anne Russell Dudley and her cohort of investors; Elizabeth Morison; and Bridget, Countess of Bedford.[47] Yet the path to finding these women was circuitous and often non-obvious. What can be learned from this story of *informational* discovery?

Tools like indexes and dictionaries have their own irregularities of recall and reference: using them can tell us both something about the resources that exist in the record and something about the way the record has been structured (deliberately and accidentally). Travel writing itself has some particular quirks: *any* travel narrative is likely to exist in multiple versions and stages.[48] As Patricia Akhimie's essay on Lady Catherine Whetenall's travel in this volume reminds us, between these multiple versions, women and other facts can appear and disappear. Comparing *all* the versions of any "travel writing," even apparently almost identical texts, can provide us with both new evidence and new questions.

Finally, "search" is an ever more pervasive and yet underscrutinized part of our lives. Scholarly communication is indispensable for sharing the dispersed evidence that others may help to assemble into a meaningful picture. Yet, a former reference librarian at the Library of Congress writes that "most library users . . . miss much more of what is actually available to them than they ever realize" because the explicit or implicit model of practice we use to conduct our research defines "—and usually limits—the range of what users expect from libraries, what questions they permit themselves to ask . . . and what they judge to be satisfactory results."[49] In other words, most of us have access to tools that we don't use as we might to discover information both in depth and with precision; we walk away from the archive (or the computer) with what we think we can get, not what we really want. Our capacities for discovery themselves call for scrutiny, exploration, and expansion in the service of turning the blank walls often encountered with difficult queries into widening gates.

Notes

1. For examples of these stories, see Few, *Women Who Live Evil Lives*.
2. For instance, see Michael Slater's essay in this volume considering the character of Desdemona in light of the different expectations of conduct for aristocratic women.
3. Ambrose's account of Clifford's multistage life writing recalls work by Ian MacLaren, "Evolution of Explorers," on the iterative "stages" of travel writing, from rough field notes or logs through narrative journals and, only after multiple transformations, published narrative accounts.
4. Hakluyt's two editions of *Principal Navigations*, whose titles differ only by a letter, are nonetheless substantially different books in length, content, organization, and principles of inclusion; it is often worthwhile to consult them independently. For references to the first edition, *Principall Navigations* (1589), I have used the Quinn and Skelton modern facsimile edition in two volumes, cited as *PN* (1965); page numbers will be identical to those of the single-volume original. For the second edition, *Principal Navigations* (1598–1600), in the absence of a satisfactory modern edition I have used the original, cited as *PN* (1598–1600). The twelve-volume modern edition of *PN* (1598–1600), cited as *PN* (1903–5), is referenced only for paratextual material specific to that edition. An indispensable aid to navigating the

collections is Quinn, *Hakluyt Handbook*, particularly the section on "Contents and Sources" (2:338–460). A critical edition of *PN* (1598–1600) is currently in preparation for Oxford University Press.

5. Appleby, *Women and English Piracy*, 191, cited in Moore's essay in this volume.
6. Borough, "Voyage of . . . M. Stephen Burrough, An. 1557," PN (1965), 1:328.
7. Hakluyt, *PN* (1965), 2:834. Citations from Hakluyt's documents will be to this edition unless otherwise noted.
8. Eden, "Second Voyage to Guinea . . . in the Yeere 1554," *PN* (1965), 1:96. This account has a complex authorship that Hakluyt's paratext only confuses further: reprinted from Richard Eden, *The Decades of the New World or West India* (1555), this text was written *by* Eden, using a pilot's log from the voyage to which he added the oral testimony of "our men," as well as materials drawn from his library and his personal observations of objects the voyagers brought back with them. The narratives were also included by Richard Willes in *History of Travayle* (1577). In the first edition of Hakluyt's collection, *Principall Navigations* (1589), the running heads misleadingly attribute the account as a whole to Robert Gaynsh, pilot of one of the voyage's three ships; in the second edition, *Principal Navigations* (1598–1600)—where this text appears for the fourth time—running heads attribute it to John Lok, captain of the small fleet. In both editions of *PN*, Hakluyt's title describes the voyage as "set out" by its principal investors: Sir George Barne, Sir John York, Thomas Lok, Anthony Hickman, and Edward Castelin (*PN* [1965] 1:89; *PN* [1598–1600] 2:2:14, misnumbered as "326"). Readers consulting the account in *PN* (1598–1600) should be aware of some additional issues; the second half of volume 2, where this account appears, is paginated separately from the first, and with many errors, as described in *The Hakluyt Handbook* (2:510).
9. Quinn's index to *Principall Navigations* (1589) appears in the Quinn and Skelton facsimile edition, *PN* (1965). An index to the second edition of *PN* (1598–1600) occupies most of volume 12 in the Maclehose–Hakluyt Society edition of 1903–5, and despite its limitations, remains worth consulting.
10. Quinn concludes an article on her own index by commenting wryly on Hakluyt's "women" entry: "what would Hakluyt have said of an index to his *PN* made by a woman and a Scot? Barbarous and undecent" (Quinn, "Modern Index," 107, 112).
11. Quinn, "Index," *PN* (1965), from the entry, "women."
12. Lambard, "Testimony of the Rights and Appendances of the Crown of the Kingdom of Britain," 1:245.

13. The list, titled "The names of all the men, women and Children, which safely arrived in Virginia, and remained to inhabit there, 1587," appears at the end of a narrative document which in the first edition of 1589 is titled "The fourth voyage made to Virginia, with three shippes, in the yeere, 1587. Wherein was transported the second Colonie." Despite the titular specification of those who "arrived ... and remained," the list includes John White and the Portuguese pilot Simon Fernando, both of whom left Roanoke and returned to England ("Fourth Voyage," 2:769–70).
14. Family names for both male and female colonists are: Dare, Harvey, Powell, Archard, Jones, Tappan/Topan, Chapman, Colman, Payne, and Vicars.
15. "Fourth Voyage," 2:764, 768, 769.
16. "Fourth Voyage," 2:768. Raleigh, "Assignment from Sir Walter Raleigh," 2:815. Richard Hakluyt is listed among the adventurers.
17. In *PN* (1598–1600), for instance, see "Testimoniall of the Company of the Desire," 3:845–46; "Petition Made in the Streight of Magellan.... 1589," 3:840–42. Unlike the Roanoke document referenced in "Fourth Voyage," these documents include the names of signatories.
18. "Fourth Voyage," 2:768.
19. See, for instance, Barlowe and Amadas, "First Voyage Made to the Coasts of America, ... 1584," 2:730.
20. White's drawings are housed in the British Library. The two images are plates 2 and 8 in Harriot, *A Briefe and True Report of the New Found Land of Virginia* (1590). De Bry's edition of Harriot was also printed in French, Latin, and German.
21. Roanoke and Meta Incognita both left a multimodal record: a variety of narratives (both print and manuscript), planning, financial and legal documents, objects, visual art, cartography, and archaeological evidence. These features afford the opportunity to place in dialogue evidence and perspectives from an unusually large variety of fields, ranging from material science and linguistics to literary and historical scholarships. See, for instance, the essays in Symons, *Meta Incognita* and (on White's drawings), Sloan, *New World*. For literary takes on Roanoke, see Powell and Powell, *England & Roanoke*.
22. On Guiana and Raleigh's career at court, see the essays by Montrose and Fuller in Greenblatt, *New World Encounters*; for a more recent perspective, see Lorimer's introduction to Raleigh, *Ralegh's Discoverie*.
23. See the materials by John Ley in Raleigh, *Ralegh's Discoverie*, 308–29, along with Lorimer's introduction.
24. For an account of Newfoundland as counterexample to the imaginative feminization of the Americas, see Fuller, "Images of English Origins."

25. See Schleck, "Forming the Captivity of Thomas Saunders," and MacCrossan, "Framing 'the English Nation.'"
26. Willes, "For M. Captayne Furbishers passage by the Northwest," *History of Travayle*, 230v.
27. Willes, "Certaine other reasons," 2:613–14, emphasis mine.
28. Willes, "For M. Captayne Furbishers passage by the Northwest," 236r.
29. Willes, "For M. Captayne Furbishers passage by the Northwest," 231r, emphasis mine.
30. Willes, "For M. Captayne Furbishers passage by the Northwest," 232v, emphasis mine.
31. Willes, "For M. Captayne Furbishers passage by the Northwest," 232r.
32. Gilbert, "A discourse written by Sir Humfrey Gilbert Knight," 2:602. R. C. D. Baldwin's entry for Clement Adams in *The Oxford Dictionary of National Biography* cautiously refrains from identifying the Cabot map at Chenies to which Willes refers with the Cabot world map engraved by Adams ca. 1549. However, Willes's several references to "Cabota his table," presumably the *same* "table" or map, confer its evidence with globes and world maps by others, suggesting persuasively if not conclusively that he refers to the Cabot-Adams world map, and not to another, unknown collaboration.
33. Willes, "To the right worshipfull, my singuler good Mystres, M. Elizabeth Morisyn," 236v. This address precedes Willes's translation of Galeote Pereira, *Noui auisa delle Indie di Portugallo* (Venice, 1565), also reprinted by Hakluyt in *PN* (1598–1600).
34. Settle, "Second Voyage of Master Martin Frobisher," 2:626. The vagaries of indexing for women's names again require persistence: under "Warwick" in Quinn's index, we find a cross reference to an entry for Ambrose Dudley, Anne's husband, but only under "Dudley" do we find entries for Anne as well as her husband, the earl. The sources I have cited regarding Anne Dudley have widely varying practices for indexing her name.
35. Related documents have been printed and reprinted in numerous editions, including *PN* (1598–1600). In addition, the Hakluyt Society's edited volumes are a reliable source of documents from manuscript (see especially those by Collinson and McDermott.) Alden and Landis, *European Americana*, is a useful guide for finding primary sources in print, at least for the Americas, and covers sources in all European languages.
36. Best's *True Discourse* is excerpted at length *without* the maps in *PN* (1598–1600), and thus the 1903–5 index does not lead us to these names (although the map is reproduced at 7:336).

37. Michael Lok's list of adventurers is printed in McDermott, *Third Voyage of Martin Frobisher*, 56. Several additional women, not all of whom were aristocrats, are named on the 1578 list or had invested in earlier voyages.
38. For Sidney's connection with Chancellor in the 1550s, see Adams, "Newe Navigation," 281. The Earl of Pembroke was also an early patron of John Dee, who was central to the intellectual, social, and practical networks surrounding voyages of northern exploration in the second half of the sixteenth century.
39. I borrow the term from Deborah Harkness's chapter in *Jewel House*, "Big Science in Elizabethan London"; on funding for Frobisher's voyages, see Harkness, *Jewel House*, 166–69.
40. Willes, "To the ryght noble and excellent Lady, the Lady Brigit," n.p.
41. Willes, "To the ryght noble and excellent Lady, the Lady Brigit," n.p.
42. Letter from Richard Hakluyt to Walsingham, 1584, in Taylor, *Original Writings*, 1:208.
43. A manuscript catalog of Morison's library belonged to Francis Russell, the Earl of Bedford (Sowerby, *Renaissance and Reform*, 242).
44. For these and other biographical details, see Sowerby, *Renaissance and Reform*, 232, 238–39n91, 251. Morison was accompanied as secretary during his embassy by Roger Ascham, whose letters provide some details of the ambassador's household and his movements; the *Calendar of State Papers* has some of Morison's own correspondence, which I have not examined.
45. Searching for Bridget, Countess of Bedford in the *Oxford Dictionary of National Biography* under her maiden or married names yields only one hit, in the biography of her third husband; she is referred to elsewhere in ODNB by her first name, followed by life dates: "Bridget (1525/6-1601), eldest daughter of John Hussey" (Woolfson, "Morison, Sir Richard").
46. MacCaffrey, "Russell, Francis."
47. See Akhimie and Andrea's introduction.
48. See MacLaren, "Evolution of Explorers."
49. Mann, *Library Research Models*, vii. The claim is fleshed out in the book by convincing real-world examples. In a related paper, Mann suggests that using post-coordinated search terms—keywords linked with Boolean operators (AND/NOT/OR)—will give markedly less satisfactory results than pre-coordinated search terms—(e.g., the syntax of LoC or other subject headings), with particularly adverse consequences for research in women's studies and African American studies. See Mann, "Reference Librarian's Thoughts," 7–9, 10–12. My thanks to Greg Eow of MIT Libraries for this reference.

Bibliography

Adams, Clement. "The Newe Navigation and Discoverie of the Kingdome of Moscovia, by the Northeast, in the Yeere 1553." In Hakluyt, *The Principall Navigations*, edited by Quinn and Skelton, 1:280–92.

Adams, Simon. "Ambrose Dudley, Earl of Warwick." In *The Oxford Dictionary of National Biography* online. Oxford: Oxford University Press. Accessed June 13, 2017.

Alden, John, and Dennis C. Landis. *European Americana: A Chronological Guide to Works Printed in Europe Relating to the Americas, 1493–1776*. 6 vols. New York: Readex, 1980.

Appleby, John. *Women and English Piracy, 1540–1720*. Rochester NY: Boydell, 2013.

Barlowe, Arthur, and Philip Amadas. "The First Voyage Made to the Coasts of America, . . . 1584." In Hakluyt, *The Principall Navigations*, edited by Quinn and Skelton, 2:728–33.

Best, George. *A True Discourse of the Late Voyages of Discoverie, for the Finding of a Passage to Cathaya, by the Northvveast, Vnder the Conduct of Martin Frobisher Generall*. London, 1578.

Borough, Stephen. "The voyage of . . . M. Stephen Burrough, An. 1557." In Hakluyt, *The Principall Navigations*, edited by Quinn and Skelton, 1:326–31.

Carey, Daniel, and Claire Jowitt, eds. *Richard Hakluyt and Travel Writing in Early Modern Europe*. Farnham, UK: Ashgate, 2012.

Collinson, Sir Richard. *The Three Voyages of Martin Frobisher, in search of a Passage to Cathaia and India by the North-West, A.D. 1576-8. Reprinted from the First Edition of Hakluyt's Voyages, with Selections from Manuscript Documents in the British Museum and State Paper Office*. 1st series, 38. 1867.

Eden, Richard. *The Decades of the New World or West India*. London, 1555.

———. "The Second Voyage to Guinea . . . in the Yere 1554." In Hakluyt, *Principal Navigations* (1598–1600), 2:2:14–23, "14" misnumbered as "326."

———. "The Second Voyage to Guinea . . . in the Yeere 1554." In Hakluyt, *The Principall Navigations*, edited by Quinn and Skelton, 1:89–98.

Few, Martha. *Women Who Live Evil Lives: Gender, Religion, and the Politics of Power in Colonial Guatemala*. Austin: University of Texas Press, 2002.

"The Fourth Voyage Made to Virginia, with Three Shippes, in the Yeere, 1587. Wherein Was Transported the Second Colonie." In Hakluyt, *The Principall Navigations*, edited by Quinn and Skelton, 2:764–71.

Fuller, Mary C. "Images of English Origins in Newfoundland and Roanoke." In *Decentring the Renaissance: Canada and Europe in Multidisciplinary Perspective, 1500–1700*, edited by Germaine Warkentin and Carolyn Podruchny, 141–58. Toronto: University of Toronto Press, 2001.

———. "Ralegh's Fugitive Gold: Reference and Deferral in The Discoverie of Guiana." In Greenblatt, *New World Encounters*, 218–40.
Gilbert, Sir Humphrey. "A discourse written by Sir Humfrey Gilbert Knight." In Hakluyt, *The Principall Navigations*, edited by Quinn and Skelton, 2:597–610.
Greenblatt, Stephen, ed. *New World Encounters*. Berkeley: University of California Press, 1993.
Hakluyt, Richard. *Principal Navigations*. 3 vols. London, 1598–1600.
———. *The Principall Navigations, Voiages and Discoveries of the English Nation*. London, 1589.
———. *The Principall Navigations, Voiages, and Discoveries of the English Nation*, edited by David B. Quinn and R. A. Skelton. 2 vols. Cambridge: Hakluyt Society, 1965.
Hakluyt, Richard, and Walter A. Raleigh. *The Principal Navigations, Voyages, Traffiques & Discoveries of the English Nation*. 12 vols. Glasgow: J. MacLehose and Sons, 1903–5.
Harkness, Deborah. *The Jewel House: Elizabethan London and the Scientific Revolution*. New Haven: Yale University Press, 2007.
Harriot, Thomas. *A Briefe and True Report of the New Found Land of Virginia: Of the Commodities and of the Nature and Manners of the Naturall Inhabitants*. Frankfurt, 1590.
Lambard, William. "A Testimony of the Rights and Appendances of the Crown of the Kingdom of Britain." In Hakluyt, *The Principall Navigations*, edited by Quinn and Skelton, 1:244–45.
MacCaffrey, Wallace. "Russell, Francis, Second Earl of Bedford." In *The Oxford Dictionary of National Biography*. Oxford: Oxford University Press. Accessed June 13, 2017.
MacCrossan, Colm. "Framing 'the English Nation': Reading between Text and Paratext in *The Principal Navigations* (1598–1600)." In Carey and Jowitt, *Richard Hakluyt*, 139–52.
MacLaren, I. S. "In Consideration of the Evolution of Explorers and Travellers into Authors." *Studies in Travel Writing* 15, no. 3 (2011): 221–41.
Mann, Thomas. *Library Research Models: A Guide to Classification, Cataloging, and Computers*. New York: Oxford University Press, 1993.
———. "Is Precoordination Unnecessary in LCSH? . . . A Reference Librarian's Thoughts on the Future of Bibliographic Control." Washington DC. http://www.loc.gov/catdir/bibcontrol/mann_paper.pdf. Accessed June 12, 2017.
McDermott, James. *The Third Voyage of Martin Frobisher to Baffin Island 1578*. 3rd series, 6. London: Hakluyt Society, 2001.

Montrose, Louis. "The Work of Gender in the Discourse of Discovery." In Greenblatt, *New World Encounters*, 177–217.

Powell, Virginia W., and William S. Powell, eds. *England & Roanoke: A Collection of Poems, 1584–1987: People, Places, Events*. Raleigh: North Carolina Department of Cultural Resources, 1988.

Quinn, Alison M. "The Modern Index to Richard Hakluyt's *Principall Navigations*." *The Indexer* 5, no. 3 (1967): 106–12.

———. "The Modern Index to the 'Principall Navigations.'" In Hakluyt, *The Principall Navigations*, edited by Quinn and Skelton, 2:836–975.

Quinn, David B., ed. *The Hakluyt Handbook*. 2 vols. 2nd series, 144–45. London: Hakluyt Society, 1974.

Raleigh, W. "Assignment from Sir Walter Raleigh." In Hakluyt, *The Principall Navigations*, edited by Quinn and Skelton, 2:815.

———. *Sir Walter Ralegh's Discoverie of Guiana*. Edited by Joyce Lorimer. London: Hakluyt Society, 2006.

Schleck, Julia. "Forming the Captivity of Thomas Saunders: Hakluyt's Editorial Practices and Their Ideological Effects." In Carey and Jowitt, *Richard Hakluyt*, 129–38.

Settle, Dionyse. "The Second Voyage of Master Martin Frobisher." In Hakluyt, *The Principall Navigations*, edited by Quinn and Skelton, 2:622–30.

———. "The Second Voyage of M. Martin Frobisher . . . Anno 1577." In Hakluyt, *Principal Navigations* (1598–1600), 3:32–73.

———. *A True Reporte of the Laste Voyage into the West and Northwest Regions, &c. 1577. Worthily Atchieued by Capteine Frobisher*. London, 1577.

Sloan, Kim, ed. *A New World: England's First View of America*. Chapel Hill: University of North Carolina Press, 2007.

Sowerby, Tracey Amanda. *Renaissance and Reform in Tudor England: The Careers of Sir Richard Morison, ca. 1513–1556*. Oxford: Oxford University Press, 2010.

Symons, Thomas H. B. *Meta Incognita: A Discourse of Discovery: Martin Frobisher's Arctic Expedition, 1576–1578*. 2 vols. Hull, Quebec: Canadian Museum of Civilization, 1999.

Taylor, E. G. R., ed. *The Original Writings & Correspondence of the Two Richard Hakluyts*, 2 vols., 2nd series, 76–77. London: Hakluyt Society, 1935.

Towerson, William. "The First Voyage Made by Master William Towerson . . . to the Coast of Guinea . . . in the Yeere 1555." In Hakluyt, *The Principall Navigations*, edited by Quinn and Skelton, 1:98–112.

Willes, Richard. "Certaine other reasons, or arguments to proove a passage by the Northwest." In Hakluyt, *The Principall Navigations*, edited by Quinn and Skelton, 2:610–15.

———. "For M. Captayne Furbishers passage by the Northwest. To the ryght honourable and vertuous Ladie, the Lady Anne, Countesse of Warwyke." In Willes, *History of Travayle*, 230v–236r.

———. *History of Travayle in the West and East Indies*. London, 1577.

———. "To the ryght noble and excellent Lady, the Lady Brigit, Countesse of Bedforde, my singuler good Lady and Mystresse." In Willes, *History of Travayle*, n.p.

———. "To the right worshipfull, my singuler good Mystres, M. Elizabeth Morisyn." In Willes, *History of Travayle*, 236v.

Woolfson, Jonathan. "Morison, Sir Richard." In *The Oxford Dictionary of National Biography*. Oxford: Oxford University Press. Accessed June 13, 2017.

CONTRIBUTORS

PATRICIA AKHIMIE is associate professor of English at Rutgers University–Newark and the author of *Shakespeare and the Cultivation of Difference: Race and Conduct in the Early Modern World* (Routledge, 2018). She has published essays in *The Oxford Handbook of Shakespeare and Embodiment: Gender, Sexuality, and Race* and *Early Modern Diplomacy, Theatre and Soft Power*.

LAURA WILLIAMSON AMBROSE is associate professor of humanistic studies at Saint Mary's College (Notre Dame). Her published work includes essays in the *Journal of Medieval and Early Modern Studies* and *The Cambridge Guide to the Worlds of Shakespeare*. She is currently completing a monograph entitled "Technologies of Transport: Travel Thinking and Travel Writing in Early Modern England: 1600–1660."

BERNADETTE ANDREA is professor of literary and cultural studies at the University of California, Santa Barbara. She is the author of *The Lives of Girls and Women from the Islamic World in Early Modern British Literature and Culture* (University of Toronto Press, 2017), and *Women and Islam in Early Modern English Literature* (Cambridge University Press, 2007).

LAURA AYDELOTTE is principal investigator for the Philadelphia Playbills Project and project coordinator for the Provenance Online Project at the University of Pennsylvania's Kislak Center for Special Collections, Rare Books and Manuscripts. She is also project coordinator for the Lapidus Reperta Project at Princeton University Rare Book and Special Collections Library.

RICHMOND BARBOUR is professor of English literature at Oregon State University. He is the author of *Before Orientalism: London's Theatre of the East, 1576–1626* (Cambridge University Press, 2003) and *The Third*

Voyage Journals: Writing and Performance in the London East India Company, 1607–10 (Palgrave MacMillan, 2009). He is completing a scholarly edition of John Saris's 1611–14 East India Company journal, and a monograph on another voyage, "The Loss of the 'Trades Increase': An Early Modern Corporate Catastrophe."

STEPHANIE CHAMBERLAIN is professor of English at Southeast Missouri State University. Her most recent publications include "Investing in Matrimony: Loss and Gain in *The Merchant of Venice*," in the *Journal of the Wooden O Symposium*, and "Domestic Economies in *Taming of the Shrew*: Amassing Cultural Credit," in *Upstart Crow: A Shakespeare Journal*.

RUBEN ESPINOSA is associate professor of English at the University of Texas, El Paso. He is the author of *Masculinity and Marian Efficacy in Shakespeare's England* (Ashgate, 2011) and coeditor of *Shakespeare and Immigration* (Ashgate, 2014). He is currently working on a book project titled "Shakespeare on the Border: Legitimacy, Legacy, and La Frontera," which scrutinizes the intersections between Shakespeare and Chicanx culture and identity.

MARY C. FULLER is professor and head of the Literature Section at MIT. She is author of *Voyages in Print* (Cambridge University Press, 1995) and *Remembering the Early Modern Voyage* (Palgrave, 2008). She is currently working on a study of Richard Hakluyt's *Principal Navigations* and preparing a volume for the Oxford University Press edition of Hakluyt's collection.

EDER JARAMILLO is a doctoral student in the English Department at the University of Nebraska–Lincoln, where he is affiliated with the Medieval and Early Modern Studies Program. He is currently working on a dissertation titled "Prospero's Books: New World Colonization in Anglo-Spanish Texts."

GAYWYN MOORE is assistant professor of English at Missouri Western State University. Her recent publications include "'You turn me into nothing': Reformation of Queenship on the Jacobean Stage," in *Mediterranean Studies*, and a coauthored chapter on *Henry VIII* in the *Greenwood Companion to Shakespeare*.

CARMEN NOCENTELLI is associate professor of English and comparative literature at the University of New Mexico. She is the author of *Empires of Love: Europe, Asia, and the Making of Early Modern Identity* (University of Pennsylvania Press, 2013), which garnered the Aldo and Jeanne Scaglione Prize for Comparative Literary Studies and the Roland H. Bainton Prize in Literature.

ELISA OH is associate professor of English at Howard University. She has published on Elizabeth I and Shakespeare's Isabella in *English Literary Renaissance* and on Ben Jonson's *Masque of Blackness* in *Upstart: A Journal of English Renaissance Studies*. Her current project examines representations of race and gender in early modern dance, travel, and ritual movement.

KAREN ROBERTSON is senior lecturer at Vassar College in English and women's studies, and has been a visiting senior lecturer at Exeter University. She is coeditor with Susan Frye of *Maids and Mistresses, Cousins and Queens* (Oxford University Press, 1999) and is completing a monograph, "Pocahontas Among the Jacobeans," for which she received a National Endowment for the Humanities fellowship.

AMRITA SEN is associate professor of humanities at Heritage Institute of Technology and affiliated faculty at Heritage College, University of Calcutta. She has coedited a special issue of the *Journal of Early Modern Cultural Studies* on the "Alternative Histories of the East India Company," and is currently coediting a collection of essays "Civic Performance: Pageantry and Entertainments in Early Modern London" (Routledge).

MICHAEL SLATER is assistant professor of English at the State University of New York's College at Brockport. His recent publications include "The Ghost in the Machine: 'Emotion' and Mind-Body Union in *Hamlet* and Descartes" (*Criticism*) and "Spenser's Poetics of Transfixion in the Allegory of Chastity" (SEL *Studies in English Literature 1500–1900*).

DYANI JOHNS TAFF is lecturer in English and writing at Ithaca College. Her article "Gendered Circulation and the Marital Ship of State in Jonson's *The Staple of News*" is forthcoming in *Renaissance Drama*. Her current book project is titled "Navigating Ships of State: Gender,

Authority, and the Maritime Environment in Early Modern English Literature."

SUZANNE TARTAMELLA is associate professor of English at Henderson State University, where she teaches Renaissance and eighteenth-century literature. She is the author of *Rethinking Shakespeare's Skepticism: The Aesthetics of Doubt in the Sonnets and Plays* (Duquesne University Press, 2014), as well as articles in *English Literary Renaissance* and *Studies in Philology*.

INDEX

'Abbas [Abbas] I (shah), 67, 69, 83, 96n18, 102 104 109
Acheson, Katherine, 161, 162, 175n11
adventure (term), 211
Akbar, 45
Alba de Tormes, 109, 110, 112
Alberti, Leon Battista, 81
'Ali Quli Beg, 105, 106
Amazons: historical representations of, 186, 337; Teresa Sampsonia Sherley as, 82, 86, 87–88, 90, 94
Amboyna (Dryden), 57
Amonute. See Pocahantas
Andrea, Bernadette, 66, 70
Anglican Church, 46, 47
Anna [Anne] of Denmark (queen), 143, 145, 146, 149, 154n18, 164
Antony (character), 22, 181, 193, 194. See also *Antony and Cleopatra* (Shakespeare)
Antony and Cleopatra (Shakespeare), 8, 10, 32, 181, 182, 191–95, 252–66
Appadurai, Arjun, 103
Arbeau, Thoinot, 139, 152n2
Armenia, trade and Christianity of, 45, 58n18, 59n19
As You Like It (Shakespeare), 10, 292–96, 299–300, 304–8
Atkinson, Richard, 32

Azores, 313–14, 323–24, 326

Balvaird, Lord, 133, 137n27
Barbary Coast, 185, 186, 325, 329n26
Beatriz [Beatrice] de Jesús, 84, 108, 112
Beeston, Eleanor Cave, 68, 77n15
Berger, Harry, 184
Bess (character), 11, 314, 316–27, 328n22, 329nn26–29. See also *The Fair Maid of the West* (Heywood)
Best, George, 340
Best, Thomas, 31
Bevington, David, 217
The Bible in Shakespeare (Hamlin), 295
Bichitr, 46
Birnbaum, Lucia, 254
Black Madonna, 10, 250–51, 253–66. See also Marian imagery and worship
The Blazing World (Cavendish), 10, 273–75, 279–80, 286, 287n9, 288n11
Boaz (character), 292, 296, 297, 299, 303–6. See also *As You Like It* (Shakespeare)
Boesky, Amy, 275
The Boke Named the Governour (Elyot), 202–3
Boling, Ronald, 207, 211

357

Book of Ruth, 10, 47, 292–99, 303–8, 308n1
The Book of the Courtier (Castiglione), 220, 221
Brabanzio (character), 199, 200, 201–2, 205, 223, 228, 240. See also *Othello* (Shakespeare)
Brathwait, Richard, 218
Brayton, Dan, 282
Britton, Dennis, 46
Bronzini, Cristoforo, 85–86, 86–88, 92, 93, 95n4
Brookes, Kristen G., 241–42
Broomfield, Ann, 26, 27–36

Caesar, Julius (character), 193–94, 263–64. See also *Antony and Cleopatra* (Shakespeare)
Caliban (character), 236, 239, 241, 245–47. See also *The Tempest* (Shakespeare)
Callaghan, Dympna, 215
canary (dance), 139
Canary Islands, 139
career (term), 108
Carmelite order, 84, 86, 102, 104, 109–10. See also Catholicism; Teresa de Ávila (saint)
Carroll, Michael, 265
Catholicism: Carmelite order, 84, 86, 102, 104, 109–10; of Robert Sherley, 105, 106, 114; of Teresa Sampsonia, 105, 107, 115n26. See also Marian imagery and worship
Cavendish, Margaret. See *The Blazing World* (Cavendish)
Cecil, Robert, 337
Celia (character), 292, 294, 298–302, 306–8. See also *As You Like It* (Shakespeare)

Cerimon (character), 277–79, 283. See also *Pericles, Prince of Tyre* (Shakespeare)
Chakravarty, Urvashi, 50
Chamberlain, John, 148–49
Chamberlain, Stephanie, 248
Charles I (king), 124, 160
Charles II (king), 57
Chaudhuri, K. N., 42, 43
Child, Josiah, 57
childbirth at sea, 33, 54, 70–71, 273, 287n4
chivalric romance, 82, 90–91, 93, 98n52, 316, 322
choreography (term), 140
Christianity: in Armenia, 45, 58n18, 59n19; racial debate in, 46–47
Christine of Lorraine, 96n28
Cinthio, Giovanni Battista Giraldi, 20
Circassians, 106, 115n24. See also Sherley, Teresa Sampsonia
Civil Conversation (Guazzo), 9, 220, 225
Clement VII (pope), 104
Clement VIII (pope), 105
Cleopatra (character), 22, 181, 192–95, 197n17, 253, 254, 258–66. See also *Antony and Cleopatra* (Shakespeare); Black Madonna
Cleopatra (queen), 259
Clifford, Anne: family of, 160, 162; legacy of, 7, 158, 163–64, 173–74; marriages of, 158, 160, 165; residences and properties of, F3, F4, 158–59; travel of, 164–73; works by, 158, 161–62, 174n9
Clifford, George, 160, 162
Clifford, Henry, 160
Clifford, Margaret Russell, 160, 162, 164, 175n21
colorism (term), 46. See also racial difference

A Comedy of Errors (Shakespeare), 20, 33
consort *vs.* wife, 6, 82–83, 92–93, 98n65, 191
Conway, Edward, 36
Cook, Ann Jennalie, 217
Copland, Patrick, 74
Coryate, Thomas, 74, 78n41, 84, 95n15
Cottegnies, Line, 279, 285–86, 289n26
Court Book of the EIC, 27–28
Crashaw, William, 256
cross-dressing, 322–23, 325
Cyprus, 19, 21, 184, 185, 204, 209

Daileader, Celia, 252, 264–65, 267, 268n8
dance, 139–40, 145–46, 152n3
Dash, Irene, 216, 232n3
Davis, Natalie Zemon, 148
"Day Book" diary (Clifford), 158, 161–62
Deats, Sara Munson, 216, 217
Della dignità e nobiltà delle donne (Bronzini), 86, 90, 93, 96n28
Dell'historia naturale (Ferrante Imperato), F5, 203
"Description of Italy" (Lassels), 133
Desdemona (character): agency of, 217–18; courtly codes of conduct for, 9, 225–31, 344n2; desire for travel of, 8, 184–85, 199–211, 219; divided figure of, 215–16, 232n3; and gender constraints, 8–9, 219–24; "greedy ear" of, 196n7, 242–44; petition for travel by, 19–22, 23–24, 27; relationship with Othello of, 22–23, 183, 222–23, 226. See also *Othello* (Shakespeare)
diary (term), 174n8
diplomacy: by Eleanor Cave Beeston, 77n15; by Pocahontas, 149, 336; by Queen Elizabeth, 333, 342; by Sherley brothers, 5, 67–68, 83, 91, 102–8, 114n13; by Teresa Sampsonia Sherley, 84; by women travelers, 64, 76, 96n24
Discoverie of Guiana (Raleigh), 337
Domańska, Ewa, 108
domesticity. *See* patriarchal domesticity
Dowd, Michelle, 281, 283, 288n17
Downton, Nicholas, 47, 48, 52, 65–66
dowry, 47, 59n30, 190
Dreher, Diane Elizabeth, 217
Dudley, Anne Russell, 338–41, 347n34
Duke Senior (character), 300–301. See also *As You Like It* (Shakespeare)
Duncan, Helga L., 302–3
Dusinberre, Juliet, 293, 295

East India Company (EIC): on Ann Broomfield's travel, 19, 27–35; benefits for sailors's wives, 24–25, 32, 37n5, 42, 44, 49–51; business arrangements with women of, 76n2; communication system in, 60n48; early company struggles of, 42, 43–44; on Mariam Khan's benefits, 44, 49–50, 51, 53; record of women travelers with, 67–76; reorganization of, 57; and Virginia Company, 5, 27. See also Roe, Thomas; Smythe, Thomas
Ebert, Christopher, 314, 327n7
educational travel, 123, 128, 174n4. See also women's travel
Egypt, 191–95, 253. See also *Antony and Cleopatra* (Shakespeare)
Elizabeth I (queen), 11, 160, 242, 259, 333, 342
Elsky, Stephanie, 163, 166, 168
Emilia (character), 20, 33

English Aristocratic Women, 1450–1550 (Harris), 228
Erickson, Peter, 142, 217, 253
errare (term), 90, 98n51
Espinosa, Ruben, 7, 282
An essay of the meanes how to make our travailes (Palmer), 1, 125
exoticism, 42–43, 196n11, 199–203, 332–34
Expedition (ship), 67, 69, 70

The Fair Maid of the West (Heywood), 11, 282, 313–27
Fashioning Femininity (Newman), 216–17
Feerick, Jean, 46
femme covert, 148, 154n31
Ferrante Imperato, F5, 203
Fiennes, Celia, 2
Florencio del Niño Jesús, 107, 115n30
Foster, William, 25, 53
Fraser, Russell, 295
Freeman, Charles, 109
Fuchs, Barbara, 237, 241, 244, 316, 329n26
Fuller, Mary C., 239
Fuller, Thomas, 87
Fumerton, Patricia, 315, 328n14, 329n25, 329n31

Garber, Marjorie, 303
Geary, Patrick, 108, 116n37
Gender, Genre, and Identity in Women's Travel Writing (Siegel), 2
Generall Historie of Virginia (Smith), 142–43
Giles, Mrs., 48, 52
Gli Hecatommithi (Cinthio), 20
The Global Lives of Things (Gerritsen and Riello), 103, 104
Godelier, Maurice, 112

Golding, Mr. (chaplain), 55, 73–75
Gonzaga, Cesare, 220–21
Goodlack (character), 316, 325–26. See also *The Fair Maid of the West* (Heywood)
Gorges, Fernando, 148
Gower (character), 274, 275, 277, 283–84
Gracián, Jerónimo, 109
Great Books of Record (Clifford), 158, 161, 174n9
The Great Picture (Clifford), 158
Griffin, Eric, 239, 307
Guazzo, Stephano, 9, 220, 225

Habib, Imtiaz, 201
Hakluyt, Richard. See *Principal Navigations* (Hakluyt)
Hall, Kim F., 142, 259, 270n45
Hamlin, Hannibal, 295
Hamor, Ralph, 140
haram/harem, 42–43, 50, 83
Hawkins, Charles, 50
Hawkins, Mrs. *See* Mariam Khan
Hawkins, William, 25, 41, 44–49, 58n16, 77n30
Hector (ship), 24, 25, 48
Helgerson, Richard, 189
Hendricks, Margo, 186
Henry IV (Shakespeare), 182, 187–90
Henry V (Shakespeare), 182, 187–91
Herbert, Mary Sidney, 340
Herbert, Philip, 158, 160
Herbert, Thomas, 85, 107, 113
Hercules, 22
Historia generalis (Saint-André), 90
The history of our B. Lady Loreto, F2. See also Madonna di Loreto
History of Travayle (Willes), 337–38, 345n8

Hobson, John, 36
Hobson, Mrs. *See* Broomfield, Ann
Hoby, Thomas, 220
Holy Bones, Holy Dust (Freeman), 109
Holy House of Loreto. *See* Madonna di Loreto
The Honourable Company (Keay), 44
Hopkins, Lisa, 260
Hudson, Mrs., 53–54, 56, 65, 66, 72
Hudson, William, 53
Husain 'Ali Beg, 105, 106
Hypsicratea, 87, 96n29

Iago (character), 199, 200, 202, 211, 222, 229. *See also Othello* (Shakespeare)
Il Mercurio Italico (Raymond), 130
Inalienable Possessions (Weiner), 112
index, women's names represented in, 332–41, 345n10, 347n34, 347n36
India. *See* Mughal empire
Indian Ink (Ogborn), 57
Isis (goddess), 255, 257, 263–64, 269n28
Islam: and Anthony Sherley, 105; of Circassians, 106, 115n24; conversions to, 83, 124, 201; in English drama, 201, 241, 306, 329n26; and Teresa Sampsonia, 105, 106–7, 110–11, 115n26
The Island Princess (Fletcher), 57, 61n84
Ismail I (shah), 104
Itinerary (Moryson), 81, 123

Jahangir (emperor), 41, 44–46, 49, 50. *See also* Mughal empire
Jahangir preferring a Sufi mystic to three kings (Bichitr), 46
James I (king), 67, 84, 141, 145, 151, 160, 164

Jewel, John, 256, 260, 264
Jones, Ann Rosalind, 220, 221, 232
Jonson, Ben, 145, 148
Journeys to the Other Shore (Euben), 102

Keay, John, 44
Keeling, Mrs. *See* Broomfield, Ann
Keeling, William, 26, 29–32, 35–36, 38n48, 208
Kempe, Margery, 12n7
King Lear (Shakespeare), 189
kinship, definition of, 50
Kintgen, Eugene R., 238–39
knights-errant, 90–91, 98n55
Kopytoff, Igor, 108

Lady Anne's Way, 158–59. *See also* Clifford, Anne
Lady Percy (character), 190. *See also Henry V* (Shakespeare)
Lal, Ruby, 43
Lassels, Richard: background of, 121; "Description of Italy," 133; on traveling, 125; *Voyage of Italy*, 121–22, 133–34; "The Voyage of the Lady Catherine Whetenall," 6, 121–22, 126–28, 131, 132
The Launching of the Mary (Mountfort), 24, 27, 58n15
Lawrence, Karen, 13n17, 275–76, 280, 289n23, 298, 309n26
Leachland, John, 76
Lefkowitz, Mary, 257
Levant Company, 24
Levine, Laura, 259
library research methods, 344, 348n49
Literature and Domestic Travel in Early Modern England (McRae), 2
Lithgow, William, 43, 131

Lok, Michael, 340, 348n37
Loomba, Ania, 185, 186, 196n11, 200, 241
Luccicos, Marcus (character), 212n5. See also *Othello* (Shakespeare)

Maddalena, Maria, 84, 88, 96n28
Madonna di Loreto, F2, 9, 122, 130–35, 135n5, 250, 254, 262–63
Malay, Jessica, 162
Marcus, Leah S., 306
Mariam Khan: background and influence of, 41–43, 50–51, 52, 55–56, 66; Downton on, 66; dowry for, 47, 59n30; and Frances (Webbe) Steele, 53–55, 72–75; husbands of, 25–26, 42, 44, 49, 77n30; and Nur Mahal, 52, 53, 55; racial debate on, 44–46; weddings of, 25, 46–47, 50, 52–53; widows benefits for, 44, 49–50, 51, 53
Marian imagery and worship: Black Madonna and Cleopatra, 10, 250–51, 253–66; Madonna di Loreto site, F2, 9, 122, 130–35, 135n5, 250, 254, 262–63; Virgen de Guadalupe, 266–67. See also Catholicism
Markley, Robert, 49, 61n84
marriages: femme covert, 148, 154n31; of Mariam Khan, 25–26, 42, 44, 46–47, 49, 50, 52–53, 77n30; of Sherleys, 83–84, 92, 95n8, 105; women's rights in, 45, 47–48, 93, 98n65, 205–6
The Masque of Blackness (Jonson), 145
masques, court, 145–46, 148–49, 154nn17–18
Master, Streynsham, 57
Matar, Nabil, 201
Matchinske, Megan, 163, 170
material culture, 103, 104

Matoaka. See Pocahantas
Matthee, Rudi, 111
Maunder, Chris, 255–56, 269n28
Mauritania, 139
McInnis, David, 202
Membré, Michele, 104
memoir (term), 174n9
memsahib (term), 64, 76n1
Meri, Josef, 111
Mexico, 266–67
Middleton, Henry, 48, 59n43
A Midsummer Night's Dream (Shakespeare), 8, 182, 186–87, 196n10, 240
Mind-Travelling in Early Modern England (McInnis), 2
Miranda (character), 236–41, 244–47, 248n22. See also *The Tempest* (Shakespeare)
Mirza, Malik, 69–70
Mistress Quickly (character), 189–90, 195. See also *Henry IV* (Shakespeare)
Monox, Edward, 54
Montagu, Mary Wortley, 2, 12n9
Montaigne, Michel de, 250
Moor, 19–22, 44–46, 184–86, 329n26
Morison, Richard, 342, 348n44
Moryson, Fynes, 81, 123, 124–25, 125–26, 133
Mowat, Barbara, 237
Mughal empire: cultural influences of, 75; exoticism of women of, 42–43, 196n11; rights of women in, 45, 48; supposed wealth of, 49, 50; trade of and racial debate in, 44–47, 61n86. See also Mariam Khan
Munday, Anthony, 262
Myers, Anne M., 163
My Ladies Looking Glasse (Rich), 218–19

Namontack, 148
Native Americans, transatlantic voyages by, 147–48, 154n28
Natural History Cabinet (Ferrante Imperato), F5, 203
Negro (ship), 323, 326
Neill, Michael, 230–31
Nightingale, Carl, 46
Nur Mahal, 52, 53, 55

Oberon (character), 183, 186–87. See also *A Midsummer Night's Dream* (Shakespeare)
Odyssey (Homer), 125, 136n16
"Of Travelling in Generall" (Moryson), 123
Oglander, John, 35
Old Fortunatus (Dekker), 273
Old Testament. See Book of Ruth
Oleszkiewicz-Peralba, Małgorzata, 255
Olson, Rebecca, 223
Omphale, 22
On Monsters and Marvels (Paré), 200
Orchesography (Arbeau), 139
Orlando (character), 295, 298, 301–5. See also *As You Like It* (Shakespeare)
Orlin, Lena Cowen, 218, 232n18
Othello (character), 19–23, 46, 183–85, 199–211, 222–23, 226, 254. See also *Othello* (Shakespeare)
Othello (Shakespeare), 19–24, 27, 182–86, 196n7, 199–211, 212n5, 253–54
Ottoman Empire, 19, 21, 58n8, 83, 103, 184, 203–4. See also Turkey
Our Lady of Guadalupe, 266–67
Our Lady of Loreto. See Madonna di Loreto

Palmer, Thomas, 1, 125, 136n12

Paré, Ambroise, 200
Parker, Patricia, 185, 243
Parsons, Robert, 105
patriarchal domesticity, 33, 42, 44, 82, 215–20, 224–25, 228, 328n24
Paul V (pope), 105
Payton, Walter, 68, 69, 72
Penelope Voyages (Lawrence), 13n17, 275–76, 280, 289n23, 298, 309n26
Pericles (character in Shakespeare play), 71, 277–78, 281–84
Pericles, Prince of Tyre (Shakespeare), 10, 33, 70–71, 273–87
Persians. See Safavid Empire
Pettie, George, 220
Philip III (king), 105
Philips, Miles, 266
Philo (character), 181. See also *Antony and Cleopatra* (Shakespeare)
pirates and piracy, 50, 315–18, 321–23, 326–27, 328n13, 329n26. See also women sailors and wives of sailors
Pocahontas, 7; and John Smith, 142–43, 149–52; marriage and family of, 140, 147, 152; movements of, 140–49, 154n14; name of, 153n4; storytellers on, 153n5
Popham, John, 148
Porter, Carolyn, 219–20
Powell, Michael, 70
Powell, Thomas, 67, 71
Powell, Tomasin, 65, 66, 67–72
Powhatan Confederacy, 142–43, 144, 151–52. See also Pocahontas
pregnancy and childbirth at sea, 33, 54, 70–71, 273, 287n4
A Preparative to Marriage (Smith), 219
Pridgeon, John, 127, 136n20
Principal Navigations (Hakluyt), 332–36, 337, 338, 344n4, 345n8, 345n10

Index | 363

Pring, Martin, 73–74
privateering. *See* pirates and piracy
A Proclamation touching Passengers, 123–24
Prospero (character), 236–41, 244–46, 248n22. *See also The Tempest* (Shakespeare)
Puckle, William, 57
Purchas, Samuel, 44, 91, 140

Quinn, Alison M., 333–34, 345n10

racial difference: and Black Madonna, 250–51; in Christianity, 46–47; "colorism," 46; on English colonial settlements, 142; in India, 44–47, 61n86; in Shakespeare plays, 199–201, 251–58, 267
Rackin, Phyllis, 217, 227
Radcliffe, Frances Sidney, 340
Rahimi (ship), 50–51
Raleigh, Walter, 11, 293, 313, 335, 337
Rampalle, Jean-Antoine. *See* Saint-André, Pierre de
Raymond, John, 130
religion: of Circassians, 106, 115n24; of stranger wives, 44, 48, 52. *See also* Catholicism; Christianity; Islam
remove (term), 169, 176n33
Roanoke. *See* Virginia colony
Robertson, Karen, 141
Roderigo (character), 230. *See also Othello* (Shakespeare)
Roe, Mrs. *See* Beeston, Eleanor Cave
Roe, Thomas, 26, 37n14, 41, 42, 54–56, 68, 72–75
Rolfe, John, 140, 147, 151–52
Rolfe, Rebecca. *See* Pocahantas
Roman Catholicism. *See* Catholicism
romance. *See* chivalric romance

Rosalind (character), 292, 294, 298–308, 310n51. *See also As You Like It* (Shakespeare)
Rosalynd (story by Lodge), 293–94, 306
Rossi, Gian Vittorio, 86, 87, 95n4
rubies, 49, 59n42
Rudolf II (emperor), 104
Russell, Bridget Hussey, 342–43
Russell, Francis, 342–43
Ruth. *See* Book of Ruth
Ruth Revived (S.R.), 10, 292, 296–99, 300, 303. *See also* Book of Ruth

Sackville, Richard, 158, 160, 165–66
Safavid Empire, 5, 67–68, 102–11, 113, 114n14
safety and restrictions of women travelers, 1, 19, 24, 27–35, 69, 123–28
sahib (term), 64, 76n1
sailors's wives. *See* women sailors and wives of sailors
Saint-André, Pierre de, 86, 87, 90, 95n4
Sampsonia, Teresa. *See* Sherley, Teresa Sampsonia
Santa Casa, F2, 7, 122, 130–35, 135n5
Santa Maria della Scala, 87–88, 106, 107
Saris, John, 48
Schleck, Julia, 69
The Seaman's Honest Wife. See The Launching of the Mary (Mountfort)
sea travel. *See* women sailors and wives of sailors
Segregation (Nightingale), 46
Settle, Dionyse, 340
sexuality and gendered violence, 69, 322, 328n22
Shakespeare, William. *See specific titles of works by*
Shakespeare and the Geography of Difference (Gillies), 183

Shakespeare on the Map project, 182
Sherley, Anthony, 85, 86, 104–7
Sherley, Henry, 53, 66
Sherley, Robert: death of, 106, 107; diplomacy and trade by, 5, 67–68, 83, 91, 102–8, 114n13; marriage to Teresa Sampsonia, 83–84, 92, 95n8, 105; plots and violence against, 69–70, 89, 114n14; religion of, 105, 106, 114; reports to, 49, 52–53, 65–66; son of, 53, 66
Sherley, Teresa Sampsonia: alternate names for, 87, 97n33, 105; background of, 66, 82–83, 95n8; companions of, 66, 67, 71–72, 75–76; comparison to Teresa de Ávila, 83, 94n3, 107; as consort vs. wife, 6, 82–83, 92–93; death of, 116n33; language skills of, 82, 86, 88, 97n39; marriage of, 83–84, 92, 95n8, 105; physical abilities of, 88–89, 91–92, 93–94; relationships of, 65; religion of, 105, 106–7, 110–11, 115n26; as represented in archives, 84–88, 94, 95n4, 96n18; son of, 53, 66; Teresa de Ávila's relic of, 102–3, 107, 108–13, 116n47, 116n52
Sherley, Thomas, 85, 86
Sixtus V (pope), 110
Smith, John, 140, 142–47, 149–52, 153n10, 153n12
Smythe, Thomas, 24, 25, 27, 30–31, 32, 34, 35, 71. *See also* East India Company (EIC)
Spencer (character), 316–18, 320–25, 328n14, 328n24. *See also The Fair Maid of the West* (Heywood)
Squanto, 148
Stallybrass, Peter, 217

Steele, Frances (Webbe), 53, 54, 65, 71, 72–73, 75
Steele, Richard, 53–54, 73
Strangers in Blood (Feerick), 46
Subrahmanyam, Sanjay, 106

Taff, Dyani Johns, 70
Ṭahmāsb (shah), 104
Talbot, Catherine, 135n1
Talbot, Charles, 137n30
The Tempest (Shakespeare), 9, 237–39, 241, 244–47
Teresa de Ávila (saint), 83, 94n3, 107; death and burials of, 109–10; relic of the flesh of, 102–3, 107, 108–13, 116n47, 116n52
Thaisa (character), 10, 33, 70–71, 273–87, 287n4, 288n17. *See also Pericles, Prince of Tyre* (Shakespeare)
Thell, Anne, 281
Thomas (ship), 25, 48–49
The Three English Brothers (Nixon), 85
Three Ways to Be Alien (Subrahmanyam), 106
Thrush, Coll, 147–48
Tisquantum, 148
Titania (character), 183, 186–87. *See also A Midsummer Night's Dream* (Shakespeare)
Towerson, Gabriel, 25, 41, 48, 49, 56–57
Towerson, Mrs. *See* Khan, Mariam
travail, definition of, 273
The Travailes of the Three English Brothers (Day, Rowley, Wilkins), 85
The Traveiler of Jerome Turler (Turler), 1
travel, definition of, 2, 273. *See also* women's travel
Travel Knowledge (Kamps and Singh), 2
travel writing, as genre, 126, 162, 174nn8–9, 329n27, 343, 344n3

Turkey, 184, 185. *See also* Ottoman Empire
Turning Turk (Vitkus), 43

Ufflet, Nicholas, 44, 46, 50–53, 58n16
Uruch Beg, 105, 106
Uttamatomakkin, 148–49

Valle, Pietro della, 85
Venus and Mars (Botticelli), F1, 22
violence. *See* sexuality and gendered violence
Virgen de Guadalupe, 266–67
Virginia colony, 140, 149, 333–37, 346n13, 346n21
Virginia Company, 5, 27, 140, 151
Virgin Mary. *See* Marian imagery and worship
A Vision of Delight (Jonson), 148
Vitkus, Daniel, 43, 70, 201, 243–44, 273
Voyage of Italy (Lassels), 121–22, 133–34
"The Voyage of the Lady Catherine Whetenall" (Lassels), 6, 121–22, 126–28, 131, 132
Voyages and Visions (Elsner and Rubiés), 2

Weaver, Jace, 147–48
Webbe, Frances. *See* Steele, Frances (Webbe)
West, William N., 237, 240
Whetenhall, Catherine, 6–7, 121–23, 126–35
Whetenhall, Thomas, 121, 129, 131

widows, benefits for: from EIC, 24, 37n5, 42, 51; for Mariam Khan, 44, 49–50, 51
wife vs. consort, 6, 82–83, 92–93, 98n65, 191
Willes, Richard, 337–39
Willoughby, Robert, 124, 127, 128, 136n11, 136n20
Wiseman, Susan, 166
women sailors and wives of sailors: benefits for, 24–25, 32, 37n5, 44, 49–50; in Heywood's *The Fair Maid of the West*, 315–25; pregnancy and childbirth at sea of, 33, 54, 70–71, 273, 287n4; prevalence of, 318; in Shakespeare's *Pericles, Prince of Tyre*, 273–87; travel restrictions on, 1, 19, 24, 28–31, 69
women's marriage rights, 45, 47–48, 93, 98n65, 205–6
women's travel: as consort vs. wife, 6, 82–83, 92–93, 98n65; for diplomatic purposes, 64, 76, 96n24; documentary record of, 67–76, 331–32, 343–44; as educational travel, 123, 128, 174n4; exoticism of, 42–43, 196n11, 199–203; ill reputations of, 328nn18–19, 329n22; justifying, 128–30; overview, 1–11, 64, 81–82; as religious pilgrimage, 293; restrictions on, 1, 19, 24, 27–35, 69, 123–28. *See also* women sailors and wives of sailors
Worthies of England (Fuller), 87

In the Early Modern Cultural Studies series:

Courage and Grief: Women and Sweden's Thirty Years' War
By Mary Elizabeth Ailes

Travel and Travail: Early Modern Women, English Drama, and the Wider World
Edited and with an introduction by Patricia Akhimie and Bernadette Andrea

At the First Table: Food and Social Identity in Early Modern Spain
By Jodi Campbell

Separation Scenes: Domestic Drama in Early Modern England
By Ann C. Christensen

Portrait of an Island: The Architecture and Material Culture of Gorée, Sénégal, 1758–1837
By Mark Hinchman

Producing Early Modern London: A Comedy of Urban Space, 1598–1616
By Kelly J. Stage

Words Like Daggers: Violent Female Speech in Early Modern England
By Kirilka Stavreva

Sacred Seeds: New World Plants in Early Modern English Literature
By Edward McLean Test

My First Booke of My Life
By Alice Thornton
Edited and with an introduction by Raymond A. Anselment

The Other Exchange: Women, Servants, and the Urban Underclass in Early Modern English Literature
By Denys Van Renen

To order or obtain more information on these or other University of Nebraska Press titles, visit nebraskapress.unl.edu.